Foundation Acti

Sham Bhangal

friendsof

DESIGNER TO DESIGNER™

Foundation ActionScript

© 2000 friends of ED

With thanks to Marthinus C. Versfeld for his artwork.

Trademark Acknowledgements

friends of ED has endeavored to provide trademark information about all the companies and products mentioned in this book by the appropriate use of capitals. However, friends of ED cannot guarantee the accuracy of this information.

Published by friends of ED

30 Lincoln Road, Olton, Birmingham.
B27 6PA. UK.
Printed in USA

ISBN 1-903450-32-2

Foundation ActionScript

Credits

Author	Sham Bhangal
stun:design	Sham Bhangal, Anders Dhyr, Jake Smith
Content Architect	Mel Orgee
Editors	Mel Orgee, Matthew Knight, Michael Urwin, Ben Renow-Clarke, Jon Hill, Julia Gilbert
Graphic Editors	Deborah Murray, William Fallon
Technical Reviewers	Jeremy Beacock, Kristian Besley, Leon Cych, Gaynor Riopedre, Rita Ruban, Emma Shakeshaft, Gabrielle Smith, Jake Smith
Project Administrator	Fionnuala Meacher
Index	Adrian Axinte, Martin Brooks
Cover Design	Katy Freer
Proof Readers	Fionnuala Meacher, Katy Freer, Ben Renow-Clarke, Michael Urwin, Andy Corsham

Sham Bhangal originally started out as an engineer, specializing in industrial computer based display and control systems. His spare time was partly taken up by freelance web design, something that slowly took up more and more of his time until the engineering had to go.

He is now also writing for friends of ED, something that is taking more and more time away from web design... Funny how life repeats itself!

Sham lives in Manchester, England, with his partner Karen.

Thanks to Anders and Jake for their input into the stun:design project. Hope I didn't work you too hard.

I learnt web design over a period of about a year whilst tucked away in a little farmhouse in deepest Somerset, owned by Roger and Annie Williams. This book is dedicated to both of you. Thanks for putting up with my strange working patterns whilst keeping up a day job and web freelancing at the same time. Sorry about the 300Watts/channel (RMS) sound system that used to keep me (and presumably the whole village) awake at night.

Particular thanks to Roger for all the beer and barbequed dead animal on hot summer days. Meat is like a glass of water in a desert for a man with a vegetarian girlfriend...

Table of Contents

Table of Contents

10 Modular Actionscript 327

11 Sprites 379

Table of Contents

Table of Contents

stun

/stʌn/ *v(·sg)*
   (a) [tn] daze or shock (sb) eg with sth unexpected
   (b) [tn esp passive] impress (sb) greatly

setyour*browser*to**stun:**

Introduction

Welcome

Flash 5 ActionScript interactivity is setting the new standard in web design. ActionScript has been the biggest enhancement between Flash 4 and Flash 5, changing from a simple animation scripting language to a fully-fledged object-oriented programming environment, with a better interface for text entry and editing, new commands for a richer set of actions and new actions applied to movies. The long awaited dot notation makes commands easier to learn and more streamlined to implement than they were in Flash 4.

All in all, ActionScript now become a much deeper and more professional tool, allowing you to add mind-blowing effects to your web site but keep that all important file size down and letting you increase the level of user interactivity to your designs.

All these enhancements, and more, combine to give you as a Flash designer more control. It's this finer level of control that top Flash designers are taking advantage of to build the amazing effects you've seen. They're not just following the rules, they're re-defining them and teaching Flash to act in totally different ways. This is what you'll be doing by the end of this book.

We aim to give you a solid foundation in the skills you'll need to run with the crowd. You'll begin by learning how to plan your ActionScript project, adding actions that provide simple timeline control and taking the full tour through re-usable code, adding sound and building your first interactive Flash 5 game! ActionScript may look like a whole new ball game, but this book will show you that the rules aren't all that different and the end result is more exhilerating than you know!

A word of reassurance - learning to use ActionScript won't stop you from being a designer. This book will open up the new ActionScript gateway and take you through the transition from linear animation to cutting edge dynamic Flash web sites, all the time remembering that what's more important to you as a designer is how ActionScript will empower you to create the designs you want. We don't want to turn into a programmer, speaking in ones and zeroes and only coming out after dark. Ideas are still your most valuable commodity, and, for us, showing you ways of smoothing

▶

the path from imagination to reality is just as important as teaching you about all those spidery things involving brackets and scary symbols.

Our Aims and Philosophy in this Book

Admittedly, we can't teach you everything there is to know about ActionScript in 500 pages, but we're going to give you a secure foundation that covers the core aspects of ActionScript in depth. Right from the beginning of this book, we're going to be considering methods like dot notation that others have labeled "advanced" but which offer simple ways to access the immense power offered by Flash 5.

We don't believe in books that show basic coding principles using non-commercial quality mock-ups that would never be used in real life. Teaching with theoretical examples – that's not us. We decided that the best way for you to see the power that ActionScript can bring to your designs is to relate what you learn here to a **real** web site. As we work through the book we're going to build **stun:design**, a fully ActionScripted professional web site that's out there in the real world as a commercial project. This will help reinforce the skills you learn in a real-world situation where deadlines rule, clients moan and things go wrong.

With the emphasis on practicality rather than theory, each chapter will follow the Foundation model and introduce a new topic, backed up with step-by-step examples that combine into a working web site full of ActionScript tricks.

Take a look at stundesign.com to see what you'll be doing by the end of this book:

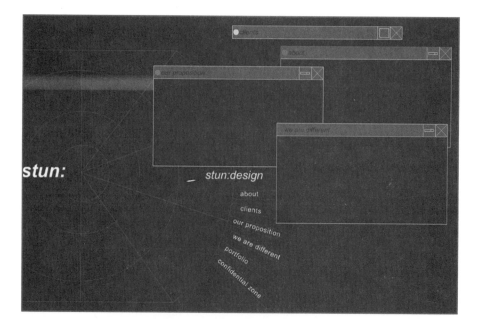

FLAs for Download

We've also included fully completed FLA files for every exercise, ready for you to download chapter by chapter from friendsofed.com. Use them and abuse them however you like within your own designs, but certainly take advantage of them to compare what you've done with Sham's finished product if you lose track of what's going on.

What You'll Need to Know

You've picked up this book so we guess that you've got the Flash basics under your belt. We think that you've built your typical timeline-based movie but you know that Flash 5 has a lot more to offer your creativity.

You may even have read books like friends of ED's own **Foundation Flash 5**, which have given you a solid grounding in Flash essentials and whetted your appetite for the next step on your journey.

ActionScript is the powerdrill in your designer's toolbox, replacing that old hand drill that was, well, useful but limited. Like all powertools, the extra potential that comes flowing down that electric lead brings with it the possibility of a far bigger mess if you get things wrong. To make sure that this doesn't happen, please read the following brief safety instructions. We're going to go through a few of the things that you'll need to set up before you begin work to start scripting straight from chapter 1.

When you were simply putting things onto timelines in Flash, you knew where they were. With ActionScript, we're going to be doing all types of things that you won't be able to see on a timeline. This means two things: firstly, ActionScript has to know how to find these items, and secondly, you need to know how to find them if you lose them.

You'll be used to turning things into symbols in Flash (with *F8* or **Insert > Convert to Symbol**) as good practice that saves download time. If you drag two instances of a symbol out of the library, then ActionScript is going to have a problem telling them apart, so we have to **name** things so that ActionScript knows where each instance is and can control them. Don't worry - we'll show you how to this when we get there. You can only give names to movieclips, so we'll be using a lot of movieclip symbols in this book!

The Movie Explorer

Later on in the book, your FLAs are going to start to get complex, and you're going to create a movieclip or a bit of script and then lose it somewhere in that vast, echoing Flash universe. The answer lies with the **Movie Explorer**, which allows you to find your symbols, movieclips, and scripts with ease. You can bring up the Movie Explorer at any time with **Window > Movie Explorer**.

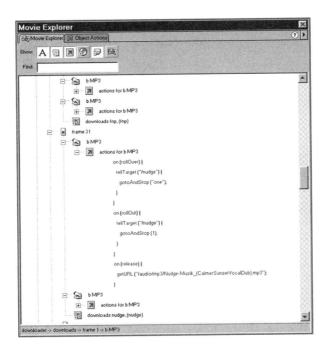

Have a little play with the Movie Explorer, and you will find that you can do quite a few things. You can print out from it, which can be particularly useful to help you understand what's happening when we start doing strange structural stuff in Flash, like embedding movieclips within movieclips. You can find all the instances on the timeline by selecting the button with the two squares on it 🔲.

You can also use the really useful **Find:** field to find all the ActionScript lines that control a particular instance. If you have an instance somewhere doing something rather strange and unexpected, then this is a particularly useful way of checking on it. You can go from a library template to all instances of that library symbol, so you can check what will change if you change the library version of that symbol. Filter on ActionScripts only by selecting the box with the arrow on it 📄, and the Movie Explorer will let you print a full listing of all your code together, which is the only place that Flash lets you do this. You might not see the point of some of these functions now, but make friends with the Movie Explorer – in a crisis, you will need it by your side.

The Stage

If you bring up the rulers in Flash with **View > Rulers**, you'll notice that the ruler measurements start from the top left corner and increase as they go from left to right (*x* direction) and from the top left corner going downwards (*y* direction). These are the directions used by printing presses and graphic designers, but not the directions used by

Cartesian geometry and mathematicians, who usually take y going from bottom to top, so that the origin sits at the bottom left corner.

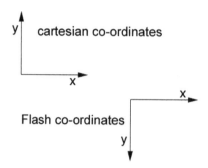

This can get particularly confusing for someone with a math background when you have to add something to the *y* co-ordinate to make your object go downwards, so be careful.

Flash Settings

We're going to be coding from Chapter 1 onwards, (don't be scared, it's much easier than you think!) so it's important that we co-ordinate our preferences before we start, so that Flash behaves in similar ways for all of us. Bring up the preferences window in Flash by selecting **Edit > Preferences**.

The options we need to look at are all in the **General** tab. In the **Selection** options check **Shift Select**. This defines how you select multiple objects in Flash. In many graphic programs (such as Adobe PhotoShop), you have to press the *Shift* key to select more than one item or add to a selection. If you select something without the *Shift* key, all previous selections are lost. To make Flash work in this way, you have to check **Shift Select**. If you leave it unchecked Flash allows you to make multiple selections simply by clicking. You then unselect by clicking on a blank area. Doing things this way can be a little confusing for anyone who's used to the Shift Select method, which is the standard way of selection in most other graphic and 3D programs.

The second option to look at is **Timeline Options**. Flash 5 has a slightly different way of allowing you to select frames to Flash 4. Flash 5's methods are a step forward for timeline-based animations, but they can be confusing when we want to select individual frames for ActionScript editing, so we need to change this. Tick the **Flash 4 Selection Style** box, and then tick **Flash 4 Frame Drawing** too. **Flash 4 Selection Style** makes the Flash 5 frame drawing style redundant.

While you're in the **Preferences** window, make sure that **Show Tooltips** is selected, because the tooltips often show some valuable information. Your **Preferences** window should now look like this:

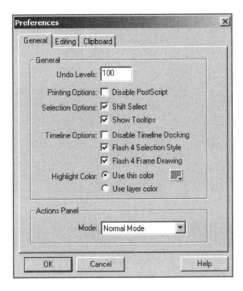

Support: we're here for you

If you have any questions about the book or about friends of ED, check out our web site: there are a range of contact e-mail addresses there, or you can just use feedback@friendsofed.com.

There are also a host of other features up on the site: interviews with renowned designers, samples from our other books, and a message board where you can post your own questions, discussions and answers, or just take a back seat and look at what other designers are talking about. So, if you have any comments or problems, write us, it's what we're here for and we'd love to hear from you.

Layout Conventions used in this Book

We've tried to keep this book as clear and easy to follow as possible, so we've only used a few layout styles:

- When you first come across an important word it will be in **bold** type, then in normal type thereafter.

- We'll use a different font to emphasize **technical words**, **phrases that appear on the screen**, and **code**.

- Menu commands are written in the form **Menu > Sub-menu > Sub-menu**.

- When there's some information we think is really important, we'll highlight it like this:

> *This is very important stuff – don't skip it!*

- Worked exercises are laid out like this:

    1. Open up Flash.

    2. Start a new movie file, and save it as TestMovie.fla.

    3. Etc...

PCs and Macs

To keep the book as easy to read as possible, we've used PC commands as a default, so that every time you come across a mouse command you don't have to read something long-winded like, 'right-click on the PC or CTRL-click on the Mac'.

We've only written *both* instructions where there is a difference between the standard Mac substitute command, and the actual command required. When we just say 'click' we mean *left*-click on the PC or simply *click* on the Mac. The common substitute commands are:

PC	Mac
Right-click	CTRL-click
CTRL-click	Apple-click
CTRL-Z (to undo)	Apple-Z
CTRL-Enter	Apple-Enter

We're now ready to start. Let's go!

stun

/stʌn/ v (-nn-)
    (a) [tn] daze or shock (sb) eg with sth unexpected
    (b) [tn esp passive] impress (sb) greatly

setyourbrowsertostun:

1

Starting Out

What we'll cover in this chapter:

- *A little programming theory to introduce you to the basic building blocks of ActionScript*

- *How to add an action to a keyframe*

- *How to use basic programming syntax*

- *How to make one line of ActionScript add interactivity to a basic timeline-based animation*

In this first chapter I'll introduce you to a little programming theory. But don't worry – it'll be just enough to get you started with an understanding of important terms. We'll end the chapter with a look at how even two lines of ActionScript can give you some basic interactivity. Coding already in Chapter 1? Yeah it's not as bad as you think...

You think of ActionScript, you think of interactivity, you think of the user reacting to your site and *making things happen*. That's why we're here isn't it? – to add that interactive power to your designs? For Flash, this interactivity is made up of **events** and the instructions that it's given on how to react to them. These events are the first of our programming building blocks.

Events and How to Handle Them

When I was a child, I was given a cuckoo clock as a present. Well, actually, a cuckoo clock only in the loosest sense of the word, given that it was in the shape of a cartoon lion with a swinging tail as a pendulum. Every time the clock struck the hour, the lion would wake up, open its mouth and growl. He could act as an alarm clock too, giving an almighty roar as the alarm went off. The point of this reminiscing is to introduce you to one of the basic building blocks of ActionScript: **events**.

As I've said, there were two things that set my lion into action:

When the clock reached the beginning of the hour, it was time to growl.
When the alarm time arrived, it was time to roar.

These were the two **events** that the lion was waiting for. As soon as either event occurred, the lion would perform the appropriate **action**. ActionScript is called an **event-driven language**, which sounds complicated programing-speak until you realise that, just like the lion, it's set up to wait for something to happen. It reacts to events – nothing more comlplicated than that.

So what is a Flash event?

It can be something obvious that happens externally, say the user pressing a button on your web site or typing on the keyboard. An event can also be something less obvious that happens internally within the Flash engine room, like loading a movie clip or moving to the next frame. When Flash moves to the next frame, it will look to see whether there are any instructions attached to it and run them accordingly. This is called an **internal event** because Flash generates it on its own.

Whether it's dealing with an internal or external event, Flash ActionScript follows the same pattern:

1. ActionScripts are set up to detect a particular event.

2. Once the event occurs, a set of ActionScripts is executed to handle that event.

The ActionScript that kicks into action in step 2 is sometimes referred to as the **event handler** and always forms a pair with the main event. So, that's the first rule of ActionScript: if you have an event, you **must** have an event handler.

In the real world, you can see all sorts of event/event handler pairs around you. For example, your electric kettle waits for the water to start boiling (the event) and has a special circuit that switches the power off (the event handler) when this occurs. Or your central heating: you set your thermometer to a certain temperature. When it gets that cold in your apartment (the event) your heating kicks in (the event hander) to make things warm and toasty again.

Events in Flash

Back in the Flash world, we'll take a look at the simplest event/event handler partnership: a button press.

The button sits there waiting for some user interaction.

press me for something to happen!!!

The user presses – the **event**.

Flash detects this event and runs the ActionScript attached – the **event handler**.

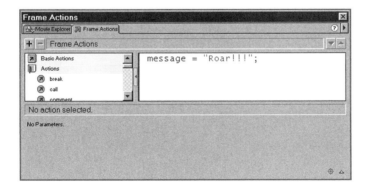

The user hears the result.

Roar!!!

This event/event handler relationship is easy to identify when we're talking about something like buttons, but the event isn't always obvious when Flash is generating it itself in the background. However, if you have this basic understanding – that events always have a corresponding event handler – it will make the discussions we have later in this book as we delve deeper into ActionScript a lot easier.

Whether you're new to this programming business or even if you've already had experience of other languages like BASIC or Pascal, you're probably not familiar with the event/event handler structure. You may be saying "OK, you've told us what each half of the pair does, but why do we use them? What are the advantages?"

One strength that event-driven ActionScript brings to Flash is the ability to react to the unexpected as soon as it occurs, or in **real-time**. I'll explain in a little more detail.

Real-time Events

Programming languages like BASIC work well on problems where there is a well-defined path. A program that calculates your grocery bill at the checkout goes along the same path in the same order every time:

1. All the prices are keyed in

2. The computer adds them up

3. The screen shows your total bill

Step 3 can happen only once 1 and 2 are done.

Unfortunately, real life isn't so easy. When we're actually *buying* the items on the grocery list we tend to forget things and have to go back and forward in the store. We don't seem to remember that we need milk until we're six aisles away from dairy products and looking at dog food. Things don't seem to happen in the order we'd like them to; there's no logical pattern to the way we walk around the grocery store.

In real life, we can't expect things to happen in the order that we'd like so we might as well deal with them in the order they actually occur. We can't be sure that event A will happen first, followed by B and C in that order. We have to tell ourselves, "Either A **or** B **or** C may happen at any time. While I'm dealing with B I may find that A happens without waiting for me to be ready."

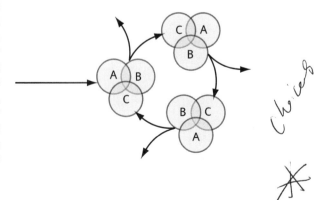

This is a defining feature of **real-time** events: they happen in a random order, either singly or in a group. They may not happen in a nice sequential, easy to follow pattern, as Pascal and BASIC assume they will:

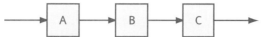

So ActionScript has to be ready to react at a moment's notice – or even quicker! This is the function of the event/event handler pair. The first half (the event) is looking for something to happen, but doesn't know when that will be. The second half (the event handler) is always ready to respond, to give you what you want as soon as you want it.

So, the difference between event-driven languages, like Flash, and other more linear languages, like BASIC, is:

- Event-driven Flash is concerned with real life environments and processes.

- Linear BASIC is more suited to analytical problems where the data has already been collected and can be processed off-line from the real environment.

OK, we've been through our first exploration of ActionScript theory. It's already time to get our hands dirty and attach our first piece of code to part of a Flash movie.

You can attach ActionScript to three things within your movie:

- A keyframe

- A button on the stage

- A movieclip on the stage.

Let's start with the easiest: adding ActionScript to a frame.

Attaching ActionScript to Keyframes

I'll show you here that adding an action to a frame involves nothing more complicated than a keyframe, the **Frame Actions** window and one line of code. Take a look.

1. In a new movie, select the first frame of Layer 1:

2. With the frame still selected, bring up the **Frame Actions** window.

You have a choice of how to do this:

- Right-click or Ctrl-click on the frame and select **Actions** from the drop-down menu.

- Double-click the frame.

- Select **Window > Actions** (or use the keyboard shortcut listed next to it on the menu).

- Click on the little arrow icon at the bottom right of your screen. (In Flash, actions are always represented by this arrow symbol.)

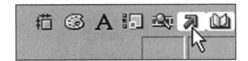

If you chose either of the first two options and click on a frame, be careful to note how you've set up your Preferences. (Go back to the Introduction for our recommendations if you need to.) If you have left the Flash 4 Selection Style box unchecked, you could be creating trouble for yourself: if you have a timeline with a few tweens and keyframes on it, not checking that option makes it difficult to select certain keyframes and add actions to them.

Whichever way of opening the Frame Actions window you choose, this is what you'll see:

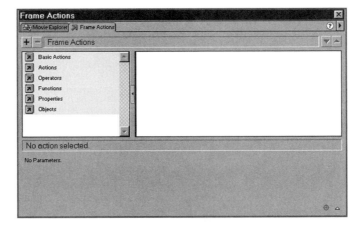

If the lower part looks a little too small and the window is shaped like this you might be in Expert mode by mistake:

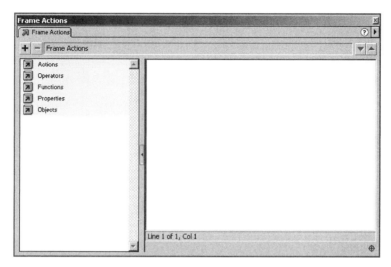

To check, click on the little arrow button at the top right of the **Frame Actions** window and select Normal mode. I'll go through what these two modes mean in more detail in a later chapter, and I promise you that we'll have you using Expert mode all the time by the end of the book. For now, we'll stick to Normal.

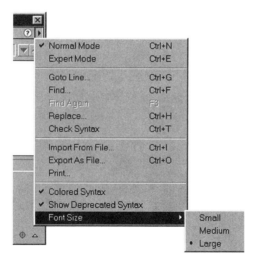

Towards the end of this menu, make sure that **Colored Syntax** and **Show Deprecated Syntax** are both ticked, and **Font Size** is set to a value that fits your monitor and eyes. I'm getting on a bit right now, so I've gone for **Large** on the font front. Again, you'll find out more about these options later. Here, I don't want to hold up your hands-on experience.

OK we've set the basic options, back to the main window.

The Actions window will lie at the centre of all the ActionScript that you will write. We'll be taking a much more detailed tour as we work through this book, but for now I'll just show you what you need to know to create your first piece of ActionScript: a simple action.

In the left pane you'll see six closed book icons, each with a little actions arrow on it. They are labeled:

- Basic Actions
- Actions
- Operators
- Functions
- Properties
- Objects

and all contain ready-made pieces of ActionScript that we'll get to know well as we go through this book. You'll see that if you hold the mouse over them, the tooltip will give you a short definition of the contents and where they're used:

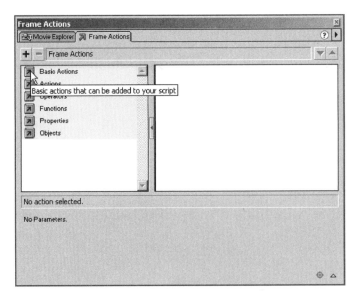

3. Click on the **Basic Actions** book to open it. The icon will change to show (quite logically) an open book. All the actions contained within will drop down. These are individual actions, or commands, and are the building blocks of ActionScript.

Again, get more information on each action by rolling over them and pausing to bring up a tooltip that confirms what that action does:

As we progress through the following steps, bear in mind that the frame must always be selected until we have finished with the ActionScript. If your Actions window suddenly goes blank, it's probably because you've clicked outside the window, and this has caused your frame to become de-selected. You can get your Actions back by re-selecting the frame, so don't start panicking and wondering where all your ready-made actions have disappeared to!

4. Double-click on the **Stop** action and you'll see the relevant piece of code jump straight across to the right-hand pane. If it doesn't, remember what I said about checking that you still have a frame selected:

```
stop ();
```

That's your action added.

You can carry on adding actions in this way or try something different.

In the left-hand corner of the **Frame Actions** title bar you'll see a **+** button:

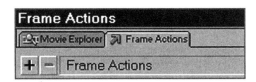

5. Hold the cursor over it to see the tooltip **Add a new item to the script**. Click on that and you'll see a drop-down list identical to the closed book icons, from **Basic Actions** right down to **Objects**. Hold the cursor over **Actions** and select **Stop** from the alphabetical list of available actions. In the same way as we've already seen, the code you want appears automatically in the right-hand window.

Notice that this selection method has the advantage of showing you the keyboard shortcuts for adding each action – something that you may like to use once you're more familiar with all the actions.

6. If you've tried out both these methods, you may have now added two Stop actions to your frame. We only need one, so delete the extra one by clicking on it to select it, then either by pressing the backspace key or by clicking on the – button, again to the left of the **Frame Actions** title bar:

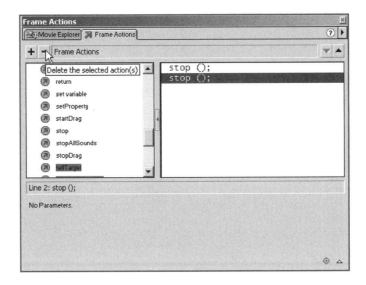

We've added a very simple Stop action. It's obviously not too hard to understand what that action does. At this stage we're dealing with just one line of code that is quite self explanatory, but I'll show you something now that will help you make sense of the the larger pieces of code that you'll be writing as you become more experienced. If you get used to using these, even in these early days, you'll save yourself a lot of headscratching later on....

We'll go through that adding process again, but this time we'll add something slightly different: a **comment**.

Comments

Think of a comment as a personal reminder for your use, a note in the margin if you like. Comments don't contain any instruction to Flash, they just provide space within your ActionScript for you to remind yourself what's going on. Add one and you'll see.

Adding a Comment

1. Again, click on the **+** button in the **Frame Actions** window and hold the cursor over Actions. From the drop-down list, this time select **comment**:

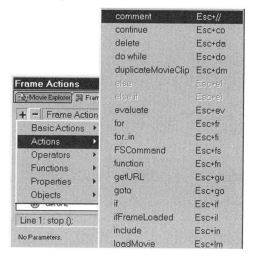

In the right-hand pane a new line appears, with **//** at the beginning. This symbol defines what is about to follow as a comment and tells Flash to ignore it.

Also, the bottom of the Actions window has changed a little: a text box has appeared, labeled **Comment**. You can type in here whatever you need to describe your script, to help you understand the code that follows. A well-commented piece of code makes it easier to understand and therefore easier to debug six months later when you've forgotten what was going through your mind when you wrote it.

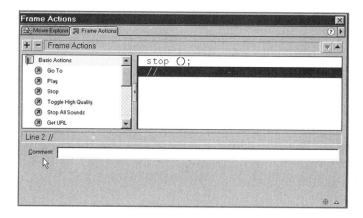

2. To add your comment, click inside the **Comment** box and type **stop the movie**. See how the ActionScript in the top right-hand pane changes to reflect your input:

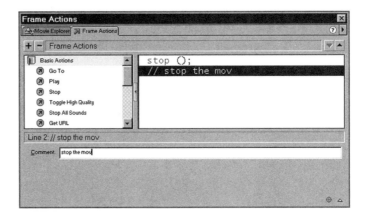

You've made a note for yourself on what the action that you've just added actually does.

You might think it more logical if the explanatory comment came before the `stop ();` action. At any point as your ActionScript grows, you can re-arrange the order of actions or comments with the up arrow and down arrow icons at the top right of the window:

3. Make sure that your comment is still selected (against a blue or yellow background depending whether you're on Mac or a PC). Now press the up arrow, and your comment will move up one line to become the top line. You can move it back down with the down arrow if you feel like it.

Although the script that is created as you add actions begins to look rather complicated, with brackets and punctuation all over the place, remember that **Flash is writing it for you**. This is the help you get when you select to code in Normal mode, as we did a while ago. All you have to do is choose the appropriate actions and fill in the boxes that are presented to you. As a beginner you don't have to know the ins and outs of ActionScript syntax straight away because Flash will give you a lot of help.

4. Finally, close the **Actions** window. If you look at the frame, you'll see there is now a small **a**. This is to show that there are actions attached to this frame:

Attaching actions to buttons and movieclips is no more complicated: select the target button or movieclip on the stage, open the Actions window and enter your scripts. We'll look at this more closely in Chapter 5.

Now, after our first hands on experience of ActionScripting, we need to get back to some of that programming terminology.

Programming instructions have to be very exact, so, just like any other programming language, ActionScript has a fairly rigid structure. Instructions can come in three well-defined parts:

- Commands

- Arguments

- Properties

Commands, Arguments and Properties

Commands and arguments will make sense if you think back to when your parents used to tell you to clean your bedroom. I don't mean that they commanded you to do it and you responded by arguing. Sure, that's probably what actually happened, but it's not what I am getting at. Linking that analogy up to ActionScript, there are two possible cases:

- You had a normal upbringing and had only one bedroom. Your parents didn't have to specify *which* bedroom to clean, because it's implicit in the command "Get up there and clean that damn bedroom *now*!"

- You were one of the Getty children and had at least twelve bedrooms, in which case your parents would say "Get up to bedroom number seven this instant or it's no rum truffles for you!"

In the first case, your parents needed to add no more details because what you had to do was obvious. You received a simple **command**. In the second case, John-Paul's parents had to add an extra bit of information – exactly *which* bedroom he had to clean. This extra piece of information that qualifies the initial command is called the **argument**.

The `stop();` command that we've just looked at has no arguments because Flash already knows what to do. It means stop *this* timeline. You don't have to specify which timeline because Flash understands that this action can be attached only to the timeline that it's placed on.

In a while, we'll use a different command: `gotoAndPlay();` which tells Flash to skip to a new frame. Obviously, we need to tell tell Flash exactly *which* frame to go to, so we'll add an argument:

```
gotoAndPlay(10);
```

Flash has been told it needs to go to a new frame (the command), and the frame it needs to go to is 10 (the argument).

If you drive down to another level of programming detail, you get to **properties**.

The property for your bedroom is either clean or dirty. The property of a sound that Flash is playing in your movie is volume. The position of an object on your screen has two properties of *x* and *y* to define its postion.

The list of properties that exist in ActionScript's world are listed in one of the book icons in the Actions window, called (unsurprisingly), **Properties**. Click on the **Properties** book and hold the mouse over some of the properties to see which attributes they control:

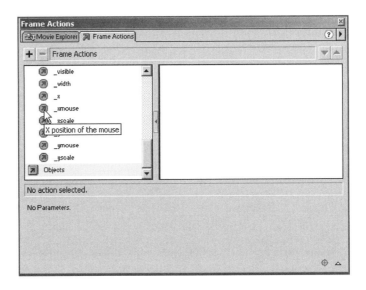

Fit together these jigsaw pieces of commands, arguments and properties and what do you get? A whole instruction:

Instructions

There are many different types of instruction, but they all fit into one of these categories, or general functional types:

1.   Do this *command*.

2.   Do this *command* using this *argument*.

3.   Change this *property* of this *argument* to that.

4.   If this *statement* is true then do *this set of actions*.

5.   Keep doing this *group of instructions* until that is true.

If you've never really done any programming before, test this out by thinking of something that you do every day: pouring a glass of water:

```
keep doing this...
pour (water)
until the glass is full.
```

Pour(water) is number 2 from our list. The **command** is *pour* and the **argument** is *water*.

Keep doing this... until the glass is full is number 5 – keep pouring until the glass is full.

If you break down every day actions like this, you'll begin to see how programming isn't about creating a complicated set of instructions in a foreign language. It's just about breaking down each process into its basic building blocks, taking each process back to its bare bones of instructions so simple that we usually do them without thinking.

You don't have to be clever to program, you just have to be able to think at the right level. The problem is that this level is so low down and basic that most of us have to force ourselves to think that simplistically! It comes with practice and has nothing to do with math or long sums or all the other things you might be expecting.

When you're trying to build up programming commands, even ones far more complicated than the `Stop this movie` instruction that we've just looked at, you can make life a lot easier for yourself by breaking down what you want to achieve into these simplified terms. Either in your mind, or even on paper, lay out what you want to do in sentences like this to help you slot the ActionScript together.

As simple as they are, all instructions have to be made in an understandable order so that they are clear to whoever has to act on them – whether that's John-Paul Getty knowing which bedroom he has to clean or Flash which frame it has to jump to. Amongst chaos, there has to be order.

The order that we need here is a clear structure for our ActionScript commands, so that Flash understands what we want. Programming syntax gives us that order.

Syntax

An important part of every language from Chinese to Serbo Croat is the accepted order in which sentences are constructed: the **syntax**. No matter what languge we speak, we expect to hear words in a certain order so that we can construct the proper meaning and understand what we're being told. If someone says "The cow lives in the big green field", you know that the field is big and green, not the cow.

We have extra rules to separate out written words with punctuation so that we make as much sense on paper as we do verbally. We can write down information about the timing of speech as well as its meaning. Syntax and punctuation combine to give us questions, exclamations and statements – the detailed level of expression that makes our language interesting.

Computers don't need to be expressive, they need to be precise, which means that learning a programming language is far easier than learning how to speak or write. I'll show you now how ActionScript organizes and expresses itself.

Unlike English, with its expressive forms of communication, ActionScript has to convey only a few nuggets of information in its syntax. These divide into three categories:

1. When an individual action has started or finished
This is a bit like saying 'when does a sentence start and when does it stop?' In English, a sentence can start on a new line or on the same line as the previous sentence. It can end with a full stop, a question mark or an exclamation mark. In Flash, things are a lot simpler.

Each basic action starts on a new line and ends with a semi-colon:

```
stop();
```

The only exceptions to this rule are:

- Comments which as we've seen begin with // and can end with whatever we like because Flash ignores them completely

- Nested commands, where additional related commands are enclosed within {} brackets to be handled independently, just as sentences are grouped in paragraphs to be read together. I'll explain in more detail shortly.

2. Which part of the action is the command, the argument or the property?
In this example, the first line is a comment that defines what's happening in the following lines. As we said earlier, Flash doesn't really understand or read anything after the // so we can put anything here:

```
                    // set x to 10 and stop the movie  ⬅——— comment
                    x = 10;                                    (magenta)
action ——➤ stop ();
(blue)              ⬆
            argument (black)
```

We have two actions: **x=10;** and **stop ();**. Both start on a new line and ends with a semi-colon. Actions *always* follow that syntax. In English, punctutation marks can mean more than one thing (**.** can be either a period or a decimal point). In ActionScript, a semi-colon *always* means the end of a line. (Isn't *always* reassuring here? It means that now we've learnt this we don't need to think about it later and say "but in this case...").

Defining which part of an action is the command, argument and property can actually be quite tricky, so Actionscript has two ways of telling us: **position** and **color**. Understanding the code by its position will come as you develop a good working knowledge of specific ActionScript commands, so for now concentrate just on the colors. Flash displays code in three colors to signify different parts of ActionScript speech. They are:

- Magenta for comments

- Blue for actions (and a few other reserved words)

- Green for properties

- Black or grey for everything else

Obviously it's difficult for us to show you these in this black and white book, so as you can see, I've flagged them up in the diagram earlier. As you add different ActionScript over the next few chapters you'll see the proof on the screen, but for now I promise that I'm telling the truth.

3. **Which lines to run when a certain condition is met or when the answer is not met. Which block of actions are to be repeated.**
   This is the 'everything else' that was covered by the color gray in that last list. We'll come to this in a later chapter, but for those who are already familiar with Flash 4 ActionScript or programming in general, it includes;

   - Variable names

   - Paths to variables or properties

   - Brackets and operators (`( )  +  -  /  *  etc.`)

As your experience with ActionScript grows you'll find that you won't always want a section of actions to run in a straight line, one after the other. Sometimes you want to perform particular sequences of actions only if something else has happened. That will be our first look at conditional, decision-based statements, in which we ask Flash to check whether something is true or false and give it a choice of what to do depending on the answer.

Our last look at basic syntax will show you how {} brackets and indentation are used to keep things happening in the order you intend and how to nest commands inside one another.

Nesting

I hate anything that has lots of brackets and commas and dots and stuff. Rather like some people hate spiders because they have too many legs, I just hate lines with too many brackets. It looks suspiciously like math, and I don't want anything to do with it. The way I got my head around this with ActionScript was realizing these are the sort of brackets that don't require you to reach for a calculator and start thinking. These are the sort of brackets that are to do with arranging things into groups, like this:

All small dogs (including dachshunds and terriers) should go to the tree on the left, but all other dogs (including beagles and alsatians) should go to the tree on the right.

I like that because it looks a lot less frightening than:

$$s = \_(u+v)t +5(a2+20c) -1$$

Urgh! Spiders! I know a lot of the stuff below will look like the awful equation, but it's not as bad as all that. Most of the time, it's just a shorthand way of writing the 'dogs and trees' sentence. When any sort of math gets involved, it's usually of the 2 = 1 + 1 variety.

The command below is an **If** action:

```
                    ────────────── is this true?
         ┌──────────┐
if (x<10) {
    y = -10;      ←───────── if yes, run this
    z = 15;
} else {
    y = 10;       ←───────── if no, run this
    z = 45;
}
```

Don't worry too much about all the y and z values for now. I just want to show you the syntax of an instruction that tells Flash to decide whether something is true and then act accordingly.

This is what's happening:

1. Flash looks at what is in the brackets of line 1.

2. If it's a correct, or true statement, lines 2 and 3 are run.

3. If it's not a correct statement, or false, the lines following the else action are run.

Lines 2 and 3 are enclosed by curly brackets and indented. Lines 5 and 6, the same:

```
. . . . . . . . . . . . . .{
    y = -10;
    z = 15;
}. . . . . . . . .
```

This syntax tells us that lines 2 and 3 are to be run as one sequence. Lines 5 and 6 are to be run as an alternative sequence depending upon whether $(x<10)$ is a *true* or *false* statement.

I need silly ways to remember things. The way I think of this rather complicated syntax is as a string of sausages, with the contents of each { } being a sausage. Written as a string of sausages, the syntax looks like this:

```
if (x<10)    {y=-10; z=15;}    else    {y=10; z=45;}
```

or more generally:

if **(this is true)** **{do this sausage}** else **{do this sausage}**

Don't try to learn the if...else structure now, but be aware of how indentation and curly brackets tell us when individual actions will be executed.

Looping structures are much the same, except this time you have only one sausage that keeps repeating:

```
while (x<10) {
    x = x+1;
    y = y+5;
    z = z-10;
}
```

In my foolish sausage notation this equates to:

while **(x is less than 10)** **{keep giving these values to x, y and z}**

We'll end this chapter with a simple example. We'll use a simple animation to give you an idea of how much adding some simple ActionScript can improve the normal timeline-based animations that you're already familiar with.

Adding ActionScript Interactivity

We know that Flash is cool. We know that it takes away a lot of the hard work behind creating animated effects. We know that it needs us to add keyframes and just the start and end points of our animation and generates the tweening itself. This is basic stuff I know, but we'll go through a basic timeline-based animation to form a comparison with the power that even simple ActionScript can add.

Before we begin, make sure you start a new movie so you don't have that Stop action we were using earlier attached to any of the frames that we'll work on now.

1. Make sure that the grid is visible on your stage. Select the Circle tool from the toolbar. Make sure you have a fill color selected and draw out a small circle somewhere to the left of your stage.

2. Change to the Arrow tool and select the circle and its outline. Press **F8** or select **Insert > Convert to Symbol** and in the **Symbol Properties** window that will appear, enter the name **circle** and make sure that the **Graphic** behavior is selected:

Flash 4 users will notice that the order of behaviors is different in Flash 5, so don't go picking the wrong one on autopilot!

3. Now we have everything we need to create our simple animation. In the timeline, select frame 40 and hit **F6** to create a new keyframe. We want to add a motion tween between the two keyframes:

4. Select frame 1 and bring up the **Frame** panel (**Window > Panels > Frame**). In the **Tweening** drop-down menu select **Motion**:

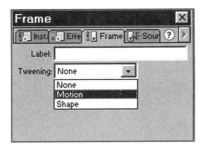

You'll now see a blue bar extend from frame 1 to 40, representing a motion tween between the two keyframes:

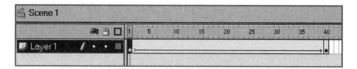

5. At the moment, the circle doesn't do anything between the two keyframes, so there's no movement. Select frame 40 on the timeline and move the circle a short distance to the right:

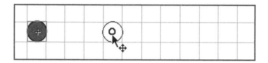

6. Now test the movie with **Control > Test Movie**. You'll see your circle move from left to right as it tweens between the two keyframes:

I'm sure that you're already familiar with this type of basic Flash animation. It always goes from left to right, always takes the same time and is pretty boring. The animation is *fixed* to repeating the same movement every time. It ignores anything we might do to try to change it, because it's not *interactive*.

Let's change that.

ActionScript-based Animation

1. Start a new movie with **File > New**. Create a circle again but, this time, put it in the middle of the stage and make it a movieclip symbol, not a graphic. Call it **circle**:

2. With the circle still selected, open the **Instance** panel (**Window > Panels > Instance**). Give the circle movieclip the name **ball**:

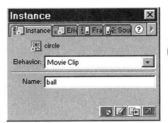

> *If the Instance panel is ghosted out and won't let you enter a name, make sure that you have the circle selected in **Scene 1** and that you haven't double-clicked so that **Circle** is highlighted at the top left of your window. Click on the Scene 1 tab to take you back to the circle surrounded by a square.*

Why did we just do that?

ActionScript needs to know what the movieclip is called before it can control it. We could leave it with the name **circle**, which is also the name of the movieclip in the library, but we would be stuck if we wanted to use it again somewhere different with new bits of ActionScript. So we have a *different* name that is particular to each *individual circle* movieclip - its **instance name**. Think of it as being like addressing identical twins. They might both be *boys* but you would have to give them individual names to be able to refer to them separately.

> *Creating individual instance names is particularly important in programming. It's an example of **instantiation**. This is the process of taking a general item and making it individual by giving it distinct properties, the simplest of which would be a unique name. Instantiation can involve giving the new individual more than just a name, and is an important concept that we'll look at towards the end of the book when we start to cover object-oriented programming.*

3. We want to add some ActionScript to control **ball**. One thing that I would recommend even in this early stage of your ActionScripting career is that you help yourself out by keeping your ActionScript always on a separate layer. Use the **Insert Layer (+)** button to add a new layer. Call the new layer **actions**.

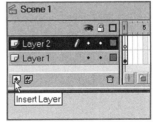

4. In the **actions** layer add a new keyframe at frame 2 (with **F6**). Add a new frame in layer 1 (with **F5**). The timeline should now look like this:

We're now ready to add our first bit of ActionScript. You may not understand exactly why you're doing what I'm asking of you at the moment, but don't worry. I'll explain everything in more detail in later chapters. For now, I want to show you what you can do with just two short lines of ActionScript code.

5. Select frame 1 of the **actions** layer. We now need to work inside the **Frame Actions** window. Remember how to bring it up? The easiest way to do it right now is to click on the little arrow icon on the bottom right of your Flash window:

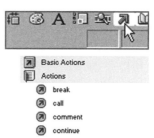

6. We need to select a set variable action. **Set variable** - sounds strange? Don't worry, set variables will make much more sense in later chapters. For now just be impressed by what it *does*. Bring up the list of actions either by (think back)... clicking on the **Actions** book icon or selecting **Actions** from the drop-down list under the **+** button. Click on **set variable** and the right-hand pane will suddenly contain the beginnings of our code:

```
<not set yet> = "";
```

But that's not the finished ActionScript. You'll see that parts of the code are highlighted red and that the Frame Actions window has expanded to give us an extra text line and two text boxes, labeled **Variable** and **Value**. Flash is expecting something from us.

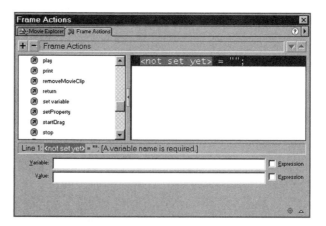

The text boxes tell us what values Flash needs and the red highlighted **not set yet** shows us where they will appear in the final ActionScript.

Line 1: `<not set yet>` = `""`; [A variable name is required]

So, we'll give Flash what it wants.

7. In the **Variable** field enter the text exactly as you see (don't forget the dot!):

        ball._x

8. In the **Value** field enter _xmouse

    Once you've entered this value, check the **Expression** box to the immediate right of the **Value** field. We'll look at this in more detail later, but for now know that an expression is a statement from which Flash knows it has to calculate a value – in this case the *x* position of the mouse. If we didn't check the **Expression** box here Flash would treat _xmouse as a literal piece of text that it should try to add to the ball – and quite rightly get confused!

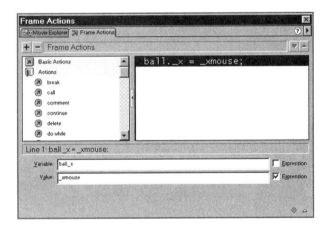

Once you've entered all the code correctly all the red highlighting disappears:

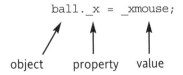

What have we done here?

Firstly, `ball` is our basic object – the ball movieclip.

`_x` is a property of that ball – its x co-ordinate position, or where it is horizontally on the screen.

We're setting this property (the horizontal position of the ball) to the x co-ordinate (horizontal) position of the cursor (`_xmouse`). Because *position* is obviously a visual property, we'll see the ball move:

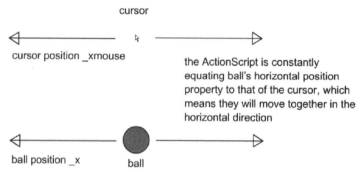

If all has gone well, we can now attach the final action to the second keyframe in the **actions** layer.

9. In the main timeline, click on frame 2. As frame 1 becomes deselected, you'll see a little **a** above the keyframe. This shows that the frame has a piece of ActionScript attached to it.

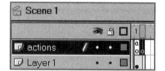

The right-hand pane in your Actions window should now be blank because, as yet, there are no actions atached to frame 2. Not for long.

10. Either from your open **Actions** book or the drop-down list under **+ > Actions**, select **Go To**.

```
gotoAndPlay (1);
```

will appear in the right-hand pane. This action gives Flash the obvious instruction to go to and play a frame. Cast your mind back to the beginning of the chapter when we were looking at commands and arguments. The number in brackets here is the argument that tells Flash *which* frame we want it to go to and play. By default, it offers to send us to frame 1, which, obviously, won't always be what we want. For now, though, that's fine so we don't need to change that number. The movie is sent back to frame 1, which makes the ball constantly follow the cursor through a looping timeline that keeps repeating our actions.

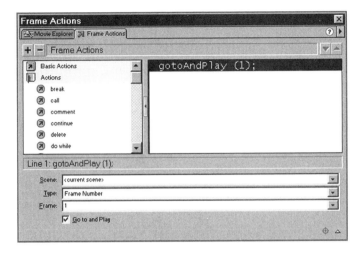

We're ready to test this movie. Do so with **Control > Test Movie**.

What happens?

The ball will sit there until you move the mouse. As soon as you do, it will move so that it's always in line with the cursor. Move your mouse to the left and the ball will roll the same distance in the same direction. Move the mouse to the right and, just like Mary's little lamb, our ball is sure to follow.

Notice that:

- The ball seems to be constantly watching for what you do.

- The ball reacts to what you do, and moves accordingly.

- The ball never performs the same fixed animation (unless you make it do so).

This animated effect is much more advanced than the last one. It's **interactive**. It watches for what the mouse does and immediately changes its own position to keep up. Our last animation just moved the ball from left to right. It will always do this. This time, we can control it.

Interaction even as simple as this opens up possibilities that we didn't have before. It could be the paddle from one of those old TV video games consoles...

Tennis anyone? You can see how easy it is to convert this ball to the paddle by looking at **chapter1_2.fla** in the download zip file. All I've done is change the ball to a rectangle, move it a bit lower down and make the background color black.

Or another thought – maybe a litle more exciting – you could just as easily change the paddle to a spaceship, so it could be The Lone Crusader© on his mission against the evil alien hordes...

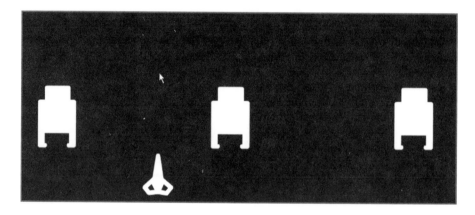

This time, the mouse lets us move our Starfleet SpaceCruiser™ as it dodges the alien plasma bolts... *save those cities young pilot!* Have a look at **chapter 1_3.fla** in the download zip file if you want to see this screen moving...

Sorry, we're not advanced enough to start adding the alien horde or associated bloolly bloolly bloolly blooop! sound effects just yet, but hey, we've only been learning this stuff for twenty minutes.

All this movement came about from two lines of ActionScript! Even better, it's the same two lines of ActionScript every time, and the whole thing is just two frames long! Two lines and we're already up to the maximum interactivity offered by home consumer entertainment systems when I was a kid. Just think what we could achieve with Flash and another forty or so lines of ActionScript...

This is why you need to know ActionScript. It's just so much more versatile. It can be dynamic in a way that leaves traditional Flash animation standing.

Summary

In this chapter, I've gone quite quickly through some basic programming concepts, along with a little ActionScript practice to give you a feel for things.

We've taken a look at:

- How basic events, like a button press, happen in Flash and how an event handler is set up to deal with them.

- How to add a simple action and a helpful comment to a keyframe.

- How commands, arguments and properties combine to give Flash instructions that it understands.

Don't worry if you didn't grasp the totality of the examples – from here on in we'll move through the concepts in greater depth and at a more leisurely pace!

In the next couple of chapters we'll take some time to prepare our workspace so that soon we're set up to add intelligence and power to our Flash animations – big time.

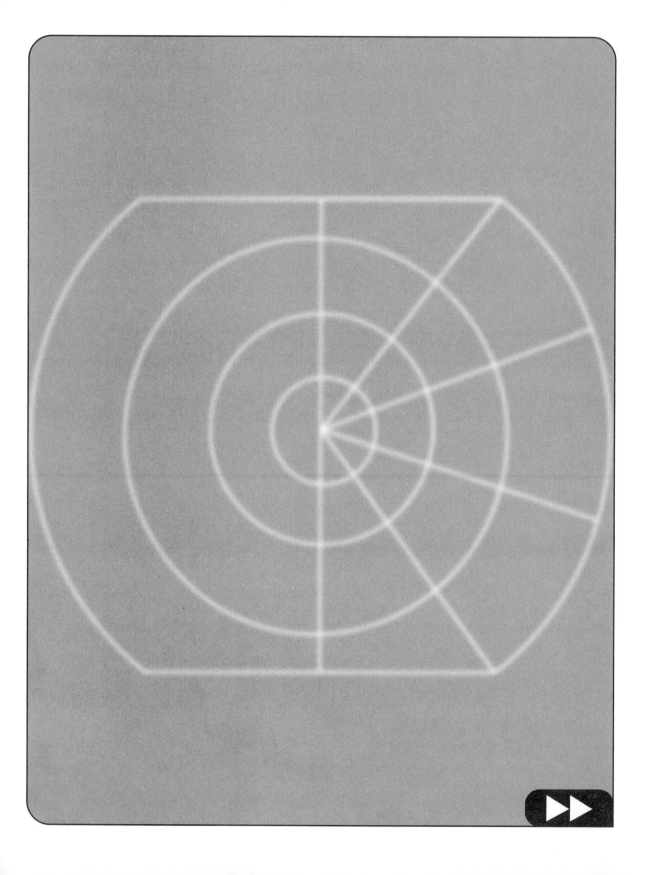

2 Making Plans

What we'll cover in this chapter:

- *How to plan your design project with the client and also in your own mind*

- *How to plan your ActionScript stage-by-stage to create the effect you want and to make your code easy to change if necessary*

- *How to plan the flow of your ActionScript within individual effects*

- *The planning stages of the **stun:design** web site*

▶

I've been involved in programming and design for some time now. My original discipline was engineering, and I've been close to computers of one form or another since the late 1980s. My engineering discipline has taught me a lot about computers and coding, and there is one fundamental rule that I've carried over with me into multimedia design:

If it doesn't work on paper, it won't work when you code it.

The single lines of ActionScript that we used in the last chapter, adding a simple Stop action and making our ball follow the mouse, are straightforward enough to not need too much planning. You have one Flash animation, you know when you want it to stop and there's one action that will do that for you.

By the time you've finished this book, though, you should be getting near to your goal of coding advanced interfaces and cool graphic effects. That's where things get a little too involved to hold the full plan in your head.

In this chapter, I'd like to show you how my first step at the beginning of a project is to establish the design goals from the client's point of view. From there, I split that problem into manageable sections and structure my ActionScript within them so that it gives me exactly what I want in a way that's easy to change if I need to.

I'll round off the chapter with a little reminder that web design isn't just a cold coding process. I'll introduce you to stun:design, a web site project that we'll work on as we go through the book and learn how to plan interfaces that are usable and cool vehicles to show off your cutting-edge ActionScript skills.

The best place to start is always the beginning, and that beginning is where you define what you need to do and plan how to do it.

Making Plans

If this were a textbook on writing novels, this chapter would be all about defining your plot. Without plot, your characters would have no motive and your audience would quickly realise your book was going nowhere.

The same holds true for your ActionScript coding. If you don't have a good idea of what you want to achieve with your design before you open up that Actions window, you're stuck. Most designers love to play around with ideas and end up with a toolbox of little demos and cool effects that they can put together later to build up a full web site. Even this organic way of working (which is the way I work too) requires you to think about how your effects will fit together and what your aim actually is for a web site. You should have a fair idea of your direction before you start programming.

In real life you have a further complication that thwarts your ideas and clean, structured designs. That complication is the client. A good plan is a safety net that helps you guard against those little requests, "Can we just move everything half a pixel to the left", or "No, we can't use that, didn't I tell you we wanted an advertising banner to go on top?" (uhh, no you didn't), and the all time classic, "That's great, and I know we go online in two days, but here's a list of 35 minor changes that Bob and I would like...".

The primary driving force of design must be managing the expectations of the client and discussing their real needs. Formulating the project beforehand and getting agreement early on goes some way to solving this, but I would be making false promises if I were to tell you that in a typical project your design objectives won't change at least once. You have to live with this and make sure that you define your designs well enough so that you can go backwards as well as forwards, and branch out onto a new path if the client (or technical problems) force you to do so.

Your plans will help you through this, so you can point to them and say things like, "Well, if you want to make that change, this will have to go, this will have to move here and that will go there, is that okay?", without having to take the time to actually do it first to see what it will look like. This is a fact of web design, and you won't really see it until you have finished a few paid jobs.

A Library of Ideas

Working in a field that requires me to think creatively doesn't mean that I can come up with all the design ideas exactly when I need them. Just when I could use something like that great mosaic effect I saw in a magazine ad three weeks ago, the magazine's gone and you can bet I don't remember exactly how it looked. I've learned over the last few years to always carry with me a hardbound book of lined paper where I note down ideas as they come to me. My other companion is a book of black card pages (black because it makes things much easier to scan into a computer), where I keep pictures that catch my eye.

I have a real collection of images in my book now, from Polish Nightclub flyers to stylized text-less instructions for inserting camera film told through icons. It's all great reference material. For example, I've kept the edge of an old pay slip of mine from a few years ago, one that was obviously printed by a big fast industrial computer printer. It has those funny sprocket holes in it, some print registration marks and some optical character recognition numbers. I would have normally put this straight into the trash, but one day is struck me that it had a real *made by computer* feel, so I kept it. Several years later, I used it for the opening titles of a graphic novel that I'm writing and illustrating which has an intelligent supercomputer as a main character.

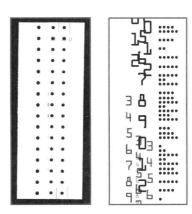

You can see the progress from the grubby bit of paper on the left to the finished article on the right. Download the files for this chapter and take a look at **chapter2_01.swf** to see how the final design turned out. You may think that it looks similar to the data animations from *The Matrix*, but mine was based on a scrappy bit of paper and not a thousand-dollar computer animation... Inspiration comes cheap.

What you see around you is the richest source of inspiration that you'll ever come across. The first piece of advice that I give to any new designer is to get into the habit of noticing and collecting. You're in a bar, you see a great color combination on a beer mat, take it home to put into your design library. Anything that may spark off an idea in your head is worth hanging on to.

OK, you've talked to the client, you've gathered a collection of ideas from things that you see every day and perhaps any assets (sound, music, video clips) that will play a part in your final site design. The next step is to tie down these ideas, to form a concrete shape that shows you how you need to implement any ActionScript as part of the project.

There are a number of ways for you to do this:

1. Write down the essence of the site in plain English.

2. Quickly code up a basic sample site and discuss it with the client if possible.

3. Storyboard the site, perhaps as a set of static Photoshop or PaintShop Pro mock-ups, and present them for approval.

4. Or most likely, a mixture of all the above.

I find the storyboarding option the most useful, both in terms of communicating with the client, and for my own use, to see how the site develops stage by stage.

Storyboarding

The term **storyboarding** is a throwback to the film industry, referring to the sequence of pictures drawn by cartoonists to plan how characters would move during the animation. Starting your designs in the same way, with sketches and pictures, I think is the best way to get a preliminary feel for what you want. It allows you to define navigation, visualization and style early on in your site design before you get involved in the finer details of animating and programming.

Some people may ask, "Why waste time creating static sketches when you could just as easily start drawing in Flash?" I find that the little extra work I put into storyboarding really lifts a presentation and allows me to fully explore my creative ideas before I need to concentrate on developing and animating them in Flash itself.

Remember, if it doesn't work on paper, it won't work when you code it.

A storyboard can be whatever you want: a sketch on a piece of scrap paper, just for your own use, or a fully blown presentation of the site from beginning to end to show to the client, like this:

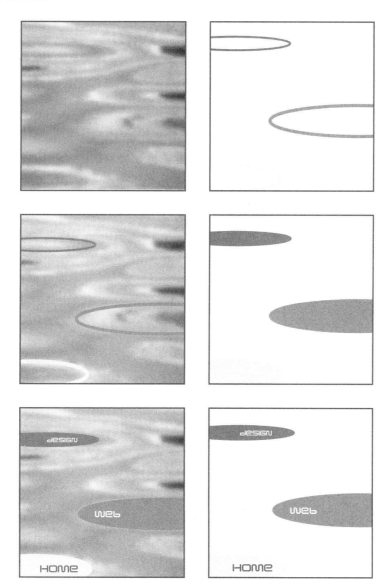

I've seen complex storyboards showing a full web site mocked up, with arrows and typed notes saying how everything will work. My advice is to find the middle road between those two.

I rarely do more than a few sketches and perhaps a preliminary mock-up of one page in Photoshop to set the feel of the site. The client is paying you for the finished site and not the intermediate artwork, so make the storyboarding functional and don't go overboard - it isn't a finished product in its own right.

Assuming that the client hasn't requested to see it, this is the kind of sketch that I begin my work with:

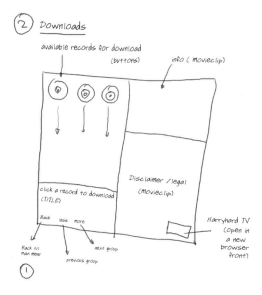

This one is for the part of a site I designed where you can select from a number of different band names, and download available (and I hasten to add, legal) MP3 files. It probably took me a maximum of ten minutes to draw, but if you look at the final page based on this sketch, you can see that the final interface is very true to the initial sketch.

Storyboarding also gives you an opportunity to start figuring out how to begin coding effects for particular areas of the site. On the music site, I had to deal with the fact that the user might choose to skip the intro before the essential components of the main site had downloaded. To cater for this, I needed something to show the viewer how long they would have to wait and keep them amused for this short time. I thought a VU meter would be quite a novel way of showing this, with the needle flickering up the scale to show the percentage loaded. As you can see, in this part of the storyboarding and sketching, I'm already starting to think about how the needle needs to be animated by ActionScript.

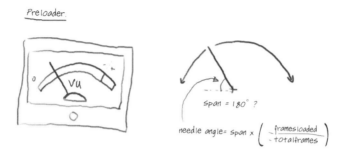

Here's the final work. Again, quite close to the initial three-minute scrappy sketch...

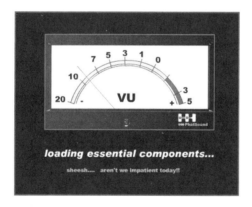

It's worth remembering that Flash isn't necessarily the best environment for you to develop your initial ideas. Playing around within graphics packages like Adobe Photoshop or PaintShop Pro, along with making your own sketches, can be a much richer way of working. Twenty minutes at the beginning of your project with a sheet of paper and a biro planning the interface and storyboarding how the ActionScript will work is time well spent.

Once you've sketched what you want to do with your ActionScript, you can again save yourself a lot of time by staying away from your monitor just a little longer and not diving headfirst into that Actions window. Take some time to plan in more detail how your code will be structured to fit with your designs. I'll show you here that you have two options for building your ActionScript:

- From the bottom up

- From the top down

Building your ActionScript

As you begin to think in ActionScript terms, you're always starting from the same point: you know how you want your designs to work. What you need to think about is the best way to get there.

There are two main ways of breaking down programming problems: top down or bottom up. **Top-down** design routes involve looking at the overall task and breaking the problem down into smaller and smaller chunks, whereas a **bottom-up** design would mean starting by looking at the basic building blocks, adapting them and building upwards towards the final solution.

Thinking from the Top Down

The top-down method is called a **functional** method, because it looks at the functions that you have to carry out, or *what you have to do at every stage*, to reach the *solution*. You begin by looking at the aim in general terms, or **high-level requirements**. Then you break each of those general stages up into separate steps that become easier and easier to manage. They are the individual **requirements** that you can deal with in turn on your way to building the final solution.

Sound strange? Let's say that we're looking at breaking down the high level requirement of making a cup of tea. If we took the top-down approach, we'd first define the top-level design statement, which is:

Make a cup of tea

...and then break it down by one level to its main stages:

1.0 Boil some water.

2.0 Put some sugar and a teabag into a cup.

3.0 If the kettle has boiled, pour some water into the cup.

4.0 After 2 minutes, remove the teabag, add some milk and stir.

Breaking the task down to this level is called the **first iteration**.

We'd then look at each of these tasks and break them down even further:

1.1 Fill kettle with water, 2/3 full.

1.2 Switch the kettle on.

2.1 Add one teaspoonful of sugar to the cup.

2.2 Add one teabag into the cup.

3.1 Wait until the kettle has boiled.

3.2 Pour water from the kettle into the cup, until the cup is 3/4 full.

4.1 Wait two minutes.

4.2 Remove the teabag from the cup.

4.3 Add milk to the cup until the cup is 7/8ths full.

This is the **second iteration**:

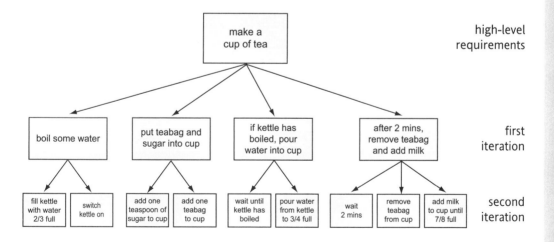

The top-down approach fits well when you're dealing with a tightly defined problem. A tight definition eliminates the need for too many iterations, or breaking the task down again and again, and makes each stage easy to change if necessary. For anything more complex, though, it throws up some pretty basic problems. The most important of these is that if the high level requirement changes, that change must filter down through all the iterations, making you think about what you do at every stage all over again.

For example, if you preferred coffee, you'd have to start at the beginning all over again with a new top-level design statement:

Make a cup of coffee

... and change all the instructions at every stage below that, to replace *teabag* references to, say, *spoon full of coffee*, take out that *wait two minutes* stage, because now we're not waiting for the tea to brew, and so on and so on. You may think that this isn't such big job in this domestic real-world example, but if your top-level design statement read:

Build a navigation computer system for a combat helicopter with satellite position systems, radar and weapons management facilities

... you'd have a bit more of a problem changing things around when the boss changed his mind about what he wanted his helicopter to do. You'd have to look at all ten thousand of the requirements for the system and see what the impact of the change that your boss was asking for was on each requirement. This can take an extremely long time (I know, I've been there in similar civil projects!) and even longer if you have to prove that you did the analysis of the changes properly. This experience has taught me to go for the easier option when I can. Speaking of which...

Thinking from the Bottom Up

Making a change in a bottom-up design is nowhere near as difficult. Taking the bottom-up approach involves looking at the problem, splitting it up into very general areas and asking, "What are the basic building blocks here?" You look for basic structures within your problem and write general solutions for them, before adding specific details to these general solutions to make them suit the problem that you're dealing with.

Going back to our tea example, the general building blocks of the problem are:

- Moving things around from one container (such as a sugar bowl) to another container (such as a cup).

- Measuring quantities.

- Waiting for particular processes to complete (boiling the kettle).

If we were tackling this in ActionScript, we'd begin to create actions based around these general building blocks. We could start with a *moving* action, to which we could add details of whichever containers and substances were involved:

move (from_container, to_container, thing)

a *measuring* action, where we can display *how much of what substance* we want measured:

measure (quantity, substance)

a *switching on the kettle action*, using basic commands:

kettle (on)

an event/event handler structure like we saw in the last chapter to detect when the kettle has boiled and switch it off:

if (water has boiled) {switch kettle off}

We could then look at the problem and see how to build up to making a cup of tea using these structures. For example, to fill the kettle we'd want to use the *move* routine to fill it with water from the tap, so:

from_container	is the tap
to_container	is the kettle
thing	is water

My *thing* is not just any amount of water, but two thirds of the kettle. I can express it as:

measure (water, TwoThirdsOfTheKettle)

  2/3

So my full statement to fill the kettle would be:

move (tap, kettle, measure (water, TwoThirdsOfTheKettle))

    2/3

Taking it all in this way, my basic solution might look like this:

```
move (tap, kettle, measure (water, TwoThirdsOfTheKettle))
kettle (on)
move (sugarbowl, cup, measure (sugar, OneTeaSpoon))
move (teacaddy, cup, teabag)
        repeat {
        }
        until (event (kettle_boiled))
move (kettle, cup, measure (water, TwoThirdsCup))
repeat {
}
until (event (tea brewed))
move (cup, trash, teabag)
move (milkBottle, cup, measure (milk,OneEighthCup)
stop
```

This looks suspiciously like ActionScript already! We've built in all the details to the general actions that we've identified as the building blocks for the making the tea process. But we've also streamlined that process by taking out some of the stages defined in the top-down approach. Point 4.1 up there was to wait two minutes for the tea to brew. We haven't had to specify that amount of detail here – we've been able to set up an event/event handler pair like we saw in Chapter 1 to say:

```
repeat {
}
until ( event (tea brewed) )
```

or

```
do { nothing } until (the tea has brewed)
```

We don't care how long that takes, just that the program carries on with the appropriate action when that event is met.

With the top-down approach, if we bought cheap and nasty teabags that took an age to brew, we would have to rewrite the program to tell it to wait ten minutes instead of two before it went to the next stage. With our bottom-up approach, we're concentrating on what happens once the tea has brewed, not on how long that takes to happen, so our code can stay the same.

So, I hope you can see that the bottom-up method can save us a little work and is also useful when the main problem or design aim is likely to change often, which could happen more than you think.

I'll give you another example. We used a *move* routine to fill the kettle with water from the tap. Once we've written that general routine, we can use it over again, with just minor adjustments for several other actions, including:

move (teacaddy, cup, teabag)

With our top-down solution, wanting coffee instead of tea caused us a major problem and we had look again at the whole process. If we're faced with that problem here, the basic building blocks stay the same, we just have to change a few minor details again:

move (coffeejar, cup, coffeepowder)

Much easier. Because our bottom-up design didn't look just at the top level problem (making tea), we generalized the problem, or **abstracted** it. So, we don't care whether it's tea or coffee or crude oil - we can still use our basic **move()** and **measure()** building blocks again, and won't have to change them when we do. Bottom-up design digs the foundations before building on top of them, while top-down just puts itself down in any old way. In the winds of change, you can guess which one stays standing longer.

This bottom-up design method can be much harder to understand than the top-down alternative because, as adults, I guess we all prefer to think *functionally*. Common sense says that bottom-up design shouldn't work, but it seems to work rather well. It really comes into its own with problems that can be reduced to a few types of building blocks, which means that it works particularly well with animation and graphic interfaces.

I recently provided technical support for *New Masters of Flash*, a book from friends of ED in which Flash designers, including Yugo Nakamura and Manuel Clement, wrote about their work and showed how they had put together some pretty impressive effects. It struck me that all the designers featured were, without exception, using a bottom-up approach to their ActionScripting. This was despite the fact that these were all creative people who were the first in their field and taught themselves ActionScript – in other words, the type of people you may expect to find using a top-down approach. The work that we'll do in the final few chapters of this book will be based on a bottom-up approach, as it looks like a required skill for those of you who want to be in the next volume of *New Masters of Flash*.

When you code in Flash, matters aren't usually as clean cut as a straight choice between a top-down and bottom-up approach. Most ActionScript structures will require a mix of the two. We'll talk about what approach to take with different ActionScript structures later. The aim of this section was to enable you to look at a problem and start to think about the best way to code it. Thinking and looking before jumping straight into coding will mean that your Actionscript changes from a 'keep coding until it works' mindset to something altogether more elegant in thought and design.

We've just taken a look at the type of general approach you might want to take as you build large sections of ActionScript. I'll now show you something that I use to help me work out what my code will look like on a smaller scale, how the ActionScript to solve a particular problem will flow.

Flowcharting

When I've got down to thinking about what happens even within a single frame, I still find it useful to think in structural terms before I start to code in detail. Again, I think you'll find that thinking in general terms like this for a few minutes helps you build your ActionScript much more fluently and with a lot more logic. As always, my favorite tool at this stage is a visual one: a flowchart.

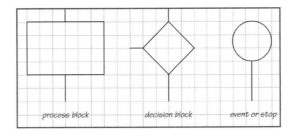

To build an ActionScript flowchart, you use three kinds of flow symbol:

The process block represents a set of linear actions that occur one after another.

The decision block is like a junction. You can either go forward or turn, depending on whether the answer to your question is true or false (yes or no).

The event/stop circle represents the event that starts or finishes a particular flowchart.

Let's look at this with a concrete example. Say we wanted to build a menu of buttons that allowed the user to control how a movieclip plays, just as if it were a videocassette in a video machine. Once we'd created a set of buttons a bit like these, we would want to attach some ActionScript to each of them. I'll show you how we could use flowcharts to help define what each button does.

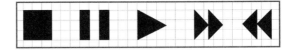

As we begin to plan, we'll make a note of some main points:

1. We're interested in two main properties of the movieclip, **_currentframe** and **_totalframes**.

2. The **_currentframe** property describes the frame that Flash is currently playing.

3. The **_totalframes** property is the total number of frames within the movieclip (which is, of course equal to the number of the final frame).

4. The first frame is when **_currentframe = 1**.

With these in mind, we'll build some flowcharts.

The **Stop** button is fairly straightforward. When the user presses it, we want the movie to stop. The flowchart shows that when a press event is detected on the stop button, we need to have some ActionScript that stops the movie exactly where it is, at its **_currentframe**:

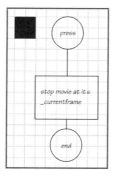

The **Pause** button is slightly more complicated. When the user presses it we need the movie to stop just where it is as if the Stop button had been pressed. But we also need to set the movie playing again when that Pause button is released. So, we have two events in our flow diagram:

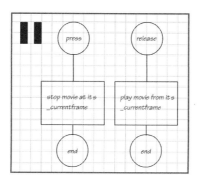

When the viewer presses the **FastForward** button we need the movieclip to advance at a much faster rate than normal. To make it move at, say, five times the normal rate, we would ask it to go to **_currentframe + 5**, every time the user presses FastForward.

Houston, we have a problem. If we press FastForward when we're within five frames of the end of the movie, that means that we're asking the movie to go beyond the last frame. We need to make sure that we don't ask our script to go further than the end of the clip. This means that our ActionScript will have to make a decision: if the **_currentframe** is within five frames of the **_lastframe**, we want the movie to go to the **_lastframe**. If it isn't, we want it to go to **_currentframe + 5** as normal.

If we draw a flowchart for this, we can see that we have to build in code to check whether **_currentframe** is greater than or equal to the **_lastframe − 5** and two routines to tell the movieclip what to do, depending on the answer:

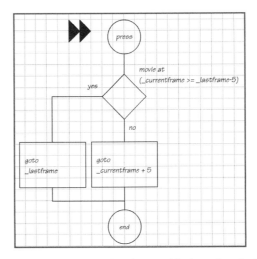

These diagrams show how you can use a simple graphical tool to help yourself to work out the advanced level of logic that the final code must have. You could very quickly sketch these diagrams on a piece of scrap paper before you begin to build the ActionScript behind each button to give yourself some pretty useful visual clues.

Don't go overboard though. Flowcharts are useful, especially for designing a single event handler that consists of lots of decisions or loops, or both, but they do have their limitations. If you try to flowchart really long sections of ActionScript, you'll quickly run out of paper and you may find that drawing the flow diagrams can become more difficult that writing the code in the first place. I use flowcharts to get a simplified bit of ActionScript going. Then, once it's working, I forget about flowcharts and slowly start building up the ActionScript itself.

For example, with our FastForward button the simple structure that we saw in the flowchart is fine as a beginning, but if things were left this way, the user would find that they had to click the button over and over again to keep the movie playing FastForward. The solution for this would be to build a **toggle** mechanism into the button, something that makes it continuously alternate between two actions each time it's pressed. The first time the user presses, it's set to run on FastForward and carry on running until it's pressed again, when it's set to stop. I could have flowcharted the solution to this, but taking the skeleton that we've seen here, coding it and then adding this additional function would be quicker.

I've shown you a lot of theoretical planning over the last few pages. I'll admit that this has held up our hands on practice temporarily, but you'll thank me in the long term, I promise. Working in these thoughts and planning processes to your designs will save you a lot of head-scratching and sleepless nights as you find that you have to start over when the client changes his mind or because your ActionScript doesn't work how you thought it would.

We'll get back into the real world now, where I'll introduce you to a project that we'll be coming back to throughout the book.

stun:design Web Site

Anders Dhyr and I have worked together to create stun:design.com especially for this book. Sure, its first purpose was to be a case study for the topics that we cover here, but at the same time we don't believe in books that show basic coding principles using non-commercial quality mock-ups that would never be used in real life. So, we decided to treat this as a fully commercial project, acquiring the URL and building the site just as you would – as a shop window that we're happy to use to show our skills. We wanted something that an accidental visitor would believe was a real design house. Who knows, it might even tempt them to offer us work!

My first idea for stun:design came two years ago as I heard the TV in the background while I was concentrating on some work. I heard the phrase *'set your phasers to stun'* but mistook it for *'set your browsers to stun'*. That went straight into the notebook that I talked about earlier, with the word *stun* circled and a note saying "Good name for a site. Instant strapline!" (In case you've not come across that term before, it means a sort of subtitle, a phrase beneath the title that adds to the logo.)

As I began working on this book I looked back at my ideas library and picked that out as the name for the case study site. I had to communicate this idea graphically, so I opened up Photoshop and Flash and started playing. I thought about the main word **stun** first. I wanted it to be bold and have a bit of movement. This is what I came up with:

After following the full design route of stun:design with us, you will be able to understand the workings of advanced Flash sites. This means that you'll be able to start a site to showcase your newfound skills.

My big idea so far is a bit of text in Arial italics! In my defense, I always start simple. It's less work to do later when you come back to refine your ideas.

Next, I had to include the line **set your browsers to stun**. Well, I knew this came from the sentence *set your phasers to stun*, so thought that this might work:

I thought the stun: gun logo was something that might look better in print than on a site, perhaps as a letterhead. I kept it as food for thought, put it back into my ideas book and went on to think along the stun gun theme. That threw up three images for me: laser beams, targets/crosshairs and gun flashes when you fire.

I liked the idea of a target because it would be easy to draw. As I started to draw I began to think that it could look like a radar screen too, which fits in well with the stun > phasers > Star Trek train of thought, so I modified it to look like a radar grid:

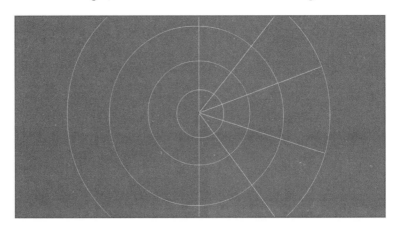

The gun flash was potentially my weakest idea, but here it is anyway. This is just an asterisk that I slanted in Flash, with the rightmost arm extended:

Here's my first attempt at putting it all together. The movie is long because I wanted to retain the ability to make the site a 'side-scroller' in a later chapter. Until then, we can use the browser scrollbars. I also thought about adding a starfield in the radar bit as well, which you can see in **stun_beta.fla** once you've downloaded it.

I passed my ideas on to Anders (who, unlike me, actually finished art school) to see what he would do:

As you can see, Anders replaced:

- Arial with the better proportioned Humanist font to stop the site looking like every other site that uses it in the same way (Arial, along with Helvetica, is a very popular font). He also changed the stun: logo 'because it represented such a good typographic opportunity' in Humanist. I consider myself told regarding my fontographic faux pas.

- The two different stun logos with just one. More than one logo tends to confuse the viewer and weaken the impact of an individual image. (I put them all on so that Anders could experiment and pick the one he liked best – that's my story and I'm sticking to it.)

- My nice web-safe colors with colors chosen purely for their aesthetic value. Anders reckons that all those old books on HTML design which told me to use web-safe colors are outmoded and that anyone still viewing the internet from a screen set to 256 colors won't know what Flash is either. I think I need to get out more. The only other reason for using a web-safe palette is to make sure that the site looks the same across platforms, but since only the most diligent Photoshop operator actually calibrates their monitor, we passed on that one.

He also added:

- A definition of the word **stun** that he picked up from a dictionary, to emphasis the way we are using it – **to impress greatly**, obviously.

- A movie clip of lightning striking, which fits in with the theme of stun and electricity.

- Some custom HTML using the default Flash HTML publish settings to get rid of the gutters around the site, which you can have a peek at if you're feeling adventurous.

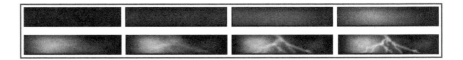

You'll soon be looking at preliminary FLAs written for the site by Anders and myself. As we work through the book we'll be adding some ActionScript details to this basic design. The text will eventually rotate around the radar screen. We'll also be adding pop-up windows and drop-down menus and some other ActionScript magic.

Summary

Until then, remember what we've said in this chapter about making sure that things work on paper:

- Keep a supply of design ideas as you come across them.

- Talk to the client to establish a clear idea of your design goals.

- Storyboard your ideas either for your use or to present to the client.

- Plan your ActionScript from the bottom up to give yourself plenty of room for maneuver.

- Use a flowchart to work out the logic of small pieces of ActionScript.

We've now scaled the foothills of Mount ActionScript. We've prepared our design, bought the boots and learnt the techniques necessary to climb those steep crags. Now we can embark on ActionScripting for real from our snug little tent at base camp one. Hold your breath....

stun:

3 Timeline Actions

What we'll cover in this chapter:

- *A first look at the new Flash 5 dot notation and how to use it to specify paths of communication between timelines*

- *The use of the **Play** and **Stop** and **Go To** actions*

- *Adding labels to our timelines*

- *How to move between scenes with ActionScript*

You now have a grounding in the fundamentals of site planning and underlying ActionScript concepts so it's time to introduce the basic structures of ActionScript. We're going to start with timeline-based actions.

One of the major steps forward with Flash 5 is the control that we now have over our movies through adding just the simplest Stop, Play and Go To actions to our timeline. Those simple commands have been given a surge of power by the Flash 5's long-awaited **dot notation**, a form of ActionScript syntax that has opened opportunities to build communication between timelines and to control how one movieclip plays from deep within another. We'll use an advanced form of dot notation to create dynamic animation by varying properties in a later chapter but over the next few pages we'll look at how it's used to specify paths for simple commands.

While we're on the subject of the timeline, let me give you a quick piece of housekeeping advice. When you're writing ActionScript it's always a good idea to keep all your code in its own layer. When I'm starting a new Flash presentation, one of the first things I do is create a layer for all of my ActionScript, called...um Actions, and place it at the top of the timeline:

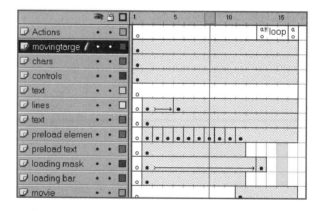

If you get into this routine too, you should find that you've made your life easier because:

- You know where all your ActionScript is, and can quickly follow it from frame to frame.

- You won't accidentally delete or move important ActionScript frames by moving their layers around, as you would if your ActionScript was on several layers.

- You can quickly 'switch off' your Actionscript. For example, if you wanted to run through a timeline animation to see what it would do without all the pauses and jumps created by the ActionScripting, you could save your file, temporarily delete the Actions layer, test your movie and undo the deletion to bring the layer back.

- If you put actions on separate layers and you had two scripts on the same frame but on different layers, it's sometimes difficult to know which one will run first (normally, the bottom one would run first, but it can be changed in the publish settings).

OK, that's the housekeeping over. Let's get into the meat of this chapter. We'll look first at how to communicate between timelines, using dot notation to specify different routes or **paths**.

Timeline Paths

You may be used to thinking of the main timeline operating in isolation from any other timeline in a movieclip. As soon as you start adding ActionScript, your timelines can start to talk, and you can build in mechanisms to control one timeline from within another. Think of how much power that will give to your designs.

Sure, you may have come across this capability within previous releases of Flash, but the ActionScript involved was a lot more contrived and long-winded. The bottleneck is no longer there in Flash 5, as the old TellTarget command is now deprecated. This means that, although you can still use the old method, Flash 5 now offers you a much better and easier way of doing the same thing: **dot notation**. This method requires an understanding of timeline levels and the relationship between timelines.

To get that understanding we'll look at an example that we all know well.

What's on your hard-drive? Lots of Files. If it's anything like mine, there are all sorts of things, from Word files to bitmaps from art packages, 3D files and textures from 3DMax and all sorts of Internet file formats like Flash, HTML and Shockwave for Director. There's even the odd game hidden away for when I need a bit of relaxation after typing away for hours on end.

How do we sort all these files into something meaningful? We use folders or directories:

Look at the picture of the hard drive that stores the Word files for chapters in this book, and you'll see that I've diligently set up a meaningful directory structure for my publishing work. For each chapter, there's a **files** folder that contains the Word document, the FLA and other files used for that chapter, and a **snaps** directory for the picture files used for the chapter. Finally, there's a directory called **stun design**, which holds all the files for the stun:design site. I'm sure that none of this is new to you – you have something similar of your own.

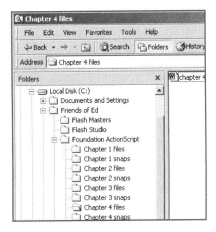

It's pretty obvious that everything starts at your hard drive. However many directories you set up, each containing sub-directories and folders of their own, they all have the same anchor point: the hard drive. This level in the filing system has a special name: **root**.

All the directories that you create for your work within your hard drive are **daughters** of that root.

Looking at it another way, the daughter directories have root as their **parent**. The second row of daughters have daughter **D** from the upper level as their parent.

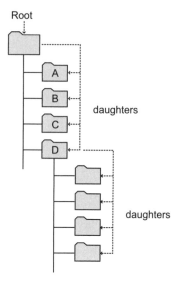

We all know that when we want to move between directories, we move up and down this hierarchy. I have all the files for this book in a folder called Foundation Actionscript, which has daughter directories where I store the material for individual chapters. If I want to get to a file within the Chapter 4 folder of Foundation ActionScript, I specify a route, which can either take along an **absolute path** or a **relative path**, to where I want to be.

The **absolute path** is so called because it takes me back to the very beginning of the directory structure, the hard drive, down through all the daughter directories and files until I get to the file that I want. So, that absolute path looks like this:

F:\Friends of ED\Foundation Actionscript\chapter 4.wp

The more direct route is the **relative path**. Instead of taking the long way round from the very top of the hierarchy, the relative path sets is starting point relative to where I am now in that directory structure and sees where I need to go from there. If, say, I was already at the folder, friends of ED, and I wanted to get to that Chapter 4 folder, I could use the relative path:

\Foundation Actionscript\chapter 4.wp

This understands that I'm already half way there and that the path just needs to take me the final few steps.

So how does this match up within Flash?

Just like that hard-drive, the main Flash timeline is called **_root**. That _root timeline can have movieclips nested within it with, obviously, timelines of their own. Flash 5 ActionScript has given us more power to make those nested timelines communicate along paths similar to those that we've just seen.

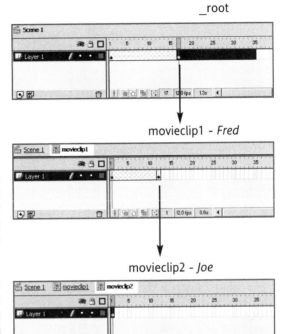

_root

At the top of the hierarchy pictured here, you can see the **_root** timeline that has 35 frames. In our hard-disk analogy, _root is the root directory.

movieclip1 - *Fred*

Frame 17 is a keyframe, and on this frame there is a movie called **movieclip1**. It's called this in the library, but its instance name is **Fred**. Fred is a **daughter** directory within **_root**. If Fred is the daughter of _root, then _root is obviously the parent of Fred.

movieclip2 - *Joe*

Movieclip1 has a second movie on its own timeline, called **movieclip2**. This movieclip has an instance name **Joe**. Joe is a subdirectory, or daughter, of Fred and Fred can specify that Joe is his parent. Joe is where our family tree ends because it has one keyframe with no further movies embedded within.

OK we know how are timelines are related. How do we generate family harmony by getting them to talk?

We want one timeline to send an action to another, so:

- We need to tell the message which way to go to the timeline you want: the **path**.

- We need to define the message: the **command**.

- We need to add any extra details that qualify that command: the **arguments**.

In ActionScript terms that structure looks like this:

```
path.command(arguments);
```

To stop the _root timeline from within itself, we would use the action:

```
stop();
```

which you've used already. Behind the scenes of this command and, in fact, all the others that you'll use, Flash adds a path at the front to make things even clearer:

```
this.stop();
```

this is useful as a path, because we'll see in another chapter it allows a movieclip to change its *own* properties.

To stop the **Fred** instance from within the root timeline you can use either the **absolute** path:

```
_root.fred.stop();
```

or the **relative** path:

```
fred.stop();
```

In the same way, to stop the **Joe** instance from within **Fred** you could either take the absolute path:

```
_root.fred.joe.stop();
```

or the relative path:

```
fred.joe.stop();
```

Going away from the root like this, to all the timelines nested within, is called **moving down the hierarchy**. I'll show you now how things are a little different if you're controlling things from the other direction, moving **up the hierarchy**, from **Joe** to the **root** timeline.

Because we're no longer controlling from the root timeline, the absolute and relative paths will now look completely different. To stop **Fred** from within **Joe** we can use the absolute or relative commands:

_root.fred.stop();   absolute path   _parent.stop();   relative path

The absolute path, as normal, says "Forget where we are now, just go back to the beginning and get to Fred from there".

The relative path uses the _parent pathname. This means **go up one level in the hierarchy**. The _parent path is different from any other path that we've seen so far because it doesn't *explicitly* refer to Joe. This means that if you did a _parent.stop(); command from a nested movieclip, it would always stop its parent timeline, whatever it was called. If you dropped it into a totally new timeline, it would still stop its (new) parent timeline. Had you built the path including the movieclip instance name, dropping it into another timeline obviously wouldn't work.

> To put it a different way, you don't have to know the instance name of the movieclip that you're controlling when you write the code. This is the basic premise of a powerful branch of programming called modular design.

Anyway, to control the root from within Joe, we have two options again:

```
_root.stop();        absolute path    _parent.parent.stop();        relative path
```

The absolute path says "Go back to the top and get to root from there," which is obviously just one step because root is at the very top.

The relative path says, "Start from here and go back through all the levels between here and the root." So, go back to the first parent, which is **Fred**, and from there to the parent above, which is **root**.

Our last piece of theory before we get some hands-on action (again) is a reminder of the term that I introduced in the introduction: **instantiation**.

From the tween animations that you've been creating, I guess you already know about library symbols and instances and that all instances are still linked to the version in the library. Change the library version and all the instances change too.

As far as ActionScript is concerned, the top dog in the library is the movieclip symbol because it has a particular property that the instances before now do not have; it has a name that makes it unique. That's instantiation for you: making a symbol unique, with properties and a name of its own that won't carry through to other instances of that symbol.

> *Once you've made a symbol unique by giving it a name, ActionScript can use that name to control that symbol. ActionScript can't control any of a symbol's properties without a name **because it would have no way of differentiating between two otherwise identical instances.** This is a fundamental point in ActionScripting practice.*

We've already seen how movieclip1 was instantiated, made unique by receiving the name Fred. Movieclip2 was turned into a unique being with the name Joe. It was those names, those unique properties that ActionScript needed to be able to build efficient communication paths.

As we move onto using specific timeline actions now, you'll see that the same applies to the symbols that we use: we have to either make them into movieclips or give them the behavior of movieclips so that they can have a name for ActionScript to refer to.

I'll start by giving you a brief recap of the basic Stop and Play actions, before we go on to the slightly more interesting Go To.

Adding Basic Timeline Actions

The first three actions in the Actions window toolbox list are **Go To**, **Play** and **Stop**. These are all actions that work on the timeline. Essentially, they do what they say.

Pretty obviously, the Play action makes the timeline play. It's not much use on the timeline on its own because, if you think about it, to reach a frame that contains a Play action, the timeline has to be playing already. So what's the point then? Well, the Play action does have purpose in life. It's useful for restarting a stopped timeline from another timeline or button. We'll be seeing this in detail later as we look at how to make timelines talk to one another.

We've already had a brief look at the Stop action in Chapter 1 but zip through this exercise quickly if you need to remind yourself.

Adding a Stop Action

The Stop action stops the timeline at the current frame. Let's go back to the ball that we last saw in the Chapter 1.

1. Just as we did before, create a 40-frame motion tween of a ball moving from left to right. Don't forget to make the circle into a symbol.

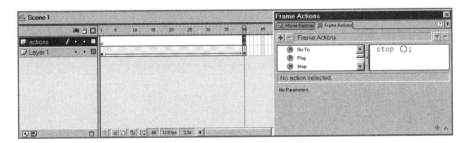

We now have that boring ball-moves-left-to-right sequence repeating itself.

2. Create a new layer called **actions** and add a keyframe at frame 40 on this new layer:

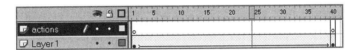

We're now ready to start adding actions to this movie. So that it only plays once, we'll add a Stop action to the last keyframe.

3. Bring up the **Actions** window and open the **Basic Actions** book in the toolbox pane. The commands will all be grayed out until you select a frame, so select the keyframe at the end of the **actions** layer. Double-click on the **Stop** action and stop (); should appear in the actions list on the right:

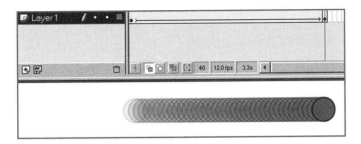

Test the movie. Now the ball only goes left to right once.

The Stop action can be a useful little number when you use it in conjunction with other actions. For example, you could stop your movie on a blank frame and jump to a frame with something on it when the user does something. You can use this strategy to create all sorts of effects, such as drop-down menus that are invisible until the button area is clicked. Play around and you'll see.

The next action in our **Basic Actions** toolbox is the Go To action, which allows you to jump from the current frame to a specific frame. We'll look at it in more detail.

Adding a Go To Action

1. Start a new movie and create the ball again. Convert the ball to a graphic symbol called **circle** and then convert it to a movieclip too. Call the movieclip **animation19**:

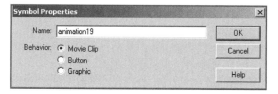

What kind of stupid name is that? Well, I'm going to show you an interesting effect using nothing more complex than looping movieclips and the Go To action. The sly thing here is the number 19...

2. Once you've converted your circle into a movieclip, double-click on it to go into edit in place mode (you'll see **animation19** highlighted to the right of the Scene 1 clapperboard, as shown). What you see in front of you may not look as if it's changed, but you're now in your **movieclip's timeline** and not the root timeline. To show this, insert a blank keyframe at frame 19 of layer 1:

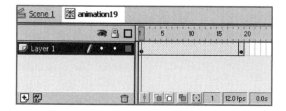

Now click on **Scene 1** to take you back to your main timeline. You'll see that, although the keyframe exists on your movieclip's timeline, the main timeline knows nothing about it.

Having two timelines running at the same time could, of course, lead to chaos but Flash makes sure two things stay constant. First, all timelines advance through their frames at the same frames per second (fps) rate specified in **Modify > Movie**. Secondly, all timelines will change frame at the same time. This makes sure that if the main timeline is about to go from frame 31 to frame 32, and another timeline in a movieclip is about to go from frame 67 to 68, they will both reach their next frame at the same time. This makes co-ordinating events in Flash productions nice and easy.

3. Go back into **animation19** and create the ball tween over 19 frames:

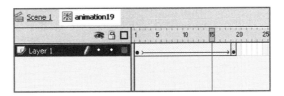

4. Still in **animation19**, add a new layer called **actions** and give this a keyframe at frame 19 too. Select this keyframe, bring up the **Actions** window. In the **Basic Actions** folder, double-click on the **Go To** action.

   You'll see `gotoAndPlay (1);` appear and notice that it has the default argument of `(1)`. This sends it to frame 1, which is just what we want here, so leave it as is:

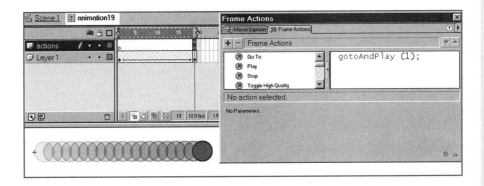

5. Once you've done this, test the movie.

   You should now have the ball going from left to right again, but we're not going to stop there.

6. If you haven't already done so, go back to the main (or root) timeline. Add a new layer, again called **actions**.

7. While you're in that layer, go to the **Actions** window and add a Stop action in the first keyframe:

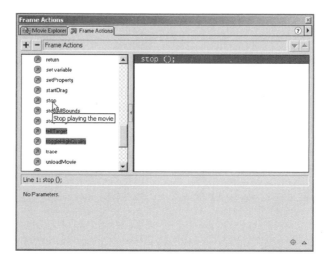

8. You should now have two layers on the main timeline, one called **Layer 1** which holds the **animation19** movieclip, and one called **actions**, which you've just created:

Test the movie and you'll see that nothing has changed. Even though you've 'stopped' the root timeline, the movieclip sitting on it has carried on playing.

> *In Flash, timelines within movieclips are always independent. When you stop a timeline, that Stop action has no effect on the timelines of any movieclips that are sitting on that timeline and currently running.*

This is an important point to take on board, because it means if you stop the main timeline, you can re-start it from any movieclip that is still running, something that will be very useful later.

Before we continue, we're going to make use of our tween movieclip and create an animation that never repeats itself. Well, hardly ever.

Creating a Looping Animation

1. On the main timeline, go into your library and select **animation19**. Click on the **Options** box within the library window and select the **Duplicate** option. Duplicate **animation19** as **animation23**.

2. In **animation23**, increase the length of both layers to 23 frames by inserting another four frames (with *F5*):

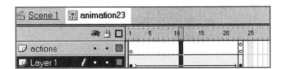

3. Return to your main timeline. Drag **animation23** out of the library and place it above and in line with **animation19**. Save this animation and test.

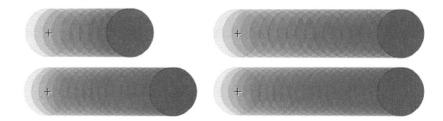

You'll see the top circle move slower than the bottom circle because it has more frames. Watch it for a while and something may strike you as odd: the two circles never seem to pass each other at exactly the same point. They actually *do*, but only once in 19x23 = 437 frames. 19 and 23 are prime numbers, which means that the only numbers that they are divisible by to create a whole number are themselves and 1. This means that there is no number on the way to 437 that they repeat at.

This is a useful technique if you have some sort of background that you don't want to repeat too often. For example, if you're wanting to show a view from a train window, with trees and hills passing by, you could make it look pretty random just by making the separate movieclips with a number of frames equal to a prime number (2, 3, 5, 7, 11, 13, 17, 19, 23, 29, 31, etc).

With **animation19** saved for future reference, I'd like to take you through a couple of other animations that I've made to further illustrate what we've done here.

Have a look at **nexus_animation.fla** in the download file for this chapter. This has an animation representing data shooting down transmission lines, that I built in exactly the same way as our movie with two balls. The data moves from left to right, but each 'blip' is a separate movieclip with a prime number of frames. The whole animation won't repeat until the number of frames equals the individual movieclip prime numbers multiplied together, so the whole animation will repeat once in about 200 lifetimes.

This is quite a powerful way of creating very long animations that to all intents and purposes never repeat. If you're asked to do something on a short deadline, it's something you can use to build complex animations quite quickly. I timed myself for the Nexus animation, and it took exactly twenty-two minutes to create from scratch (and I spent five of those looking for the groovy techno font on the Web).

If techno isn't your scene, have a look at **butterfly.fla** to see how subtle these loops can become. This FLA is my attempt to emulate a butterfly on a flower. Life is short for butterflies, and they never stay still. Even when they're resting, they are constantly twitching their wings and antenna. This effect is again created by looping prime numbers along with the simple `gotoAndPlay(1);` action to create a 'non-repeating loop'.

I hope these examples give you some clues for how to use the techniques that we've been looking at here. We've been seeing how to communicate between timelines, controlling how one movieclip plays from within another. I'll move on now to show you how to build that communication between specific keyframes. Remember that ActionScript needs to know exactly who it's talking to via unique instance names. We can give those unique names to keyframes using **labels**.

Adding Labels to the Timeline

As you're building your ActionScript and your timeline is getting busier, it's useful to be able to **label** keyframes. Although you can just as easily tell ActionScript to go to a particular frame by specifying a frame number, you could be creating work for yourself later. It's not uncommon to have to add or subtract keyframes from timelines, so if you've specified a numbered keyframe in your ActionScript, you'd have to go back and change every argument of every Go To action in every script that referenced the keyframe. Heaven help you if you miss one! If you add labels to your keyframes, you can move them around as much as you like without having to change the ActionScript.

To add a label to a timeline, simply select your keyframe and bring up the **Frame** panel (**Window > Panels > Frame**). In the **Label** field, type a meaningful label:

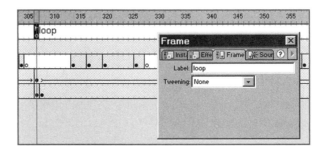

▶ A flag symbol will appear in the keyframe to signify that a label has been added.

If your timeline is too short to display the label text, or you have lots of labels close together that make it difficult to make sense of which is which, remember to hold your cursor over the flag symbol to see a tooltip. It will show exactly what your label says:

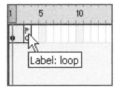

If you're already in the habit of adding labels to your timeline animations, I have a tip for when you're mixing timeline and ActionScript animations together. It's sometimes better to make any labels that are there just for your benefit, and not to be referenced by ActionScript into **comments**. Remember that I showed you how to add comments to you ActionScript in Chapter 1, like notes in the margin to remind yourself what's going on. Comments on keyframes are exactly the same.

To add a comment, select a keyframe and bring up the **Frame** panel, just as you would if you were adding a label. This time, though, add **//** before you type in whatever you want to help you remember what's going on here. The comment will appear on the timeline with a colored **//** symbol in front of it so you'll easily tell the difference between a label and a comment.

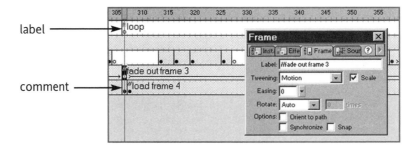

Comments aren't exported to the final SWF file, so you can make them as large and detailed as you want to.

OK, adding labels takes no time. Let's see how you can actually use them as part of your ActionScript.

In the final stages of the last exercise, we added a Go To action that used the argument 1 to direct the timeline to go to and play frame 1: `gotoAndPlay(1);`. I'll show you here how you can amend this slightly to go to and play a frame, specified by a label, not a frame number: `gotoAndPlay(<label>);`

Adding a Label to a Go To Action

1. Go back into **animation19** from our earlier example. Select frame 1 in the **actions** layer and using the **Frame** panel as I've just shown you, give it a label name **start**:

   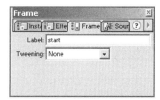

2. Select the last keyframe in the same layer and bring up the **Frame Actions** panel. Making sure the keyframe is still selected, click on the **Go To** book and check the **Go to and Play** box to bring up `gotoAndPlay(1);` in the right-hand window.

3. Click on the **Type:** drop-down menu and select **Frame Label**. In the **Frame:** text entry box, type `start`. The action will change to show that you have specified that label name as part of the `gotoAndPlay` instruction:

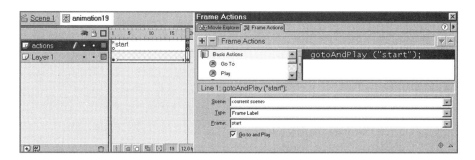

We've given that first keyframe a Go To action and then given it a label that will follow it around wherever it goes. Now, even if we make changes to the timeline order, Flash will be able to find our keyframe when it runs the `gotoAndPlay` action.

The last place we'll be using the Go To action here is between different scenes within our movie. Here, we'll look at how to organize scenes and build the same lines of communication between them.

Using Go To with Scenes

1. Start a new movie and in the top left-hand corner of the stage add the text **scene 1**. Extend the timeline to frame 40:

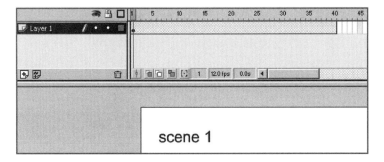

2. Open the **Scene** window with **Window > Panels > Scene**. This window lets you edit and arrange your scenes:

This window will have a single scene, called **Scene 1**, at the moment. The three icons at the bottom right of the window allow you to:

duplicate a scene

add a scene

delete a scene

3. In the **Scene** window press the duplicate icon twice to create two duplicate scenes. Your window will now list three scenes:

(If it says Scene 1, Scene 2 and Scene 3 at this stage, you've pressed the 'add scene' ➕ button and not the 'duplicate scene' 🗗 button. Delete scenes 2 and 3 and start again.)

We're going to be imaginative and rename these so that they read **Scene 1**, **Scene 2** and **Scene 3**. For this you'll need to double-click on each of them in turn and enter the new names.

4.   Once you've done this, double-click on the clapperboard icon 🎬 for Scene 2. Although nothing much appears to have changed, you can tell that you're in Scene 2 because it says so above the root timeline:

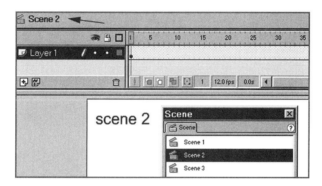

Change the text on the stage to read **scene 2**, and do the same for **scene 3**, so that it reads... it's too obvious so I won't say it.

5.   Go back to Scene 1. We want to add some actions here, so add a new layer called **actions** and add a keyframe at frame 40 of this layer. Add a keyframe at frame 40 of Layer 1 too:

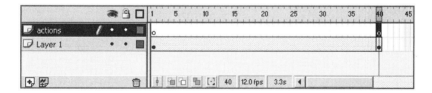

If we made no changes to this FLA, after it had completed Scene 1, the root timeline would go straight to frame 1 of Scene 2 and continue playing. We don't want that to happen. We want it to go straight to Scene 3, and stop once it gets there. So...

6.   Make sure that you're in Normal and not Expert mode and attach a Go To action to the keyframe. Change the **Scene:** drop-down menu from **<current scene>** to **Scene 3**. Notice that scenes 1 to 3 are listed here, as will be any subsequent

scenes you add. Change the **Type:** to **Frame Number**, if it isn't already. Leave the **Frame:** as 1, but this time un-check the **Go to and Play** tick-box.

Your Action will now read:

```
gotoAndStop ("Scene 3" , 1);
```

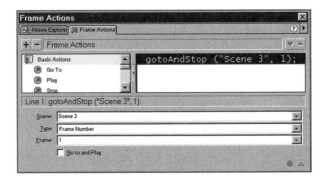

7. Test the movie. The text on the stage changes from **scene 1** to **scene 3** after a short pause. The timeline stops once it reaches Scene 3 because we've put in a `gotoAndStop` action.

8. Test the movie again but this time, once you're inside the test bring up the bandwidth profiler either with **Ctrl-B**, or by selecting it from the **View** menu. You'll see that the frame counter goes from frame 1 to frame 40, and then skips to frame 81. This is as you would expect, but notice that frame 1 of Scene 3 was called **frame 1** in the FLA, but in the final SWF it's called **frame 81**. Remember this if you have problems and ever need to debug movements between scenes.

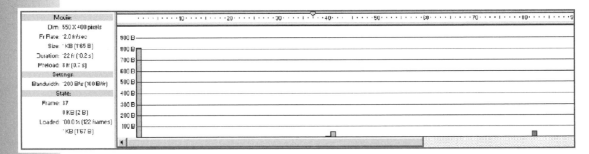

If you want to change the order of the scenes, open the Scenes window (with **Windows > Panels > Scene**) and simply drag the individual scenes up or down in the list, just as you would do with layers. This may seem fairly trivial now, but scenes are a good way of structuring your site. Just like a theater play is broken into separate acts, scenes let you add structure to your FLA. You could have different scenes for your preloader and your main page. Obviously, only the main or root timeline can be split into scenes - you can't do the same for timelines in movieclips.

Look back at the **Nexus** picture. If we had scenes called **about**, **home** and **products**, we could make the individual text items in this FLA into buttons that had a Go To action that went to the **about** scene or the **home** scene, or whatever. This is something that we'll be looking at in the next chapter.

Let's see what we can do with the actions and paths that we've learned about in this chapter. This exercise requires precise typing of a few actions, and won't work if you get them wrong. If you get stuck, look at **chapter03_01.fla** in the download file for this chapter. We're already going to do something that is impossible without ActionScript: stop and restart a timeline.

Stopping and Restarting a Timeline

1. Create a new movie. Draw a filled circle on the left of the stage and convert it into a graphic symbol. Call it **circle**. Delete it from the stage – it'll be in your library when you need to use it.

2. Now create a new movieclip called **mccircle**. Drag an instance of the **circle** graphic symbol onto the stage. Inside the movieclip, create a tween animation of the circle moving from left to right over 40 frames:

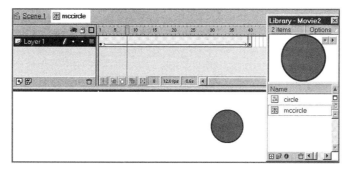

3. Go back to the root timeline and drag your movieclip **mccircle** from the library onto the stage, somewhere to the left. Use the **Instance** panel to give it the instance name **ball**:

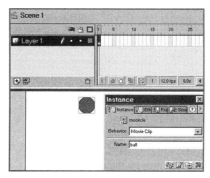

If you test the movie you'll see the familiar ball moving from left to right. We'll develop things now by adding some commands to control **ball** from the root timeline.

4. Add a new layer above Layer 1, called – you guessed it – **actions**. Extend both layers to frame 50:

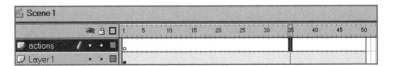

We'll add a `ball.stop();` command at frame 35. The notation that we're about to use is considered *advanced* by Macromedia, so they only allow you to do it in Expert mode. Don't worry – we'll enter Expert mode without losing the safety and error checking available in Normal mode.

As you'll have found by now, Normal mode is very much a drag-and-drop mode which gives you lots of prompts and sorts out the syntax for you, not to mention pointing out your mistakes with lots of red highlighting. If Normal mode is a wordprocessing package with spell checker, grammar checker and lots of nice menus, then Expert mode is the equivalent of Notepad, letting you get on with things without checking your syntax and assuming that you know the arguments for each command. Expert mode doesn't include the Basic Actions group and won't format your text by adding the appropriate indentations, semi-colons and curly brackets either. You can drop back into Normal mode to add the correct indentations, semi-colons and curly brackets - but only as long as your script doesn't contain any errors (if it does, then you're barred from Normal mode). As your confidence increases, you'll get fed up of all the pesky boxes and drop-down menus getting in your way and find yourself moving naturally towards the more efficient climate of Expert mode. We're just going to be paying a flying visit this time, but you'll be back...

5. Add a keyframe in the **actions** layer at frame 35. Select it and bring up the **Frame Actions** window. You'll be in Normal mode at the moment. Double-click the **Stop** action from the toolbox pane:

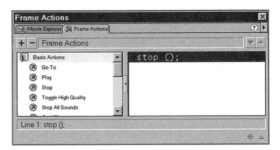

We now have the Stop command, but not our path.

6. Click on the right-facing arrow at the top right of the **Actions** window to bring up the drop-down menu. Click on **Expert Mode**:

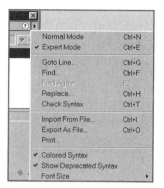

You might want to note the keyboard shortcuts to move between Normal and Expert mode while you're here. But be careful – **Ctrl+N** means **File > New** when you haven't got the **Actions** window selected! Another triumph for ergonomic design...

There's actually a way to add paths without going to the trouble of ever using Expert mode, which uses the Evaluate action. This is quicker in the short term, but makes matters more complex in the long term, which is why we're not using it here. Dipping into Expert mode early lays good foundations for your future as an ActionScript expert. As your knowledge of ActionScript and its syntax increases, you'll start staying in Expert mode more often.

7. We want to add the path at the beginning of the `stop();` command, so place the cursor before the command (press the left arrow key on your keyboard a few times to make sure). Now click the **Insert Target Path** icon in the bottom right of the **Actions** window to bring up the **Insert Target Path** window:

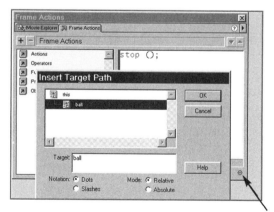

Insert Target Path icon

In the top pane you can see the available targets. You can select **this** (which you'll remember is the non-specific timeline that your action is attached to, the root), or ball. You want **ball**, so double-click on its icon.

You'll see that name appear in the **Target:** window. (If it doesn't, you didn't name the movieclip instance properly. Simply shut down the Actions window, go back and name the movieclip, and reopen the Actions window on frame 35.)

*Using the **Insert Target Path** window is a useful way to select the instance name you wish to control. It's particularly useful because you click from a list of names available to the current script. This means that you won't give your ActionScript a headache by mis-spelling the instance name or by specifying an instance name that isn't available to your script – both easy errors that can make your code grind to a halt.*

You have a choice to make here. You can either select the relative path or the absolute path by clicking on the **Mode:** radio buttons. As we mentioned earlier, **Relative** gives a path relative to where you are at the moment – within the movieclip, **ball**, in this case. **Absolute** will give you a full path from the very top of the hierarchy: `_root.ball`.

The **Notation:** radio buttons refer to Flash 5's way of expressing paths via dot notation rather than the old Flash 4 use of the forward slash **/**.

8. Leave that **Dots** radio button selected. Check the **Relative** radio button to specify a relative path back to **ball**:

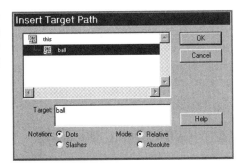

9. Flash doesn't add the dot automatically, so click inside the **Target:** window, move your text cursor to the end of `ball` and add a dot after the last `l`. Click the **OK** button to return to the **Actions** window.

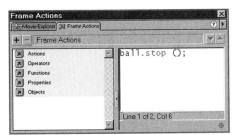

You'll see that the command `stop();` has now changed to `ball.stop();` You can check that the syntax is correct by looking at the color (which we first talked about under the heading *Syntax* way back in Chapter 1). The path `ball.` and the final brackets and semi-colon should be black, the command `stop` should be blue. You could have just as easily gone straight into Expert mode and just typed `ball.stop();` directly using this color codings to check that your syntax is right. Maybe try this later when you've had more practice?

Drop back into Normal mode by bringing up that drop-down list with the ▶ arrow button. Assuming that you've entered the command correctly, you'll be returned to the safety of Normal mode again. If there are mistakes within the command (any part of the blue text) Flash will alert you and tell you that it won't let you back into Normal mode until they're fixed. Proper little task master!

Now test the movie. You'll see the ball move left to right for a while, but then stop. If you open the bandwidth profiler, you'll see that the main timeline is still running, so we have the option to control ball further. How about we now restart it?

10. In the root timeline add a new keyframe at frame 45 in the **actions** layer. Attach a Play action to it:

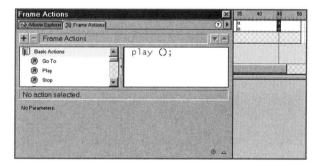

11. Go into Expert mode in the same way as you did for the last command and change the command to

    ```
    ball.play();
    ```

    You can just type `ball.` in front of the `play();` action rather than using the **Insert Target Path** window if you wish, but don't forget the dot.

Test the movie again. You'll see **ball** pause on its journey because it is stopped between frames 35 and 45. This is something you could never do with timeline methods. You could just split your timeline up so that the ball did nothing for a few frames, but if you wanted to pause in a different place, you would have to change the tween substantially. We can make the **ball** movieclip pause wherever we want by just moving the keyframes.

Later, we'll do this interactively as a pause button that can be applied to a movieclip - you can probably already see how this would work.

When we're controlling a movieclip from lower down in the hierarchy as we've just done, we have to know the *instance name* of that we're controlling. If we control the movieclip from a higher level, we don't need to know the instance name, because we could just use:

```
_parent.stop();
_parent.play();
```

If you think about it, this is a pause function that will work on *any* timeline.

We've started and stopped our timeline where we've wanted it to, and now we're going to look at how we can see it all over again.

Running a Timeline Backwards

1. Without closing your current movie, create a new movieclip and call it **rewind.behavior**.

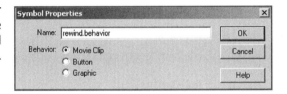

2. In the movieclip give Layer 1 100 frames and rename it **actions**. This movieclip will be a strange one with only actions in it. It will impart a behavior on its parent, which is any movieclip you put it into. The behaviour is not complex. It only needs two simple Go To actions and will make the movie run backwards.

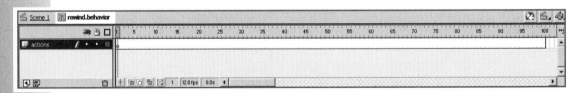

3. At frame 99 on the **rewind.behavior** timeline, add a keyframe. With that keyframe selected, bring up the Frame panel and assign it a label, **loop**:

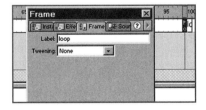

4. With the keyframe still selected, add a **GoTo** action. Leave **Scene:** at **<current scene>** and change the **Type:** drop-down menu at the bottom to Previous Frame. This will change the command to prevFrame();:

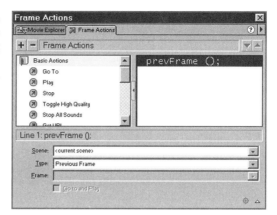

5. We now need to add the path for this command, so go into Expert mode. Because it can be used in any Flash movie, Flash sees the path _parent. as a command and not a path, so it isn't in the **Insert Target Path** window. You'll have to type _parent. in front of prevFrame (); yourself. Don't forget the dot, and make sure that all the text except the (); at the end is blue when you've finished:

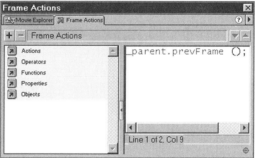

6. Return to Normal mode and add a keyframe at frame 100. Add a Go To action. In the **Type:** drop-down, select Frame Label, and in the **Frame:** drop-down, select loop (which is the label we've just created):

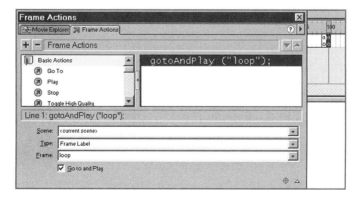

If you're hot on timeline-based animations you may have wondered if there was an easy way to run a tween backwards. This is it.

We now need to plant this behavior into our unsuspecting movieclip **mccircle**.

7. In **mccircle** add a new layer and call it **behavior1**. Make sure that it extends as far as Layer 1, because the behavior will only last as long as our **rewind.behavior** movieclip is on a timeline.

8. Go back into your **mccircle** movieclip and place the **rewind.behavior** movieclip on the stage. When you place it, you'll see a tiny circle. That is how Flash shows movieclips with blank first frames. In fact, all the frames of this movie are blank. I've placed mine just above the center pip of the **mccircle** movieclip so that I know where it is.

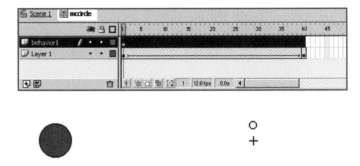

Test the movie.

Notice one very important feature of this setup. You already have the pause commands coming in from the root timeline. These still work, but as soon as the **rewind.behavior** kicks in, the ball goes backwards to its start. The behaviors are working together at the same time. If you added more embedded behaviors, they would work too.

As you can see, you can have lots of little embedded movieclips imparting their own little behaviors on the timeline. It may be a poor little movieclip, but look at the amount of control it's given us over the simple ball animation. We've gained another video rewind behavior here.

I know that Go To, Play and Stop commands aren't that glamorous and that you'll be wanting to get on with things, so I've attached something much more subtle and powerful to them. If you have FLAs lying around that you've created already, before embarking on this ActionScript exploration, you can start attaching behavior movieclips like the rewind behavior to them to give yourself much finer control of the movieclip animations.

Let's round up this chapter with a look at how all of this comes into play at stun:design within an advert for the site.

The stun:design Web Site

Go To, Play, and Stop commands are useful for building animations that are not timeline-based. When you use these ActionScript commands you remove the need for multiple frame timeline animations. This in turn makes the animations small in file size. A good time to use this method and the small file size that goes with it is when you're building a Flash advert. You get them as pop-ups on some sites and they're slowly replacing the old animated GIF banner adverts.

I'm guessing that if you take a job in an established web design house, you may be asked to make something simple like a Flash advert as your first job. So let's do one here ready for the day when stun:design becomes an organization that can afford to advertise itself on other sites.

Our first step is to practice what we preached in Chapter 2 and make some plans for our advert. The one thing I was taught in the five minutes that I attended art school was that if you want to get an objective perspective on what something will look like, you need to look at it in a way that prevents your mind from applying any preconceptions. The easiest way to do this is to look at it upside down, or through a mirror. I knew Anders had come up with the goods and done us proud with the new stun logo, but to be sure, I viewed it upside down:

What does that look like to you?

To me, not only did it show off the nice curves and forms that Anders had added, it looked like a different language - Sanskrit or Arabic, or even some alien off-world hieroglyph. Even if you've seen the stun logo before, you wouldn't immediately recognize this as the logo upside down. You'd see it as a hieroglyph. I liked that, and started sketching and writing notes. I wanted a simple animation that used small file sizes to create something that will download immediately. The final SWF file must be no bigger than 4k if we want it to download immediately – which is pretty important for an advert.

After a page of rubbish, I came up with a storyboard where the Stun logo is upside down in frame 1, and we have the text:

Speak a new web language

The logo then rotates to its proper orientation and we see the words:

Stun Web Design

Nice. Simple. I can work with that.

What I wanted was a simple motion tween of the logo turning, and then to use ActionScript to do something weird and fancy to the rotation.

Have a look at the **stun_banner.fla** in the download for this chapter. First of all, use the library to open the movieclip **stun1**, which is the logo rotation. I've added a Stop command to the start and end of this movieclip so that it doesn't play until it's told to and stops after playing once.

I love that ethereal fade effect that appears when you switch on onion-skinning mode. I've seen a lot of beginners on newsgroups who have knowledge of tweening but not ActionScript asking how to achieve it. This is the effect we're going for.

If you look at the main timeline of **stun_banner.fla**, you'll see that there are six layers named **one** to **six**, as well as the **actions** and **strapline** layers. Each one of the six has an instance of the movieclip **stun1** on it. Layer one has a version of **stun1** with an instance name **one**. There are six instances in all, named **one** to **six**, each on a layer of the same name.

If you hide layers two to six, you'll see that the logo **one** on its own is quite faint, because it has an Alpha of 20% applied to it. If you make layers two to six visible again, one by one, you'll see that each layer copies a new version of the logo over the original logo to slowly make it darker.

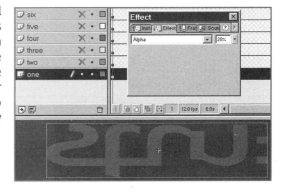

The real trick is in the **actions** layer. You'll see six keyframes, each of which starts off one instance of the **stun1** movieclip. The first keyframe starts **one** with a one.play(); action and so on, in sequence, until **six** is started with a six.play(); action:

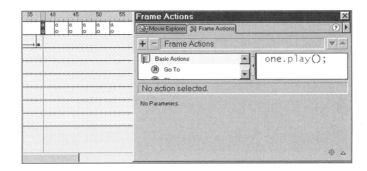

By delaying the six instances from starting, I've created the onion-skinning effect. You could have done the same animation with tweens only, but you would've had lots more keyframes and motion timelines and therefore a much bigger file. Later, we'll learn about variables in loops, which enable us to set all the instances off in a loop thus making the file even more efficient. As it stands, this whole animation comes in at about 3453 bytes, which means it would run instantaneously on the web. The movie pauses to let you read the initial text **learn a new web language**, by which time the whole movie has loaded in!

As an aside, this book ignores all the legacy commands and half way house commands in general (such as setProperty and others), which become redundant as soon as you learn dot notation (which you are now). This is fundamental to efficient Flash 5 coding, and avoids you wasting time on learning old commands that might not even make it to Flash 6.

Summary

This chapter has covered a lot of ground. We've looked at:

- Flash 5 dot notation.

- Adding basic Stop and Go To actions.

- Directing a Go To action to different scenes.

- Stopping, restarting and playing a timeline backwards.

Can you feel it? You've just moved up a level in your knowledge of Flash. We'll keep moving in the next two chapters, looking at the basic interactivity behind normal buttons, and then using buttons in a way that you wouldn't expect...

stun:

4

Basic Interactivity

What we'll cover in this chapter:

- *Adding simple actions to a button to detect that the user has pressed and to control the timeline*

- *Building interactivity into a movie clip to create a 'continue' screen for a web site*

- *Controlling the root timeline from within a movieclip*

- *Using button events to build a game and some simple site navigation*

In Chapter 1 we learned that ActionScript is an event-driven language. Just like that lion clock, Flash and the ActionScript behind it react to events happening. So far, the event triggering off our ActionScript has been Flash entering a new frame in the timeline. This is an internal event that Flash creates itself, like the clock reaching the hour and chiming, so it doesn't really seem like a real event to the user.

We're going to have a look at external events that we have some control over, like setting the alarm time on the lion clock. We'll look first at how to attach basic interactivity to a button to make it detect that a user has pressed it, stop the main timeline and jump to a different frame. We're also going to have a look at Flash 5's new event type - **movie events** - and how we can use these to build interactivity into movieclips to control the root timeline.

As we build a better understanding of the events that lie behind buttons, I'd like to show you how we can take away preconceptions of buttons as just 'point and click' circles and think about using them to build a simple game that doesn't have a 'button' in sight. After a few moments playing we'll come back into the grown-up world and look at some standard navigation tools.

All of that sounds like a lot of work so we'd better get going. We'll start with a recap on what you may be familiar with already – creating a simple button - but at least it will form a solid foundation for what we do in the rest of the chapter.

Creating a Button

1. Draw another filled circle and make it a graphic symbol, called **circle**. Once you've converted it into a symbol, delete the original circle from your stage.

2. Create a new symbol and make it a button, called **button1**:

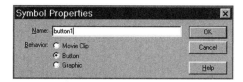

You'll end up with a **button** timeline with four states: Up, Over, Down and Hit, like this:

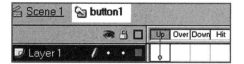

Each frame represents a *state* that the button can be in:

- The **Up** state shows what the button will look like when it's in the 'up' or 'not selected' position.

- The **Over** state shows how the button will look when the mouse is over the button, showing the user that they are over a button which will make something happen if they click on it.

- The **Down** state shows the button when it is pressed.

- The **Hit** state defines the area in which the button will detect the mouse.

The button timeline is a special one controlled directly by Flash, which takes it to the appropriate frame depending on what the mouse is doing in relation to the Hit area. You can also add layers for sound and drop movieclips into the frames.

> *The Up, Over, Down and Hit states have frames, but remember that a button doesn't have a timeline. Any actions that you attach to the button shouldn't be attached to the keyframes on the button's individual frames, but to the button itself once it's on the stage, as we are about to see.*

3. Select the **Up** frame and drag the **circle** symbol onto the stage. Unless your button state is in exactly the same place in every frame, your button will 'wobble' as Flash moves between frames. It's a good idea to set the shape center to something easy to remember so that you can quickly fix any untoward movements. The best way of doing this is by setting the center of the shape to be at 0.0, 0.0 in the **Info** panel:

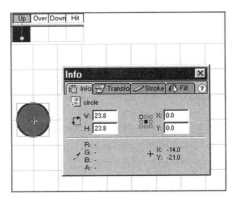

4. Add a keyframe in each of the other button frames. Your circle should be visible in all of the button frames. Return to your main timeline and drag **button1** from the library onto the main stage.

Test the movie and you'll see that, although the cursor changes to a hand icon to show that it's over a button, there are no other button changes. This is because all the button states are the same. We'll change this.

5. Go back into your button and, in the **Over** frame, make the button slightly larger by using the **Info** panel to increase the width and height of your circle. This will mean that your *x,y* co-ordinates are no longer 0.0 but the center of your circle will stay the same, so there's no need to change them back to 0.0.

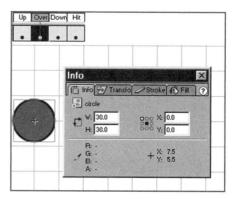

6. Select the **Down** frame, click on the circle and bring up the **Effect** menu (**Windows > Panels > Effect**). Select **Brightness** from the drop-down menu of effects. (If you can't open this menu, make sure that the circle is selected and try again.) Make the circle noticeably brighter, say around 50%, with the slider bar accessed through the drop-down menu to the right of the current percentage brightness.

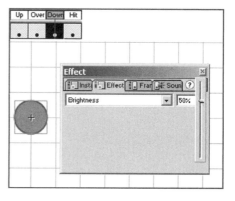

The **Hit** frame is the one most beginners have problems with. To make your button selectable, you must have a Hit state that includes some pixels that the mouse can move over. Most people find it difficult to define a Hit area that, after all, will never be seen. My advice is to use this 'difficulty' to help yourself out: as no-one will ever see it, why not make the Hit area a solid square of color so that any gaps show up. This extends to buttons that use text – people sometimes define the Hit area as the text itself, which means that the button won't work if your mouse is over the space between letters.

Now's a great time to practice.

7. Select the **Hit** state and draw a filled square of color around your circle. Remember that no-one ever sees this, so don't worry if you can't see your circle behind the square.

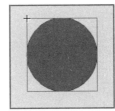

Test your button movie and make sure that you can see the different Up/Over/Down/Hit effects that you've just given it.

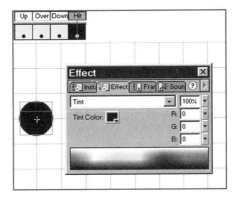

Now that we have our basic button, let's look at how to add some simple actions to it. You can use the button in **chapter04_01.fla** in the download file for this chapter if you want to skip this section but I wouldn't recommend it – this is going to be a very complex button by the end of the chapter.

Adding a Stop Action to the Button

1. Go to the main timeline of the button that we've just been working on. Change the layer name to **button** and extend it to frame 40. Add two new layers called **text** and **actions**:

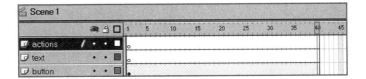

2. At frame 20 add keyframes to the **text** and **actions** layers. In the **actions** layer select that keyframe, bring up the **Frame** panel and give it the label **detect**:

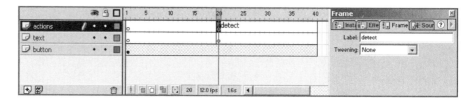

3. At frame 20 in the **text** layer add the text **event detected** on the stage, below your button:

4. Add a keyframe in the **actions** layer at frame 35. Attach a `gotoAndStop(1);` action by selecting a **Go To** action and un-checking the **Go to and Play** checkbox at the bottom:

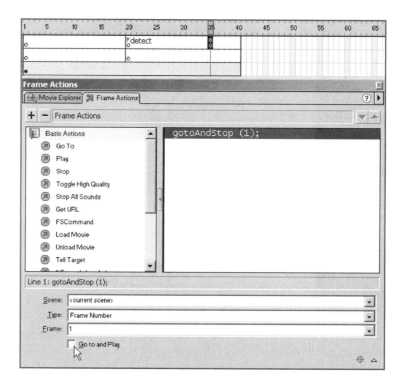

5. Finally, add a `stop();` action in frame 1 of the **actions** layer:

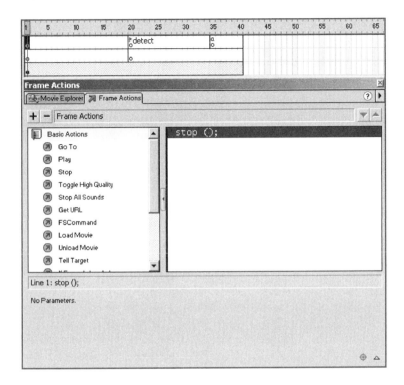

We've set up a simple timeline with a button on it. The timeline will stop as soon as it sees the `stop();` in frame 1of the **actions** layer.

Now we'll set the button up to detect that the user has clicked on it by adding an **On Mouse Event** action. We'll make the button tell the timeline to jump to the label **detect** and start playing as soon as it's there. This will bring up the **event detected** text. At frame 35, the timeline will be told to go back to the start and stop there, ready for the user to press the button again.

Adding an On Mouse Event Action

1. Select the button we've just created and bring up the **Actions** window. (If you double-click on the button, you'll go into edit in place mode and you'll need to click back onto the Scene 1 clapperboard to the top left of your screen). Notice that the window now appears as the **Object Actions**, instead of the **Frame Actions** window that you've used before:

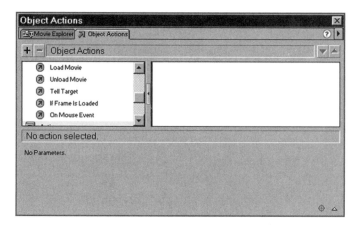

There's not actually that much difference between the **Object Actions** and **Frame Actions** windows. They both display the same basic list of actions but shadow out those that aren't applicable to the frame or the object that you have selected. For our button object, we'll be using the **On Mouse Event** action (the last action in **Basic Actions**) which you'll see is selectable.

2. Double-click the **On Mouse Event** action. You'll see an **Event:** set of checkboxes at the bottom of the window. These are the events that the button can detect. I won't delay things by going into them all here, so if you want to know what the others do, now's the time to pay your first visit to the very useful appendix at the end of the book. The one that we're interested in here is the **Release** event:

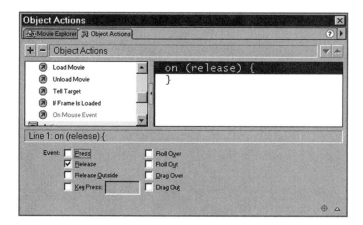

Cast your mind back to the section on nesting back in Chapter 1, where I showed you my simple sausage notation.

If I re-write:

```
on (release) {
}
```

in a more user-friendly way, what it's actually saying is:

on (release) {do this sausage};

Our sausage is currently empty, so it's time we added some meat to it to tell ActionScript what to do next.

3. With the on (release) { line highlighted, select a **Go To** action and double-click on it. In the drop-down menu at the bottom of the **Object Actions** window, change the **Type:** to Frame Label and add the instance name detect to the **Frame:** textbox. Notice that the line gotoAndPlay ("detect"); is indented to show that it's to be run as one sequence once the on (release) event has been met.

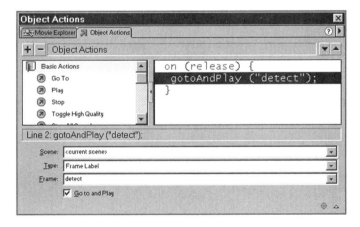

4. Test the movie. You'll see the circular button sitting in the middle of the stage. Press and then release it to set off the event. The movie will jump to frame 20 and you'll see your **event detected!** text appear on the screen.

That's our first look at interactivity and buttons. It's very simple, but we now have some ActionScript that responds to what a user does, rather than just carrying on and minding its own business in the background. We're now going to move on and look at a cunning way of implementing that same timeline control not with a button, but with a movieclip. The user clicking on a movieclip? Believe me, it's possible...

Interactivity and MovieClips

Adding events to movieclips is a new feature that was introduced with Flash 5. Some of the events that you can attach are actually quite complex internal events, so we'll steer clear of those and stick to a simple one to begin with. The process for attaching events to movieclips is the same as the one we've just seen for buttons, but what actually happens when the event occurs is totally different, so watch closely.

Imagine this situation: you have an animation or other effect that takes a while to load. Just like you, the average user is probably going to get bored while the effect loads and open another browser window to keep themselves amused. If this happens, the user is probably not going to return to your window at the exact same moment that your effect starts, and is going to miss some or all of your hard work. You need something to alert your user to the fact that your effect has loaded and is ready to go – you need a *continue* button.

Using a button for a *continue* option means that the user has to move to the button and click it before your effect will run. If we wanted the user to be able to click anywhere, we could make a button as big as the screen, which would make the user's cursor change from a pointer to a hand icon. This means they will know how you've achieved the effect and, as a designer, I don't like the user to see the cogs and smoke behind things. We're going to look at how to create a continue screen where the user can click anywhere to continue without using a button. You can find the completed Flash file for this as **chapter04_02.fla** in the download file for this chapter.

Creating a Continue Screen

1. Create a new movie and make the background a dark gray in the **Modify > Movie** menu. Call layer one **movie** and create another layer, called **actions**:

   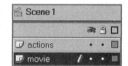

2. On frame 1 of **actions** add a Stop action. In the **movie** layer, add the text **click anywhere to continue** in the center of the screen:

   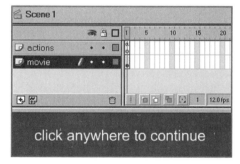

3. We need to animate this text, so make it a movieclip symbol and call it **enter**:

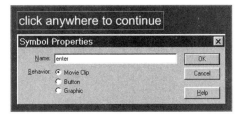

We want to edit the movieclip whilst it's still on the stage because we want to do something that depends on the size of the stage. Do this by double-clicking on the text on the stage. You can tell that you're editing the movieclip **enter** and not the main timeline because of the movieclip symbol that has appeared next to the **Scene 1** title above the main timeline:

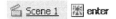

4. Once you're inside the **enter** movieclip timeline, rename layer 1 to **message** and add two more layers, **box** and **actions**:

Select the text on the stage and convert it to a graphic symbol, called **text**.

5. In the **message** layer, add a new keyframe at frame 20. Select frame 1 and select the **Motion** tween option from the **Frame** panel. You should now have the familiar blue background and arrow between frames 1 and 20 on this layer:

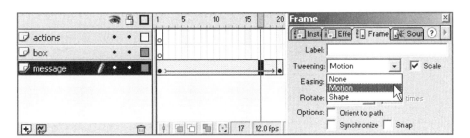

6. Select frame 20, go to the **Effect** panel and select **Alpha**. Give the text an Alpha value of 0%:

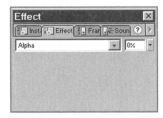

If you run your playhead through the tween you'll see the text slowly fade.

7. In the **box** layer, add a keyframe at frame 2. In it, draw a white box outline (turn off the fill) that just encloses the text:

8. Select all the lines of the box with **Shift select**, and convert it to a new graphic symbol called **box**.

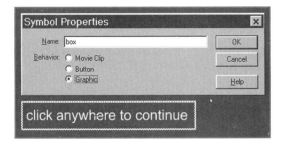

9. Still in the **box** layer add a keyframe at frame 30. Highlight frame 2 and select a motion tween from the **Frame** panel. Your timeline should look like this:

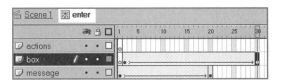

10. With frame 30 selected, select the Scale tool from your main toolbar and scale the box up until it encloses the whole stage. You may have to zoom out so that you can see the whole stage to do this. It doesn't matter if you didn't

get your box in the middle of the stage and your scaling means that the top line is further out from the stage than the bottom line – we're going to make it disappear anyway.

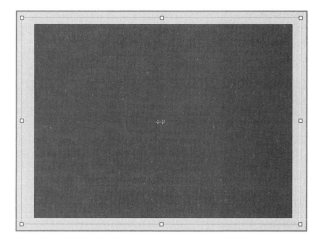

11. Still at frame 30, select the **Effect** panel and set the Alpha of the box to 0% in the same way you did with the text just now.

We've set up our movieclip so that the text fades away at the same time as the box around it moves outwards, fading as it moves further away from the text. We now want to look at the actions required in the movie. When our nice effect or whatever it was we were loading has finished loading and starts playing, we want to immediately stop two things. We want to stop our **click anywhere to continue** movie and make it wait for the user to click, and we want to stop the root timeline that our effect is on, so that this also waits for the user.

When our **click anywhere to continue** movieclip ends, we want to restart the root timeline that has the effect we've been waiting for on it. So, what we need to do is make everything stop where it is and do nothing until the user clicks. Once that happens, our **click anywhere to continue** movieclip has done its job and needs to restart the root timeline. So let's get started...

Controlling the Root Timeline from a Movieclip

1. In our **enter** movieclip, in frame 1 of the **actions** layer, take yourself into Expert mode and add this script:

```
_root.stop ();
stop ();
```

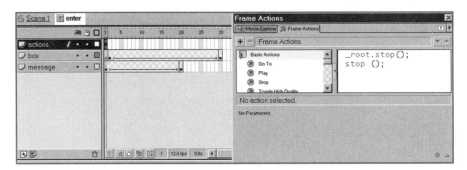

These are the Stop actions for the root and movieclip timelines. Notice the order in which the timelines are stopped. If we stop the movieclip timeline first, we have no way of controlling the root timeline. We need the movieclip timeline to tell the root timeline to stop first, before stopping itself.

> *You have the option of adding these actions in Normal mode and then zipping across into Expert mode to add the _root path to the first. Choose whichever way you prefer. I directed you to the Expert mode option first to help you become more familiar with typing actions in rather than selecting ready-made ones.*

2. Once our little movieclip, **enter**, has finished we can safely continue the main timeline, so on Frame 30 of the **actions** layer, create a keyframe and add this script, again in Expert mode:

```
_root.play ();
```

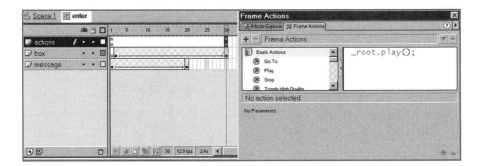

We now have a movie that stops everything and just sits there. Once the main timeline has started, we'll have no way of knowing that this is what's happened.

In other words, inserting our *click to continue* screen has no further bearing on our SWF once the user has continued.

3. Go back into the root timeline and extend the **actions** layer (but not the **movie** layer) up to frame 40:

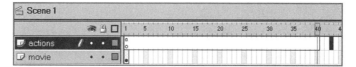

Doing this simulates what would happen in a real situation: once the user decides to continue past our **click anywhere to continue** screen, the **enter** movieclip has served its purpose. We can stop its timeline and return to the original timeline with our effect, now fully loaded, on it.

Now here's the magic.

4. Select the **click anywhere to continue** movieclip on the stage and bring up the **Actions** window in Normal mode. From the **Actions** book, find the On Clip Event action. Select it and check the **Mouse down** event.

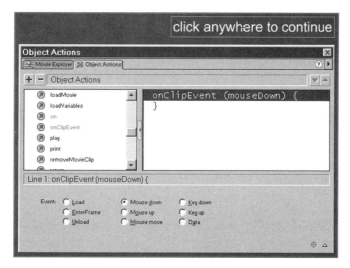

The difference between doing this with a button and with a movieclip is quite subtle, and could easily be missed. We haven't attached this action to the movieclip's timeline or the root timeline. We've attached it to **the movieclip itself**. The actions that we're attaching are specific to the instance of **enter** on the stage. If we dragged another instance of the **enter** movieclip from the library onto the stage, it wouldn't have this action attached to it so this instance of **enter** is unique.

We now want to tell Flash what to do when it detects the Mouse down event. We need to restart our movieclip timeline.

5. Make sure that the first line of code, `onClipEvent (mouseDown) {` , is highlighted and add a `play ();` command:

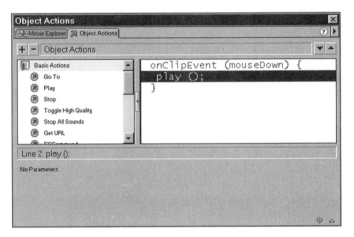

If that first line isn't highlighted, Flash will add another `onClipEvent`, which you'll need to highlight and delete.

6. Test the movie. To start with, you will see the **click anywhere to continue** message. Try it! The mouse is still a pointer because we're not using buttons:

As soon as you click, the box will grow and get fainter as it expands outwards:

If you open your bandwidth profiler, you'll see that the main timeline is still halted but once the movieclip **enter** has finished, the main timeline restarts. So, in our example, the timeline loads up our fantastic effect and then goes to the movieclip, which stops everything until the user proves that they're paying attention and clicks. At this point our movieclip will finish and the main timeline will resume to play our great effect. Think of our movieclip as the trailer to a film – it makes sure that everyone has finished buying popcorn before starting the film.

When I first found out that Flash 5 allows you to add actions to a movieclip itself in the same way as a button, I thought, "That's stupid! You can already add actions to a movieclip's timeline, why add them to the movieclip itself as well?" As soon as I tried it, I realized the difference. If you add actions to a timeline, every instance of that movieclip performs the same actions. If you drag a movieclip onto the stage and attach actions to its movieclip events, that code is unique to that instance. In our example, every instance of the **enter** movieclip that we drag out of the library will have the scripts that we attached to its timeline, but none of them will have the script that we added to the instance of the movieclip on the stage at the end. In practical terms, every instance of **enter** that we drag out of the library will fade slowly away, but only the particular instance of **enter** on the stage will do something when we click the mouse.

This lets us modify the basic actions that the movieclip contains straight from the library by attaching new actions that are specific to each instance, which is what we can do with our **enter** movieclip. We can configure our basic movieclip to do what we want without having to alter the library version. So, for example, we could change the text in our original movieclip, drag it out of our library and change the actions attached to it to react to a keypress instead of a mouse click.

If we wanted this particular instance of **enter** to do something more than just restart the root timeline, we could add that as an Unload event in the OnClipEvent action. For example, we could get the Unload event to go to another URL, jump to another scene, or start some music playing. We can configure each instance to do something slightly different, without changing the version in the library. This makes it possible to:

- Re-use movieclips.

- Build up a library of movieclips, and tweak them for particular applications.

- Make individual instances behave slightly differently.

Although the exercise above may seem a little simplistic, consider this game as an example:

Zarg, Blard and Lard are three space invaders in your game. Zarg is the run of the mill alien, quite happy to move from left to right, spitting plasma at the enemy. Blarg is more of a professional, and moves and fires faster. His father was the xenomorph in the original Aliens film, so he has a lot to live up to. Lard isn't really cut out for all this invading lark, and would much rather stay in with the lads and get his tentacles round a few tins of beer. His slow movements and inept firing are testament to his diet of pies and lack of exercise.

Imagine you had a movieclip called **alien**, consisting of three frames, each one containing one of the three images above. The first frame would show Zarg, Blarg would be in frame two, and the last frame would hold our reluctant alien Lard. You could then drag instances of **alien** out of the library, and once it was on the stage attach an On Load event with a gotoAndStop to tell it which of the three frames to go to – in effect which of the three aliens you wanted it to be.

In addition to containing the three images of our three aliens, the **alien** movieclip could also contain a set of ActionScripts to move itself around. These could take in values to set how fast the alien moves and fires and how accurate the firing is. Don't worry – we'll be looking at this later, but the important fact here is that you could have just one **alien** movieclip and change all these values after you've dragged it out of the library. You could use OnClipEvent to make one instance of the **alien** movieclip a slow inaccurate version of Lard for an opening level, and then make another instance of **alien** into a super shooting Zarg for a point later in the game.

That is the real power of the OnClipEvent. Like its cousin the SmartClip (which we'll also meet later), it allows you to configure particular instances to exhibit more differences from the library version than just their instance name, making them much more versatile.

Now you know how to detect events, we're going on to look at how you would use these events and simple event-event handler pairs to build up complex overall behavior.

Using Button Events to Build Interactivity

In the download for this chapter you'll see a file called **stuntoy_01.fla**. This is a game based on those toys where you have a wire and a loop that you must pass around the wire without touching it. If you touch the loop to the wire, a buzzer sounds. It's not long after you start the game by placing your mouse over the left electrode that you realize why this is a stun:toy - watch out for the electricity!

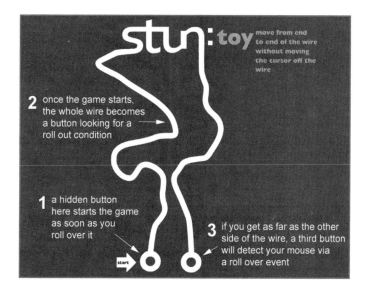

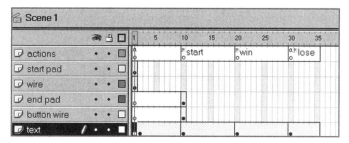

The 'start electrode' has an invisible button in layer **start pad** that detects your mouse rolling over it. We haven't learned how to make invisible buttons yet, (that comes in Chapter 5) but in terms of actions, they're the same as normal buttons. As soon as you roll over the button, the whole wire becomes a button that watches for you to roll off it. This happens in frame 10 of the layer **button wire**. If you slip off, the button sends you to the **lose** label. If you make it to the 'end electrode' to the right, you'll roll over another invisible button (in frame 10 of the **end pad** layer) whose roll over action takes you to the **win** label. You can see how this game is nothing more than buttons set up to detect particular events.

The three events are:

- If the player rolls onto the starting area (the left electrode), the game is started by the action attached to the start electrode's button;

```
on (rollOver) {
    gotoAndStop ("start");
}
```

- Once the game commences, the wire becomes a button that's looking to see whether the player's cursor rolls out of the wire pixel area. If this happens, the Rollout event sets off an action to go to the **lose** label and show the losing screen

```
on (rollOut) {
    gotoAndPlay ("lose");
}
```

- If the player gets as far as the right-hand side of the wire, they will roll onto a second hidden button that takes them to a winning screen as soon as it detects a Rollover event:

```
on (rollOver) {
    gotoAndPlay ("win");
}
```

That's more or less the ActionScript for this whole game. The game actually only uses three buttons, and took me very little time to build once I'd devised it (as usual, the creative input was the most difficult thing).

Making the most of buttons in Flash doesn't mean thinking of them as something that is pressed and released like a doorbell. Thinking of buttons more as 'mouse event detectors' allows you to use them to create Flash structures that react to user input but look less and less like physical buttons.

So far in this chapter, we've only used one button or one movieclip to allow our user some say in what happens next. Our next chapter is going to look at using ActionScript to come up with an entire navigation structure for our web site. As a lead in to that, we're going to have a look here at the ActionScript behind multiple buttons as a simple navigation tool.

Using Button Events for Navigation

One of the things that struck me about the e-commerce boom as a designer was the search for recognizable URL names. All the big e-commerce sites need a short, snappy address, and some were prepared to pay a lot to acquire them. We're now told that the big Internet carve up has finished, and all the good names have gone. Just before starting this chapter, I had a look to see what was still out there by way of snappy URL names. On just my second attempt I found one that's a lazy designers dream because you could use it to build up a web site that sells anything from women's handbags to used cars. All you have to do is make sure the design uses lots of circles. This is great for building up a simple web site to show how buttons can be used for navigation, because most buttons are circular. We're going to have a go at coming up with something for **polka dotcom**.

The final FLA for this site is in the download file for this chapter as file **polka.fla**. I've created a bare template for this site and also added a short Swift3D animation in one of the scenes to start showing how you can start building up this bare template. The font I've used is HandelGothic. In case you don't have this, and to make the FLA look the same on every machine, I've converted all text to vectors with **Modify > Break Apart** so that Flash stores the text as a graphic rather than asking your machine for a font.

We're going to create some buttons that you'll be used to seeing on e-commerce sites. If you get stuck, the completed version of this exercise is in the zip as **polka_cutdown.fla**, along with the final FLA.

Creating Navigation Buttons

1. Create a new movie and set the background colour to the jade green you can see in the FLA with **Modify > Movie**. If you really want to get the color precisely right, go to the **Mixer**, enter #639A9C into the hexidecimal values and make it a custom colour. You'll then be able to access it from the **Modify > Movie** menu.

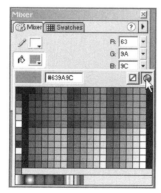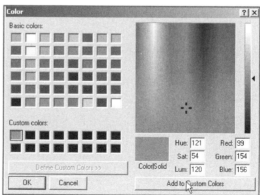

2. Create a small button about two centimeters in circumference and make it look different for each of the Up, Over, Down and Hit states, like this:

Look back at the previous button exercise if you can't remember how to do this. If you're confident about buttons and feeling lazy, the button is in the library as **bu.circle** in the final FLA, so you can get it by opening **polka.fla** with **File > Open as Library**.

3. Place three of these buttons in a row on the stage:

It's fashionable in Flash to have simple buttons like this, but the user has no way of telling what each button will do because they're too small to fit text onto. You can solve this by using a movie with the button captions on it. Suppose button one went to a section of the site called **about**, the second button went to a section called **products** and the third was a **contact** button. We'll have the three buttons pop up those corresponding names before the user presses them, so we want something to happen on rollover, just like the wire game. This means attaching an action to the Rollover state of each button to make a movie to bring up this text.

4. Create a new movieclip called **buttontext** in this movie and add the word **text** at position 0.0,0.0 using the **Info** panel to help you place it precisely:

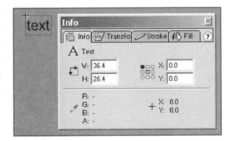

5. Go to the main stage and drag the **buttontext** movieclip out of the library to where we want it to be, just under the first button:

We're doing this now because, in a second, we'll make the first frame of **buttontext** blank, which means that it will be difficult to place it accurately.

6. Now that we've placed it, go back into **buttontext** and add three consecutive new keyframes, one for each button. Add a new layer called **actions** and give that four keyframes too:

7. In frame 1 of the **actions** layer add a stop ( ); action. You'll notice we do this a lot with movieclips that we want to control externally with ActionScript. It's a good trick to learn - a stopped movie is the easiest thing to control because you know where it is when you start playing about with it in ActionScript.

    Add labels **blank**, **about**, **products** and **contact** to the four keyframes on the **actions** layer:

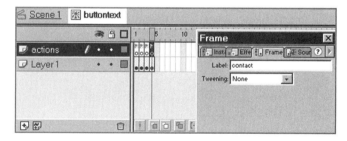

We'll now look at the layer with the text in it. Each keyframe currently says **text**. This is just a placeholder, so we'll change each one to what we really want.

8. In frame 1 of the **actions** layer, delete the text. In frames 2, 3 and 4 change the text to read **about**, **products** and **contact**.

9. Now go back to the main stage. Notice that the **buttontext** movieclip has been replaced by a small circle. Told you!

10. We have to animate **buttontext** from the ActionScript attached to the three buttons. We're missing one important element to allow us to do this, though: the *instance name*. With the **Instance** panel, give **buttontext** a **Name:** of **text**.

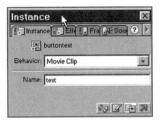

We can now control the instance of **buttontext** with this name, so let's get to it! The first button will be the one that navigates us to the **about** section.

11. Click on the first button and bring up the **Actions** window. Click the **On Mouse Event** action in **Basic Actions**. It will come up like this:

```
on (release) {
}
```

but we want the text to come up on roll over, so un-check **Release** and check **Roll Over** to give you

```
on (rollover) {
}
```

We want to make **text** show the text **about**. Or in ActionScript terms, we want to make the instance **text** goToAndStop at frame label **about**, which is the frame containing the text we want. Here's the command we need:

```
text.gotoAndStop('about');
```

path   command

As a bit of revision to let us catch our breath: the `text.` part of this command is the path that the command will affect. Everything to the right of the final period is the command. You should remember this from the last chapter but I'll run through the first one with you.

This is what you've got so far:

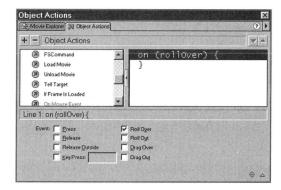

12. Select the `on (rollover) {` line and add a **Go To** action from **Basic Actions**:

We need to change the default action so that it goes not to frame 1 (gotoAndPlay(1);) but to our label: gotoAndStop("about");

13. Un-check the **Go to and Play** tick box and change the **Type:** to frame label. In **Frame:** textbox, type about.

The label we want won't appear in the **Frame:** drop-down menu because it's not in the root timeline, and the **Actions** window doesn't look any further than that. This is why we have to type it in by hand.

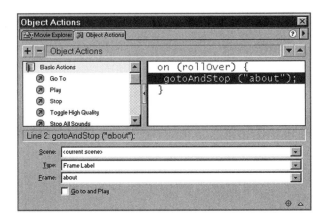

We now have our command, but it's currently pointing at the wrong path, which is this.gotoAndStop("about"); The this. part is not written because it's implicit; we always expect an action to affect the timeline that it's attached to.

We can only add our path in Expert mode, so switch to that with the drop-down menu accessed from the arrow at the top right of the window.

14. Place the cursor before the goToAndStop ("about"); command, and type text., taking care not to forget the dot:

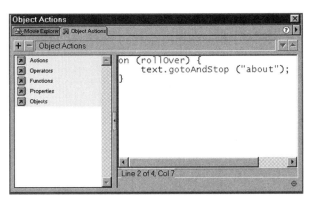

When you're dipping into Expert mode, remember to check the syntax with the color coding:

```
text.gotoAndStop ("about");
```
black   blue   black

Once you're happy, jump back to Normal mode.

We want to do almost the same thing with the Rollout event that comes next. This gets rid of the text when the mouse rolls outside the button, so we want to use the **blank** label that we carefully prepared earlier.

15. Repeat steps 11-13 but this time select **Roll Out** rather than **Roll Over** and use the label blank instead of **about**. Don't forget to uncheck the **Go to and Play** box to make your action into gotoAndStop before you drop into Expert mode to add text:

16. Your ActionScript should look like this when you're done:

```
on (rollOver) {
   text.gotoAndStop("about");
}
on (rollOut) {
   text.gotoAndStop("blank");
}
```

Now test the movie. Well, that's one button working.

The actions for the other two buttons are almost identical, so we can block copy them when we're done with this button. At the moment, though, if we click on the buttons they won't take us anywhere so we'll need to build this in before we start duplicating the code we've just created.

The first two buttons will take us to specific sections of the web site, so we might as well create those sections as scenes. There are other ways of doing this, which we'll be looking at in the next chapter but we'll stick to scenes for now.

17. Bring up the **Scene** panel with **Window > Panels > Scene**. Rename **scene 1** to **main** and add two new scenes (using the + button at the bottom) called **about** and **products**:

18. All the scenes are currently identical, so go to each scene with the **Scene** panel and add some text at the bottom to differentiate them.

19. We now have enough information to complete our button. Go back to the **main** scene, click on the **about** button and bring the **Actions** window up again. In **Basic Actions**, double-click on **On Mouse Event** and check the **Release** checkbox to give you an on (release) event. For this event, we want to go

to the **about** scene. Keep on (release) highlighted and select **Go To** from **Basic Actions**. The new code will look like this by default:

```
on (release) {
    gotoAndPlay (1);
}
```

We want to change the directions in the Go To action so that it goes to the **about** scene.

20. Change the **Scene:** drop-down menu to about. This will go to frame 1 of scene **about**. We also want Flash to stop once it gets there, otherwise it will just run through all the other scenes. Un-check the **Go to and Play** checkbox to make this a gotoAndStop action and we're done with this button:

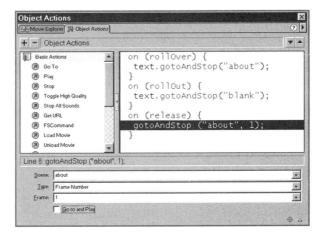

Our main timeline doesn't show this because the new frames are in our extra scenes, but we now have a timeline of more than one frame. The timeline will start to play as soon as we run the SWF. This will make our whole SWF flicker because we'll effectively be continuously playing through all three scenes, only one of which has our buttons on.

21. To stop this happening, add a new layer to the **root** timeline, call it **actions** and add a Stop action:

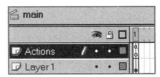

22. Click on the first button and bring up the **Object Actions** window. Select all of the code by clicking on the first line and then *Shift*-clicking on the last line (the last **}**). You should now have all the actions selected. Either right-click or **Ctrl**-click to bring up the edit menu pictured.

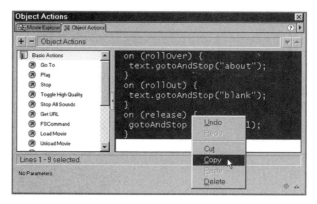

Click on **Copy** to.... y'know.

23. Select the second button, **products**, and bring up an Actions window. Click inside the right-hand window and paste there everything that we've just copied from the **about** button. Do the same for our third button, **contacts**.

We have actions attached to our last two buttons, but we need to make a few changes to make them do exactly what we want. Amending parts of the ActionScript that we already have will be far quicker than doing everything from scratch again.

24. In both the Rollover and Release states for the **products** button we need to change the label within the gotoAndStop action to read products rather than about so that clicking on this button takes the user to the relevant part of the web site. Although we've used Expert mode to add a path to the Rollover command, we can still edit it in Normal mode by clicking on it and altering the text in the **Expression** box at the bottom of the window. So, select it and delete about and replace it with "products", like this:

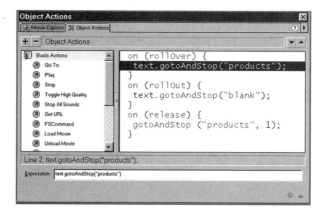

25. With the `gotoAndStop ("products", 1);` line selected, click on the **Scenes:** drop-down menu and select **products**:

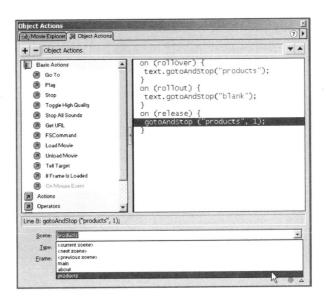

For the **contact** button, we're going to do something different and add a new action: **Get URL**. Normally, you'd use this action to jump to a new site by adding the full URL in the **URL:** field that comes up at the bottom of the window after you double-click on it to include it in your script. This should include the http:// part as well, so if you wanted to have a button that jumped to the Macromedia Flash 5 page, you'd enter http://www.macromedia.com/software/flash/. We're going to use **mailto:** which is a little different because it's a protocol that any system with a properly configured e-mail program will take to mean 'open a new email message'.

26. Select the **contact** button and bring up the **Object Actions** window. To make sure that the **contact** text comes up on mouseover, change the ActionScript from `gotoAndStop("about");` to `gotoAndStop("contact");` in the Rollover state at the top. Then, highlight the `on(release)` event at the end of the list and delete it. In its place, add the **Get URL** action from the **Basic Actions** list. In the **URL:** field add mailto:people@polka.com?subject=info. This will open a new mail message addressed to people@polka.com, with a subject of **info**.

Your code should look like this:

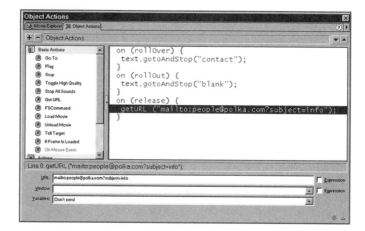

We've finished with the buttons. Test your movie and click on, say, **products**. You'll go to the Products scene. We still have some work to do though, because now you're there, you'll find that you won't be able to move from there to another scene. This is because our buttons only exist in the **Main** scene at the moment.

27. To fix this, *Shift*-select both layers on the main timeline (selecting the layer title selects all frames in that layer so this is a good shortcut for layers with a large number of frames). Then, right-click/*Ctrl*-click on any frame that has been used (in this case, frame 1 in both layers) to bring up the menu you see here:

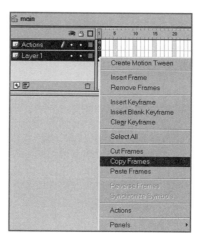

Select **Copy Frames** and then go into the **about** and **products** scenes.

28. Right-click/*Ctrl*-click on the currently empty frame 1 and select **Paste Frames**.

You can now test the file. Depending on how your system is set up, you might get a browser window appear as well as the e-mail, but this won't happen to other people when you publish it or put it on the Web, so don't worry about it.

You might have noticed that if you're at scene x, there's still a button that takes you to scene x even though you're already there. For example, it's quite possible to go from **products** to **products** and have Flash reload the screen. To clear this up, go into the relevant scene and delete the on (release) event. In the **about** scene, you would go to the **about** button and delete the on release event there. Do the same for the **products** scene and we're done. This means that we can't go to the same place again (e.g. from **products** to **products**) but can only go somewhere else.

This might not affect our one-frame scenes now, but if we chose to modify the scenes by adding more frames, the user would end up back at frame 1 every time they pressed these buttons. This might start to get annoying because the whole scene and any associated movieclips would all start again and, having seen it once, they're not likely to want to see it again.

Summary

In this chapter we've made our first exploration into how ActionScript can add varying degrees of interactivity to buttons and movieclips. We've been through some pretty intense exercises that have shown us how to:

- Use a Stop and Go To action on a button to control the timeline.

- Add an On Mouse Event action to detect that the user has pressed the button and bring up text that signifies an event has taken place.

- Attach actions to movieclip instances to make them act like buttons and control the root timeline.

- Build basic site navigation using multiple buttons and scenes.

Our next chapter carries on where this one leaves off. We're going to meet the invisible button and take a look at building a structured, interactive and generally funky Flash interface.

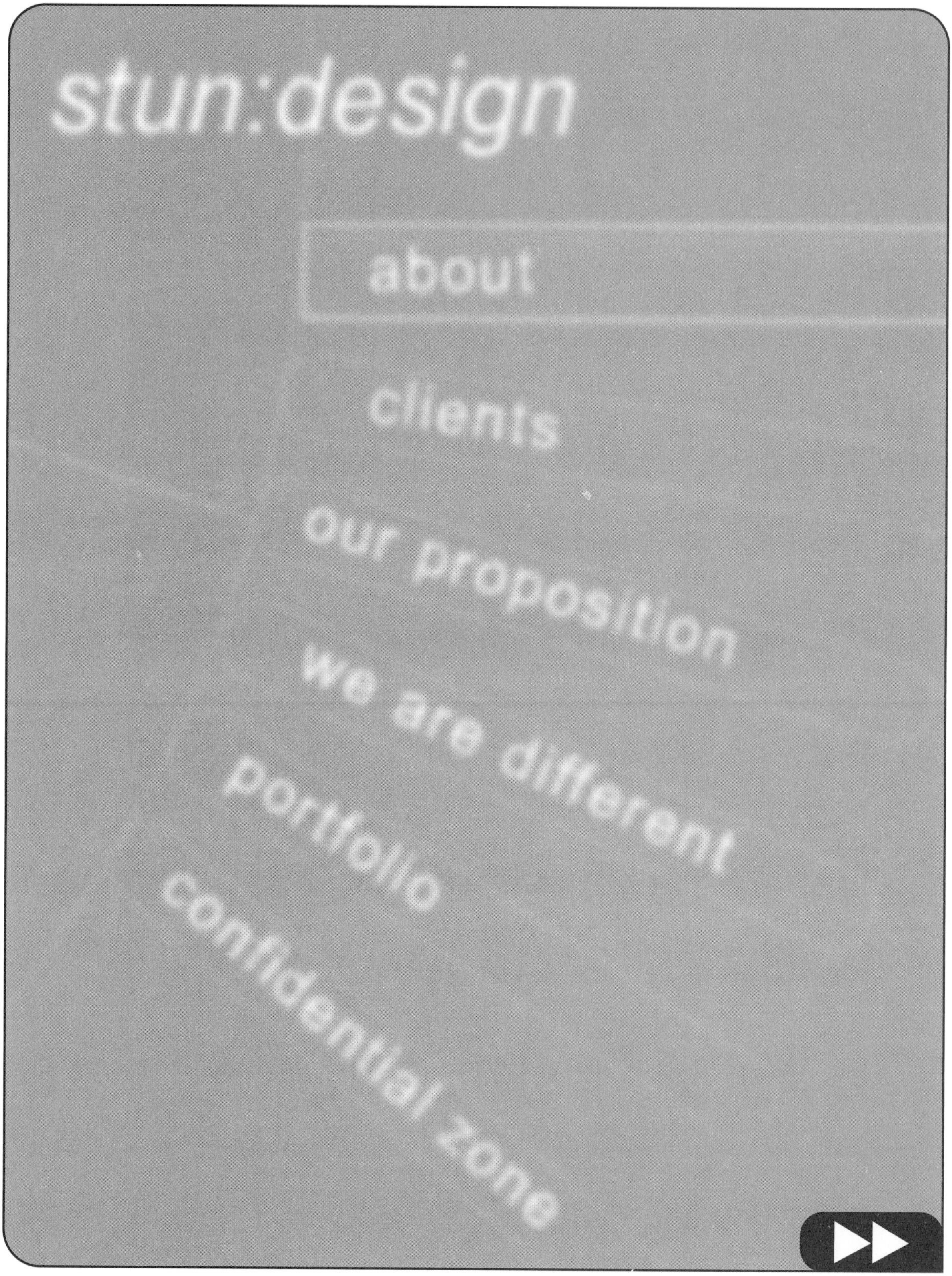
stun:design
about
clients
our proposition
we are different
portfolio
confidential zone

5 Navigation Tricks

What we'll cover in this chapter:

- *Creating invisible buttons and implementing them as more sophisticated elements in site navigation*

- *Choosing the most efficient site structure for streamlined ActionScript navigation, using either scenes, movieclips or levels*

- *Creating draggable windows for the stun:design web site project*

With our **Polka** project in the last chapter we started to look at the wider navigation possibilities that ActionScript opens up. Even there, though, we were just using buttons at their very basic level. We'll carry on with that theme in this chapter to look at how we can use buttons more subtly to form part of a larger navigation effect using draggable windows. As we're starting to build up more complex ideas for navigation we'll need to take some time to think about how we structure the different parts of a site to give the user the streamlined experience we want them to have. We'll round off with a pretty detailed look at stun:design and how I've implemented there everything that we'll talk about in this chapter.

There's gonna be lots to look at.

Our first step towards building a true ActionScript interface is creating a sophisticated little number: an **invisible button**.

Invisible Buttons

An invisible button can receive all the usual button events that we've seen, but has no Up, Over or Down states, only a Hit area. This means that your button is invisible to the user, but can still detect when they pass the mouse over its Hit area, which designers often call the **hotspot**.

Invisible buttons will obviously never replace the usual buttons that we see every day for navigation – can you really imagine a user hunting around the page, waiting for the cursor to change to tell them that they've found the button to take them to your portfolio page? – although some sites will use invisible buttons for all their navigation by placing them over graphic symbols that just look like buttons (but don't actually do anything). When the user clicks on them, they're using an invisible button without knowing it. Other designers drop invisible buttons over static button shapes and add audio so that the user receives some musical reward when they roll over, rather than a visual effect.

Flash also allows you to use invisible buttons for something completely different: to create a **draggable area**. I'll take you through an exercise now where we'll use the button not as a user input device, but rather as a handle with which to drag a movieclip around the screen, in much the same way as we drag a heavy bag around the airport by its handles – but with less effort. Later, we'll see how they're used to full effect when we look some more at the stun:design web site. Some practice first, though...

Creating an Invisible Button

1. Open a new movie, create a new button symbol and call it **dragbutton**. Insert a keyframe in the Hit area. Define the Hit area as you normally would using a button, with a filled square or circle:

2. Return to your main timeline, open your library and drag the button onto the main stage. You'll notice that the button will appear as a semi-transparent cyan shape, the same size as the Hit area you've just defined.

    Just as with any other type of button, the user won't be able to see the Hit area but, as the rest of the button is invisible, Flash is giving you the cyan as a guide for placing the button accurately.

3. In the same movie, create a new movieclip called **draggable** and draw something that looks like a file folder. Make sure that you give your shape some kind of fill, because we'll be changing that later. See my pretty standard attempt here, or on the other hand be as creative as you like:

    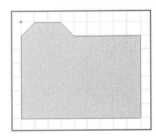

4. Drag the invisible button from the library, placing it roughly over the tab area of the file. Use the Scale tool from the main toolbar to shape **dragbutton** so that it covers the tab more exactly, like I've done here. This will make the tab our draggable area (or handle in our heavy bag analogy):

    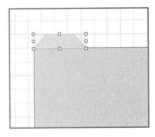

    Why are we using a button for this? It's not really the first function that comes to mind when you think of a button, is it? The reason is that Flash has a wider definition for a button than we do. We tend to think of a button as geometric shape that begs to be pressed. For Flash, it has a more general purpose – it can be anything that captures mouse (and key) positions. Think back to the Stun:toy game that we saw in the last chapter.

4. Select the button and bring up the **Object Actions** window. In the **Actions** book, scroll down and click on **startDrag**. `startDrag ("")  ;` will appear with an automatic `on (release)` event on the line before:

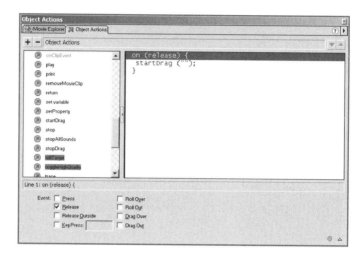

Obviously, we need to change this so that the user can drag once they've *clicked* on the invisible button.

5. Select the first line, `on (release)  {` to bring up the different **Event** checkboxes at the bottom of the window. Check **Press** and uncheck all the others. We'll get the `on (press)  {` that we want:

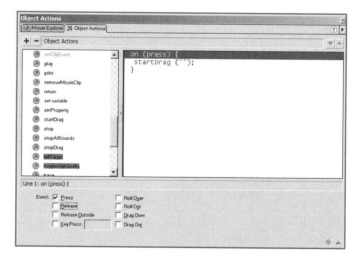

6. Click back on the second line, `startDrag ("");` and you'll notice that the bottom of the **Object Actions** window changes to let you specify a **Target**:

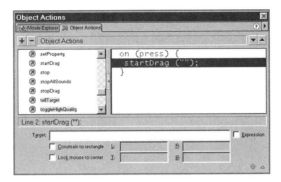

This allows you to specify an instance name. Leave it blank. A target of `this` is assumed, which will be the timeline that the button is on. That's what we need.

If you put the button on the main timeline, you can drag the whole SWF, which is useful if your site consists of different SWF levels. It almost gives you a navigation system of windowed and draggable movies straight away! You can also constrain the dragging to a rectangular area within the stage, but I'll leave that for you to play around with.

Our button now knows what to do when someone clicks on it, but what about when they let go?

7. Select the last line of the **startDrag** action and double-click on **stopDrag** in the **Actions** book. The default for this is `on (release)` so we can leave it as it is. We don't need to add any arguments to `stopDrag ()`, because you can only drag one thing at a time, so it only has to stop the current drag in progress.

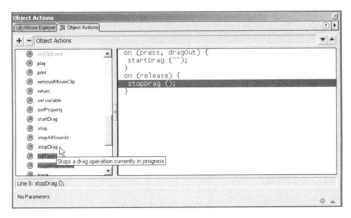

8. Test the movie. You should now be able to drag your file shape around the window and drop it wherever you want. Just like our good ol' suitcase handle.

That's our basic process for creating a draggable window. We'll take a couple more steps to create some more and give them colors so that we have something that looks as if it's ready to use on a real site.

9. Drag another two windows out of your library onto the main stage. Select one of the windows and bring up the **Effect** panel. Select the **Advanced** option from the drop-down menu and select an Alpha value of 30% and a R(ed) value of 255.

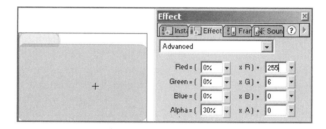

10. Do the same to the other two windows, but enter the 255 value into the G(reen) and B(lue) columns instead.

11. You should now have three draggable windows on your stage, one with a green tint, one with a blue tint, and one with a red tint. Test your movie and try dragging them over each other, watching the colors mix:

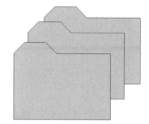

By stacking a few of these things together, you have the basis of a neat draggable files type interface. Just drag the one you want to look at out of the stack...

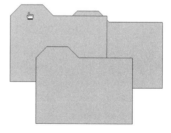

That's all the basics we need for now. We're getting to a seriously professional level here. We're creating buttons, Jim, but not as we know them - our first little playthings to amuse site visitors as they view our work. We'll use these draggable windows again later when we look at how I've used them at Stun. Before that, though, we need to take a break from work, some time to think about the structure of a site.

Site Structure

We're extending our portfolio of ActionScript effects and techniques, so if we're not careful things will get jumbled up like spaghetti when we put things together. We need to get back to the drawing board a little to plan how we can structure all these labels, scenes and the ActionScript within them so that things are easy to manage as a site builds in complexity. We're creating buttons to give the user access to deeper parts of a site but before we get carried away with how that navigation interface is going to look we need to take some time out. Some thinking time is in order to look at different ways we can structure a site and deliver the goods efficiently once those buttons are pressed. Learning about basic structure is fundamental and has a big effect on how your ActionScript will work, so you'll thank yourself for taking this time out when you're sitting there with a blank stage window and a $25,000 web site to start building.

A little background theory first, then back to the real word of stun:design.

I'll look at the pros and cons of displaying different parts of your site as:

- Scenes

- Frames with labels

- Movieclips

- SWFs on different levels

Linking Scenes

If you remember our polka dotcom exercise in Chapter 4, we used buttons with `gotoAndStop(scene, 1);` actions to move around our site. Working things this way lets you look at each scene in isolation, and is a good way to build up big sites, particularly if more than one person will be working on the site at the same time. Where you have repeated elements that must exist in all scenes – a logo or a menu bar of buttons as we did in polka dotcom – you have to repeat those elements to each scene. This repetition adds a slight increase in size but as long as all your repeated elements are symbols that also exist in the library, this is minimal. This is where symbols start to come into their own because Flash only needs to load up one logo instead of one for each scene that you have.

In polka dotcom we had our scenes structured like this:

The three scenes have different timelines and we can always go to the other two scenes from the scene that we're in.

Some Flash designers don't use scenes at all, and just have labels on their main timeline for each part of their site.

Linking Labels

Instead of a button going to a `goToAndStop(scene, 1);` for a different part of a site, your button would just do a `goToAndStop(frame);`. For small sites, this can be an advantage because you can see the whole site in one timeline. You end up with a structure like this:

Put this structure into practice on a real timeline, with three labels on the first layer and this is what you'd be faced with:

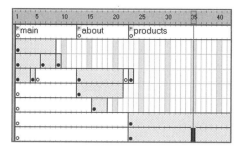

The problem's clear: all those layers spread across scenes start getting squashed into one confusing pile. This method is popular, but, as you go on to bigger sites and the number of instance names and layers increase, you'll start to lose track and not even the Movie Explorer will help you find that lost layer. This confusion will get even worse as you try to add ActionScript to anything. My advice: don't do this at home if you want to use advanced, well structured ActionScript.

Linking Movieclips

In the Polka exercise in the last chapter, we used the movieclip **buttontext** to bring up text under each button when the mouse rolled over it. What if you had a second movieclip containing all of your content instead of just the names of your four scenes? The buttons would have a path attached to them to navigate between the labels within your movieclip. This method works the same way as the one we've just talked about, but is split into different movieclips instead of different scenes so that we don't get confused with what belongs where.

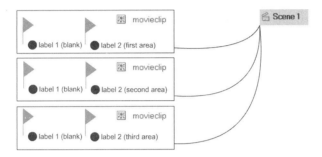

Structuring your site this way is great if you have a big ActionScript-controlled interface. It has the added advantage of letting you do all sorts of really cool things by using ActionScript to control the movieclip that contains your content. You can:

- Make your movieclip move left to right, opening the way for sideways scroller sites.

- Make your movieclip draggable, letting you emulate putting your content in windows that can also be scaled.

- Apply instance effects to your movieclip, which would affect all of your content and add things like fade out and fade in actions to your navigation buttons.

You can see why ActionScript programmers love this method.

In the same way as our Polka example had a blank first frame, you can give each movieclip a blank first frame and stack them on top of each other. As soon as you want to show some content, you just make one of the movieclips go to a non-blank frame, and keep the rest of the movieclips at a blank frame. You can also make the separate movieclips have the same internal structure, so they might even be controlling further movieclips within them in the same way.

We'll use the movieclip method in Chapter 9 to give the stun:design site a side scroller, a feature that that relies on a lot of ActionScript tricks.

There is one last way to structure your site.

Linking SWFs and Levels

This last method uses multiple SWF files stacked on top of one another. For the sake of argument, we'll call the first SWF loaded **_level0**. That SWF, **_level0**, can then load up subsequent levels and control them with any Goto command that is preceded with the path **_leveln**, where **n** is whichever level you want to control. The levels can have scenes, telltarget clips or anything that a normal single level movie would have:

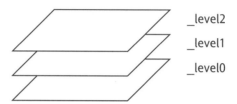

This method is very useful when your site is bandwidth heavy, because the whole site doesn't load up straight away. Each SWF works like a separate HTML page and loads up when demanded. You can make your **_level0** movie entertain the user while the other bandwidth-heavy levels load up. Levels can be things other than graphics. For example, I use this method a lot to load up *soundtracks* on top of the main site at **_level0**.

What happens if one of your other levels, as well as **_level0**, loads up more levels too?

You don't get nested levels (bah!), but **levels in the same sequence**, so any level can load/unload levels (including itself) in the same way as **_level0**. The maximum number of levels is 16000 so you're never likely to run out.

I've left this one till last because it leads me back nicely to our stun:design site. This is the structure that I used there because I find it particularly elegant, as well as bandwidth efficient.

We're going to use floating, draggable windows to provide information in the main site. These will be loaded in as separate levels on demand from the user, and not at the same time as the main site. That makes for a site that loads quicker and is more responsive.

We'll go through some exercises now that will show you how that structure works and how I put into practice at stun:design the invisible buttons that I showed you at the beginning of this chapter.

Stun:design Interface

Before we start, load the **stun_basic.fla** from the download zip for this chapter. You might have to alter your **File > Publish Setting** to **HTML** and then do a **File > Publish Preview > Default (HTML)** to view the site in a browser window because of its non-standard size.

Back in Chapter 2 I laid out for you the first plans for general stun:design interface:

The buttons defined in the bare bones of the site there describe how the user can see the typical pieces of information that they're after on a corporate site. They describe aspects of the company, what we do and how we operate:

- About

- Clients

- Our proposition

- We are different

- Portfolio

- Confidential zone

To carry on the theme of lightning that runs across the top of the home page, I wanted to add some small animations to give a flash of lightning as the user rolls over these buttons:

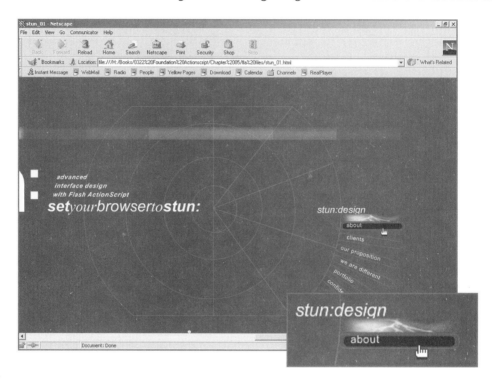

Once they've decided which piece of information they want and clicked on the relevant button, my idea is that Flash will bring up a draggable window with the content they're after.

Look at **stun_basic.fla** and you'll see that, at the moment, the buttons have been set up to run that little animation, but they don't produce any navigation. That's for later. For now, I'll show you how I added those lightning animations.

Adding Animations to Buttons

Animated buttons aren't complicated - they simply have movieclips in the Up, Over and Down states. I'll give you a little advice here: unless you like antagonizing your audience, it's best not to animate the Hit area as well.

I created a movieclip **mc.thunder_spark** and arranged a sequence of bitmaps on the timeline. You can see them in the library as **stun_01** thru **stun_08**:

Here's the **mc.thunder_spark** timeline. You'll see that there's an action in the last frame. It's a stop(); action to prevent the movie from cycling:

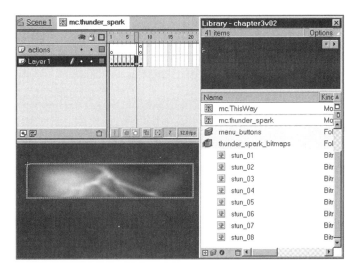

Next, I added **mc.thunder_spark** to the Over state of the first button, **About**, on its own layer. Notice that I haven't added subsequent keyframes in the Down or Hit state, so the movie will be present (and continue to play) for those states as well.

As you can see, the **About** button has more than one layer on its timeline. I'd recommend that you get into this habit when you're building complex buttons like this. In general, add a new layer to the button timeline for animated movieclips, soundtracks, and where you want things to go in front of or behind each other. Whatever you do, though, **don't add an actions layer**, because buttons should only have actions attached once they're sitting on a timeline, and **not** while they are in the library.

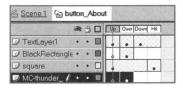

That's our animation added. Told you it was going to be simple. We'll move on now to those draggable windows.

Draggable Windows

A combination of these draggable windows and the background structure of SWFs on different levels that I've talked about has made the Stun interface pretty elegant, if I may say so, as well as responsive to the user. It means that we don't load the window content until after the main site has loaded, and lets us put fairly bandwidth-heavy content in one of the windows, knowing that it won't affect the rest of the site and its responsiveness – there are other things the user can do whilst they're waiting for our content to load.

Because each window has its own separate SWF, the FLAs are different too. Content will change more often than the basic web site framework itself, so by separating out the main web site and the pieces of content, we have effectively created plug-in content. If you want to add new content in any one window, you'll just need to change the contents of that windows' FLA and SWF – there's no need to access or change the FLA or SWF of the other windows or the site itself. The SWFs can be loaded in from a separate location to the main site, which allows two different people, or even organizations (such as the client and the host) to maintain the two halves of the site – the main site and the content – independently. If you're ever building a site and it looks as if you'll have to wait a while for the client to come up with pieces of content for you, you can carry on your design and fully test it with empty windows – a client's lack of speed is their problem, not yours!

Creating stun:design Draggable Windows

As I've said, the structure of stun:design uses loaded levels. An important point to remember when you use this method is that the loaded levels must have the same stage size and background color as the lowest level movie or, in other words, the first movie to be loaded. In our case, that's the main stun:design interface.

1. Create a new movie. Use **Modify > Movie** to change the background color to dark gray and the dimensions to 2880 x 600 Pixels, the same as the stun:design web site:

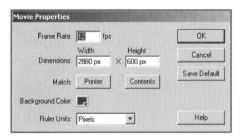

We'll need some buttons for our windows. The easiest thing is to make the buttons invisible so that we can re-use them for the different window functions.

2. Create a button, insert a keyframe in the Hit state and place a borderless square in it, like this:

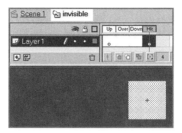

Before you move on, make sure that there's nothing in the Over and Down states and that the keyframe in the Up state has nothing in it, otherwise our button won't be properly invisible.

3. Create a new movieclip called **window**. Rename Layer 1 **window** and create within it a window of your own design. Take a look at this basic window shape if you need inspiration:

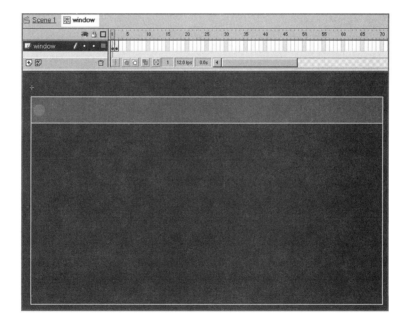

We just need an outline because we want to get the ActionScript working before we start going overboard on the graphics. Check with the **Info** panel that your window isn't bigger than 360 by 206 pixels and if it is, scale it down. The little blue dot in my example serves no purpose but I just like little flashes of color – they seem to really lift web sites with otherwise neutral color schemes.

4. Create a new keyframe at frame 2 in the same layer. We want this keyframe to contain the minimized state of the window, with just the title bar showing. Make sure that you have the keyframe in frame 2 selected and delete the bottom half of your window so that it looks like this:

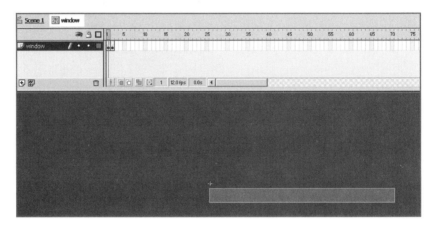

5. Now create a new layer and call it **icons**. We're going to use this to hold the icons on our title bar that will close, maximize or minimize the window. This layer needs to be in front of (above) the **window** layer so that the icons are on top of the title-bar. Move it above **window** if it isn't already there:

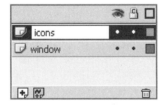

The icons on that layer will be the standard three: close, minimize and maximize.

6. In frame 1 create the minimize and close icons like these:

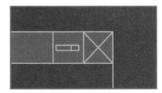

You probably want to zoom in on your window to make sure that you get this right. Don't forget to make sure that you're in the **icons** layer.

If the window is minimized, we want an option to maximize it.

7. Create a new keyframe in frame 2 of the **icons** layer. Leave the close icon as it was but where the minimize icon was in frame 1, make a maximize icon like this:

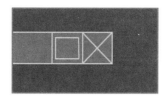

Now we add our buttons. As you'll have guessed, we need to add an invisible button behind each of the two icons that we've just created on the right-hand side of our title bar. We'll be attaching actions to them in a moment.

8. Create a layer above the two existing layers and call it **buttons**. Create a new button and add a filled rectangle in the Hit state, as we've done before. Drag two instances of our invisible button out of the library and resize them to fit the minimize/maximize and close icons like I have here:

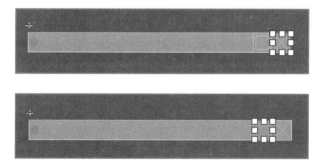

9. We also need a button to cover the rest of the title bar, so drag another invisible button out of the library and resize this to fit:

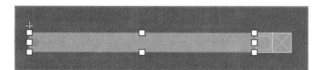

10. Add two layers to the movieclip, called **content** and **title**. In **title**, add the text **about** on the title bar, like this:

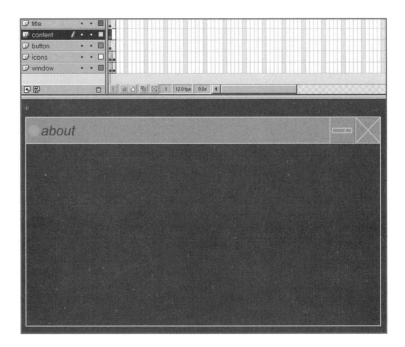

If you want to use these windows in other sites, you could enter something more generic such as **<title goes here>** and then make a copy of the window before you enter **about** for our stun:design site. We'll leave content empty for now but we'll be putting some in later.

It's now time to get all this working.

11. Add an **actions** layer at the top of our other layers, and give it keyframes in the first three frames.

12. Give the first keyframe in **actions** a label of **full** and attach a Stop action to it.

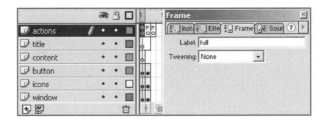

When the window first appears, we'll make the movie stop at label **full**, which shows an open window complete with content.

13. Label the second keyframe **bar**. If we make the window gotoAndStop at **bar**, the content will no longer be displayed and the window will change to a title bar only.

14. Label the third keyframe **blank**. If the window is made to gotoAndStop at **blank**, the window will disappear completely. Delete frames 2 and 3 from the **content** layer and check that your timeline matches mine:

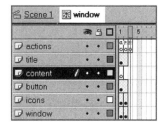

We'll now add the functionality to turn the title bar into that suitcase handle that the user can use to drag the windows as much as they like.

15. Select the invisible button and open the **Object Actions** window. As we did before, click on **startDrag** in the **Actions** menu. Click on startDrag (""); in the actions list to bring up the **Event** checkboxes at the bottom of the window. Uncheck **Release** and check **Press**:

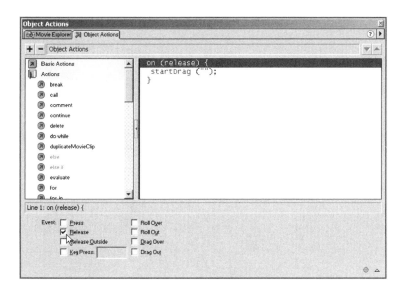

16. Go back to the **Actions** menu and click on **stopDrag** action. As it did before, the action will appear with a default `on (release) {` event. This is the ActionScript that you're left with when you're done:

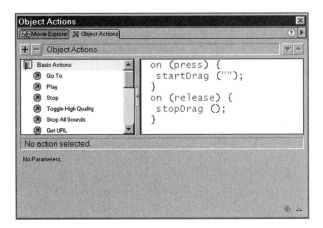

17. In frame 1 of the **buttons** layer select the minimize icon. Bring up the **Object Actions** window and click on **On Mouse Event** in the **Basic Actions** book. Leave the **Release** box checked.

18. With `on (release) {` still selected, click on **Go To** to bring up `gotoandPlay ("1") ;`. We need to change this to `gotoAndStop`, so uncheck the **Go To and Play** checkbox at the bottom of the window. Change the **Type:** to **Frame Label** and select **bar** from the **Frame** drop-down menu:

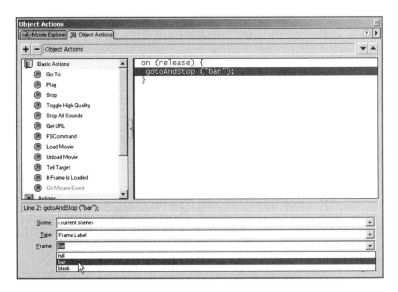

19. Select the close icon and bring up the **Object Actions** window again. Follow the same steps as for the maximize button that we've just dealt with, but specify the label blank this time. Here's your finished ActionScript:

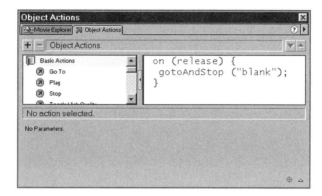

20. Add a keyframe in frame 2 of layer **buttons**, where you have your maximize icon. Bring up the **Object Actions** window again, select the gotoAndStop action and change the **Frame:** drop-down menu to full:

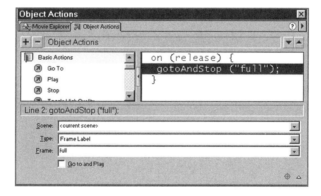

This sends Flash to the **full** label in our timeline, where the window is displayed in its full glory.

21. When you created the third keyframe in your **actions** layer, Flash may well have tried to be a little clever and added an extra keyframe to make up the numbers on your other layers. Check that none of your layers apart from **actions** go beyond frame 2. If they do, delete them.

So where are we so far? Well:

- If we select frame 1 of the **actions** layer, we'll see the full window. We've labeled this frame **full** and it's where we've sent Flash when we need to see exactly that – the full window – when we click the logical maximize button.

- If we select frame 2 of the **actions** layer, we'll see just the title bar. We've labeled this frame **bar** and we've sent Flash here so that it shows us just the title bar when we click the minimize button.

- If we select frame 3 of the **actions** layer, we'll see the same as in frame 2 – just the title bar. We've labeled this frame **blank**. This is where Flash will go when we click the close icon, telling it that we want to get rid of the window.

- Given that we've sent Flash to the third keyframe when we want to see **blank** we need to select the remains of the window in this frame and delete them.

22. Return to the main stage and drag your window movieclip onto the stage, somewhere to the far right.

23. Test the movie. The window will appear a little small because of the overall size of the stage, but you should find that you can do whatever you want with it: drag it, maximize it, minimize it or close it. If it doesn't work, compare it with my version which is in the zip file for this chapter as **stun_win.fla**.

You'll remember our discussion about site structure earlier. Imagine our base file – in this case **stun_basic.fla** – being a piece of board and the files on top of this as transparent sheets, each with its own timeline and associated animations and movieclips. The additional sheets will have no background, so you'll be able to see straight through down to the board:

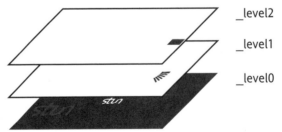

The board, or **level0**, defines the stage size, frame rate and background color for all other levels. Not only can you see down through the levels, all interactive elements (such as buttons) will also work. The transparent sheets are therefore not so much glass as totally without substance; your mouse is actually on all the levels at the same time, which is something to be aware of if levels below your top level have active buttons in their current frame; they will be active even if they're obscured by subsequent levels.

Our window movieclip will sit on top of the stun:design web site. Because everything will be visible, the windows have to be placed so that when they first appear on the site, they don't hide any of the graphics already there, or the title bars of any of the other windows. Our windows should be just the right size to fit on the extreme right of the *stun* site.

Let's make our multi-level loading windows. Loading at different levels means using SWF files, so we to make separate FLA and SWF files for each window.

Preparing Multi-level Loading Windows

1. To make the first window, delete the instance of **window** that you've just tested. Drag a new instance of **window** out of your library onto your plain black stage and place it at **X**: 2500.0, **Y**: 50.0 using the **Info** panel (with the center point set to the top left):

    Save this file as **about.fla** – we'll be using this later. Now test the file to create the SWF.

2. With the same file, change the **Y**: value to 100.0. Double-click on the **window** movieclip and change the window title from **about** to **clients**:

    Save this file as **clients.fla** and test the movie to create **clients.swf**.

3. Repeat the process again, this time set the **Y**: value to 150.0, and change the window title from **clients** to **our proposition**. Save it as **our.fla** and test it to create **our.swf**.

4. Do it all again for a final time with a **Y**: value of 200.0, and a window title of **we are different** instead of **our proposition**. Save it as **we.fla** and test it to create the SWF.

You should now have four FLA files, and the four corresponding SWFs. The final thing we need to do to get the whole setup working is add the actions to get the SWF movies containing the windows loaded up over our web site once the user presses the appropriate buttons.

There's a problem with calling the timeline of our base file **_root** because there are other root timelines in the levels above. To make things clearer, we'll call this timeline **_level0** to show that it is the lowest level. So:

- **_root** means the root timeline of the level you are currently on.

- **_leveln** means the specific SWF loaded at level **n**.

If you were trying to issue a play(); command to a movieclip **carrot** that sat on the timeline of **_level2**, you would issue the following command from any other level to get **carrot** to play:

```
_level2.carrot.play();
```

The lowest level can load up further levels via the loadMovie action, which will be called **_level1**, **_level2**, ...**_leveln**. This is what we are about to do – make **stun_basic.fla** load up the further levels with our windows on. If **_level0** (or any other level) loads up a new SWF into a level where an existing SWF is already loaded, that SWF will be replaced by the new one, even on **_level0**.

Open **stun_basic.fla**. We'll be adding the LoadMovie action required to bring up each corresponding window, starting with the **About** button.

Adding a LoadMovie Action

1. Select the **About** button now and bring up the **Object Actions** window. Click on **on Mouse Event** and check the **Release** box so that it reads `on (release) {`.

2. Select **LoadMovie** from **Basic Actions** and in the **URL:** field add **about.swf**. Make sure the **Location:** drop-down menu is set to **level** and in the field to the right of it enter **1**. Make sure that **Variables:** is set to **Don't send**:

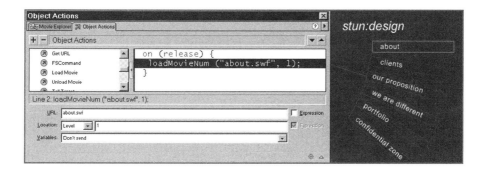

Don't worry about this **Don't send** option right now – trust me. I could write a whole book if I were to explain the ins and outs of sending variables, most of it not relevant to what you're doing at this stage in your ActionScript career. We'll look at everything we need to know about variables for what we're doing right now in the next chapter.

3. Select the **clients** button, bring up the **Object Actions** window and, as before, add an `on (release)` action and then a `loadMovie` action. This time specify the level as **2** and the **URL** as **clients.swf**.

4. Now select **our propostion** and do exactly the same again, but specify the level as **3** and the **URL** as **our.swf**. Finally, do it one last time for the **we are different** button, specifying level **4** and **we.swf**.

5. Save the file as **stun_01.fla**. Make sure that the four SWF files that we created earlier are in the same directory as **stun_01.fla** and test the movie (you'll probably need to publish to HTML as we did earlier to cope with the size of the screen). If things go wrong, compare your file with my version of this file in the zip for this chapter.

As you click the first four buttons in the stun:design menu you should see the four windows appear nicely cascaded:

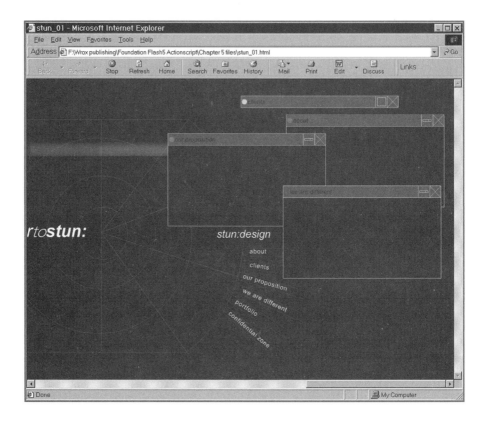

The user can drag, minimize, maximize or close these windows at will.

As they stand, the windows are quick to download and load up as soon as the user presses a button. That's as much hard work as we need for now, I think.

Summary

We've started to get into some serious stuff in this chapter, not only ActionScript, but general site organization and maintenance too. We've taken a look at:

- Creating invisible buttons.

- Creating draggable windows.

- The different options for structuring a site for efficient upload and navigation, using:

    - Scenes

    - Labeled frames

    - Movieclips

    - SWFs on different levels

- How to add animations to the Rollover states of buttons.

- Displaying draggable windows in response to a user clicking on menu options at stun:design.

We haven't really considered the fact that the content in the windows could turn out to be fairly large. If this was the case, we would need to change the window movieclips so that before they load in any content, they put up a little *loading* message in the frame before the keyframe containing the content. (We'll see how to do that in Chapter 9.) That way, the window loads up straight away, irrespective of how heavy its content is. This is a good ActionScript alternative to the scene-based web site because like HTML, it loads up content on demand, so there's no big boring download at the start.

Our final site will go one better and will have a *bandwidth manager* whose job it is to make efficient use of bandwidth. If you start (for example) to interact with one of the loaded windows so that you're not using any bandwidth, the manager will start loading up content that you *might want to see later*, and will hoard it up in the background ready for you to see as soon as you ask for it. You can't make such efficient use of bandwidth via single SWF Flash sites, so you've learnt the first step in creating efficient sites by using ActionScript... not only does it make your sites look cooler, they load up better as well. How's that for value?

We're going on to learn how to make these windows open up with all sorts of content in them, from text to still pictures to whole web sites! If this isn't enough, we'll also make the windows *scalable*, so you can scale the size of a window up or down while an animation is playing inside it.

Our ActionScript journey is starting to give us some stunning views of the valley below.

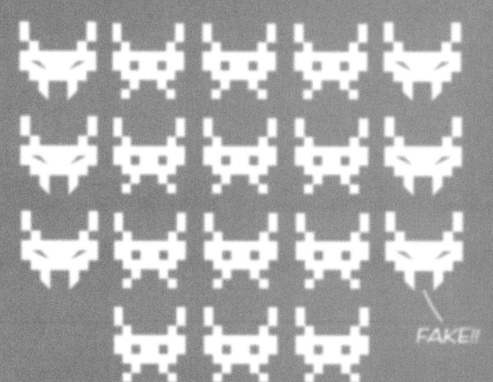

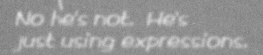

6 Variables

What we'll cover in this chapter:

- *How variables are containers for data*

- *The different types of variables – numeric, string and Boolean*

- *The use of expressions to generate values to be stored in variables*

- *Creating Input and Output fields to go beyond buttons in providing interactivity with the user*

- *How objects can store a collection of values and more*

Until now, our ActionScript has been looking at what's going on in the present – where the mouse pointer is, or what the current frame is – not what has happened in the past, or what will happen in the future. It can't do this because it has no memory: it can't remember what's happened, so it has nothing to use as a reference for making decisions or predictions, or for creating new information. In our example in the last chapter, once the movieclip had finished, Flash had no memory of it.

For Flash, having no memory means having nowhere to store **data**. Storing data will let Flash access information from events that have happened in the past. Perhaps more importantly, if Flash has somewhere to store data, it can start to ask the user to input data, and act on that when it arrives.

You have data, you need it at your fingertips and it's likely to change from one moment to another. The place you keep it is a **variable**. Here's an official-sounding definition:

A variable is a named memory location for holding data that's prone to frequent change.

In this section, we'll see what this definition really means, and look at how Flash uses variables to keep track of what's going on. We'll see how Flash can use what it knows to make decisions and predictions, or to perform calculations. Occasionally, this chapter may start to look a bit like math, but variables don't have to be used to contain things like the speed of light squared – they can just as easily be used to specify how high you want your cartoon Flash character to jump. It's not *really* math; it's just a powerful way to get Flash to do the fun things you want it to.

In Chapter 7 we'll cover looping and decision making, a topic that really makes the most of what you can do with variables. So that we can get the most out of these two subjects together, I've left the use of variables in our stun:design site until the end of the next chapter. The good news is that by then you'll have made it to Base Camp 2 on the ActionScript mountain, with the snowy peak now visible beyond those swirling clouds of mist. You'll have learned the basic ActionScript structures that underpin everything else and will be able to go on to do some really great stuff in the later chapters that specialize in sound, sprites, objects and the like.

Variables

A variable is a named 'container' in which to store data that may change. Whenever you need to use the data, you give Flash the variable name, and it will look in the right place and retrieve it for you. This concept can be confusing, so let's consider it in non-programming terms.

If you consider your wallet, it – hopefully – holds money. You have a particular amount of money in the wallet, which goes up and down depending on how much you spend. It's important to note that in general, the wallet itself isn't valuable – it's the money inside it that defines the value. Your local superstore isn't going to accept an empty wallet as payment for produce.

Put another way, the wallet is a container that you recognize as holding your money. When you hear the word wallet, you always know that what you'll find inside is money, never socks or frozen pizza. You also know that the amount of money in there will never stay the same for long.

But you might use other containers to store money too. You might have a tin in the kitchen to pay for coffee, tea and chocolate biscuits. You might have a piggy bank or a bottle into which you throw all your small change throughout the year. (If you're like me, you might spend that small bottle of money on a big bottle of something else at Christmas.) You have different containers because you need separate places to store money that's set aside for different purposes.

So, I have three different storage places, each holding separate quantities of money that fluctuate constantly:

- My wallet, containing my day-to-day money

- My tin, with money for tea and biscuits

- My bottle, containing my Christmas money

Those storage places are my 'variables', each containing different values that may change at any time. My first variable is my *wallet*, and the value it contains is the amount of money that I have to spend on everyday items. I also have a *tin* variable that holds tea money, and a *bottle* variable that holds beer money.

An important aspect of my high-level financial management is that I keep money for the right purpose in the right variable. Imagine the tragedy of confusing my *tin* variable with my *bottle* variable, so that at the end of the year I have enough cash to buy tea for the whole of China, but only $2.50 for a glass of beer on New Year's Eve!

Hopefully, I'm not very likely to confuse physical items like a tin, a bottle, and a wallet, but when we're programming we don't have that luxury. To ward off this potential tragedy, I'll have to stick labels on the front of my containers, or name my variables, so that I can be sure to know what each holds.

Values and Types

In the real world, we're surrounded by different kinds of storage spaces, designed to hold different things:

- Your wallet is designed to store money

- Your fridge is designed to store food

- Your closet is designed to store clothes

In ActionScript too, there are different kinds of values that we might want to stow away for later use. In fact, there are three such value types:

- Strings, or sequences of characters, such as Sham, or Hello, or a1b2c3. String values can be any length, from a single letter to a whole sentence, and they're especially useful for storing input from your users.

- Numbers, such as 27, or -15, or 3.142. As we'll discuss later, putting numbers in variables can be useful for keeping track of the positions of things in your movies, and for controlling how your ActionScript programs behave.

- Booleans, which are simple 'true or false' values that we'll look at more carefully at the end of this chapter.

When it comes to storing these different types of data, some programming languages mimic the real-world situation and force you to create and use variables that are able to store only one kind of value. ActionScript, however, doesn't ask you to be so explicit. It is an **untyped language**, which means that you *don't* have to specify what sort of values a variable will hold when you create it. Furthermore, ActionScript variables can hold different kinds of data at different times. When it needs to, Flash will work out what the type is.

Literals and Expressions

Shortly, we'll look at some examples that will start to demonstrate just how useful variables can be. When we get there, we'll find that Flash gives us quite a lot of help in doing so, but it's often nice to know what kind of thing to expect.

The easiest way to store a value in a variable is to use an equals sign (=). The easiest way to specify what you want to store is to use a **literal value**.

Literal Values

Imagine, then, that we have an ActionScript variable called `myname`. If I wanted to store my own name in this variable, I might do it like this:

```
myname = "Sham";
```

Here, "`Sham`" is a **string literal**: the string value that you want to store in `myname` is *literally* what appears between those two quotation marks.

In a similar way, we could have another variable called `myage`. To store a value in this variable, we might use a **numeric literal**, like so:

```
myage = 33;
```

> *Actually, we could call any number that appears anywhere in your ActionScript code a numeric literal – but plain "number" will do, most of the time.*

After these two lines, the variables `myname` and `myage` can be used in your code as direct replacements for the values they contain. That might not sound like much now, but you'll soon see just how much versatility this can provide.

Before we move on, remember that variables live up to their name: storing a value is no bar to storing a different value (or even a different *type* of value) in the same variable later on. Variable `x` may start out holding the numeric value 10, but tomorrow I could make it hold a string value just by writing `x = "Sham";`.

Expressions

The next way of generating values to be stored in variables is through the use of **expressions**. As we'll see in the exercises, this is where programming does start to look a bit like math, because expressions are often sequences of literals and variables, linked together by mathematical symbols. For example, you might have something like this:

```
result = myage - 10;
```

If `myage` were still storing 33, then the above would cause the value 23 (that is, 33 - 10) to be stored in the variable named `result`.

It's when we start to use expressions like this that we have to think carefully about the types of data being stored by our variables. The price we pay for the ease of using our untyped language is that it's *our* responsibility to keep track of what a variable is holding. If we get it wrong, we run the risk of using a value in the wrong place, and producing incorrect results.

Think back to your high school algebra. You can plan an equation like $a + b = c$, and be sure that it will work even before you know what the exact values of a and b are. Whatever happens, they're both numbers, and you know that two numbers added together will give you another number. Easy.

Programming is a little more complex than algebra. We have variables that hold not only numbers, but also other values – letters and words. We have to be aware of the types of data, and make sure that we don't try to mix two different types together.

If variable a = 2 and variable b = 3, we could add a and b to get a value for c that makes sense, because 2 + 3 = 5.

If variable a = "mad" and variable b = "house", we could add a and b to get a value for c that makes sense, because "mad" + "house" = "madhouse".

If variable a = "mad" and variable b = 3 and we add them together, the value for c is unlikely to make sense, because "mad" + 3 = "mad3".

To make variables work for us, we have to manipulate types separately and not mix them together. As a rule, if you input numbers, expect the result to be numbers as well. If you input text, expect the result to be text. If this doesn't happen, it's important that you know why, because this can be one of the most subtle and difficult errors to find if you are not expecting it.

Input and Output

So far, we've really only talked loosely about what variables are and the kinds of values they can store. It's about time we had a proper example of using them, so that you can start to see what they can do for your web sites. Because the benefits are perhaps most obvious, we'll begin by using them to store strings.

The act of storing strings is closely associated with input to and output from Flash, simply because users generally prefer to interact with a computer using text rather than raw numbers. Most complex interactions with computers are done using text of some kind, from filling in a form to order something online, to entering keywords into a search engine. Both are much more involved than, say, entering numbers into a calculator, and this is where string variables shine.

Creating an Input Field

1. If we're going to use a variable to *store* a string that the user has entered, we need to enable the user to *input* a string. Open a new movie and bring up the **Text Options** panel. The drop-down menu will currently have **Static Text** selected. Change that to **Input Text**:

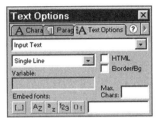

Select the Text tool from the toolbar, and click once on the stage to insert a textfield:

You'll notice that two things are different from the usual textfield:

- A static textbox has a circle at the top right-hand corner. This has a square at the bottom right to show that we've set it as an input field.

- A static textbox starts its life one character long, and grows as you add more text. Our textfield, on the other hand, immediately comes up with room to enter several characters. This is because text won't be input into this window until you publish your file. Until then, Flash needs to make a rough guess at how much you might need to enter. This default size is Flash's best guess; you can make the field longer (or even make room for more than one line of text) by dragging the little square on the bottom right of the text field.

2. Look again at the **Text Options** panel. Because we've assigned this box as an input field, Flash knows that we'll want to store that input for later use. It has made a start at creating the variable we need to do that. The **Variable** field has changed to show Textfield1 as a default name for the variable attached to the textbox we've just created. We need to rename the variable that will store our input to something more meaningful. This is our first input box, so I say we call the variable in1:

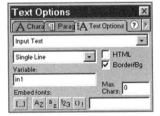

3. This is an area for inputting text, so when this runs on the web site, the user will need to click on the area before they can enter any text. Check the **Border/Bg** box to make Flash draw a box around the text area's limits. This will tell the user where to place the cursor, ready to enter text.

4. Now test the movie. You should see an empty rectangle on the stage. Click inside it, and a text entry cursor will appear. Type in whatever you want. If you type in more than the box can fit, it will scroll to accommodate your input as you type. You can use backspace, the normal copy and paste keys, and most of the other keys, although you can't use **Enter** to finish your input.

> hello Flash!!

That's all very well, but we can't see what (if anything) Flash is doing with our text as we enter it. I promise, it *is* doing something: it's storing whatever you type in the variable called in1. Let's start to use variables properly now, by sending Flash to retrieve what it's stored in variable in1 and display it in an **output field**.

Creating an Output Field

1. Click on a blank part of the stage with the Arrow tool to deselect the input field that we've just created. Bring up the **Text Options** window again, change the top drop-down menu to select **Dynamic Text**, and make sure the **Border/Bg** and **Selectable** boxes are unchecked:

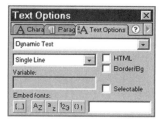

We've unchecked these options because the field that we're creating is for Flash's use, not the user's. It's being used as a display area, so the user won't need to see it drawn or be able to select it.

2. With the Text tool, add a new text field directly below the existing one. When you do so, the **Variable** field in the **Text Options** window will become selectable. Change the variable name to in1. This tells Flash where to look for the text that it has to display; of course, this is the same variable that we're using to store input into Flash.

3. Now test the movie. You'll see the same empty rectangle, *until* you start entering some text. When you do that, the dynamic text field will begin to 'echo' what you've entered. You'll also see, though, that it's of fixed length, and it won't scroll in the same way as the input box to display everything that you type in.

*The update speed of both text fields is determined by the frame rate specified for the movie. At the default frame rate of 12fps, the speed of text entry and its echo should look immediate. If you go and change the frame rate via **Modify > Movie** to 1fps, you will see a marked change in the update rate when you test the movie again. When you're done experimenting, return the frame rate to 12fps.*

At the moment, Flash is displaying a copy of what we type into the input box in real time, as soon as we type it in. If we make a mistake, Flash displays it for the world to see. We need a way to make Flash wait until we've finished entering our text and are happy with it before considering it the finished article. The easiest way to expand on what we've got to give us this extra feature is to create an **enter** button.

4. Select the lower textfield (the output box). In the **Text Options** panel, change the **Variable** from in1 to in2.

5. Add a button next to the input text. You'll know how to create your own buttons by now, so I'll leave that to you. Whichever way you do it, make sure that when you enter the **enter** text into your button, the text is set as static (in other words, it's not still set to **Dynamic** in your **Text Options** panel):

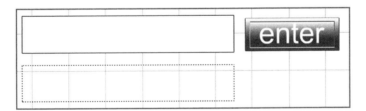

*If you don't want to create another button, you can get some predefined ones to modify from **Window > Common Libraries > Buttons**. These might not be exactly what you need, but they have been created using multiple layers, which makes them really easy to modify. I've done just that to make my button, which was derived from the push bar button in the common library. If you want to use my button, you can open as a library from the download file for this chapter.*

We now need to add our ActionScript to the button.

6. Select the button, and bring up the **Object Actions** window. Select the **On Mouse Event** action from **Basic Actions**. Keep the **Release** event checked, but also select the **Key Press** event. The textfield next to this label will immediately become selected. Press your *Enter* key to select it as the 'event key'.

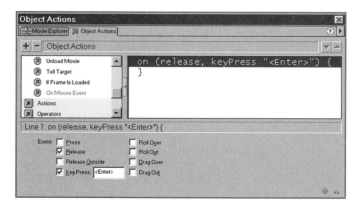

Our next step is to make Flash display in the output window (variable in2) exactly what we've typed in the input box (variable in1). Earlier, this happened automatically, because both fields displayed the contents of the same variable (in1). Now, we have to make the value of in2 equal to the value of in1.

7. With on (release, keyPress "<Enter>") { highlighted, double-click on **Set Variable** in the **Actions** book:

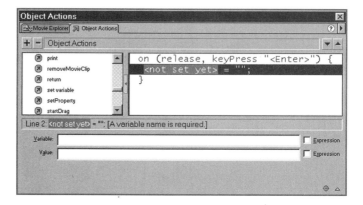

Yikes: all that red highlighting – but in fact we saw this briefly earlier on. Then, as now, Flash was showing us that we need to enter some missing information, but where previously it has been able to provide default values (for example, the default argument for gotoAndPlay() is frame 1), here it is unable to do so. Setting a variable is a rather more complex operation.

For a start, we need to specify the name of the variable that we intend this action to set. There's no way for Flash to guess which variable we might want, so it doesn't even try. Instead, it comes up with the most obvious way to alert us that we need to enter a name:

Line 2: <not set yet> = ""; [A variable name is required.]

8. In the **Variable** field, type in2. Flash is now happier, and has changed the line in the Actions window to:

    ```
    in2 = "";
    ```

    The red highlighting has disappeared because as far as Flash is concerned, this is legal: we're storing an empty string in the variable named in2. However, although Flash is happy, the command still doesn't do what we want it to.

9. In the **Value** field, type in1. Flash will now change the line to:

    ```
    in2 = "in1";
    ```

    This is *still* wrong. Although the right-hand side now contains the name of the variable containing the value we want to store in in2, those quotation marks mean that Flash will set the contents of in2 to the *string literal* "in1", rather than the value stored in the variable in1.

10. To the far right of the **Value** field is an **Expression** checkbox. Check it to tell Flash that what we've entered into the **Value** field is a variable. You'll see that Flash has finally got with it and come up with the goods:

    ```
    in2 = in1;
    ```

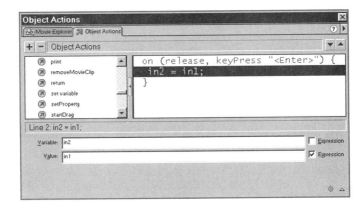

11. Now test the movie. This time, when you enter any text, the bottom field doesn't echo our input until we press the **enter** button. Save the FLA, because we'll be using it several times later on as a simple Flash user interface.

anybody home?	enter		anybody home?	enter

anybody home?

Using String Expressions

Let's recap. To start gathering together the first building blocks for inputting and outputting text within Flash, we've created simple textboxes for obtaining and displaying the values of basic variables. Now that you know how to do this, your available lines of communication with the user (and levels of interactivity) have just gone up from basic mouse-clicks, to phrases and sentences.

Having got our text input and output working, we're going to look now at how we can use string expressions to give Flash a human face and communicate with the user on a more personal level. We'll create a string expression that combines the value of the variable in1 with some extra text to display more than the user might expect.

Working with Strings

1. Load up the FLA that you've been working on, or use the original version of **chapter06_01.fla**.

2. Select the **enter** button yet again, and open the **Object Actions** window. Then, select the line in2 = in1; to bring up the **Variable** and **Value** fields at the bottom of the window. Edit the **Value** field so that it matches what you can see here:

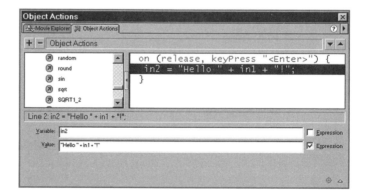

You don't need to insert a semicolon yourself; Flash will do this for you. If you get a lot of red highlighting and a message "trailing garbage found" this is probably what has happened.

When ActionScript encounters this, it takes the string literal `"Hello "`, adds the contents of the variable `in1`, appends the second string literal `"!"`, and stores the result in the variable `in2`.

3. Test the movie and enter your name. Flash should greet you like a long lost friend:

Hello Sham!

I don't want to undermine what we've done here, but I have to point out that there's a slight problem. We haven't been able to empower Flash with the grammatical knowledge to check whether what it's saying to you makes sense. Whatever you type in, Flash will give it back to you as part of the same answer:

Hello hi there!

I can't say that I have the solution to this for you here. I've shown you how to use string expressions to build in a degree of personalization, but be aware how quickly the illusion of intelligence falls apart. If you try this within a web site project, be careful. Still, it's reassuring to know that computers still can't be more intelligent than we are!

Naming Variables

Now that you've had just a flavor of how it might be possible to improve the web sites you build by using variables, and before we move on to look at storing numeric values, the time is ripe for us to look a little more deeply into the names we give to our variables. As you'll see, there are two very good reasons why this is an important thing to get right.

In Flash, we can name a variable however we like, *as long as Flash isn't likely to confuse it with something else*. Built into Flash are numerous names and symbols that are important to its correct operation, so we can't use them for our own purposes. These are called **reserved names**, and they include:

- **Commands**, or any other part of ActionScript that might be mistaken as part of an action, including {}, ;, and (). The reserved names that can't be used are: break, continue, delete, else, for, function, if, in, new, on, return, this, typeof, var, void, while and with. Obviously, don't precede your variable name with //, because then it becomes a comment! As a general rule, if your variable name is shown in black in the **Actions** window, it's probably OK. If it's shown in blue or highlighted in red when you select the line containing it, Flash has mistaken it for something else.

- **Operators**, such as +, -, and /. Otherwise, Flash may try to treat your variable as a sum to occur between two variables.

- **Spaces**. (Use underscores _ instead.)

- Names with leading numbers, such as 6y. Use y6 instead.

With these provisions in mind, valid variable names would be:

- cow

- menu6

- label7c

- off

Invalid names would be:

- on   because Flash will expect it to part of an OnEvent action

- label 7   because of the space in the middle

- 6cmenu   because it starts with a number

- my-toys   because it contains a minus operator, which will confuse Flash into thinking it means two variable names

Once you've obeyed these rules to keep Flash happy, the important thing is that your variable names keep you happy too. You don't want to spend time figuring out what types they contain or what values they're meant to hold, so be as efficient as you can. Make sure that the names say something about what the variables hold. For example, if I had three variables holding my three amounts of money, I could name them `dayMoney`, `teaMoney` and `beerMoney`. This really will make debugging a lot easier. As you become more experienced, you may find times when you need to use variables of the same name in different places. As long as you're clear on the reasons why you need to do that, that's fine.

Another thing well worth knowing is that Flash is a bit strange about case sensitivity. It *is* case sensitive for actions, so `gotoandplay(1)` wouldn't work – Flash expects the action to read `gotoAndPlay(1)`. At the same time, however, Flash *isn't* case sensitive for variable names, so `big` and `BIG` would be taken as the same variable. Take some time to remember this!

Finally for this section, a path name is part of the variable name, so if you had a variable named `igor` in the timeline of a movieclip instance called `darkcastle`, the full name of the variable would be `_root.darkcastle.igor`.

At the same time, and without causing problems, you could also have the same variable name, `igor`, in the timeline of a movieclip instance called `transylvania`. Its full name would be `_root.transylvania.igor`.

Variables can be **localized** to a particular timeline, and only exist in that timeline, so identically named variables in different paths are distinct, and can hold different values or types. Flash would recognize your two `igor`s as being different, no problem, but you would have to be very careful to make sure that *you* remember the difference!

Storing Numbers

In everyday use, numbers can represent more than just raw values. Numbered seats in a cinema don't represent a chair's *value*, but its *position*. The ISBN for this book doesn't represent its value or its position, but is a *reference* or *index* to the book.

To a much greater extent than strings, numbers lend themselves to being operated upon: they can be added to, subtracted from, added together, multiplied, divided, and so on. If you store numbers in variables, all kinds of possibilities are opened up.

Returning to those cinema seats, if we arrange to store the number booked so far in a variable called `seatstaken`, then the number of the next seat available for booking is *always* `seatstaken` + 1, regardless of the actual value stored in the variable.

Look at this:

```
seatstaken = seatstaken +1;
```

It says, "Add one to the current value of `seatstaken`, and store the result back in `seatstaken`." Each time ActionScript encounters it, the number stored in the variable increases by one. Remember: variables are all about giving ActionScript a memory.

Let's try some of this out, using the FLA you just made (if it went wrong or you didn't save it, use **chapter06_01.fla** in the download file). In this exercise, we're going to get the user to input some numbers, and then perform some calculations on them.

In the previous exercise, the values we saw going into `in1` were actually string values, which is to say that they could include more than the numbers 0 to 9 and the decimal point that we would normally expect in numeric values. Before we start using `in1` in numeric expressions, we need to take steps to prevent the user from entering characters that could spoil our work.

Performing Numeric Calculations

1. Select the input text and bring up the **Text Options** panel. At the bottom, you'll see a number of buttons with various characters on them. If none is selected, Flash will accept all characters the user may type. If any are selected, however, Flash starts to become choosier. Select the one marked **123**, as shown, and we'll only accept numbers. In order to accept decimals as well, there is a text entry field to the right of the buttons where you can enter additional characters. Click in it and type a decimal point:

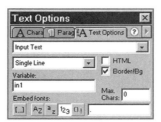

9. Now test the movie. You'll find that you are no longer able to enter anything other than decimal numbers, which is a step in the right direction.

456.565464

3. Select the **enter** button on the stage, and bring up the **Actions** window. Because we can be sure that it's safe to treat in1 as a numeric value, we can assign in2 to the result of some arithmetic to be performed on in1. We'll try:

```
in2 = 2*in1;
```

> In computer programming languages, the asterisk '*' is often used to represent multiplication in place of the traditional 'x', to remove the chance of confusion with the letter 'x'.

Change the second line in the ActionScript to this new command by changing the **Value** field from in1 to 2*in1.

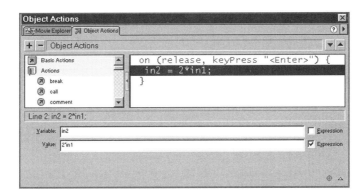

Now test the movie. Our output is now a calculated value based on our input – that is, it's the result of a numeric expression.

90

If you like, you can try changing the expression to give the following information:

```
in2 = in1*in1;
```
for the square of the amount entered

```
in2 = 1/in1;
```
for the reciprocal of the amount entered

More Uses for Numeric Expressions

Numeric expressions have a lot more to offer than making Flash do sums for us. For example, we could use the results of numeric expressions to control the position or orientation of an instance, allowing us to create some very complex movements. We could have an expression to tell our alien spaceship where to move to when Blard shot at him!

We can also use numeric expressions to jump to frames within a movie based on *dynamic* values, not just the fixed number values we have used so far, allowing us to control timeline flow to a much greater degree. We could jump to an explosion if we hit an alien, for example.

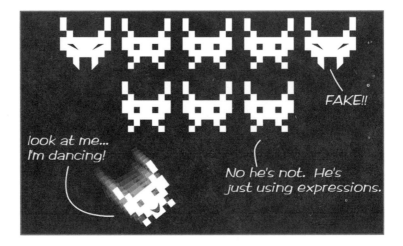

Some of the stuff we've been looking at may have seemed a little removed from space invaders flitting about the screen, and cool, ActionScript-heavy dynamic sites, but we are learning about the cogs that make these things turn. We'll continue to do that in the next section.

Boolean Values

If I buy a packet of cookies, I do so because they look tasty and I am not on a diet. This is a very clear-cut decision: if two criteria are met, then I buy the cookies. In general, however, we don't tend to make such straightforward decisions; instead we base them at least partly on a comparison, our mood, or a predisposition. We might even base some decisions on inputs that have nothing to do with the choice at all: "I don't want to talk to him because I don't like the color of his shirt." Our decisions can have many more outcomes than just, "I will," or, "I will not."

Computers, though, stick to decisions of the more clear-cut variety, which is a relief because a computer probably tracks my bank balance and transactions. I wouldn't like my balance to halve suddenly because the computer was having a bad day and I turned up to the bank wearing a lilac shirt. Computers base their decisions on statements of the yes/no or true/false variety. Their decisions have only two possible outcomes at a time, although they can apply lots of yes/no decisions in a row to tackle more complex outcomes.

Suppose, for example, that we wanted to find out whether a number was higher or lower than 100. It could be the price of a share on the stock market: if it is lower, we want to think about buying, and if it is higher, we will think about selling. Depending on which side of 100 the price is, we will perform one of two different sets of actions. Alternatively, it could be that we're writing a space invaders game, where the invaders move down the screen in their attempt to land on your planet. Once the distance of any invader from the top edge of the stage is greater than 100, we know they are at the bottom of the screen, and the player has lost.

Take the first case, and assume that the share price we're interested in is stored in a variable called price. Now have a look at this:

```
buy = price < 100;
```

When we've seen code like this in the past, the expression on the right hand side of the equals sign has been evaluated, with the result being stored in the variable on the left hand side. But what *is* the value of the right hand side? Given the title of this section, you won't be surprised to discover that it's a **Boolean value**, which means that buy will be set to true if price is less than 100, or false if price has any other value. true and false are the *only* Boolean values, and they are the only possible values of the right hand side.

> Note that true *and* false *here are neither strings nor variables. They are simply the two possible Boolean values.*

Until we start to look at conditional operators in the next chapter, which will indeed allow us to perform different actions depending on Boolean values, there's a limit to what we can do with them. However, we can at least check that what I've been saying is true, and use them in some slightly more complex expressions.

Experimenting with Booleans

1. Let's modify our movie again. Load up **chapter06_01.fla** (the file you created way back at the beginning of this chapter), making sure it's free of all the little tweaks we made after saving it for the first time. Select the input text, and on

the **Text Options** panel change the parameters so that we will again only accept numeric values, by selecting the **123** box and inserting a decimal point in the bottom right box:

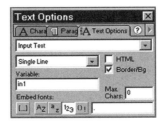

2. Now select the **enter** button, highlight the line

```
in2 = in1;
```

and change the **Value** field to

```
in2 = (in1<100);
```

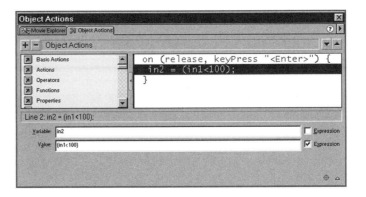

3. Now run the movie. Flash will look at any number you put in and compare it with 100. If it's lower, (in1<100) is a true statement, so you will get `true`. If it is greater than or equal to 100, then (in1<100) is not true, and you will get `false`.

false

If you need to, you can use **logic operators** to make your test more complex. That's what we're abut to do. Take our earlier example about share prices. If you were prepared to buy if the price was below 100, then you might want to stop buying if the price went below 80, because such a sharp drop would indicate unfavorable market conditions. In words, you would need something like this:

"Price is less than 100, AND greater than 80."

Bringing this closer to our expression in this example, we need:

```
(in1<100) AND (in1>80)
```

To signify AND, Flash uses the `&&` symbol, which can be found in the toolbox pane under **Operators**. In fact, Flash even has a more user friendly `AND` command, but it's really only for compatibility with Flash 4 – it is deprecated, and you should avoid it.

4. In your current button script's second line, place your text cursor in the **Value** field, and at the end of the line. Double click on the `&&` operator. You will now have

    ```
    in2 = (in1<100)&&
    ```

    and Flash will be giving a syntax error, because it expects another term after the operator. Add `(in1>80)` to the end of the Value field to give you

    ```
    in2 = (in1<100)&&(in1>80);
    ```

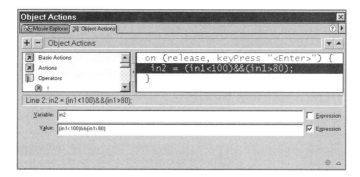

5. Now run the movie. You'll see that you get a `true` result only if the price is between 80 and 100.

Using similar techniques, you can build up very complex conditions that involve a number of other operators and terms, and we will start using them for real in the next chapter.

ActionScript Objects, Properties, and Methods

Before we go on, there's one more thing that I ought to introduce – or perhaps I should say, reintroduce. It probably hasn't escaped your attention that the act of storing values in variables looks similar to what we did in order to set the x-coordinate of the moving ball in earlier chapters:

```
ball._x = _xmouse;
```

Of course, this is no coincidence. Those "named instances" (as we called them then), such as `ball`, were in fact variables that contained **objects**, and while we'll be looking at these much more carefully in Chapter 9, we can start to say something about them here.

Objects

If you think of strings, numbers, and Booleans as the milk, dark, and white chocolate of the variable world, then objects are the boxes of chocolates that you buy people for Christmas. Objects provide a way to store whole collections of values, and can have some extra things thrown in too. They lie at the heart of a lot of what Flash 5 can do, and we've seen some of what they allow *us* to do already.

At this time, the Flash object that you know best is the movieclip. You know that it's a distinct item that you use for distinct purposes, and that it has a set of **properties** – the number of frames, the position, etc. – that relate to its physical appearance. Those properties are always part of any movieclip object that you ever use.

This is a useful feature, but it's not the only trick that objects have up their sleeves. The movieclip object also had a "stop" command that we were able to use like this:

```
ball.stop();
```

You'll see these variously called commands and actions, but the correct term for them is **methods**, and using them usually causes something to happen to the object. When you're starting out you can just call then commands and nobody will notice, but giving them their proper name will never fail to impress. Knowing how to apply methods in Flash is crucial if you are to make it as a top class ActionScripter.

It's quite easy to get a feel for a movieclip object, because its properties and methods relate to its physical appearance. However, not all objects are so intuitive – in general, they can be collections of any number of properties and methods that may or may not have an obvious visual representation. For example, Flash 5 uses objects for features such as advanced mathematical operations and sound control, and we'll look at the first of those here.

The Math Object

The Math object is always available for you to use from anywhere in your ActionScript code, but it's a rather strange object because it only has methods – there are no properties at all! It's really acting as a 'library' of commands that you can use whenever and wherever you need them. Let's see how it works.

Finding the Square Root of a Number

1. Returning again to our sample movie, and with the **enter** button selected, open the **Actions** panel and clear the **Value** field. Now look in the toolbox pane under the **Objects** book icon. You will see a number of other actions books under **Objects**, one of which is **Math**. From this, select **sqrt**, and provided that the **Value** field is selected, you should see the following:

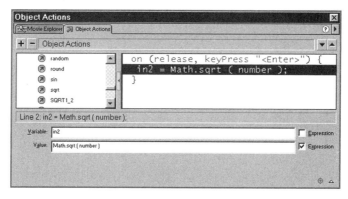

2. `Math.sqrt ( number )` has appeared, and we need to replace `number` with the variable we want to operate on, `in1`. When you've done that, run the movie.

7

As you've probably worked out, Flash is now giving us the square root of the value we enter. If you look at some of the other methods of the Math object, you will see that they cover trigonometry, logarithms, and some other things. When you progress to real-time 3D and other fairly heavy simulation graphics, these functions will become very useful.

The String Object

Lastly, and taking a deep breath, I'm going to let you in on a little secret. In Flash 5, *all* variables contain objects, even when they're apparently only holding simple values of the types we met earlier in the chapter. Numeric values, for example, are objects with just one property: their value. As we've proved in the exercises so far, this apparent complication doesn't prevent us from using them in simple ways, but in some cases it does allow us access to some more powerful functionality when we need it.

To bring this further out into the open, it's a fact that just as all movieclips have the same set of methods and properties, so too do all the strings you create. You can see the full complement of these by looking in the toolbox pane under **Objects > String**:

If you roll over any of these, Flash will give you more information about them with its tooltips. We're not going to cover the whole list here (although you'll find that they will appear from time to time as we progress through the book), but there is time to explore one or two of them. Look at this:

```
in2 = in1.length;
```

Here, in1 contains a string, and this line of code makes use of the string object's length property to store its length in in2. As you can probably imagine, knowing this value is pretty crucial if we want to split the string up, analyze it, or do other clever things with it. Let's see how we would go about doing this in Flash.

Finding the Length of a String

1. Start by typing `in1` into the **Value** field of your button's **Object Actions** panel. Then, go to **Objects > String** in the toolbox pane, and find the `length` property. Before you double-click on it, select the **Value** field, and place your cursor right after the `in1` text. Now double-click on the method:

2. To test the movie, input some text, and press **enter** to see the result. Notice that any spaces are counted in the length, because as far as Flash is concerned, a space is a character like any other.

9

As another example, you'll often want to know whether input contains a particular character. If you ask the user for a yes/no answer, then for the "yes" response you might get "yes", "y", or even " y" (with a leading space). You might also get the same answers in upper case. For robust code, you must always assume that the user will do the wrong thing, so you need to be sure that your code is tolerant of all stupid answers.

In this exercise, we'll examine a string to see whether it contains a "y". We don't care if there are any other characters, because the minimum information we need to know that a "yes" response was intended is just a "y".

Examining the Content of a String

1. Before we do anything else, we need to make sure that we're looking at a lower case "y", and not a capital "Y". To do this involves an intermediate step, so we'll create a new variable called `temp`.

   Still in the same **Object Actions** window from the last exercise, insert a new **Set Variable** action from the **Actions** list. Position it between the two lines of code you already have by using the up and down arrows in the top right-hand corner of the **Object Actions** window.

2. Enter `temp` into the **Variable** box. In the **Value** box, make sure that **Expression** is checked, and ensure that the cursor is located within it. Then, select the `toLowerCase` method from the **Objects > String** menu, click once again at the beginning of the **Value** field, and add the name of the variable containing the string: `in1`.

3. We now need to find our "y". Select the old `in2 = in1;` line, and change the **Value** field to:

   ```
   temp.indexOf("y")
   ```

   This line now looks for a "y" and gives us its position (or index) in the string. Your **Object Actions** window should now look like this:

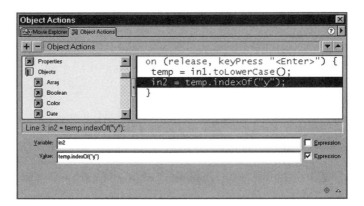

4. The first possible position of "y" is 0, rather than 1. If Flash doesn't find a "y", then it gives up and returns -1. Test the movie, and try entering different text. As long as you enter "Y", "y", "yes", or "Yes", the number displayed will be positive (or at least, 0).

As you can see, by treating strings as objects, we've been able to use their methods to perform various actions over and above simple addition. We've been allowed to apply more specialized routines that are specific to this particular type of value.

Summary

You now have a good grounding in variables and values. Although you haven't built any cool FLAs in this chapter, you have a solid foundation to move forward into Chapter 7, where every new thing you learn will allow you to do something cool and immediately useful. That's what you've built up to by slogging through this one.

In your projects, try to work with value types that are appropriate to the problem you're solving. For example, we would all prefer to be able to converse with machines in a language like the one we use to talk to each other. Strings are useful here, because they represent a friendly way for Flash to communicate with the user, but they're no good for complex calculations.

In this chapter we've looked at:

- What variables are and how Flash uses them

- Using string values to communicate with the user

- Using numeric values to perform calculations

- Using Boolean values to store the results of comparisons

As we work through the rest of this book you'll see how variables lie at the heart of many of the effects that you can create within Flash. We'll use string values to build a hangman game and look at the decision-making functionality that we can build using Boolean values.

We've quickly mentioned objects as things that can store a collection of values and do a bit more than just acting as the sum of their parts. We're going to come back to objects in Chapter 9, but now that you know a little about them, you'll be able to spot objects in everything that we do. The sound object, for example, gets a lot of press in Chapter 8.

Have a little break, and then go straight into the next chapter, where you'll really start using your variables in anger!

estr

accepted

NEO: (we have been waiting)

7 Looping and Decision Making

What we'll cover in this chapter:

- *How to make Flash look at a situation and make a decision on what to do next, depending on what it sees*

- *Giving Flash the intelligence to check a password*

- *How to use ActionScript features to deal with large pieces of data and control several items at once*

- *Creating a hangman game*

Up to this point in the book, we've made Flash perform fairly linear commands. We've jumped to new frames on button events or Go To actions, and controlled timelines externally to give some feeling of non-linear movement. However, we're still not stretching Flash and making it act intelligently. In the last chapter we learnt the basics of getting Flash to manipulate data with variables, and display the fruits of those manipulations. In this chapter we'll close the loop and get Flash to use the data it manipulates to control itself further. We're going to instruct Flash to test whether certain conditions apply and tell it to act accordingly. When we've done this Flash will be able to handle much more data with looping structures, making your Flash presentations think intelligently and act in a more convincing way.

In the first section of this chapter we'll look at **decision making** and show how you can use Boolean comparisons to decide which lines in your ActionScript you want to run. The rest of the chapter will look at **looping structures**, which allow you to repeat your actions and let you sift though large amounts of data, or control more than one item with the same small piece of code.

Decision Making

In terms of decision making within Flash there's only one main command you have to learn: the **if** statement. This statement can have additional decision making branches, called the **else** and **elseif** commands, but we can think of these as separate parts of one action because they tend to be used together.

Before we look at the **if-elseif-else** structure in Flash, let's look at how we make decisions in real life. Even when we're making everyday choices, there are certain things we consider first.

Real Life Decisions

Real life decisions are rarely as simple as:

"I'll go to the open-air rock concert if it's not raining."

You're more likely to think:

"If I have enough money, and it's not raining on the day, I'll go to the open-air rock concert. But if I'm late with my job I won't be able to afford the time."

Your decision now is not only based on whether you'll get wet if you go to the concert, but also on whether you have enough money and can spare the time.

In the same way, when you're writing ActionScript it's important to consider what the conditions of the event are and what you need to do when each one is met. Just as you do with your real life choices, you need to think in terms of the consequences, and address them all in your code.

The main problem you may have as a beginner is knowing how to express a decision in a way Flash will understand. You know what you want to say, but you need to learn to write it in a new way. That's what we're going to learn now.

Using my sausage notation from Chapter 1, we can re-write my initial concert dilemma as:

if (it's not raining)
{go to the concert}

However, as I explained, the problem is more complex than that:

If (if I have enough money) and (it's not raining on the day) and (I can afford the time)
{go to the concert}

If you were programming this decision, you'd go through exactly the same process. Writing a decision down on paper in the same way that I've done here will help you to make sure you've considered all the conditions that need to be met.

Using the sausage notation will help you to write all your programming decision branches in terms that you can use to set things clearly in your mind before you start coding. You have the added bonus that it's written in the correct ActionScript syntax, so you can convert it seamlessly into working code. Don't be put off by the silly sausage name – it really does help.

Let's apply this thinking to an actual Flash programming decision, set at the standard that you as a professional Flash ActionScript programmer would face.

Flash Decisions

We'll work out the final code later, but for now we'll take a look at expressing the decision simply and precisely to help us build a clear idea of what we want the code to do.

Here's the decision I want to make:

> I have a game of space invaders. The player's ship is allowed to fire bullets at the aliens. I'm looking at the situation when the bullet has been fired (signified by a Boolean `bullet_fired = true`), and is moving up the screen at a speed signified by the variable `bullet_speed`. I want to move it further up the screen if it hasn't already reached the top. If it's at the top I want to stop moving the bullet and remove it from the screen. In this case I want to set `bullet_fired` to `false`, which Flash will see as a sign that the player is allowed to fire again.

When you're faced with such a longwinded problem, there's only one way to simplify it: get rid of some of the words. The easiest way to do this is to draw a picture – automatically dropping your word count to near zero:

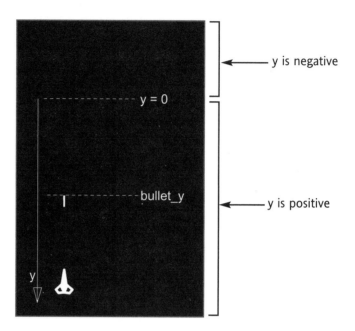

We've got our player's ship at the bottom and our bullet at some point moving up. The bullet moves up in a straight line, so only its *y* co-ordinate decreases as it moves up the screen, towards a value of zero at the top.

So we need to look at two things:

- How do we define the bullet's position when it's on the screen?

- How do we define when it's gone off the top of the screen for the first time?

We need to define the conditions relating to these variables precisely because these are the variables that'll actually drive the bullet's movements. Don't worry about how we would move the pieces – that's for a later chapter. What we're concerned with now is building up the framework of variables and decisions that will cause this movement.

So, the *y* co-ordinate of the bullet, `bullet_y`, reaches a value of zero at the top of the screen. In other words, `bullet_y` will be *positive* before it hits zero and *negative* once it's gone beyond that.

As long as `bullet_y` is positive, we want to keep subtracting speed from it, which will move the bullet upwards as its *y* co-ordinate decreases.

As soon as bullet_y is less than zero, we no longer need to animate the bullet, although we need it to disappear. We could make it disappear in a number of ways, but the easiest would be to place it off screen, say at bullet_y = -100.

When the bullet is off screen, the player would be allowed to fire another bullet, so we need to tell Flash this by making bullet_fired = false.

The decision breaks down into two branches:

If (the bullet is being fired) and (its *y* position is greater than 0)
{move the bullet}

otherwise

If (the bullet is being fired) and (its *y* position is less than 0)
{hide bullet and let user fire another}

But what'll happen if the bullet isn't being fired? Well, neither of these branches in the decision will be relevant, and neither of them will do anything. If you think about it, that's what we want. If bullet_fired == false, the bullet will be safely hidden away above the top of the screen, and we want it to stay there.

So, we transfer the sausage notation into ActionScript:

```
if bullet_fired and (bullet_y > 0)
    {bullet_y == bullet_y - speed}
```

otherwise

```
if bullet_fired and (bullet_y < 0)
    {bullet_fired == false; bullet_y = -100}
```

Notice that I've written (bullet_fired == true) simply as bullet_fired. That's because I'm basing my decision on whether the expression in each bracket is true. In other words, inside the brackets I'm always looking for:

(does this) == true

If I looked for (bullet_fired == true), I would be actually asking for:

(bullet_fired == true) == true

which is asking for the same thing twice.

> *When you're looking for conditions, it makes for neater code if the condition is simply a Boolean in its true state. Then, you just insert the Boolean and don't have to put unnecessarily long expressions all over the place.*

Placing the bullet at a *y* co-ordinate of −100 is the sort of thing that you'd look at six months after coding it and say, "Why is that −100?". A better way would be to use a variable with a descriptive name, such as **hide**. At the beginning of the game you'd set a variable, hide, to −100. In the main code you'd then be able to make statements like bullet_y = hide, which gives you a much better clue of what you're trying to do.

After all that, all you need to know is the syntax of the if action. We're going to learn that now; and you'll probably feel like you've already used it because it's so close to what we've already done so far.

The if Action

The basic structure of an if command is this:

if (the condition inside the brackets is true) {
 do this;
};

The only difference between this and my sausage expression:

if (it is not raining)
{go to the concert}

is that Macromedia have split my sausage across three lines.

Let's look at a simple example.

I've built a screen which has the sole purpose in life of extracting a password from the user. If they fail at this point, they won't be allowed to enter the site. I've used the font OCR−Extended, which you can pick up from most free font sites. If you can't find it elsewhere, try the newsgroup **alt.binaries.fonts**.

> If you want to try this exercise with my graphics, you can see *chapter07_01.fla* in the download file for this chapter. I've used **Modify > Break Apart** on all the fonts so that you don't need to have them installed on your machine to see the screens as I've designed them. If you're using this ready-made version, ignore the first two points below, as they've already been done for you. You'll notice also that scenes 2 and 3, which we'll come to later, have already been created for you too.

OK, let's get going.

Using the if Action

1. Create a similar screen to the one I have here:

restricted
>Password: [   ] _execute ▐▊▌▌▊▌▌▊▌▌▊▌

There are two active items on this screen. The hollow block is an input textfield with the variable name password:

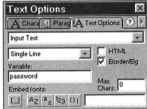

The **_execute** text is a button that the user has to press after entering the password.

2. Create a new layer called **actions** and add a simple `stop();` command in frame 1:

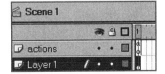

Once the user has entered the correct password, we want to take them to the next stage of the movie, which will start at scene 2, frame 1. This is what they'll see:

It has exactly the same timeline as scene 1, minus the `stop();` action because this is obviously where you would want your web site to start playing.

Before it lets the user see all your hard work, Flash will check whether they've used the correct password as soon as they press the **_execute** button. This is where we need to attach our ActionScript because it's the key to making the system work. We need to make Flash look at what the user enters and compare it with the actual `password` variable. If they're the same, it will let the user into scene 2. In recognition of one of my favorite films, I've decided that the password will be **I am The One**.

Expressed in my shorthand, the decision we need to make here is:

if (password == "I am The One")
{go to scene 2, frame 1}

To make life easier for the user, I'm going to make the password case-insensitive, so they can enter 'I am the One', or 'I am the one' or any combination of upper and lowercase letters.

Notice that I'm not considering what happens if the password doesn't match. At the moment, I don't want to do anything, which means that the user won't move from the password scene.

3. Add an `on (release) {` action to the **_execute** button.

    We'll now add a Set Variable action and one of those ready-made methods that we talked about in the last chapter to change the password to lowercase.

4. Click on **setvariable** action. In the **Variable** field, type the name `password`. In the **Value** field, type the same name and leave your cursor there. (Don't add the expected dot for the dot notation yet – it will be added automatically in a moment.)

5. Open the **Objects** book and within that, the **String** book. Click on the **toLowerCase** method to add that to the **Value** field. (See, the dot gets added too.) Check the **Expression** box to the right of the **Value** field:

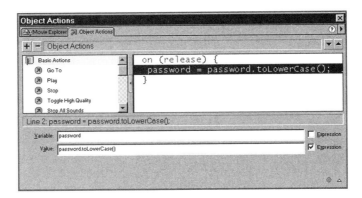

Now we can start on our if command.

6. Select the **if** action. As soon as it appears, you'll recognize it is doing the same thing we saw with `setVariable;`. The action comes up with a syntax error because there are no defaults that Flash can sensibly add to it:

The window is asking for an expression in the **Condition** field. We need to form an expression to make Flash check what the user has entered against what we set as the password.

The new syntax for just performing a check uses a double equals sign ==. This means **test equality**. You can see this command in the **Operators** book in the toolbox, but, as with any operator, it's usually faster just to type it in manually and only look at the toolbox if you need to make sure you've got it right.

7. In the **Condition** field type: `password == "i am the one"`

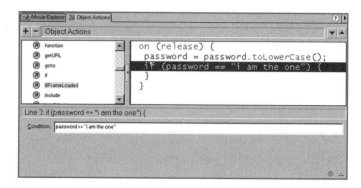

We now need to add an action telling Flash to run our movie from the first frame of scene 2 if this condition is true, that is, if the user has entered the correct password.

8. Add a `gotoAndPlay` action, directing Flash to scene 2, frame 1 by filling in the fields like I have here:

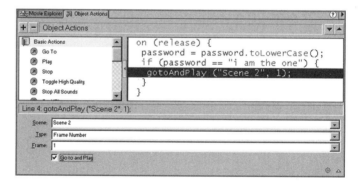

> *We could have used a Play action here instead because Scene 1 has just one frame, so we're in effect going to the next frame of our animation. However, in future you won't always be taking the viewer to the next frame on the timeline when a condition is met, so using* `gotoAndPlay` *is a good habit to get into.*

You may find that the indentation of these lines in Normal mode a little too subtle. If you jump into Expert mode you can make it more pronounced, like this:

```
on (release) {
    password = password.toLowerCase();
    if (password == "i am the one") {
        gotoAndPlay ("Scene 2", 1);
    }
}
```

Personally, I would've expected the indentation to be a lot clearer in Normal mode than it is in Expert mode. Still, you can't have everything...

9. Test the movie. If you enter the right password, you'll get as far as scene 2. If you don't, nothing happens and you're stuck.

   Let's take this up one level more. What if we wanted an executive password for a special user? I've made a screen to welcome this person and put it in frame 1 of scene 3 in **chapter07_01.fla**:

We'll now also need an executive password that only this person would know. You can see here that I've chosen **Neo**. We'll need Flash to check whether it's been entered. Some sausage notation to clarify what we're doing:

if (password == "I am The One")
{go to scene 2, frame 1}
however, if (password == "Neo")
{go to scene 3, frame 1}

> You should be getting familiar with using == instead of = when you're testing whether two things are the same. In fact, when you're writing the condition of your **if** statement there's no occasion where you'd use a single =. If you do you'll get very odd results, and it's really hard to find this kind of error in large ActionScript sites.

Don't start looking for the **however, if** command. It doesn't exist. To say this Flash uses the elseif action. It means 'if the last statement was false, check whether this next one's true'.

Let's break off for a minute and look at the elseif action more closely, as learning to use it properly will be very helpful to your programming.

The elseif Action

You can put as many elseif actions as you want after the initial if action, making Flash check whether any number of conditions have been met (are true):

```
if (a)
{do this}
elseif (b)
{do this}
elseif (c)
{do this}
elseif (d)
{do this}
```

We'll break this down.

```
if (a)
{do this}
elseif (b)
```

Here, Flash will look at (a). If it's true, it will carry out the associated {do this} instruction. If it's false, Flash will skip straight to the next elseif , which tells it to check whether (b) is true.

If (b) is true, Flash will run the associated {do this} instructions and go no further.

It won't check either (c) or (d) or run their associated {do this} instructions, **even if (c) or (d) are true**. This is an important note to take on board, because it shows that the order you enter your elseif actions decides which one has precedence.

So, you need to always remember that only one branch of your elseif command will run, and that's the first one Flash checks and finds it to be true. After the initial if, it's better to use elseif actions rather than a further string of if commands because once a condition within an elseif command has been found to be true, Flash doesn't continue checking the subsequent elseif conditions – it just follows the appropriate instruction. If we use a group of if actions we'd force Flash to check every single one, even after it had found a condition that had been met. This puts an unnecessary strain on Flash.

Essentially, as you go down the ladder of `elseif` actions, you're finding out what *isn't* true, and then homing in on what *is* true by asking more and more precise questions based on what you know it *might be.*

Imagine that you were writing a piece of code that controlled how a diving space invader attacked the player on its way down the screen, and you wanted to make your space invader do different things as it got closer to the player's ship. You'd write your decision like this:

```
if (ship_y - alien_y >50)
{make alien stay in formation}
elseif (ship_y - alien_y >25)
{make alien start to fire on the ship and dive in a random
downward direction}
elseif (ship_y - alien_y >10)
{execute kamikaze tactics}
```

If the first condition in the `if` action is found to be false, you can deduce that on the first `elseif` statement the distance is less than 50, because if it wasn't you wouldn't have got this far down the statement. If the condition in the first `elseif` statement is found to be true, you know that the distance must be greater than 25 but less than 50.

So, to make your decision, you're using what you know the distance *isn't*, as well as what it *is.*

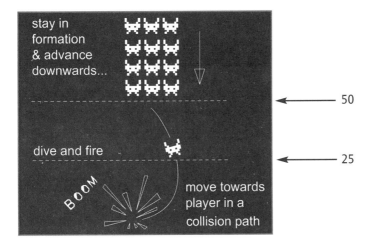

You can also see from this example that as the demarcation lines to decide the kamikaze behavior move up or down the screen, the alien will get more or less skilled. Moving the line up gives the alien more room to perform their kamikaze maneuver. So if you moved the line up as the game progressed, you'd instantly make your aliens more aggressive with time. Amazing how much an object's behavior can be modified by changing a single number.

As you can see from this explanation, elseif has many more versatile uses than we're exploiting in our simple password exercise.

Speaking of which, let's get back to that now. We've so far used Set Variables to make Flash check whether the user has entered the correct **I am the one** password. We've also set up an executive password as the first step to give the user privileged access to different parts of the site.

We'll use the elseif action here to ask Flash to distinguish between the two passwords and direct the user to the appropriate part of the site.

Using the elseif Action

Go back to your FLA, exactly where we left it last.

1. With the line gotoAndPlay ("Scene 2", 1); selected, double-click the **elseif** action. You'll get a line looking very similar to what you saw for the initial if:

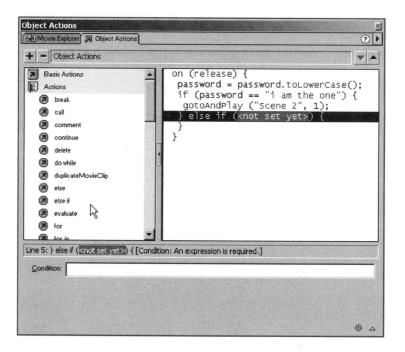

2. In the **Condition** field, enter: password == "neo"

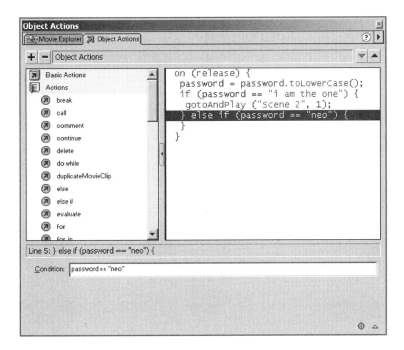

Remember that our conversion to lowercase earlier means that we're looking for lowercase text only, which is why Neo has become neo.

3. Finally, add the last gotoAndPlay to send the executive password holder to scene 3 frame 1:

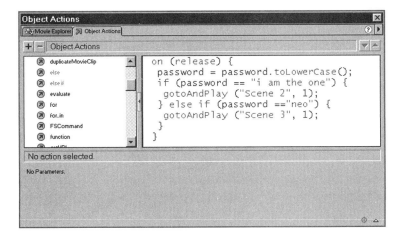

4. Test the movie and you'll see that the button will take you to two screens now, depending on whether you type **I am The One** or **Neo** (regardless of whether upper or lowercase letters are used). If you enter anything else, you remain on the initial **Restricted** screen, but the password entry field doesn't clear ready for the next attempt.

You'll remember earlier we said that the if action should be thought of as having three integral parts. The third one of these, after if and elseif, is the else command. We'll look at this now.

The else Action

The else action executes the attached ActionScript without having to look and see whether a specified condition has been met. It's usually a 'last resort' instruction at the end of the if chain that you tell Flash to execute if all the other choices turn out to be false.

```
if (a)
{do this}
elseif (b)
{do this}
elseif (c)
{do this}
else
{do this}
```

In this if chain, the last {do this} instruction will execute if (a), (b) and (c) are found to be false. By using an else, rather than an elseif, you can be sure that the last instruction you entered will be followed. You know that if all the elseifs have been found to be false, the only option left is to follow the final else instruction.

For example, from a fruit bowl you can choose either an apple, a pear, an orange or a banana. You could deduce which one you'd picked by checking only three conditions:

```
if (it's round and orange)
{it's an orange}
elseif (it's round and either red or green)
{it's an apple}
elseif (it's curved and yellow)
{it's a banana}
```

At this point you know that the only fruit it could be is a pear, so you don't need to check whether it's green and teardrop-shaped. You can definitely state that it's a pear with a final else statement:

```
else
{it's a pear}
```

This chain contains an `elseif` after an `else` statement:

```
if (a)
{do this}
elseif (b)
{do this}
else
{do this}
elseif (c)
{do this}
```

That `elseif` at the end will **never** run because Flash sees the `else` as the final option once it's seen that the `if (a)` and `elseif (b)` are false. Once it's seen an `else`, Flash won't look any further for more instructions.

> *So remember, the `else` must be the last statement in an if...elseif...else, because it will always run, causing any statements below it to be ignored.*

In programming one of the most common choices to be made is of the form:

if (it's raining) {I'll stay in} otherwise {I'll go out}

This type of decision has only two possible outcomes and is easily formed by an if...else chain:

```
if (raining) {
        what_to_do = "stay in";
} else {
        what_to_do = "go out";
}
```

More subtly, the `else` can be used if you want to check for an inverse condition:

```
if (raining) {
} else {
   what_to_do = "go out";
}
```

You might see this better in sausage notation:

if (raining) {} else {what_to_do = "go out"}

The initial `if` does nothing - irrespective of whether `raining` is true or false - because it has an empty sausage. If you reach the `else` command, however, you know `raining` is definitely false, so the `else` part only runs if `raining` is false. Sometimes this is neater than looking for:

$$(raining == false) \quad \text{or} \quad not(raining).$$

So, if we relate this back to our password system, we have:

```
if (password == "I am the one"); {
   gotoAndPlay ("Scene 2",1);
} else if (password =="neo") {
   gotoAndPlay ("Scene3", 1);
```

This has asked Flash to check whether the user has entered either password **I am the one** or **neo**, and send them to the relevant scene. If the password entered is neither of these, we have only one option left: it's the wrong password. We can handle this with a final `else` statement to clear the password field, ready for the user to try again.

Using the else Action

1. After that last `gotoAndPlay ("Scene 3", 1);` add an `}` else `{` by clicking on **else** in the **Actions** book.

2. Then select **set variable**. In the **Variable** field type `password` but leave the **Value** field blank:

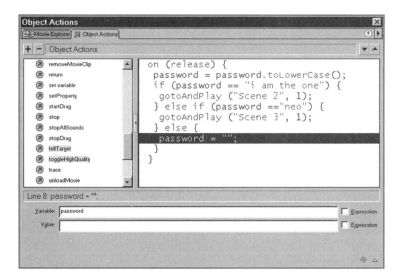

3. Test the movie now and you'll see the password entry field clear if an incorrect password is entered.

Flash has tested the `if` and `else if` statements, found them both to be false and then sees that its only option is to run the final `else`, which tells it to clear the password field.

Although your final script is shown here, you'll get a better appreciation of the code in Expert mode, because the formatting includes bigger indentations:

```
on (release) {
    password = password.toLowerCase();
    if (password == "i am the one") {
        gotoAndPlay ("Scene 2", 1);
    } else if (password =="neo") {
        gotoAndPlay ("Scene 3", 1);
    } else {
        password = "";
    }
}
```

You'll find the final FLA for this exercise as **chapter07_03.fla**.

I've used this example to take you through each stage of the `if... else if... else` structure, showing all the decisions that Flash takes at every point. You've seen, I hope, how much functionality you can gain from making Flash make simple `if` and `else if` judgments and giving it different courses of action to follow depending on the answer.

We're going to move on now to make Flash work a little harder, using **loops**.

Looping

Looping structures come into their own when you have actions to repeat, a large chunk of identical data that needs processing, or when you want to control multiple items with just one piece of code. Very often, you'll use these structures hand in hand with arrays, which we'll look at in detail in the next section.

Any loops that you use in ActionScript are loops within a single frame and distinct from the loops between frames that you've created previously with `gotoAndPlay()` actions.

The timeline that you see here is a typical **multi-frame loop**:

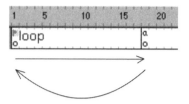

The action at frame 18 is a `gotoAndPlay("loop")` command which will loop back to frame 1. This will set up a constant loop between frames 1 and 18, and Flash is quite happy for this to go on indefinitely.

The next loop is the little number that we'll be looking at in this chapter: an **ActionScript loop**.

ActionScript Loops

An ActionScript loop exists not between frames but within a single frame that contains actions to create the loop within ActionScript itself:

We'll look at the mechanics behind them in a moment, but I'd like to first lay out some things that you should always have in the back of your mind while you're considering whether an ActionScript loop is the right thing to use.

Don't use an ActionScript loop if you want to move an object across the screen by using each loop iteration to move the object a few pixels at a time. If you do, all you'll see is the two points at the start and the end of the movement. ActionScript moves far too fast for this sort of effect – it'll have done the entire movement within a single frame. Since Flash only does one screen redraw per frame, you won't see too much in between. You should instead use a frame loop, so that the movement occurs over a period of frames. ActionScript loops are not set up to perform animation in this way.

Never use ActionScript loops to provide delays. The best way to do this is to have a movieclip that, when run, stops the main timeline with a `_root.stop()` command and then re-starts it a few frames later with a `_root.play()`. If you try to add delays via an ActionScript loop, you're trying to do something that just isn't feasible. Flash must move on to the next frame in one twelfth of a second, and adding a delay in ActionScript will not prevent this happening because all Flash will do is break your loop.

For the same reason, there are limits to how long an ActionScript loop can go on for. Flash has to maintain a constant frame rate and, as I've said, is constrained to move to the next frame in one twelfth of a second. The ActionScript loop must finish before the frame interval. Flash will also stop the loop running if it detects a looping structure that looks likely to never stop (Flash does this by counting the loops and if it is more than 200,000, it will halt the loop). You don't want this to happen because your variables will be at indeterminate values when you're ejected from the loop, and this will cause errors further down the line.

OK, there are a few issues as ground rules. Let's move on to look at the types of loop that exist and how ActionScript is structured to build them. There are four types of loop:

1. A loop that checks the looping condition at the *start* of every loop and stops looping only when it finds that condition to be false. This is a while...do loop. The syntax is:

   ```
   while (condition) {
       do these actions;
   }
   ```

2. A loop that checks the looping condition at the *end* of every loop and stops looping only when it finds that condition to be false. This is a do...while loop. The syntax is:

   ```
   do {
       do these actions;
   } while (condition);
   ```

3. A loop that is set to repeat a specified number of times.

4. A loop that repeats forever.

Obviously, number 4 is a no-no in Flash, so we won't consider it further. The third loop type is the one you'd use when, rather than looking for a condition to be met, you're attempting to do something to a big block of data, and know how much data you want to change before you start. This type of loop is very useful when used with arrays of multiple variables, which, as I've said, we'll look at later in this chapter.

We've looked at how to form the decision-making structure, so let's step boldly into the world of ActionScript loops with an example.

Gases are made up of lots of little particles that bounce around in a random motion. This is called **Brownian motion** and is caused by the particles constantly hitting each other and shooting off at random directions after each collision. We're going to simulate this effect by using a **do...while** loop to create a group of randomly moving particles. However, rather than model the collisions (which would take the biggest computer in the world a week), we'll use Flash's own random number generator. The file **plasma_01.fla** is included in your download file for this chapter and you'll find the basic effects for this exercise there. Otherwise, the first few steps in this exercise will tell you how to create them yourself before we go on to see the **do...while** loop in action.

Creating a while...do Loop

1. Open a new movie and give it a black background via **Modify > Movie**. Create a graphic symbol called **plasma** that consists of a white circle with a radial gradient that fades to zero alpha at the edges. Now create a movieclip symbol called **random plasma**:

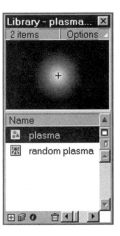

2. Place the **plasma** symbol into the center of the **random plasma** movieclip on **layer 1**, and use the **Info** panel to place it exactly at 0.0, 0.0. Add another frame to this layer and then create a new layer called **Actions**.

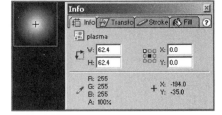

In frame 1 of the **Actions** layer, I'm going to get you to add two Set Variable actions that you may not understand at the moment. I'll explain things in Chapter 11 when we look at sprite behavior, but for now I need a little blind faith. These Set Variables will create the random motion of our gas particle:

```
this._x = this._x + (Math.random ()*4)-2;
this._y = this._y + (Math.random ()*4)-2;
```

The `Math.random ()` method creates a decimal number between zero and one. You can find it in the **Math** book, which is inside **Objects**. We'll use it again in another example at the end of this chapter, and again later when we start playing with sprites.

Let's add these now.

3. In frame 1 of the **Actions** layer add a keyframe and then add the first Set Variable. Enter `this._x` in the **Variable** field and `this._x + (Math.random ()*4)-2` in the **Value** field. Check the **Expression** checkbox:

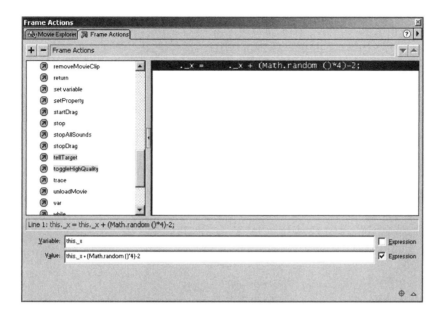

4. Still in the same frame, for the second Set Variable enter `this._y` in the **Variable** field and `this._y + (Math.random ()*4)-2` in the **Value** field. Check the **Expression** box again.

> *These refer to the x and y co-ordinates of our movieclip, and by changing them, the movieclip is essentially controlling its own position. This code is equating the position of our movieclip to the position plus a small random offset, which is our Brownian motion. We'll get to know more about Brownian motion in Chapter 10.*

5. Add a keyframe in frame 2 of the **Actions** layer and add a `gotoAndPlay(1)` action:

6. Return to the main stage, and drag **random plasma** onto the center of the stage (making sure you don't drag **plasma** instead, because they both look alike) and test the movie.

   You'll see our little circle pulsate gently. This doesn't look like a cloud yet, because we need lots of particles, which is the point of this exercise...

7. Bring up the **Instance** panel to give the movieclip an instance name, **particle**. We'll be using this instance name in an ActionScript loop to clone our bit of plasma and create a big plasma cloud:

8. In the root timeline, add a new layer called **Actions**.

   In frame 1 of this layer we'll add a loop to clone our particle and make our gas cloud. The first action is a Set Variable to set how many times we want it to loop.

9. Select the first frame of the new **Actions** layer, bring up the **Frame Actions** window and click on **set variable**. Enter counter and 10 in the respective boxes as I have here. Remember to check the **Expression** box at the end of the **Value** field to give you a string 10 and not a number "10":

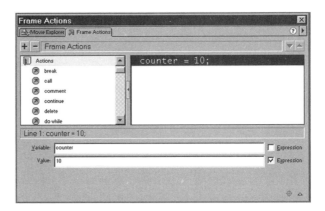

10. From the Actions book add a `while` action:

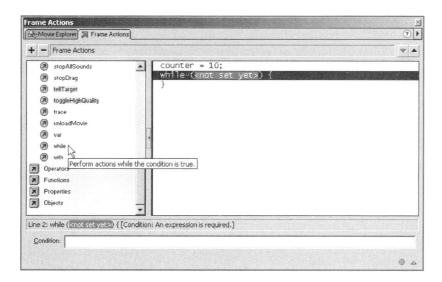

The `<not set yet>` prompt is in red, telling you an expression is needed.

11. In the **Condition** field, add the expression `counter > 0`:

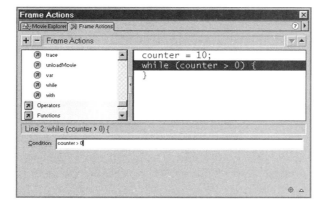

This'll make our `while` loop cycle until `counter` drops in value from 10 to 0. Since there's nothing there to make it do this at the moment, our loop will run forever if we test the movie now. You can try it if you want, but your computer might lock up for a while when Flash tries to compile the SWF until it realizes your mistake, so I wouldn't recommend it. If you do, you might have to be a little patient. For the sensible, I have taken a copy of the error message to show you what would happen.

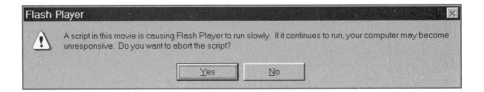

*I strongly suggest hitting **Yes** if you ever see this dialog. It means that your ActionScript has a forever loop in it somewhere. Although Flash is set up to detect them, I've seen some forever loops crash computers, which I guess is a pretty good reason for never pressing **No** here. You'd have to debug code like this by hand, I'm afraid. I've never seen this error message appear for any reason except an ActionScript forever loop, so at least that means Flash has given you a big clue.*

Be prepared....I'm introducing you to another new action here...

12. Staying in the same frame, in the **Actions** book click on **duplicateMovieClip**:

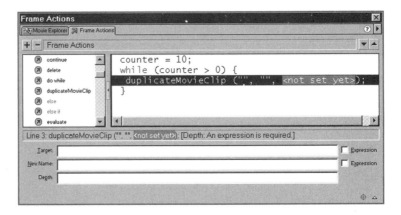

This action copies new versions of the same movieclip to the stage. As we'll soon see, we can give each new instance a unique instance name so that we can still control them individually if we want to. This is particularly suited to high-end Flash graphic effects and is used in a lot of games to quickly and efficiently populate the screen with identical sprites.

As befits such a useful command, Flash needs us to enter quite a lot of info here. I'll go through each of those fields, **Target**, **New Name** and **Depth** in turn, giving a little background information and then exact details of what to type in.

Target is asking us to tell Flash exactly which movieclip we want to duplicate.

13. Place your cursor in the **Target** field and click on the crosshair icon at the bottom right of the window to bring up the **Insert Target Path** panel. Insert the instance name `particle`. Leave all the radio buttons at the bottom at their defaults:

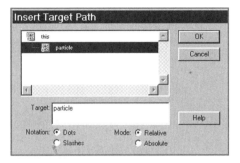

The **New Name** field is asking us to enter the name of the new instance. In this case, we don't strictly need to call the instances anything because they're controlling themselves, but we'll add one for future development. A new instance is created every loop, so why not use the counter as part of the name? This way, we could have ten instances called `particle1` to `particle10`, as well as the original, `particle`, making eleven uniquely named instances in all.

14. In the **New Name** field add `"particle" + counter` and check the **Expression** box. You need to type the speech marks, but until you check the **Expression** box, Flash won't understand the second set of speech marks and you'll get:

```
"\"particle\" + counter",
```

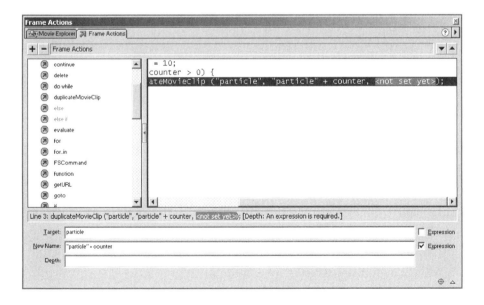

This will add the current value of counter to the end of "particle" to create a new string per loop. This process of adding strings together is called **concatenation**.

Depth is similar to the levels in LoadMovie. If you have a movie at a depth of 1 and create another instance at the same depth, the original is replaced. The original is at a depth of 0, so we need our depths to be 1 to 10. We already have a variable that cycles through these values: counter.

15. In the **Depth** field enter counter. Here's the finished action:

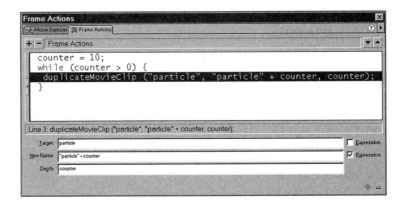

I've closed the toolbox panel on the left temporarily so you can see this rather long command from beginning to end.

> Whatever you do, don't test the movie until you've added this final command, otherwise Flash will carry on adding new instances until it realizes you're not going to stop it. This could take much more time than when I ran the loop 'forever' last time round, because this time the loop is actually doing something and eating up considerable resources as it creates the 16000 clones before it stops itself.

The loop is currently expecting counter to go down in value, which we know because it starts off as 10, all the time checking that counter > 0. So, the loop will stop when counter = 0. Why did I do it this way round and not set counter to zero, with a check whether counter < 10? Well, I like to have all the initialization at the top of my code. If I developed this effect further, I'd still have counter at the top, but may have changed its name to something meaningful, like number_of_particles = 10. By keeping the 10 at the top, I keep all the things that are liable to change at the top of the code where they're easy to find, rather than having to delve into loops that may by now be twenty lines down the window.

OK, so I need to take one away from `counter` with every loop. Normally, I would create a Set Variable like `counter = counter - 1`. However, adding or subtracting 1 from something is such a common thing, that there's a special command to do it:

```
counter = --counter
```

There's a similar command to add 1 to a variable:

```
++variable
```

Let's use them.

16. Still in frame 1 of the Actions layer on the main timeline, bring up a Set Variable. Add `counter` to the **Variable** box and `--counter` to the **Value** field. Don't forget to check the **Value** field's **Expression** box. Finally, to stop the loop from going on forever, add a `stop();` action after this, as I have here:

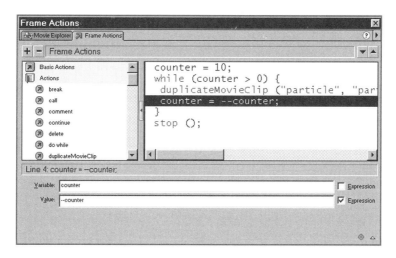

If you've got stuck, this final FLA is also included in this chapter's download file as **plasma_final.zip**.

Now test the movie. You'll see a little white circle that slowly expands into a fluffy white gas cloud or nebula-like formation. Later, once we begin to use properties, you'll be able to make the smoke cloud appear to be coming out of the cursor and make the nebula interact with the mouse.

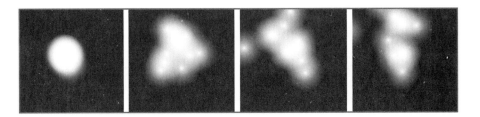

We've had hands on practice of a `while... do` loop. Before we get on to the next part of this chapter when we'll look at arrays, I'd like to quickly skip through a different kind of loop that we'll come across later and that you'll find is a useful weapon in your ActionScript arsenal: the **for** loop.

For Loops

Sometimes you don't want to keep looping until a particular condition has been met, because you already know how many times that you want to loop. For example, you might know that you have ten movieclips which need their color changing from red to blue, or that you have *max-1* names to turn into lowercase. This is where the `for` loop comes in.

The `for` loop is actually the preferred looping method for a number of practical reasons:

- Because you know how many loops it will cycle through, you're less likely to be surprised by it when you come to test your code.

- You can easily modify the `for` command so that it cycles only once during code development. Once you've got it working for one loop, you can be confident that it will run for many cycles.

- Because you're forced to know how many times your loop will run and give fairly explicit parameters to the `for` loop, your code will tend to look more structured and easier to follow.

The `for` loop doesn't work by looking at a condition, but at a counter, which is incremented (or decremented) by a set value on every loop. The counter can be very useful because we can use it for all sorts of things other than simply a counter that specifies how many times we loop: as the index for an array or a variable (one reason why this looping structure is closely associated with arrays, which we'll see in a while); or for deriving a linear sequence of numbers (such as a math times table; 5, 10, 15, 20, 25, etc...).

As mentioned before, one thing you *wouldn't* use this or any ActionScript looping structure for is for changing *visual* parameters, such as the position of a symbol on stage from x = 0 to x = 200 in steps of 5. This is because ActionScript loops complete within a single frame (for animation you want the change in x to occur over a number of frames).

The `for` loop looks like this:

```
for (Init; Condition; Next;) {
    do these actions;
}
```

When you enter a `for` action, you'll see three fields that need to be filled in. Although this may look a little scary, persevere, because the `for` loop can be very useful for advanced programming techniques, particularly when you're controlling multiple instances or sifting through a lot of structured data.

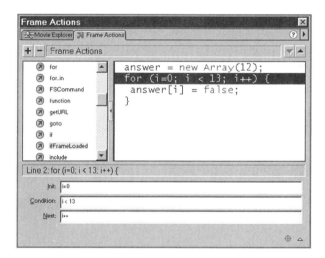

> It is a programming convention to use the variable names i, j and k for looping variables, although that convention arose in the days when even mainframe computers typically had 16K of memory. You can now use whatever variable name you want. counter is a good a name as any, although it's better to make the variable name as descriptive as possible.

The **init:** value is the initial `counter` value. You'll usually set it to zero, although if you want to start from a different value (such as when you want to count backwards), you can put any value you want. The number of loops must turn out to be a numeric variable, so valid start counter values are:

- `counter = 0`   The counter starts at zero.

- `i = startValue`   The counter starts at the value of variable `startValue`, which must be a numeric.

There are some **values** that won't work. Avoid using **methods** because not all of them work, and Flash won't let you use **properties**, so this *won't* work:

- `counter = myclip._x`

The **Condition:** value is exactly like the condition in an `if` statement: the condition must be true for the loop to continue cycling. You would normally set this to be **'counter is less than the stop value'**. Valid examples are:

- `i < 10`   Loop as long as `i` is less than 10.

- `counter <= 200`   Loop as long as `counter` is less than or equal to 200.

- `x < xMax`   Loop as long as `x` is less than `xMax`.

In the last example **don't let the loop alter the value of** `xMax`. Although it's possible to do this, it may mean that the loop turns into a *forever* loop, and you stop being aware of the maximum number of times the loop will cycle – both of which will make your code unpredictable.

One that beginners will get stuck with is:

- `counter == 10`

Although this is OK for the condition in an `if` action, it will stop a `for` loop from working, because `counter` won't be equal to 10 on the first loop, causing a stop.

The **Next:** value is what happens to the `counter` after every loop. Possible things you can add here are:

- `i++`   Add 1 to `i`.

- `counter --`   Subtract 1 from `counter`.

- `i = i+2`   Add 2 to `i`.

Notice that using the `++` or `--` operators allows you to use a shorthand way of writing **Next:**, whereas any other expression must be written out in full.

The `for` loop can look a bit daunting, but it's perhaps the most useful because it's the most **structured**. To take a look at how the `for` loop works, add the following script to frame 1 of a new movie;

```
for (i=0; i <= 12; i++) {
     trace (i);
}
```

(Hint: don't forget to tick the **Expression:** box for the `trace();` command.)

This will open the **Output:** window when you test the movie where you can see the values of the counter `i` for every iteration of the loop. Try these:

```
for (i=12; i >=0 ; i—) {
     trace (i);
}
```

That will make the loop run backwards.

```
for (i= 0; i <= 12; i = i+2) {
     trace (i);
}
```

That will count up in a sequence 0, 2, 4, 6, 8, 10, 12.

Note that the value that the counter takes up when the loop has completed is the first counter value that *doesn't* meet the **Condition:**. For the last example, `i` will be 14 at the end of the loop.

The `for` loop is useful for creating changes to a large number of variables or objects in one go, and is particularly suited to working with arrays because we can use the `for` loop's counter as the index.

Which brings me on nicely to the next section of the chapter. I'll show you something in ActionScript that's used very often in conjunction with loops. That something is **arrays**. I'll explain a little background theory first, then we'll take a look at a hangman game where you'll see them in action, in partnership with the `for` loop that we've just looked at.

Arrays

An array is a variable that has a sequential number of memory locations. In terms of the container analogy, think of an array as a cabinet. The whole cabinet may have a single name, but it then has many 'sub-containers,' or individual drawers that contain different pieces of information. You could remember that a particular piece of information in your cabinet is held in 'filing cabinet, third drawer'. In ActionScript terms, that filing cabinet is your array and third drawer is the variable, expressed like this:

```
filing_cabinet[3].
```

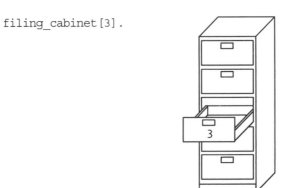

Each drawer is like a variable in its own right, and they're all kept in a common cabinet, or array, because the separate variables are related:

It's important to grasp the fact that unlike physical cabinets, our 'array cabinets' hold one thing only; data in the form of variables.

Ordering variables as arrays is useful for four reasons:

- They keep **related** information together. For example, we have a list of birds. We want to keep together information on all birds that live around water, so we have a cabinet marked **wadingBirds**. Within that we might have in drawer three the name **flamingo**. We would have other arrays such as **tropicalBirds**, with variable **parrot** and an array **tundraBirds**, with a variable **ptarmigan**.

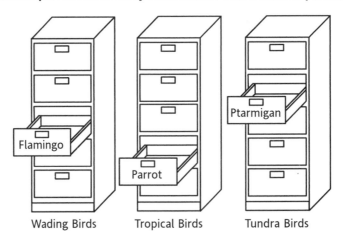

Wading Birds   Tropical Birds   Tundra Birds

- Arrays can also keep **sequential** information in a way that represents its original order. For example, we might want to have a cabinet containing the names of pupils in the order of their exam results, best first. Drawer **pupilsLeagueTable[3454]** may contain the information **Sham B**:

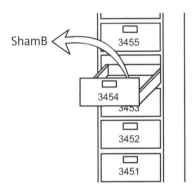

- Arrays can store **indexed** information. For example, each drawer in our cabinet represents information about a numbered item. If I had a cabinet that related to opera bookings, the name of the person who had booked seat 45, would be in the numbered drawer 45, or **OperaBookings[45]** and might be **John Lydon**.

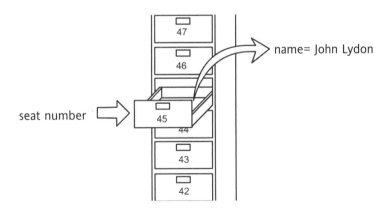

- Arrays can join **linked** information together, so that if we look at one piece of information about something, we can find all the linked information too. For example, we might want to link common plant names to their Latin names. We would have two cabinets side by side, one called **CommonName** and the other called **LatinName**. If we looked in a drawer of **CommonName**, say *CommonName[6]* and found **Common Snowdrop**, we would look in the adjacent cabinet **LatinName**, in the same drawer up, **LatinName[6]** to find **Galanthus nivalis**.

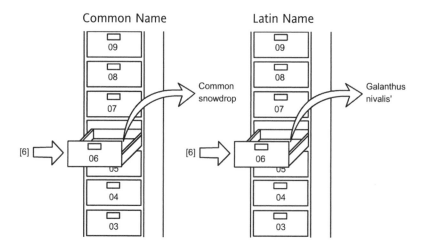

In an array, we use a number to represent the individual locations. The first location – or the bottom drawer – is the **base** location. Subsequent locations are accessed by specifying an **offset** up from the base.

For example, if your array `mycolor` had five locations or five drawers, you'd express the first, bottom drawer as:

    mycolor[0]

In Flash the array offset is surrounded by square brackets. Notice that the first array location (bottom drawer) is zero, not 1. An offset of 0 gives you the base. The second array item (first drawer up from the base) would be:

    mycolor[1]

the third is:

    mycolor[2]

and so on.

> *If the fact that there is a zero drawer confuses you, you could always just leave it empty (not recommended) or use an index of [n-1] (this is the preferred option). When we specify an index [n] we're really just saying 'look in this filing cabinet, drawer n up'.*

The beauty of arrays is that you can specify another variable as the offset. This means that you can bring a variable that you've already created elsewhere and use it to specify which drawer you want to look at. In the example below, `offset=0` is a variable, and `mycolor[offset] = 'blue'` is an array which uses the variable we'd previously created. Our array uses `[offset]` and then goes to another drawer, takes out the offset file and finds out all about it:

```
offset=0;
mycolor[offset] = 'blue';
```

You can only use a **numeric variable** as an offset in an array.

The use of arrays with variables as shown above is useful because by changing the value of your variable you can look at different drawers. This is powerful for a number of reasons:

- You can set the offset variable in one piece of code and then use that offset in another piece of code to actually manipulate the data in that array position. The beauty of this is that although your offset may change, the data to perform the manipulation *doesn't care*; it has been written to work on *any* array position.

- You can perform searches. By continuously looking in a drawer for a piece of information and if you don't find it just increasing your index by one and trying again, you are searching every drawer. This is useful for asking questions like 'what is the Latin name for the Californian poppy (Eschsholzia californica). We would search through the **commonNames** array until we found the name, note the index and then look across **LatinNames** using the same index to find Eschsholzia californaica. This method, of finding an index and applying it to another related array is called **cross indexing**.

- If you want to perform the same calculation on a list of values, you can write a general calculation that works on an arbitrary location array [offset] and then use a loop to apply it to all the data. If you want to turn a list of values between 1 and 20 into percentage values, all you have to do is write the general equation:

  percent[offset] = rawData[offset]*5.

  By increasing the variable offset in a loop, you can apply the same calculation to the whole list.

This is how arrays are closely associated with loops. You can write a general set of instructions of any array location and then apply it to **all your data via a loop**. This allows relatively small pieces of code to cycle through massive amounts of data, and is the idea behind databases and other information systems. Here's a typical looping structure used with arrays:

```
offset = 0
while (we have not done all the array) {
do stuff with mycolor[offset]
add 1 to offset
}
```

This is a useful looping structure because we're constantly re-using the same set of actions to look at *all* our array values.

For example, if mycolor contained a number from 0 to 100, respresenting the amount of red in each cabinet door, we could make the colors redder in turn by increasing each number. The beauty of doing it this way is that if we had 100 different colors to work with, we're changing them all with a small bit of code.

We'll now see how an array can be used along with the for... looping structure to handle large amounts of data in a structured way.

A new array is created via the setVariable command. To define an array myarray, you'd need to:

■ Put myarray in the setVariable **Variable** field:

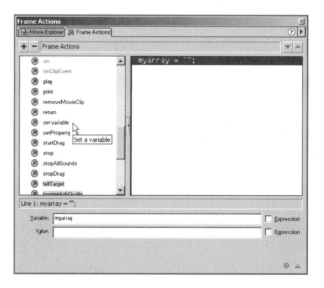

- In the **Value** field add new Array(), which is found in the **Array** book, within the **Objects** book in the **Actions** window:

```
myarray = new Array();
```

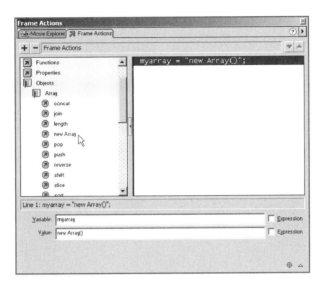

- Within the new Array() brackets add either the number of entries the array will have (remembering that zero is a number, so Array(9) has 10 entries), or enter a list of the entries. If you don't put anything, Flash will add new entries as you fill the array.

  For example:

```
myarray = new Array(2345);
```
  gives 2346 empty array entries

```
myarray = new Array(1, 45, 34.504, 3.1415);
```
  gives four array entries with numeric values

```
myarray = new Array("cat", "dog", "pelican");
```
  gives three array entries with string values

```
myarray = new Array();
```
  gives an array ready to add new entries.

In the last line, referring to myarray[19] will create a **single** array entry myarray[19]. Flash *won't* create array entries [0] to [18] as well, so using this method can be a bit dangerous because you have 'missing drawers' that subsequent code may be expecting to see filled with a sensible value (such as zero or "").

There are other ways to create arrays, but my advice would be to stick to the method I've shown you until you find your feet a little more.

Now it's time for something new that'll really test your skills. The following game uses arrays and loops together, with more than a little string variable manipulation, too. Taking this one together with the calculator means that you've seen almost everything you've learnt so far used in anger in a large ActionScript program.

The Hangman Game

We'll run through the Hangman game in outline, but I'll give you enough information to see how the arrays are set up in this game for you to be able to start using them yourselves. This way we can look at arrays without getting bogged down looking at pictures of data-structures and all sorts of academic looking stuff. A real-life example will lift the whole thing right off the page.

Graphics

Hangman is a brutal game when you think about it, and my version doesn't hide the fact that it's a game about someone getting hanged - there are no fluffy bunnies or suchlike to hide that gruesome outcome. In contrast to the shiny hi-tech feel of the calculator that we saw earlier I've tried to get it to look like it was all drawn and painted by a child.

Open **hangman.swf** to see how it all plays. You might not see the same font as I've used when you come to look at the SWF. The one I've used is called **kids**. Take a look at the fonts I've put up for download if you need help.

The main graphics are in a movie called **hanging man**, which shows the scaffold building up:

There are two possible outcomes: either our character gets hanged, or he survives to enjoy the sun and the scent of that single flower that I've given him.

Code

The code for this game will get a little hairy at times, but stay calm! If you have problems following it, don't worry. Just look at the structures you already understand and see how they're being used to form the game; how the movieclip is being controlled, for example, or how the arrays are being initialized.

Hopefully, these programs are something you'll keep coming back to as your knowledge increases. I'm hoping they'll add to the usefulness of this book as you graduate beyond the level of 'ActionScript beginner'. This and the calculator program have been designed to show you how to put all the building blocks together for everything you've learned so far.

The **hanging man** movieclip's timeline looks like this:

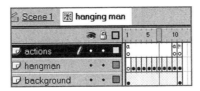

The **hangman** and **background** layers contain the hanging sequence. Frame 10 is the final *the end* frame. The last frame, frame 11, which is labeled **win**, is the *and he lived happily ever after* outcome. The important layer for us as programmers is the **actions** layer.

Frame 1 contains the actions

```
_parent.gameover = false;
stop ();
```

This sets up a Boolean `gameover` on the root timeline (which is the same as the parent timeline in this case) to `false`, telling the main timeline that the man hasn't been hanged yet. The root timeline will advance this movieclip to the next frame in the movie for each wrong answer until the man is hanged at frame 10. The action on this frame will tell the root timeline that this has happened with:

```
_parent.gameover = true;
```

If the root timeline sees a win situation, however, it will send the **hanging man** timeline to label **win**, and show us the man enjoying his freedom.

Now let's look at the root timeline. You'll see this at frame 2:

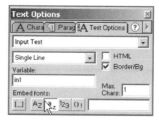

guess a letter: enter

The input is via a text entry box next to the guess a letter: text. Here's the **Text Options** panel used to create it:

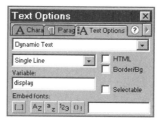

Notice that it is assigned to the variable `in1` and that it accepts lowercase letters only.

The word that the user has to guess is displayed just below the grass, and is assigned to the variable `display`. Here are the **Text Options** panel settings:

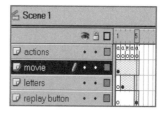

The root timeline looks like this:

- The hanging man movie sits in the **movie** layer and has an instance name **hangman**.

- The input and dynamic text areas in1 and display are on the **letters** layer.

- There's a replay button that allows you to play the game again on the last frame of the movie in the **replay button** layer.

Now let's look at the main section of this Flash game: the **actions** layer. The first frame initializes the arrays to be used in the program.

```
// initialize the program
words = new Array("computer", "apple", "coffee", "flash",
"animal", "america", "panel", "window", "import", "number",
"string", "cake", "object", "movie", "aardvark", "kettle");
wordcount = words.length;
letters = new Array(10);
guess = new Array(10);
```

Notice that there are three arrays defined here using two different methods:

- words contains all the words available to be guessed, and you can add more simply by appending them to the end of the list. Any word you add can have up to ten letters, no more. You'll see why in a moment. The new words must also be lower case only, because that's all the user is allowed to enter.

- The words are all literal strings, and are therefore surrounded with " " quotes. Use this method of array definition if you want to define an array with data already in it. Once the word to be guessed has been selected by the actions in a later frame, it is necessary to split the word into the individual letters to be guessed.

- The letters and guess arrays are used to store the letters to be guessed, and the letters the player has got right so far respectively. Because these are 10 elements long, the maximum word length is also limited to 10. letter and guess are simply defined with a number, which corresponds to the number of elements required. Remember though, zero is counted as the first element, so asking for ten elements will give you elements numbered from 0 to 9.

- The wordcount = words.length command is used to find the total number of words in the words array. You'd build this action in the same way you built up the password = password.toLowerCase() action in the password screens at the beginning of this chapter. Because Flash directly counts the number of words it knows for the game every time the program is run, you can add new words and don't have any variables at all to change to accommodate the new data. If and when you get to the heady heights of dynamic web sites, where the data is presented to Flash during run time and is different every time the web page is called up, you will see the usefulness of this sort of approach.

Frame 2 has a rather long script attached, so I'll go through all its separate parts. Before I start, see what I meant back there at the start of the book about comments being worth their weight in gold! I've added them here at the beginning of every stage, to prevent panic setting in as the code gets longer and longer.

Basically, the ActionScript initializes the word to be guessed and splits it into its separate letters using the `letters` array. It also creates another array of the same length, except this time it consists only of question marks, to indicate the number of guesses the player has had.

The first command makes movie **hangman** go to frame 1 and stop:

```
// initialize movie
hangman.gotoAndStop(1);
```

As the comment says, the next block selects the word and establishes how long it is:

```
// select word and get wordlength
index = Math.round(Math.random()*(wordcount-1));
to_guess = words[index];
wordlength = to_guess.length;
togo = wordlength;
```

This code is equating `index` to a random number from 0 to the number of words available to guess minus one. We have to use `wordcount - 1` because the array starts at element zero. To create a random whole number you'll always have to use an expression like:

```
Math.round(Math.random()*(wordçount-1));
```

so although it may look a little complicated, it's something you should try to get used to.

`Math.random()` is a method that we used back in the plasma example. It creates a decimal number between zero and 1.

The random number Flash creates is always a decimal that's less than one, such as 0.56478903454. To get a number of an appropriate size you have to multiply this number by your range. If you wanted a number between 1 and 100 you would use:

```
Math.random()*100
```

If you want a whole number such as 78, rather than 78.456734324, you have to round the number using another Math method called round, which rounds your number to the nearest integer:

```
Math.round(Math.random()*100)
```

We then get a word that the player has to guess with:

```
to_guess = words[index];
```

Finally, we also need the length of this word so that Flash can compare it with the number of correctly guessed letters to see whether the full word has been guessed:

```
togo = wordlength;
```

We have to split the word that the player needs to guess into its individual letters. Here's how:

```
// split to_guess into its letters
for (i=0; i<=10; i++) {
letters[i] = to_guess.charAt(i);
}
```

The for command takes three arguments:

- ● i=0; specifies the initial value of your loop variable, which is i in this case. Enter this in the **Init** field, as shown below.

- ● i<=10; is the condition that must be true for the structure to keep looping. Enter this in the **Condition** field.

- ● i++ tells Flash to add 1 to the i loop variable at every loop after the expression has been evaluated. Enter this in the **Next** field.

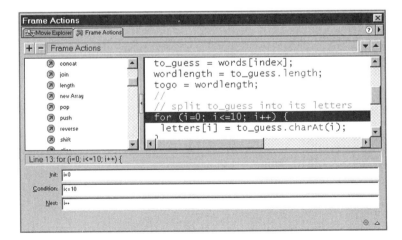

> *Notice that I've put i++ and not ++i. ++i would tell Flash to add 1 to i before the expression is evaluated, not after as I want. I've used i++ because I want i to be 0 on the first loop, and not 1. Loops are probably the only place you'll need to use variable - - and variable ++, so it's another little trick worth remembering.*

The charAt(i); method takes the character at position i in our word, so as we go through the loops, we're stripping each letter from the word and putting it into our array elements letters[i].

We're almost there now. This is another loop, but this time we are creating an array of '?' characters. This is what we'll be displaying – as we don't want to display the answer and ruin the game.

```
// initialize the players guesses
display = "";
for (i=0; i<=wordlength-1; i++) {
guess[i] = "?";
display = display+guess[i];
}
```

The variable display has been set up to receive the word to be guessed in that dynamic textbox underneath the grass. The for loop is set up to loop as long as the i counter is equal to or less than wordlength (number of letters in the word). So it counts how any letters there are in the word and adds a question mark to the variable guess for each one. That number of question marks is then fed into the display variable, which will show them to the player as an indication of how many letters they have to guess.

Frame 3 is a blank keyframe with the label loop. Frame 4 is controlling the program flow:

```
if (togo == 0) {
   hangman.gotoAndStop("win");
   gotoAndStop ("end");
} else if (gameover) {
   gotoAndStop ("end");
} else {
   gotoAndPlay ("loop");
}
```

We can either:

- Win - if we've guessed all the letters (togo = 0)

- Lose - if the hangman movieclip gets to the hanging frame and sets gameover

- Go back to frame 3 and continue looping between frame 3 and 4 if we have neither won nor lost using gotoAndPlay ("loop")

The final piece is the **enter** button. This has an attached ActionScript that looks at any letters we enter and checks to see whether we've guessed any correctly:

```
on (release, keyPress "<Enter>") {
    wrong = true;
    display = "";
    for (i=0; i<=wordlength-1; i++) {
        if ((letters[i] == in1)&&(guess[i] <> in1)) {
            wrong = false;
            togo = —togo;
            guess[i] = in1;
            display = display+in1;
        } else {
            display = display+guess[i];
        }
    }
        if (wrong) {
        hangman.nextFrame();
    }
    in1 = "";
}
```

As soon as we press on the button or press **enter** on the keyboard, the first thing the script does is initialize itself. We set a variable wrong to true, and clear display, which is currently showing a combination of question marks (letters we haven't guessed yet) or letters (letters that we've guessed already). Notice that although we've cleared the display, the script will have worked out a new value for display by the time that Flash comes to do a screen redraw. That means that you'll see straight away the changes in display as more letters are guessed correctly and change from question marks to the correct letters.

Let's run through this code assuming that the word we have to guess is **cat**. Before we start, the variables will be as follows:

```
letters[0] = 'c' letters[1] = 'a'     letters[2] = 't'
guess[0] = '?'   guess[1] = '?'       guess[2] = '?'
display = '???'
togo = 3
wrong = true
```

display will be cleared during initialization so that our loop can rebuild it to reflect any correct answers, so:

```
display = ''

on (release, keyPress "<Enter>") {
    wrong = true;
    display = "";
```

We then go into our loop. This will look at in1, the first letter that we have guessed and typed in, and use i to search through the word we have to guess (held in array letters) to see if it can find a match. We will cycle i between 0 and the number of letters, noting that zero is a number so we have to use wordlength - 1 as our last letter.

For **cat**, *i* would be 0 on the first loop, then 1, then 2.

```
for (i=0; i<=wordlength-1; i++) {
```

The next line looks at whether our guessed letter in1 is the *i*th position letter of the word we have to guess:

```
if ((letters[i] == in1)&&(guess[i] <> in1)) {
```

- For i = 0, we would be checking for ('c' == in1?) and (have we guessed this correctly before?).

- For i = 1, we would be checking for ('a' == in1?) and (have we guessed this correctly before?).

- For i = 3, we would be checking for ('t' == in1?) and (have we guessed this correctly before?).

&&(guess[i] <> in1) is the code that checks whether we've guessed that letter before. Notice that if we guessed c twice in a single game, we would lose a life the second time, so we have to remember our guesses and not enter any letter twice.

For each of the letters that match, we:

- Set our Boolean `wrong` to `false` to signify at least one letter has been guessed correctly.

- Reduce the number of letters still to be guessed, `togo`, by `1`.

- Change `guess[i]` to the correct letter `in1` (we could also have equated it to `letters[i]`).

- Add the correct letter to `display`.

```
if ((letters[i] == in1)&&(guess[i] <> in1)) {
   wrong = false;
   togo = --togo;
   guess[i] = in1;
   display = display+in1;
```

For each letter that doesn't match, we add a ? to `display` by equating it to `guess[i]`. We can't just do a `display = '?'` because if we guess the same letter twice, we wouldn't only lose a life, but the previously correct letter would now show up as a question mark, which is a bit harsh!:

```
} else {
      display = display+guess[i];
   }
```

Supposing we had guessed **a**. Once the loop had run three times we would see:

```
in1 = 'a'
letters[0] = 'c' letters[1] = 'a'    letters[2] = 't'
guess[0] = '?'   guess[1] = 'a'      guess[2] = '?'
display = '?a?'
togo = 2
wrong = false
```

Supposing we'd got it wrong and guessed **z**. In this case we'd see:

```
in1 = 'z'
letters[0] = 'c' letters[1] = 'a'    letters[2] = 't'
guess[0] = '?'   guess[1] = '?'      guess[2] = '?'
display = '???'
togo = 3
wrong = true
```

In both cases, `display` is what we would see on the screen: **?a?** for getting one letter right, and **???** for failing miserably.

The next bit checks to see whether we got any letters right this go. If we didn't, `wrong` was never set to `false`, so is still `true` as per our initialization, and we move the hanging movieclip forward by one frame:

```
}
if (wrong) {
    hangman.nextFrame();
}
```

Finally, at the end of the go, we clear the textfield `in1` ready for the user's next turn:

```
    in1 = "";
}
```

And that's it. I think after all that code dissection you need a little rest. Sit back and take a look at stun:design.

The stun:design Web Site

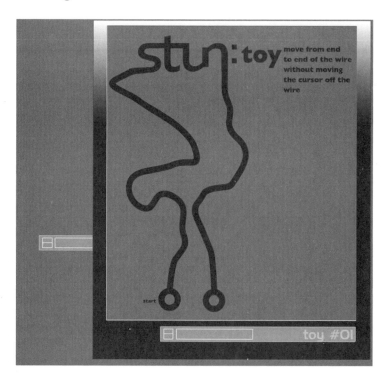

In Chapter 5 we had a look at a wire game that I created to illustrate what I was saying about invisible buttons. That set me thinking. The eternal child in me jumped at the chance of having a stun:toys option on the main menu that would bring up a few windows, each containing a different toy. Hours of fun!

As you get into professional web design, you'll realize that toys, or 'extras' like these are something that clients love. They like to have lots of toys that hold the visitor longer on the site or screensavers that the visitor can take and put onto their own machine. If you're ever involved in an initial submission to a client's specifications for a web site for a new product, re-branding or something similar, this is an ideal way to use your ActionScript skills. Put a little brand logo somewhere on the extras (just like I have with the stun wire game), or theme them to the client's specification and the marketing people will love your submission, giving you a better chance of that nice fat contract.

Something as simple as a wire game consisting of three button actions looks quite stylish here. Repackaging little games and ActionScript effects into an integrated set of extras is something that you'll find useful as a freelance designer, because it lets you take all sorts of initially disjointed ideas and put them all together. Let's see how I packaged the stun:toys.

Have a look at **stun_toys01.fla**.

While you're looking at this file, be aware that I haven't broken up the fonts for anyone that wants the original FLA to play with. This means you need to have the three fonts that are used installed on your machine to see the same thing as is shown in this book when you compile the SWF. I've put some fonts up there for you at friendsofed.com, along with all the downloads for the chapters.

When you start, you'll see two gray rectangles, each with some text inside them letting you know what they contain, a minimize/maximize icon and a dragbar:

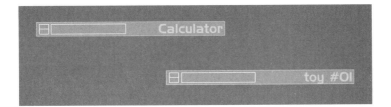

The calculator is another little piece that I created for this book. It contains a lot of the looping decision-making ActionScript that we've been through in this chapter. I thought about explaining all the detail behind it in this chapter but I felt that I'd given you enough work already. When you're ready have a look in the download file for this chapter and you'll see a document called Calculator in which I'll break down the ActionScript behind it, step by step. For now, just play with it.

Toy 01 is the wire game that you've already seen. Notice how I've repackaged something as simple as the wire game, which only consists of three button actions, into a pretty professional looking Flash item. This has nothing to do with ActionScript, but everything to do with **presentation**, which is always an important consideration.

The dragbar is a single movieclip placed into the timeline of the movieclip that it controls. So I have that same drag bar movieclip as a building block that I can use in different situations; the calculator or the wire game toy that you've seen in action. The dragbar movieclip is actually quite similar to the draggable windows in Chapter 5. It uses a dragbar and buttons to take you to frames that hide or show the main window content:

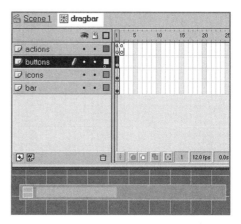

The maximize/minimize button on the far left of the dragbar uses an on (release) action to tell the timeline to go to a label and play to execute the calculator, wire, game... whatever. Because the dragbar has been inserted into a movieclip, it can simply reference a parent timeline to do this:

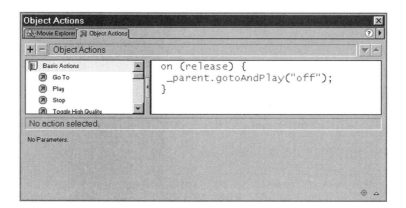

The drag button uses the combination of a `startDrag` and `stopDrag` action that we saw with our draggable windows in Chapter 5. The drag this time is aimed at the parent movieclip, which includes the dragbar:

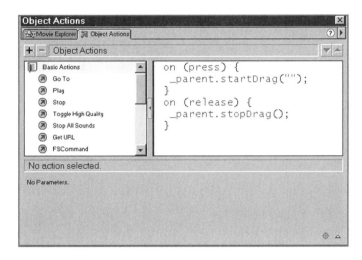

If we didn't specify the path, only the dragbar would move and the movieclip it was placed in would just stay put – obviously something we'd rather avoid!

The **actions** layer of the dragbar movieclip has two frames, each of which has a simple `stop();` command on it:

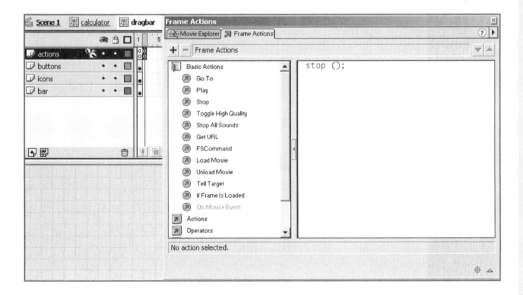

The second frame and its associated `stop action` hasn't been used yet, but it makes the dragbar disappear. When the toys are integrated into the main site, we'll add some commands to make the toy and the dragbar disappear so that the user can dispense with the toys when they're finished with them and not have them cluttering up their screen.

If we exit our dragbar movieclip and return to the parent movieclip, we'll see that the toys each consist of two frames, labeled **off** and **on**. You'll see in the **off** frame that only **bar title** and **bar** layers - which contain the drag bar and the drag bar's title - have anything to show:

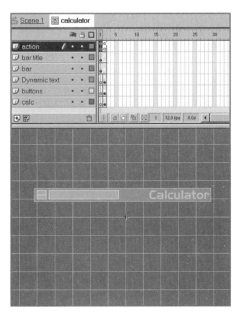

The **on** frame shows the calculator itself:

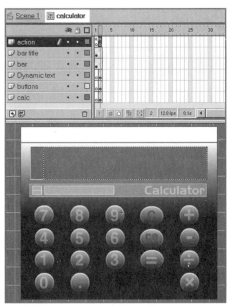

There's no `_parent.gotoAndPlay("on")` command to be seen on the dragbar movieclip, just a `_parent.gotoAndPlay("off")`. Surely this means that the dragbar only ever sends the user to the **off** state of our toy, to show only the dragbar and the title bar as I showed you just now. What about the **on** state?

I'm using a particularly fiendish shortcut here to create a *toggle* between the **on** and **off** states of our toys. This is a very useful trick to know, but it does require an in-depth knowledge of how ActionScript works to understand, so hold tight.

The calculator movieclip has `stop();` commands in both the **off** and **on** frames as the last action:

The calculator is the **_parent** to the dragbar. Whenever you press the maximize/minimize button, it **always** sends the calculator movieclip a `gotoAndPlay("off")`. If you remember our draggable windows, we used separate layers to give the minimize and maximize buttons different `gotoAndPlay` actions. Here, though, whether our user minimizes or maximizes, the same `goto` action is always used.

If we think through what happens when the `gotoAndPlay("off")` action is initialized, we'll realize that whichever frame (1 or 2) Flash is in, it will already have processed the `stop();` command for that frame. So when the `goto` action happens, it will move into the next frame and the `stop ();` command there. If it's already at the label **off**, it will proceed to the **on** frame and then obey the `stop();` action there, making sure that our toy is now visible. If the same `goto` action then happens again, because we press the same button, it will already have processed the `stop();` action in the **on** frame, so it will move to the **off** frame, and hit the `stop();` action in that frame. This diagram should make things a little clearer. You can see Flash moving between the `stop();` action in frame 2 to the label in frame 1, finding a `stop();` action there and directing itself back to frame 2:

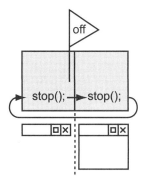

So, although we're sending Flash to the same label each time, we are taking advantage of the fact that Flash only executes the stop(); action when it enters the frame that the stop(); action is in. Our gotoAndPlay action keeps moving until it hits a stop(); action, so it effectively moves either side of the label.

So even though the gotoAndStop("off") action always goes to the same frame, the actual frame it *ends up on* is always the frame it *wasn't* on before. It therefore toggles between the **on** and **off** frames. Sly, eh?

We'll get to integrating these toys with the main web site in another chapter. We'll do this by using a LoadMovie action, which we've already used in Chapter 5, so if you wanted to, you could integrate them now. I'm really having fun now, but we must go on to the next chapter, so I'll leave you to imagine the other little toys I could have created. Better still, why don't you make some?

Summary

This chapter has had the biggest variety of examples so far, because your ActionScript skills are starting to come together. It's also the first one where you've seen what ActionScript can really do. You've learned some important techniques. More importantly, you've seen large sections of ActionScript working together in finished applications. Don't worry if you've only skimmed though these. The important thing is that the standard has been set in your mind, and you've probably picked up a lot of little snippets without realizing it.

That's what coding is all about. You're probably looking at all the long pieces of code and saying 'Why has he done that? Why didn't he do it *this* way?' The proof is when you start creating your own programs and recognize things you're trying to do in terms of the programs I've listed here.

In this chapter we've been through:

- How Flash uses if, else if and else structures to decide what to do, based on conditions that we've set in ActionScript.

- Creating while and for loops.

- Using arrays and variables together to create the maximum ActionScript functionality with the minimum code.

You've been through two important chapters. Now that you understand paths and variables, looping and decision-making, more of what you build will have the feel of a finished Flash presentation, and you'll start being able to enhance any sites you may already have up on the web. With only half a book gone, you're already moving away from the level of 'novice' ActionScripter and will soon be in a position to use ActionScript in your own projects outside of this book.

The next chapter will take you through one of the most important finishing touches to a web site and an area that has received a big boost with the new power of ActionScript in Flash 5 - sound.

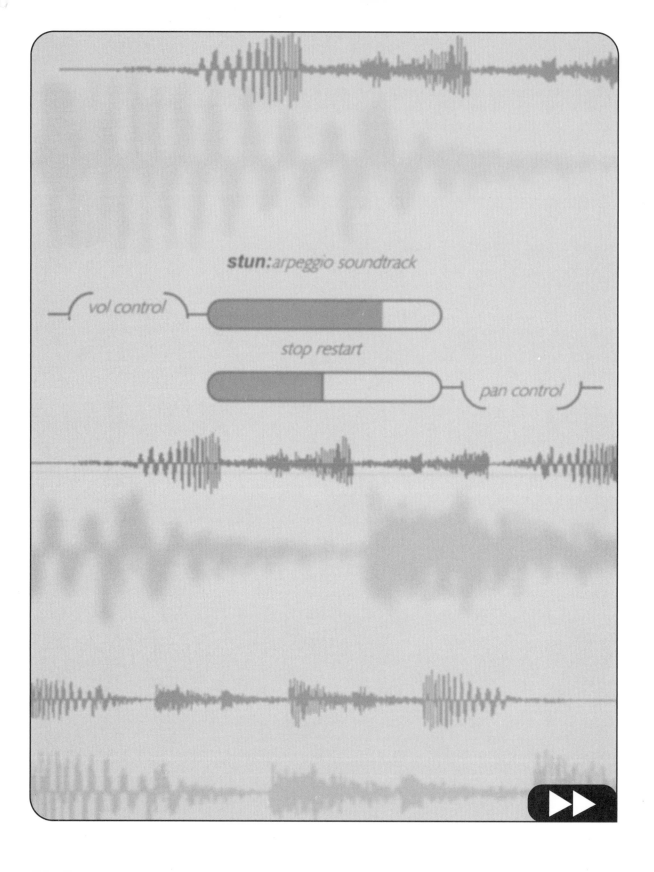

8

Sound

What we'll cover in this chapter:

- *Creating a sound movieclip*

- *Converting that movieclip into an object that ActionScript can control.*

- *Creating sound controls to alter the pan and the volume of a sound effect.*

- *Creating the soundtrack for stun:design and adding interactive graphic effects to represent a volume control.*

There are some pretty nifty new sound ActionScript commands in Flash 5. These are generally designed to create a stereo soundscape so that if, say, a car moved from left to right on the screen under control of the user, ActionScript can now make the car's engine sound pan from left to right at the same rate. In the same way, if the car moves into the distance, ActionScript can make the sound fade.

As we look at how to make the volume and panning of the sounds associated with a sprite vary as the sprite moves, we'll also use some interactivity techniques that we'll look at in more detail in Chapter 9.

The new sound commands are all used to drive a new **sound object**. The actions to create this object are actually very easy, but also very fiddly, and you can easily forget what you are doing if you blink. This chapter shows how to create a sound object and then how to use it to vary sounds dynamically.

The Sound Object

The new **sound object** is designed to control the sound on a timeline. There are four stages to creating a sound object:

- Attach your sounds onto a movieclip's timeline.

- Drag that movie onto the stage and give it an instance name.

- Create a sound object and attach it to the movie by referring to the instance name.

- Control the sound in the movieclip by referring to the associated sound object.

This might sound a little long winded, but it has the advantage of using only the things that you have learnt before; movies, dot notation and object methods.

The final file for this exercise is **chapter08_01.swf** and **chapter08_01.fla** in the download file for this chapter.

Before we start, we need to get sound that we can control. A looping sound is best. If you can't find one on the Web anywhere, you'll find **soundloop.fla** in the download file for this chapter. It contains a looping percussion sound in the library called **percussion3**.

We need to give that an instance name and the best way to give it one of those is to put it inside a movieclip.

Creating a Sound Movieclip

1. Create a new movieclip and call it **sound1.percussion3**. This name is made up of the instance name that we'll be using, followed by the name of the sound in the library. I find it useful to use this naming structure with sound movieclips because it stops you getting confused about which sound is in which movie, and what its instance name is.

2. Select frame 1 of **sound1.percussion3**. Bring up the **Sound** panel, click on the **Sound:** drop-down menu and select **Percussion 3** from the list to attach that sound to the frame. Leave the **Effect:** and **Sync:** drop-down menus at their defaults (**none** and **Event** respectively):

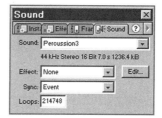

We want this sound to loop forever, and the maximum times you can loop a sound is 214748. For a 1 second sample, this amounts to almost 60 hours of looping, which *is* forever as far as a web site is concerned.

3. Add a new layer called **actions** and in frame 1 add a simple stop(); action. Your movieclip's timeline will look like this:

4. Back in the root timeline, select **Layer 1** and change its name to **sounds**. Drag the **sound1.percussion3** movieclip onto the root timeline, just off the edge of the stage:

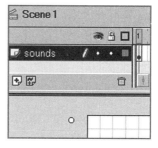

Because the movie has nothing except code and sound in its frames, it will be represented as a circle on the main timeline.

5. Using the **Instance** panel, give the movieclip an instance name, **sound1**:

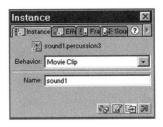

6. Test the movie now and you should see a blank screen, but hear a repeating drum beat from your speakers.

Now that the sound is inside a movieclip and has an instance name we have something that we can edit. One option is to edit the sound via the Edit Envelope window. You may have come across this in your work with Flash already. We'll take a quick look at it here but as this isn't a book dedicated to sound I won't go into detail on how to use it. I'm showing it here to show you how much more you can do with ActionScript.

Go back into the movie, select the frame with the attached sound in **Layer 1**, and select the **edit** button in the **Sound** panel to bring up the **Edit Envelope** window:

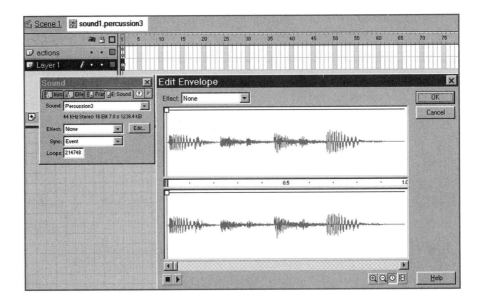

This window presents you with one way of editing sound, and if we were cowards we could stay with this. But we're here to learn the more in-depth ActionScript route. Let me convince you that it'll be worth the effort in the long run:

- The **Edit Envelope** window's effects are *fixed*. We can add believable panning and volume effects only if we know how our Flash presentation is going to turn out. We can't easily *dynamically* change the sound to reflect dynamic animation and the users' preferences. The corresponding ActionScript allows us to do this.

- The **Edit Envelope** is limited to a finite number of envelopes. In ActionScript we can effectively have as many as we want.

- The **Edit Envelope > Effect** drop-down menu is limited to just a few sound/pan effects. Although it allows us custom effects as well, we can create much more complicated effects via ActionScript.

So the advantages of using ActionScript are a pretty compelling, don't you think?

I'll prove it to you. We have our sound movieclip instance, waiting to be controlled. We'll create a sound object to do that for us.

Creating a Sound Object

To keep our programming neat, we'll put all our sound controlling ActionScript and controls in a single movieclip.

1. Create a new movieclip called **sound control** and change its existing layer, **Layer 1** to **actions**.

2. Select frame 1 and bring up the **Actions** panel. In the **Actions** book click on **set variable**. Add sounda in the **Variable:** field:

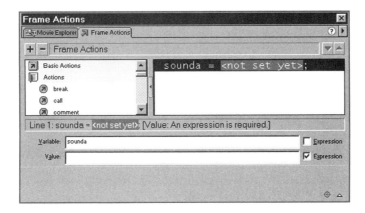

3. In the **Value:** field we'll be adding an expression, so check the **Expression** checkbox.

4. Click in the **Value** field to select it and open the **Objects** book. Within that book, click on the **Sound** book to see a list of ready-made sound methods. Hold the cursor over the **New Sound Method** to see Flash confirm that it will do what we want to do here – create a sound object:

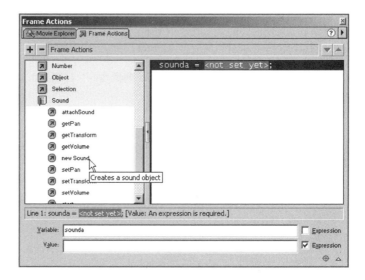

Click on the **new Sound** method and you'll see this code appear:

```
sounda = new Sound ( target );
```

Select `target` and press ***backspace*** to delete it. You're left with:

```
sounda = new Sound ();
```

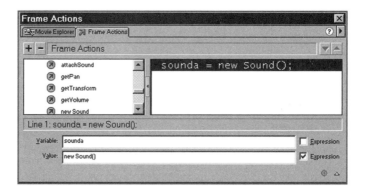

All of this is a bit fiddly, so I'll give you a recap: we've created a new sound object and told Flash to call it sounda. At the moment Flash doesn't know what the sound is or where it can find it. We need to tell it which timeline the sound is on.

The command we need for this uses dot notation, so it'll be quicker to do this in Expert mode.

5. Switch to Expert mode and add sounda below the line sounda = new Sound ();.

6. Place the cursor at the end of the code you've just added and double-click on the **attachSound** method (in **Objects > Sound**):

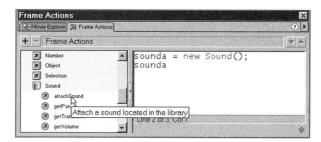

7. This will automatically add the dot, so your line will now say:

```
sounda.attachsound( idName )
```

idName is a prompt to enter the target path of the movieclip containing the sound that we want to use. We need to replace it with the path that will direct Flash to the sound movieclip that we created earlier.

8. Replace idName with _root.sound1. The dot notation tells Flash to find the sound1 movieclip instance on the main timeline.

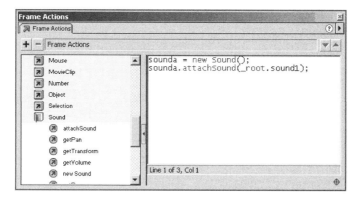

If you ever decide to create a Flash presentation with lots of sounds under the control of ActionScript, it's a good idea to follow a very methodical naming pattern because for every sound you have four names:

- The name of the sound file (**percussion3**).

- The instance name of the sound movieclip (sound1).

- The library name of the sound movieclip, which, because you are using the instance name of the container movieclip, you don't use in the ActionScript at all.

- The name of the sound object (sounda).

...and if you confuse any two of them, your ActionScript won't work!

If I added another ActionScript controlled sound, I would give it an object name soundb, and the movieclip would have an instance name sound2, so I'm being consistent and therefore have less chance of getting all the names mixed up. Anyway, once you've added the path, your ActionScript will look like this:

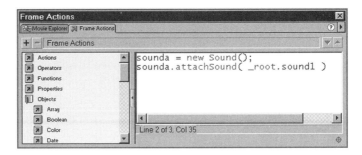

You can now go back to Normal mode, but before you do, check the syntax as we've done every time before:

- Check that new Sound, attachSound and _root are in blue, because they're reserved words.

- Check that everything else is in black.

- Check that all the dots that need to be there *are* there.

> *Notice that I haven't added a **semi-colon** at the end of the second line. When you're in Expert mode you don't have to worry about adding either semi-colons or indentations because Flash will do it for you if you forget.*

Go back into Normal mode.

We've defined sounda as our new sound object and directed Flash to the sound1 movieclip on the root timeline to retrieve the sound that we want to use.

Now we'll add some sound controls to give us some funky effects as if we were in a concert hall with a musician moving around the stage as he sings.

Adding Sound Controls

1. Create a button symbol and call it **button**. In the Up state create a small filled circle like the one you see here:

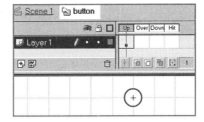

   Use the **Info** panel to make sure that its center is at 0.0, 0.0 and be sure to give it a white fill, otherwise you'll have trouble selecting it! Notice that although the other states have no keyframe in them, if you select the other states, the circle is still there. We want to use this as a draggable button, so we need to drop it into a movieclip.

   > As a recap, we drop the button into a movieclip because a draggable button will drag **everything** on the timeline it's placed on. So if you put it on, say, the root timeline, it will drag the whole SWF. We want only the button itself to be dragged, so by putting it in its own movieclip (which has a timeline containing only the button) we're ensuring that only the button will be dragged.

2. Create a movieclip called **dragbutton**, and place **button** in it. Again, use the **Info** panel to position it at 0.0, 0.0:

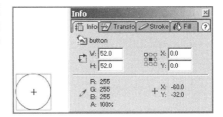

   Finally, we need to attach ActionScript to the button inside **dragbutton** to make the whole thing draggable. We'll be adding a Drag action, like we did in Chapter 5, but this Drag ActionScript is a bit more sophisticated.

3. Select the button and open the **Object Actions** window. Create an on (press) action:

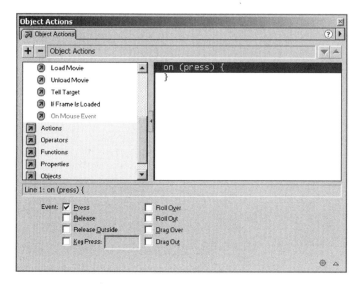

4. In the Actions book, click on the **startDrag** action and check **Constrain to rectangle**. Flash will prompt you to enter an expression containing values for the Left, Right, Top and Bottom of the rectangle:

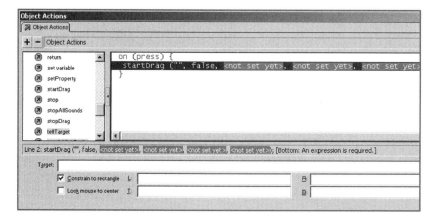

5. Enter the following in the **L: R: T:** and **B:** fields:

    L: **-50**
    R: **50**
    T: **-50**
    B: **50**

This constrains the drag to a rectangle like this:

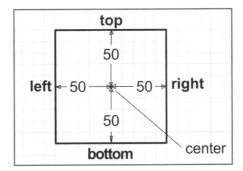

The **L: R: T:** and **B:** measurements represent the distances from the center point (which is the position the button initially starts off at on your stage). Notice that the *y* direction is measured in a *down is positive* direction (as is the stage).

6. Because the button is constrained within this area, it will get left behind when the user drags the cursor outside of the bounding box. With this in mind we need to stop the Drag action as soon as the mouse moves outside the box. We can do this by including a dragOut condition alongside the usual release condition in the stopDrag(); action:

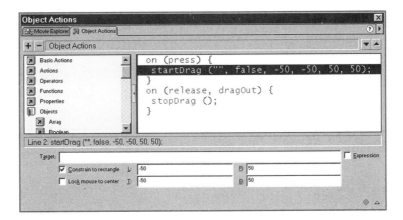

Ever since we met it you may have been wondering where that dragOut little number could possibly come in useful!

7. Now that we have our draggable button, go back to the **sound control** movie and extend the existing layer **actions** to frame 3. Then create three new layers: **text**, **dragbutton** and **back**:

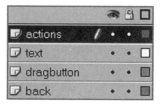

8. In layer **back** create a black-filled borderless square, roughly positioned over the center. Using the **Info** panel, alter its size and position so that it has a width and height of 100.0 and is centered at 0.0, 0.0. This is going to represent, admittedly rather basically, the birds' eye view of a concert stage:

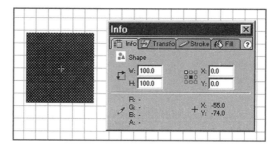

9. Now add a little black circle at the bottom of the square and make it the approximate dimensions that you see here:

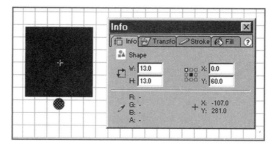

The important thing here is that it is centered at X = 0.0. This represents you sitting at the front of the stage.

10. Next, in layer **dragbutton**, place the movieclip **dragbutton** roughly in the center of the square. Using the **Info** panel again, place it at exactly 0.0, 0.0, and give it dimensions roughly equal to the circle we just added in the last step:

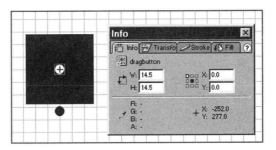

11. Using the **Instance** panel, give **dragbutton** an instance name of **drag**.

If you can't see a white circle, make sure that the **dragbutton** layer is above the **back** layer in the stack. This white circle represents a musician, in our case a percussionist, on the stage.

So, to recap on the plan. Imagine the black square is a stage viewed from above. The black dot is you sitting in front of the stage and the white dot is a musician on the stage. As the white dot is dragged around the stage area by the user, we want ActionScript to dynamically alter the stereo image, or panning, and the volume of the sound source as it moves around the stage.

If the musician is right at the footlights and in front of you, you would hear the sound at a maximum volume, from your left and right ear.

If the musician moved to the left or right of the stage, you would hear sound more strongly in the corresponding ear.

If the musician moved towards the back of the stage (and assuming they didn't have a microphone), the sound would be equally faint in both ears:

This sound effect is created by altering two aspects of the original sound: the volume and the panning, which is the direction from which the sound comes to us most strongly. ActionScript has two cunningly named methods for the sound object that allow us to make the changes that we want:

```
setPan();
setVolume();
```

The setPan(); Method

The `setPan();` method allows you to vary the sound level in each speaker. The values that we can apply to it alter the sound accordingly:

- `sound1.setPan(0);` would give us an equal balance in the left and right speakers for the sound object that we've just created.

- `sound1.setPan(-100);` would give us 100% of the current volume in the left speaker, and 0% in the right speaker.

- `sound1.setPan(100);` would give us 0% of the current volume in the left speaker, and 100% in the right speaker.

In terms of our stage, our button can be dragged −50 pixels to the left and +50 to the right from its initial starting position. We want to scale this from −100 to +100 for our `setPan();` method. This is simply a question of doubling the x co-ordinate of the button:

```
(-100 to 100) = 2 x (-50 to 50)
```

so

Pan level = 2* button's *x* position.

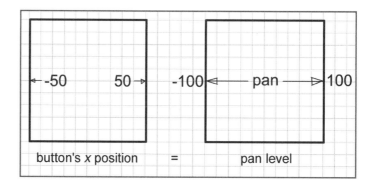

The setVolume(); Method

The `setVolume()`; method allows you to vary the total sound volume. The values that change this are pretty obvious:

- `sound1.setVolume(0);` would give you 0% volume, which is silence.

- `sound1.setVolume(100);` would give you 100% volume.

In terms of our stage again, we can drag the button 50 pixels to the front and -50 pixels to the back from its starting position. This must be scaled from 100 to 0% for the `setVolume()`; method. To do this, we just add 50 to the button's y position:

(100 to 0) = 50 + (50 to −50)

Volume level = 50 + button's y position.

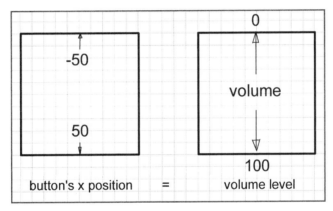

This is where we start to get the effects that we want. We'll use variables to equate the `setVolume` and `setPan` methods of our sound object `sounda` with the x and y positions of the drag button to make the user feel that they're sitting in the middle of the Carnegie Hall.

Adding setVolume and setPan Methods

1. Back in the **sound control** movieclip, in frame 2 of layer **actions** add a keyframe. Click on **Actions > set variable** twice to create these two variables:

   ```
   pan = 2*drag._x;
   vol = 50+drag._y;
   ```

   These take the x and y positions of the draggable button (or, rather, the **dragbutton** movieclip that contains is it, with instance name **drag**) and convert them to the correct pan and volume scales that we need.

Before we go on, check that you have the correct syntax. Make sure that you haven't missed out the dots and once you have entered the **Value:** fields, don't forget to check **Expression**. You can't see it in this picture but _x and _y should be green:

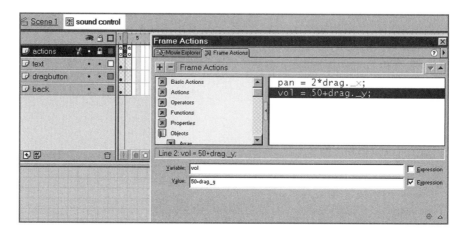

Note that these particular examples are specifically for this stage size, you will have to re-evaluate the equations for different stage sizes.

We now need to use the vol and pan variables to alter the sounda object. The setPan() and setVolume() methods both use dot notation, so it's best if we enter them in Expert mode.

2. Beneath the lines of code that we have already, type in sounda and double-click on the setPan method within **Objects > Sound**. Now repeat this using the setVolume method. Make sure your setPan() and setVolume() brackets contain the pan and vol variables respectively:

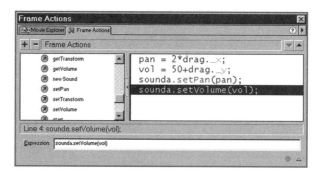

We'll now make Flash constantly re-evaluate the sound object's panning and volume based on the button position.

3. Use the **Frame** panel to give frame 2 a label **soundloop**, and in frame 3 add a keyframe and a `gotoAndPlay("soundloop");`.

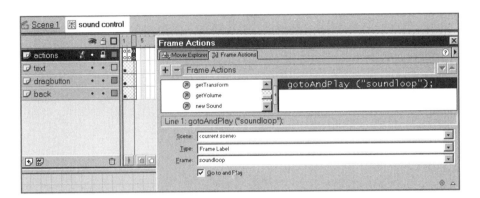

As a final exercise, you could add a text field to display the actual values that Flash is using for the `setVolume()` and `setPan()` commands to increase your understanding of what's going on.

4. In layer **text** add two dynamic text fields to show how variables `pan` and `vol` are varying:

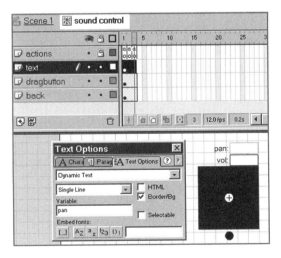

5. Finally, drag a copy of the **sound control** movieclip onto the main stage.

As I said earlier, the final FLA of this completed exercise is in **chapter08_01.fla**.

If you test the movie, you'll hear the sound volume and panning change as you move the sound source around the stage. This sound variation is occurring in real-time, in response to how you drag the button. You can see how this is a template for creating a dynamic soundscape for your web sites or Flash games. As the sound-source moves around the screen, you can create the appropriate sound effects on the fly with the sound object and ActionScript.

A pretty powerful effect, I think you'll agree, created with some relatively simple ActionScript. But that's not all that a sound object can do for you. It can stop and start all your sounds too.

Starting and Stopping Sounds

The actions to stop and start all sounds in a movieclip are:

```
instanceName.start();
instanceName.stop();
```

You can attach these actions to additional buttons to stop and re-start sounds for your sound object. To stop sound for our object sounda, you would add the following action to your mute button:

```
on (release) {
  sound1.stop();
}
```

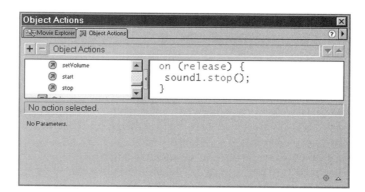

Using these two separate commands is preferable to using the stopAllSounds (); action in **Actions**, because not only would this stop your soundtrack, it would also stop all sounds you may have attached to button clicks and any other incidental effects.

We've taken a look at how the new Flash 5 sound object can give us pretty efficient control over individual sound movieclips to create some realistic effects. But hang on, I think that we can move on from here.

Forget click sounds attached to buttons or the odd incidental effect. As ActionScript experts, we'll settle for nothing less than making that sound object work a little harder to control a full, life-sized soundtrack. I'll show you in a while how I did this at stun:design, but before then I'll bring you back down to earth a little with a few practicalities.

Let's face it, sound is a big download. An important factor that always plays on the designers' minds when they think of using sound is **file size**.

There are things we can do to get the file size down via compression but that's only part of the solution.

We need to be able to **stream** the sounds in as well.

ActionScript and Streaming

The term **streaming** refers to the process by which a SWF starts to play as soon as the first frame has loaded. The SWF doesn't stop to wait for the full site to be loaded, but rather displays new frames as it downloads (streams) them in.

If we used a system of placing our entire soundtrack into a movieclip we, or rather our viewers, wouldn't receive the benefits that streaming has to offer because **Flash doesn't start to play a movieclip until the whole movieclip has loaded in**. This is unacceptable for the end user; waiting extra time for a 200K soundtrack to load in before the site appears is bad design. So, the first rule of Flash sound is that, unless you expect all the end users to be in possession of high bandwidth connections, you should avoid placing your complete soundtrack within the manacles of a movieclip.

That makes streaming a good option. Hang on, though; if you're thinking of streaming and using ActionScript, there are a few caveats to bear in mind:

- We have to be streaming in the sound continuously for a continuous soundtrack, which will limit our bandwidth to do other things.

- A streaming source locks itself to the timeline. If the timeline can't keep up, Flash misses out frames to catch up. This is OK for a timeline full of tween animations, but is disastrous for ActionScript, because any ActionScript attached to those lost frames could be lost too, causing all sorts of errors.

- Streaming sound is not really conducive to a typical timeline under the control of ActionScript, where we could be jumping about all over the place.

So streaming sounds and ActionScript don't mix. Is there any hope?

The best way, and really the only sensible way to add a soundtrack to a Flash ActionScript site without running up massive download times is to load it up as a new SWF with **loadMovie**.

This has a number of advantages:

- It loads up separately from the main site, so you can discard the soundtrack on user preference and free up any further unwanted sound download.

- Unlike Flash's streaming sound type, you can re-use the sound once it's downloaded because the soundtrack consists of event sounds.

- SWFs containing just sound are transparent because they will have nothing on the stage, so there are no issues with loading a soundtrack and obscuring lower levels of SWFs.

Controlling our soundtrack across multiple SWFs may sound a little daunting, but is actually perfectly possible and easy as long as you use the right path to your soundtrack. Funny how most things in Flash 5 tend to hinge on an understanding of the correct path!

I'll take you through now how we did just this at stun:design. As I explain, you'll see that the process fell into three stages:

1. Creating the soundtrack to overlay over our web site with **loadMovie**.

2. Creating the controls to modify the soundtrack's volume and pan levels from the stun web site.

3. Creating the sound object to control our soundtrack from the main web site.

I'll give you some background info first, then I'll round off with a little more of a hands on demonstration, where you can test what we did for yourself.

The stun:design Web Site

I created the stun soundtrack with the help of a good friend (if you've read Foundation Flash 5 you'll have met him already and seen some of our previous joint efforts). The file for my soundtrack is called **soundtrack.fla**, and the raw MP3 files that we used to create it are contained in **stunsounds.zip**.

A word of warning before you download it:

The FLA file is about 7.5 Mb, because, although we imported the six sound files as MP3 into Flash (and they were 192K each at this point), once they're in the FLA, it looks as if Flash balloons the file sizes up by converting them to raw sound data. The final SWF, though, contains compressed sound data. We imported our sounds as MP3 because this is a new feature to Flash 5 so we felt that we'd better try it out! This may cause issues with some machines, particularly Macs, which don't seem to like the combination of Flash 5 and big FLA files. Also, when you come to test the soundtrack, be aware that there's a lot of sound compression for Flash to do before it can create the SWF file, so there will be a long pause if you're using the hardware of the specification stated on the Flash 5 box (which is the minimum spec). If you want to bypass all this trouble, just download the ready-made **soundtrack.swf**, which is all you will really need for this demo.

You can just load up the separate MP3 files via the more download-friendly **stunsounds.zip**, which is 1.5Mb or so, and build up your own soundtrack. Don't forget the kicker streaming sound at the start of your composition though. The sounds have been normalized to sound OK together, so you can safely maintain them at their current levels when you play them all at once without overdriving the overall sound level (aren't we good to you, considering this is a programming book, not one about music!).

Anyway, back to business. Here's a view of the soundtrack's timeline and library:

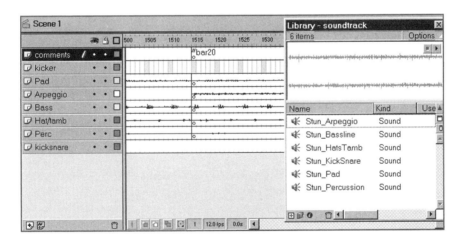

There are six sounds, all of which are loopable and last for two bars each. Using loopable sounds means that we can splice them together on the Flash timeline to create a soundtrack (or, if we're lacking imagination, we could just loop them forever).

We arranged these on the main timeline to form a musical composition. The track has been made to last just under five minutes, which is as long as I would expect a casual visitor to listen to a piece of music that was nothing more than the constant re-cycling of six basic samples. If music was to play a much more prominent part of the site, I would have considered using several different compositions that the user could select maybe by clicking on a little Deejay's bag full of records (I should stop giving away all the little ideas I am using on my current web sites....).

Of special note is the bandwidth profile for the soundtrack. The track has been arranged to stream in satisfactorily on a very low bandwidth, and will work even on a 28K modem. Notice that we're using streaming on the soundtrack timeline, which consists of event sounds. To confuse the issue, there is a type of sound in Flash called stream sounds (which we're not using). Although detailed sound issues are beyond Foundation ActionScript, look in the glossary if you're unsure about stream and event sounds.

The upshot of using event sounds that stream in is that the sound only needs to load in once. After the initial 16K preload, the soundtrack will happily stream in without crossing the limit line of the 28K modem (which took some arranging!). This is achieved by copious use of the bandwidth profiler. You can see here that we've made sure that we don't go over the 200 bytes per second bandwidth limit of a 28K modem, following initial download. That way, we can be sure of uninterrupted streaming on even low bandwidths:

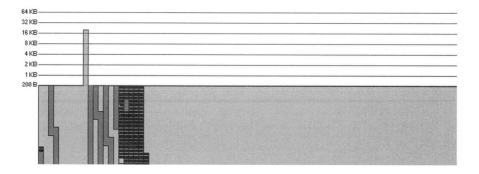

> As an aside, if you want to get into music composition for the Web using Flash you may want to look at the **soundtrack.fla** file, because it contains a lot of tips and tricks (most of which are beyond the scope of this book).

We'll have a little (well, actually quite a lot!) of that hands on experience here. I thought it would be cool to show you in detail how I created some slider controls for the volume and pan of the sound object on stun:design. I'll take you through quite thoroughly so that you can take these away to use on your own sites.

Creating the Sound Controls

You should create this control in a separate FLA from the soundtrack because that way it will load in the soundtrack as a level and play that. This is a useful technique to use in general when your Flash site consists of bandwidth heavy multimedia. Today's first lesson then: load the multimedia separately so that it doesn't affect the main site loading time.

1. In a new FLA, create an invisible button, just as we did in Chapter 6. Make the button a simple square and call it **invisible**:

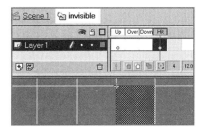

You'll probably be starting to appreciate that invisible buttons are a clever little tool for the ActionScript programmer. Don't leave home without one.

Next, we'll create a draggable bar graph, or a slider, for the sound and pan controls. This is how it will work:

We have a bar graph - the gray rectangle - inside a frame - the bezel. We'll make it draggable, so that when the user clicks and holds inside the bar graph bezel, they can drag the gray bar to the left and right. If you drag it to the left, the bar graph disappears and we are reading 0%. If it is dragged all the way to the right, then we will be reading 100%.

This shows how we'll create some nifty control:

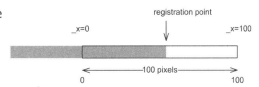

Making our bar graph and bezel both 100 pixels wide means that we automatically get a scale that changes by 100, because the _x property of the rectangle will change by 100 pixels as we drag it across the bezel area. To make things easier still, if we place the far left-hand side of the bezel at x = 0, and put the registration mark of the bargraph at its far right hand edge, we'll automatically get a bar graph _x property that varies between 0 and 100 pixels, which is our 0 to 100%. Clever eh?

Don't worry about the fact that the area of the bar graph rectangle outside the bezel might show through, we can *mask* that out with a mask layer.

OK, let's do it.

2. Create a new movieclip called **bargraph**. Inside it, create a horizontal rectangle as I have here:

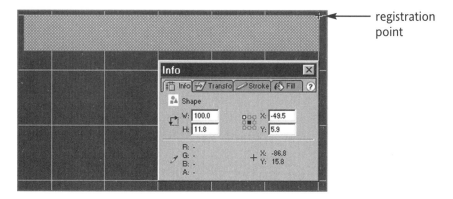

registration point

The rectangle should be exactly 100 pixels long (so that if we drag it along its full length, it will have moved exactly 100 pixels as I said before) and have its center in line with the top right corner (so that its _x property will vary 0 -100 for the 100 pixel drag). The center point is the little registration + that you see in the screenshot, and needs to be in the top right-hand corner of the rectangle. As usual, when you need exact measurements, use the **Info** panel. The height is less important, but make it 10 -15 pixels high. I've made my rectangle a light gray to match the general stun:design web site color scheme.

Now we need to make the bar draggable. We'll do this with the invisible button.

3. In the **bargraph** movieclip create a new layer called **button** and drag the **button** movieclip that we created earlier onto it. Use the **Info** panel to scale the button to be 200 pixels wide and of the same height as the rectangle. Next, drag it over the rectangle so that its leftmost part completely covers the rectangle:

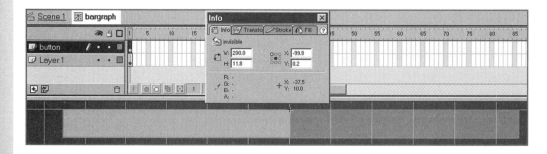

Notice that the invisible button extends 100 pixels beyond our bar graph. This is so that when we're at 0% on the final bar graph slider control, we don't have to click on the bar graph itself to drag it, we just have to be inside the bezel area.

4. To make the whole thing draggable, attach this ActionScript to the button:

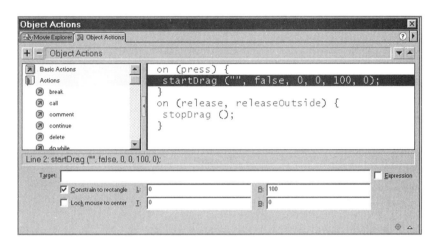

The `startDrag` action needs to be constrained to a rectangle. We want to be able to move it left from its current position by 100 pixels, but we don't want it to be able to move it up or down because we only want it to be able to slide in one direction. Don't worry about the `false` in the `startDrag`'s parameters. This just means that we don't want to lock the mouse to the center of our shape.

5. Check the **Constrain to rectangle:** checkbox, and enter these values:

    L: 0   **R:** 100
    T: 0   **B:** 0

You can now test the movie by doing a **Control > Test Scene** from inside the **bargraph** movieclip. You won't see anything if you put the registration point at the bottom right in a fit of pique, so make sure it's in the top right-hand corner.

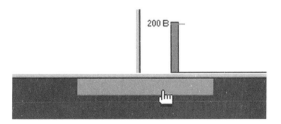

The Drag action only allows you to move the rectangle left or right, and only by 100 pixels.

So far we have a sliding rectangle. It's time to make it into a fully-fledged bar graph.

6. Create a new movieclip called **meter**. Call the current layer **graph** and in it place a copy of **bargraph**, giving it an instance name **graph** via the **Instance** panel. You need to place this instance at exactly 0.0, 0.0, so use the **Info** panel to do this:

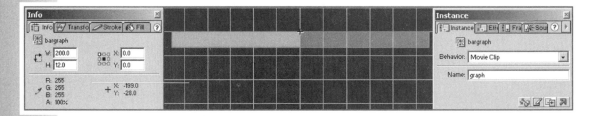

7. Extend layer **graph** to 2 frames by adding a new frame with *F5*. Now here's the clever bit. Create two new layers **mask** and **bezel** in this order:

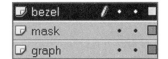

The next stage involves us putting a mask layer over the button and a bezel around the whole bargraph so that we only ever see the part of the bar graph that is actually inside the bezel area. This would normally require close positioning, but here's a cool shortcut that's worth remembering whenever you want to build any kind of meter or dial in Flash.

8. Make sure that **View > Snap to objects** is on. Select the Rectangle tool, and give it a light gray outline and black fill. Click on the **Round Rectangle Radius** icon (try saying that with a mouthful of rice), and enter a value of 10 for the **Corner Radius**:

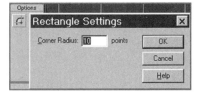

9. In layer **bezel** drag out a rounded rectangle to cover the right side of the **bargraph** instance:

10. The outline of this rectangle is our bezel, but we want the fill to be a mask, so copy the fill area only, and then delete it from the **bezel** layer. You should now only have the bezel outline in layer **bezel**:

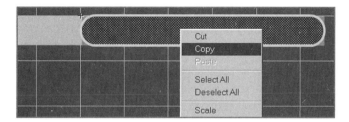

11. Next, select the **mask** layer and **Paste in place** the fill. Make this layer a mask. Your layers and graphics should now look like this:

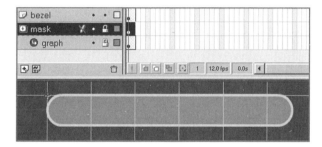

You can click within the bezel and drag the bar graph in from the left now, to create a cool looking slider control. Test it via **Control > Test Scene** if you don't believe me. Notice that the masked-out areas of the drag button don't register. This means that a button (or part of a button) that is masked is disabled. That's something that I didn't know until I tried this, but now that I do I can see that it will be useful for doing all sorts of clever stuff with menus. Play around a little to see if you can work out what I'm thinking...

OK, we need to convert the slider's movement into a value that we can use.

12. Create an **actions** layer.

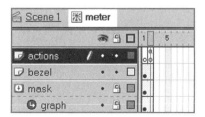

13. Add a keyframe at frame 2 and add this script:

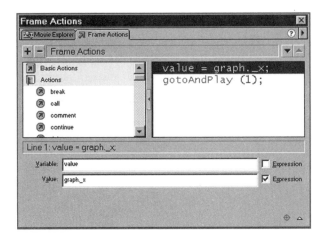

This will constantly convert the amount you've dragged the bar graph to a variable called value, which will vary between 0 and 100, which is where our 100% scale will come from.

You can't get the debugger window up in **Test Scene**, but if you bring up the **Output** window at different drag values, you'll see value change as you drag the buttons bar graph about:

For these four positions, I see value being 0.0, 28.85, 75.9 and 100.0 respectively. The actions are constantly looking at the position of the bar graph via its x property and assigning this to value.

Cool. We now have a generic slider control. You can rotate this to make it into a scrollbar (and you would also have to make the bar graph shorter), or a numeric slider to 'scrub' through frames in a movieclip, or even as a way for the user to answer questions like 'how strongly do you believe that the political system in America is democratic?'. The stronger the belief, the more to the right they pull the slider bar. Note that if you want your slider to give integer values, you'll need to add a math.round(); action in the script to round value up or down to the nearest whole number.

You can look at my generic slider control via **slider.fla**.

Here are the sliders that I've made for the sound controls:

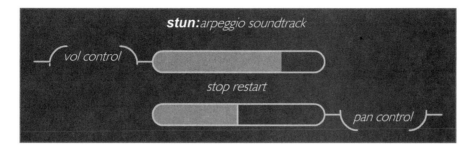

The whole thing is contained in a single movieclip called **soundcontrol**. This handles everything to do with the soundtrack, including the volume and pan controls, so we'd better take a good look at it.

Creating the Sound Object

The **soundcontrol** movieclip has been built to be *modular*, so that we can simply drop it into our web site (or your web site if you like the soundtrack!), and it will work as long as it can find the **soundtrack.swf** file. Simply open the **soundtrackcontrol.fla** as a library, and drag the **soundcontrol** movie where you want it. And you thought Microsoft had plug-and-play sewn up.

The **soundcontrol** layers look like this:

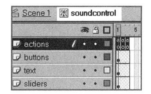

The two sliders are generic sliders, with instance names soundvol and soundpan, and are in layer **sliders**. The text and graphics are on layer **text**. Before we look at layer **buttons**, we need to have a peek at **actions**. Here' what lies behind frame 1:

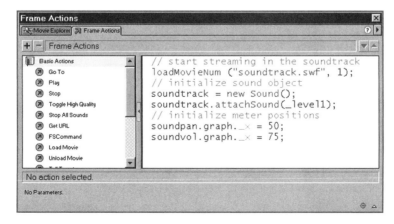

```
// start streaming in the soundtrack
loadMovieNum ("soundtrack.swf", 1);
// initialize sound object
soundtrack = new Sound();
soundtrack.attachSound(_level1);
// initialize meter positions
soundpan.graph._x = 50;
soundvol.graph._x = 75;
```

Frame 1 initializes everything:

```
//start streaming in the soundtrack
LoadMovieNum ("soundtrack.swf", 1);
```

This script starts loading the soundtrack into level 1 via the loadMovieNum action. Because it's optimized for streaming, it will start playing as soon as 16k of it has loaded in. (The bandwidth profiler shot earlier tell us this.)

```
//initialize sound object
soundtrack = new Sound();
soundtrack.attachSound(_level1);
```

The next few lines initialize a new sound object called **soundtrack** and attach it to the root timeline of _level1, which is the soundtrack we've just started loading in. Notice that we can point the sound object to a **timeline** as well as to a movieclip.

```
//initialize meter positions
soundpan.graph._x = 50;
soundvol.graph._x = 75;
```

When you look at these last two lines, you may need to look back at the generic slider we built. These lines are essentially looking inside the two slider instances soundpan and soundvol and moving the bar graphs (which we gave an instance name **graph**) to non-zero start values.

The frame 2 actions simply look at what *value* is in each of the two sliders and set the pan and volume values for our soundtrack:

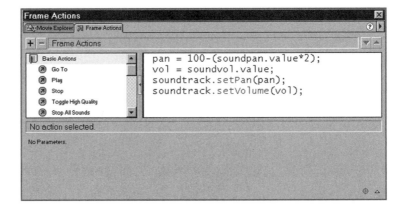

274

Notice that each slider has its own value. Although the variable names are the same, the **path is different**, which makes the two value variables unique, so we're OK (although we're probably getting too smart for our own good).

The final frame in **actions** frame just does a `gotoAndPlay(2);` so that we keep performing the script that we've just seen to update the sound level based on any movements that the user has made with the slider. You could do a `gotoAndPlay("label");` but I passed on that, given that there are only three frames.

The only things left are the **stop** and **restart** buttons. The two buttons are bits of text with invisible buttons over them:

The **restart** button has this script:

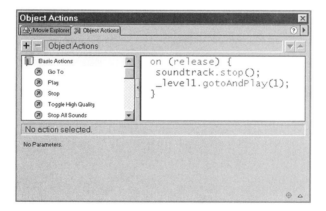

This does two things. First it stops all the sounds in our soundtrack, and then it makes the soundtrack's timeline go back to the start and begin replaying. We have to stop the soundtrack object from playing anything else before we do this, otherwise we would still hear the current samples until they finished the number of loops that we'd specified when we attached them to the **_level1** timeline (which is generally 2 loops or 14 seconds).

The **stop** button is the same except that it has no `goto`.

And that is it!

You can test everything by playing this FLA **from a location that includes soundtrack.swf**. You can use my versions from the zip, which are:

soundtrackcontrol.fla
soundtrack.swf

The use of dynamic sound control can really add to a web site by adding sound cues to what's happening on screen. This is a powerful ability, because many home users now have fairly advanced audio equipment attached to their computer's audio-out ports. The use of the sound object with soundtracks offers the user fairly advanced sound control options, which are very easy to implement in ActionScript once you've overcome the very precise steps that need to be taken to set up a sound object in the first place.

Pump up the volume!

Summary

This chapter has taught you something that a lot of people seem to be struggling with: how to totally tame and understand the sound object. Believe me, this took me some time, so you're benefiting from my late nights, and can use the time you've saved building your own Oscar award-winning soundtracks.

In this chapter we've covered:

- Creating a new sound object

- Adding pan and volume controls

- Creating stun:design sound control interactivity

In the next chapter we'll look in more detail at some of the interactivity tools that we've touched on here to ultimately create a scroll bar for stun:design. We're getting to a pretty professional standard now, you know...

02

9 Advanced Interactivity

What we'll cover in this chapter:

- *How Flash thinks of instances as objects*

- *How different parts of ActionScript are structured around those objects to affect what they do and how they look*

- *How to use those properties to build some advanced interactivity*

- *How to create a scroll bar for the stun:design web site*

The use of **properties** is an essential part of ActionScripting, allowing us to create everything from efficient site pre-loaders to video games. There has been very little written about properties for the non-programmer. What has been written seems to assume that if you want to know about properties, you must know the basic concepts behind them because you're a hot ActionScripter and you know all about objects and object-oriented programming.

Um, well, I just wrote that, and it scares even me. In this chapter we'll go though properties from step one and build up to see why they're so useful. Rather than just say 'properties are cool, so use them', we'll look at the general programming structure of which properties are a part. This chapter also goes some way to explaining what all this fuss about Flash 5 being object-oriented is, what that means, and what an object actually is.

If you've come to Flash 5 from Flash 4 you'll find this chapter particularly useful because Flash 4 wasn't object-oriented (well, it had one true object, which was the string object). Unless you're aware of what objects and classes are, you won't understand the fundamental framework that Flash 5 is now using.

We'll start by looking at what properties are, where to find them and what the deal is with all the ActionScript gurus out there telling us all they're really cool. In this book, I've taken the bold step of teaching you dot notation, paths and the use of Expert mode in ActionScript as basic skills rather than the advanced Actionscript abilities that everyone else seems to assume they are. As a result of this, you're actually closer to using properties than you think, and already know the fundamental skills required.

Once we've looked at the properties basics, we'll see how they're fundamental to how Flash creates animation, and how we can use this fact to create our own custom animations using properties through practical examples. We'll be creating a scroll bar for stun:design that you can take for your own use wherever you want it.

Let's start at the beginning, with a reminder of how Flash thinks of instances as objects.

Instances Re-visited

When you began at elementary school, in your English lessons you started off by learning 'naming words' and 'doing words', and slowly moved on to think of them as pronouns and adverbs as your grasp of the language increased. In physics, you start off believing that matter and energy are separate, until you advance to the level where you're told that matter is just a special case of energy, and can be converted back to it.

So it is with learning Flash. Instances are only one step in a learning pattern that gets more complex as you continue. Flash 5 uses a particular model to represent almost everything that can be changed, and that model is called an **object-oriented approach**. Instances are just another way of saying **objects**. Just when you think you've got your head around that one, you find out that the object is one part in a two-part process of **classes** and **objects**.

This section is all about changing your perspective from whatever you thought Flash did before, to what it *actually* does. As I said, you already have the basic skills needed to understand this new perspective. You've already been moving in this direction because of the way in which the exercises in this book have been structured.

How Flash Thinks

Let's consider Flash's library elements – buttons, graphics and movieclips. You'll remember that we discussed the importance of instance names earlier, and how once you assign such a name you can control that element with ActionScript because you now have a name with which to reference it. We also said that buttons and graphics couldn't have instance names unless you changed their behavior with the **Instance** panel so that they behave like movieclips.

This gives the impression that it's the instance name that's important, but this isn't entirely true. If you don't give a movieclip an instance name, Flash will assign one itself. The truth is that **all** movieclips have instance names - it's just that if you don't assign one yourself, you don't necessarily see Flash doing it for you behind the scenes. Flash actually names the first movieclip that it hasn't got an instance name for as **instance1**, and the second one **instance2**, and so on. You can see this in the **Debugger** window if you do a **Control > Debug Movie** with an FLA that consists of movieclips that are still without instance names.

I created a FLA with three nameless movieclips on the stage. You can see here that they've inherited names from Flash, and all have a full path and instance name:

So, if the *instance name* isn't the important thing, what is? It's the fact that the thing you are controlling is a movieclip, or rather, that it is an **object**. You'll remember that we first discussed objects in Chapter 6.

Similar objects are grouped together in **classes**.

Classes

A **class** is a programming term that describes a template for an object. It describes a general list of things that all objects within that class will have. A class called **plant bulbs** might have a template that includes:

- Name of plant

- Height of plant

- Color of flower

- Flowering month

- Soil type to plant the bulb in

Any particular **plant** object would be a full list of actual values for this list, so you could have an object of the class plant that read: daffodil, 20cm, yellow, March, normal.

In Flash, each class has three main features that we're interested in:

- Methods

- Properties

- Behaviors

We're going to look at each of these in turn.

> *As an important aside before we begin, don't get confused by the Macromedia* ActionScript Reference Guide *that came with your Flash 5 program (you can also access it with the help menu in Flash). This makes no distinction between objects and classes. I'm teaching you why as well as how in this book, so I'm not making any shorthand approximations.*

Let's recap again on something that we introduced in Chapter 6: the ActionScript that you can attach to objects to make them *do* something – methods.

Methods

Methods are commands that can be used to *do* something to objects of a particular class. You already know all about methods. When you used the action

```
instancename.play();
```

you were using a command that is only applied to the movieclip class. You can't play a button or a graphic symbol. In this case, the **method** being applied is play();.

You've already done this for the sound object and array object when you did:

```
sound1.setVolume(100);
wordcount = words.length;
```

setvolume and words.length are both **methods** that can only be applied to objects of a certain class.

In the first example, you're using the set the setVolume method to set the volume of an object of the sound class called sound1. In the second you're retrieving the length of an object of the string class.

As you can see from our examples, you always apply methods in the same way:

instancename.<method><arguments>;

The only slight complication with this handy annotation is that with movieclips you sometimes also want to add the **path** as well as the instance name at the beginning of the method. The syntax would become:

path.instancename.<method><arguments>;

We've already seen how to do this too, so this is a quick section!

The important thing to get a feel for is that methods are the same general structure for all classes. Once you understand one method, applying methods is the same for all objects in Flash irrespective of class. They all follow:

instancename.<method><arguments>;

Now number 2 in our list: properties.

Properties

Properties are pieces of data that together define everything we want to know about the members of a class. Remember our **plant bulbs** class with its five values? (Name, height, color, flowering month, soil type.) In programming, properties can do more than just *describe* elements of the class we're talking about. The property can represent a current *value* of something to do with the class, and this value affects how the object *looks* or *behaves* from instant to instant.

If we defined a class called **sprite**, it could have these properties:

- Name of sprite

- Current *x* position

- Current *y* position

- Current speed in the *x* direction

- Current speed in the *y* direction

- Whether the sprite has hit another sprite

- The *name* property of the sprite that we've hit

You would typically *read* some of these properties by assigning the property value to a variable. You might want to *write* other properties by changing their current value. If you *write* the property *current y position*, you would physically alter this property. The *current y position* property affects the position of your sprite, so the sprite would move. This is the basis of animation based on changing properties. Rather than using tween animation, you can change properties over time through ActionScript.

Flash lists all the properties you can access in the **Properties** set of the **Actions** panel:

Almost all of these are only for use with the **movieclip** class, which is what the movie symbol really is. Hold the cursor to see tooltips that describe them. You'll see that most are self-explanatory. (Remember that _highquality is highlighted green because it's deprecated.)

Some of these properties refer to things you would want to know about the movieclip, such as:

- `_framesloaded` shows the number of frames of the movieclip that have been loaded from the internet. This property can be applied to the root timeline as well as a movieclip, so you can use it to easily tell how many frames your entire SWF has.

- `_totalframes` shows the number of frames in the movieclip. Again, this property can be applied to your root timeline. When used in conjunction with the `_framesloaded` property, `_totalframes` can tell you how much of your Flash presentation has streamed in. We'll be using both of these when we make an ActionScript preloader later on in this chapter.

- `_droptarget` specifies the `_name` of the movie that the movieclip was dropped onto. You would use this if your movie was being dragged and you wanted to know if it had been dropped onto another movie.

- `_url` tells you the URL that the movieclip was loaded from. This might seem like something you wouldn't normally want to know, but it allows your ActionScript to know the address of your web site, and therefore load up subsequent SWF files without you having to tell it where they are. This is useful if you tend to move your web site from a development area to a final URL when it's finished, which you would do if you were working professionally for a client.

Other properties in the list refer to internal attributes that specify what movieclips do or are:

- `_currentframe` refers to the frame your movie is on at the moment. If you change it, the movie's playhead will be forced to a new frame. You can do all sorts of things to a movieclip (or even the *root* timeline), such as make it play backwards by reducing `_currentframe`, or do a fast forward by increasing `_currentframe` by more than one every frame.

- `_quality` refers to how the Flash player renders each frame. It can either render them at LOW, MEDIUM, HIGH or BEST quality, depending on the string value you assign to `_quality`. The string value is one of the strings just listed, e.g. `quality = "LOW";`. You could use this to dynamically alter the rendering quality so that your Flash presentation is able to detect and allow for slow computers. Hurray for intelligent self-configuring Flash web sites!

- `_target` finds the path of a specified named movieclip, so you don't even have to bother with knowing the path of a movie to be able to control it. Boy, you must be *really* lazy if you use this one!!

- `_name` allows you to change the instance name of a movieclip. Why would you want to do this? Say that you had a general movieclip *control* sprites that controlled the movement of another movieclip `_root.sprite`, making sure that it never went off screen and checking that it hadn't collided with any other sprites (and changing variables `_root.sprite.collide`, `.xpos` and `.ypos` as it did the checks). Changing each of your movieclip's instance names on the root timeline temporarily to *sprite*, and then running *control sprites*, means you could get the movieclip to control all sprite movieclips, and update each set variables, in turn! How's that for efficiency?

Instead of holding background information about the movieclip, some of these properties refer to its physical appearance: the Alpha values, the height, the position etc. Although the fact that you can't apply these changes to buttons or symbols may seem a little restrictive, you can actually work around this factor surprisingly easily in each case, as we'll see in the next section under the heading **Behaviors**. I won't go into more detail on these appearance properties here. I've listed and explained them all in an appendix at the end of the book. Take some time to have a look there. These are the magic properties related to ActionScript-based animation, and as a top ActionScripter you'll come to know them by heart.

Finally, there are a few properties that apply to the mouse cursor. You can use these properties to track where the mouse is, which is a useful thing to know because you can then have all sorts of interactive processes looking at where the mouse is and acting accordingly.

`_xmouse`, `_ymouse` tell you the current position of the mouse cursor. These are read only values. Asking for the mouse position from the root timeline and asking for the same thing from a movieclip's timeline will give you different results because the mouse position is calculated from the origin. For the stage, 0,0 is at the top left-hand corner. For a movieclip, it's the little **+** registration mark, which could be anywhere. So it's different because the 0,0 point is different.

Behaviors

All objects of a class like our sprite class have the same behaviors, and this behavior is something that is useful to us as programmers. In Flash, behaviors are implicit - the movieclip class behaves like a movie, with frames and a playhead, the sound class makes sound and so on.

There's not much to know about behaviors that common sense doesn't already tell us. The one exception here is when we want to give buttons or graphic symbols properties which allow us to animate them like the movie class.

To animate a graphic you just change its **Behavior** in the **Instance** panel to make it a movieclip. As soon as you do that, **cir** becomes a one-frame movieclip, you can gain use the standard movieclip properties and begin to animate the symbol with ActionScript and properties.

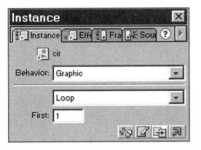 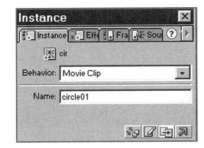

To give a button movieclip properties is easier still; just drop it into a movieclip! The movieclip then acts as a wrapper, and as you vary the properties of the movie the button inherits them and changes as the movieclip is changed. The only thing to be aware of is that the path of the button will change to the timeline of the movieclip it is inside. If I use this method, I tend to just change the button actions to now have `parent` in front of them, so that:

```
on (release) {
stop();
}
```

becomes:

```
on (release) {
parent.stop();
}
```

This is preferable to using `_root`, because with `parent` you have greater flexibility - the button will always affect the timeline the wrapper sits on, even if you move it again.

OK, so where are we up to? We've said that objects are made up of methods, properties and behaviors. When do all these things come into being? When is our object defined?

Defining Objects

An object in Flash is a class that has been initialized to include a full set of properties that make it unique. For example, giving the six categories in our sprite class values make it a unique object. You make movieclips unique in a slightly different way than you do for the other objects because movieclips are both graphic symbols and objects, so we'll look at movieclips first, before we look at how to turn classes into objects.

Movieclips

A movieclip has no properties while it's still in the library, and so is still a class. As soon as you drag it on stage, it gains a full set of properties (so our Sprite class would get an *x*, *y* position and speed etc.), and becomes an **object**. The most important property is the *instance name* and you won't know what this is until you assign one. In practical terms, your movie can't really be treated as an object until you've assigned it an instance name. Until then, you won't be able to apply methods to it or look at its properties. You can therefore assume, as most professional programmers do, that **instance** and object are the same thing.

What about the other objects?

Non-graphic Objects

All other objects still follow the general rule that a class becomes an object as soon as you give it a full set of properties to make it unique. They're not drag-and-drop graphical items like movies, so the way of defining any other Flash object is slightly different because you have to do it with code and use the `new <object class>` action to create a new object. As usual, you've done this many times so far in this book, so it shouldn't be new to you. Only the context of talking about it all in a *class – object* perspective has changed. Here are a couple of reminders of examples that you prepared earlier:

```
letters = new Array(10);        which defined a new array object
sounda = new Sound();           which defined a new sound object
```

Both commands still follow the general rule that the object comes into being as soon as you have assigned it a name, and you're then able to look at properties and apply methods.

Now that you know all about what properties are, and what their relevance is, and can even define what objects and classes are, you are ready to start using object properties to start doing some **really** cool stuff...

Advanced Interactivity and Object Properties

We can use what we've learnt about Flash structure to take direct control of what happens at the heart of Flash with ActionScript. We no longer have to bother with tween animations at all because we can do it all with code, and will have a much finer level of control when we do so.

I'll illustrate the power of this method by taking you through with two practical examples: a preloader and a cache detector.

Planning our Preloader and Cache Detector

Most beginners want a preloader on their site. A common error is to mistake the preloader for the intro, making the preloader part of a bandwidth-eating mega intro that's not so much there to entertain as to show off the skills of the Flashmeister who built the site. This means that the user will have to wait for the intro to load in before they see the lifesaving **Skip** button to take them to the main site, which potentially holds content that they *actually want to see*.

So, we want an intro that will allow the user to start loading the main site before the intro has finished if they're in a hurry. Oh, and we'd like the main site to be loading itself at the same time as the intro as well...

You might have noticed a problem here: what if the user skipped to the main site before it had loaded, maybe because they had seen the intro before and pressed the **Skip** button as soon as they saw it?

This is exactly when a preloader should make itself known. It should quickly and efficiently load what remains of the main site and keep the user informed of how long they should have to wait. That's what a preloader should be. No fuss, no hassle. Just something that loads the main site up without taking up any bandwidth itself.

This is what happens the first time a user visits our site, but now that we've decided what we want to happen then, we've got to consider what happens if the user has visited our site before. If they have, it will probably have been cached into the browser's memory. More importantly, the user will have already seen the intro once, and is probably using the browser's *back* button to get back to your Flash site, perhaps after having visited some links from it. If the site is cached, we want the preloader to send the user back to the main site.

Even some professional designers don't know how to handle this situation adequately, and end up opening all the links from their sites in a new browser window, cluttering up the user's desktop with all sorts of windows and generally giving Flash sites a bad name.

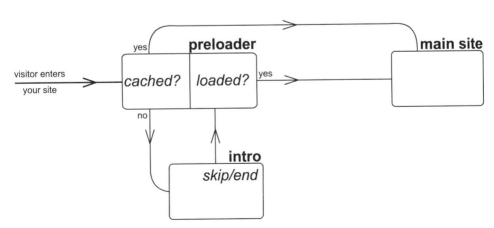

The preloader shown in the flow diagram comes in two sections. The first part looks at whether the main site is already cached. This asks "Is the site still in the browser's memory?" If the user has visited the site before, it will be still in the browser's memory. In this case, the preloader doesn't have to do anything except send the user seamlessly back into the main site.

If the visitor hasn't been to the site recently and it's not in the browser cache, the preloader should hand over to the intro. The intro will attempt to play, but if the user decides to skip straight to the main site, the preloader should be cope with the situation if either of these things happen:

- Not enough of the main site has yet loaded to run, and the user should then be given some sort of countdown to how long they have to wait before they can enter the main site.

- The main site has fully loaded in the background, and the preloader should take the user seamlessly from the intro to the main site.

If the user watches the intro all the way through, the main site will have loaded by the time the intro ends and they will be seamlessly dropped into the main site... the user will never realize their visit was controlled by a preloader because they never saw it. That's the trouble with good ergonomic design – it's designed not to be noticed!

ActionScripting our Preloader and Cache Detector

The preloader will use a couple of the movieclip properties that we met in the last section: `_framesloaded` and `_totalframes`.

Open **preloader.fla** from the download file for this chapter and make sure there's a **intro.swf** file in the same folder/directory as **preloader.fla**. This is important because the preloader needs the SWF file to work. You'll see that this FLA consists of two parts:

- A preloader and main site that are the first and second scenes in **preloader.fla**

- An introduction FLA, **intro.fla**.

Test the movie. You'll see a short repeating animation taken from the stun:design web site. I've set the JPEG quality of the bitmaps in this sequence to 100% so that this is fairly bandwidth heavy. This may not be all that much, but until we add anything else, this constitutes our main site (you might have guessed that from the text that says **main site**...).

Testing the preloader as we've just done makes Flash ignore bandwidth constraints and assume that the full web site is already in memory, as if it was in the browser cache once you'd been to the site already. Because of this, our movie skips straight to our main site screen, without showing us the preloader screen or the intro that we went through in Chapter 3.

To simulate loading up the site for the first time, stay in test movie mode and select 56k modem with **Debug > 56K(4.7Kb/s)**. Now use **View > Show Streaming**. You'll see the intro for the first time. As this runs, notice the green band on the bandwidth profiler.

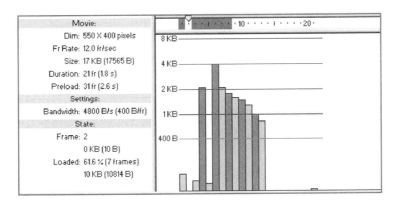

This is your main site loading in the background. Don't press the new *Skip* button at the bottom right of the intro just yet, and watch what happens when the intro finishes: the presentation switches straight to our **main site** animation. In this case, the preloader knows that the main site has loaded in, so when the intro hands back to the preloader, it jumps seamlessly to the main site.

What happens if we want to jump straight to the main site from the intro before the main site has loaded? Well, to handle this, you'll have to be pretty quick with a 56K modem, because the main movie is still fairly empty. Set the **Debug** menu to a 14.4K or 28.8K modem, and use streaming again (the **Show Streaming** selection is a toggle, so you may have to select it twice). Hit the *Skip* button before the main site loads up.

This time you actually get to see the preloader. As you can see, it shows a little bar graph and a percent loaded meter that increases with time, giving a visual and numerical progress of how much of the site has loaded, and therefore an indication of how long the user will have to wait:

How does this work? Let's look at the preloader in detail.

The Preloader

Bring up the **preloader** scene in **preloader.fla**. If you want to attach this preloader to an existing site, you'll have to add this first scene as the first scene of your FLA, although you won't have change anything in the site itself.

The preloader consists of three layers:

- **Actions** as usual contains the actions.

- **Meter** contains the bar graph.

- **Text** contains all the text.

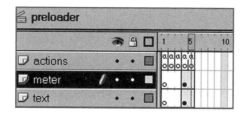

Frames 1 to 3 in all layers only contain actions, so let's start by looking at those.

Frame 1 contains actions that look to see whether this SWF has been loaded into cache before. If it has, it will jump to the main site, in this case to the scene **main**, frame **startmain** (although you would obviously need to change this if you dropped the preloader into another site). If this SWF hasn't been loaded before, the preloader assumes that the user may want to see the intro and starts loading that at level 1.

Here are the actions:

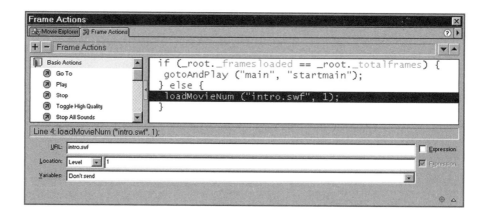

Let's take this line by line.

```
if_root._framesloaded == _root._totalframes
```

By preceding the property with _root, we're asking Flash to look at properties of the main timeline. We're comparing the frames loaded with the total frames. If both amounts are equal, (as signified by ==) Flash knows that all the frames are loaded in. We haven't told Flash to start loading our site yet, so the only way that this could have occurred is if the user has visited the site before. If this is the case, we skip the intro completely with:

```
GotoAndPlay ("main", "startmain");
```

This goes to the main site, which is in the next scene.

```
} else }
    loadMovieNum ("intro.swf", 1);
```

These lines set up an alternative course of action for Flash if it finds that all the frames haven't loaded. We start loading **intro.swf** in the level immediately above us. As you'll remember from Chapter 5, the base level is level 0, so the level immediately above us would be level 1.

Select this frame and bring up the **Actions** window. Take a look at the stage and you'll see that it's empty, so the loaded SWF will be shown against a blank background.

The actions in Frame 2 simply stop the preloader with a `stop();` action:

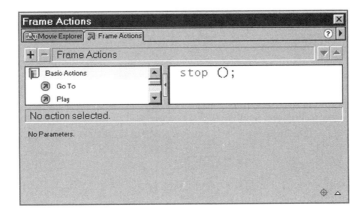

In the first frame we gave control to **intro.swf** if the site hasn't been loaded before. Here, we're stopping **intro.swf**, again in a frame with an empty stage. That means that we'll stay here in frame 2 until the intro finishes. Just because we've stopped doesn't mean that **preloader.swf** has stopped loading. At this point, **intro.swf** is loading as per our instructions in frame 1, and **preloader.swf** our current file, is also loading.

Let me take you back to the relevant part of the flow diagram that we saw earlier:

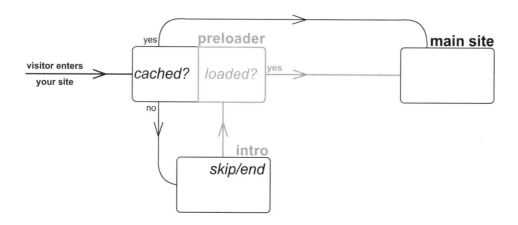

The first part of this asks the question *Cached?* and specifies what should happen if the answer to this question is yes or no. The actions we've been looking at in frames 1 and 2 address this, using `if` and `else` commands to tell Flash to go straight to the main site if the site has been cached, and to start loading up the intro sequence if it hasn't.

Let's move on to dealing with the next section of our flow chart: the intro.

The Intro

The intro has two things in it that will give control back to the preloader: the **skip** button and the last frame of the intro. The last frame has this control because by the time we get there we want to go to the main site anyway because there's nothing left to do. **intro.fla** has so far appeared in our **preloader.swf** courtesy of its SWF which we've loaded in at level 1.

If you go and load **intro.fla** into Flash, select the **skip** button and bring up the **Actions** window, you'll see this script:

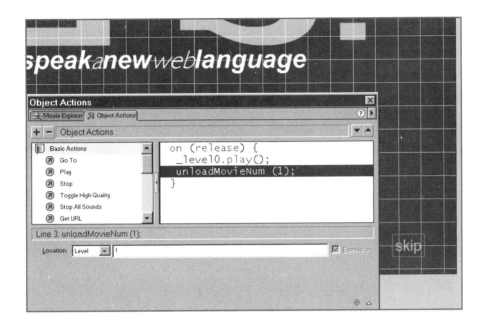

```
on (release) {
_level0.play();
```

These lines restart the preloader by returning to level0.

`unloadMovieNum (1);` simply unloads the intro.

These actions mean that the intro will not only stop running, but will also stop loading *even if it's partway though its download*. This is a big advantage: as soon as the user decides they don't want to bother with the intro anymore, the intro is discarded completely and all the bandwidth then goes towards loading up the main site.

Back in **preloader.fla**, there's one more blank frame before the **loading essential components** text and bar graph appears on the stage: frame 3.

Select frame 3 on the **actions** layer and bring up the **Actions** window:

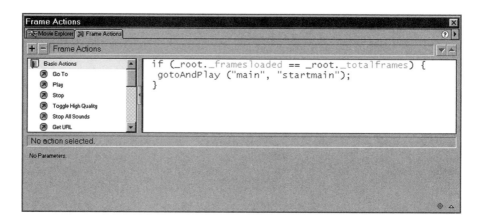

You'll see that the actions here are identical to those in frame 1, except that they're missing:

```
    } else {
        loadMovieNum ("intro.swf", 1);
    }
```

By now, either the intro has finished or the user has skipped the intro so there's no need for these lines. In either case, our preloader scene has just been re-started by the _level0.play();, and is now at frame 3.

If we return to our preloader flowchart, we can see that we've dealt with the *cached?* and the *intro skip/end* choices. The only part we have left to deal with is the *loaded?* box.

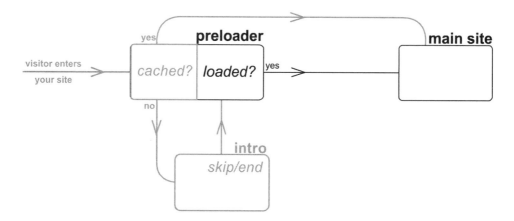

We can see from the flowchart that we need Flash to notice when the main site has loaded, and jump to it only when this has occurred.

Frame 3 checks whether the main site has loaded with the same `if` action that we saw in frame 1, checking whether `_framesloaded` is equal to `_totalframes` for the root timeline. If it has, the `gotoAndPlay` command takes the use directly to the main site without seeing the preloader. We're using the same actions here that we used in frame 1 because we're looking to do the same thing: take the user to the main site if it has loaded. Instead of throwing an `else` action to take us somewhere else if this hasn't happened, as we did in frame 1, we can simply leave the timeline to naturally progress to the next frame, which contains the preloader bar graph and text.

Frames 4 and 5 contain ActionScripts to continuously monitor how much of the site has loaded, and jump to the main site as soon as it has fully loaded up. It contains a percentage bar to show the user how much of the site has loaded. Making a basic animated bar graph like this is actually very easy and we're going to go through this now. It will be easy enough to transfer our preloader into another site by copying it across as the first scene, as we discussed earlier, but we may well need to change the bar graph to fit in with the style of the new site.

Creating an Animated Bar Graph

1. Create a long rectangle roughly the shape of your bar graph, and make the fill color and outline color the colors you want for the bar graph and bezel (the border of the bar graph):

2. Now select the rectangle's fill without selecting the outline, and convert it to a new movieclip symbol called **bargraph**. Double-click on it to enter **edit in place** mode.

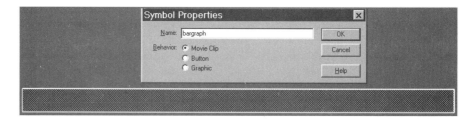

The new movieclip will have its center – shown by the **+** symbol – at the center of the rectangle. This is not what we want, because we only want to scale it from one end, that is left to right. The solution is to move the rectangle so that its left edge is touching the **+** denoting the center of the movieclip, as shown.

3. Move the rectangle to the right by selecting the rectangle and using the arrow keys to move it (holding down **<shift>** and an arrow key will make the rectangle move faster). Zoom in to make sure that your positioning is exact. Make sure the center point is just touching the rectangle's left edge (you could also use the **Info** panel if you have problems). If you don't get it right, the bar graph will move as well as get bigger when you scale it, so it's worth double checking.

4. Go back to the main timeline and move the rectangle back inside its outline bezel. You'll notice that the **+** symbol is now on the left-hand side, rather than in the middle. Give the **bargraph** movieclip an instance name **bar** with the **Instance** panel:

5. We've now got to sort out the ActionScript to drive it all. Go to frame 4 and bring up the **Actions** window. We can use _framesLoaded and _totalFrames from the **Properties** section in the **Actions** window to give us the figures we need to work out our percentages. We need to assign both to a variable, so our first two lines of code read:

```
framesLoaded = _level0._framesloaded;
totalFrames = _level0._totalframes;
```

These lines assign variables framesLoaded and totalFrames to _level0._framesloaded and _level0._totalframes respectively. I could have used _root instead of _level0, but because this is a multi level presentation, I want to keep it obvious that I'm talking about the root timeline for level zero, and not the root timeline for any other level.

6. For a percent loaded value, we need to do a calculation that works out the value of *(framesLoaded / totalFrames) x 100*. In ActionScript, we specify a variable to contain the percent loaded value and then tell it to perform the calculation, so we end up with:

```
percentLoaded = ((framesLoaded/totalFrames)*100 );
```

7. It's going to simplify things a great deal if the result of this calculation is a rounded figure that eliminates decimals. Fortunately, Flash has an object (in **Objects > Math > Math.round**) which does just this. We need to add it to our script just before the calculation, like this:

```
percentLoaded = Math.round ((framesLoaded/totalFrames)*100 );
```

8. The bar graph is at an _xscale of 100%. (You can check this via the **Transform** panel if you don't believe me.) As the last line of our code, we need to enter:

```
bar._xscale = percent loaded;
```

so that the width of the bar changes as our SWF loads in.

9. We now need to create our text. Use the Text tool to write in **loading essential components...** or whatever you feel is fitting. For the numerical percentage value that you see on the screen, we need to create a text box and specify it as dynamic text. For this dynamic text, we also use the `percentloaded` value that we so carefully created earlier, so you can just enter `percentLoaded` into the variable box in the **Text Options** panel as you see here. Add a percentage sign in the correct font just after the dynamic text box and we're done.

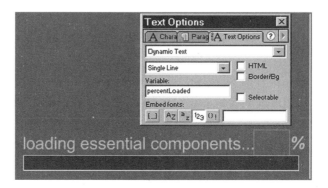

We've just been through all the code needed for our nice bar graph and text and have placed this in frame 4 of our **actions** layer. What happens when the bar graph and text get to 100%? The next frame needs to make the decision between jumping to the main site when this happens, or jumping back to frame 4 if it hasn't. To be able to reference frame 4, we need to give it a label – I've used `preloaderloop`. We then need to use an `else… if` action to tell Flash to go to the main site when it has loaded, or return to frame 4 (labeled `preloaderloop`) if it hasn't. As before, we're going to use

```
(frames Loaded == total Frames)
```

to tell us whether the main site has loaded. This means that we need something like this:

```
if (framesLoaded == totalFrames) {
    gotoAndPlay ("main", 1);
} else {
    gotoAndPlay ("preloaderloop");
}
```

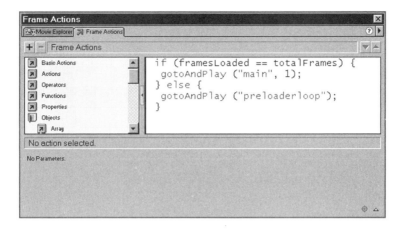

```
if (framesLoaded == totalFrames) {
  gotoAndPlay ("main", 1);
} else {
  gotoAndPlay ("preloaderloop");
}
```

10. Enter this all into frame 5, test your movie and it should all be working.

This example shows you how properties can be used not just to create animations but to tell you something about what the Flash player itself is doing. The preloader uses only three properties (the `framesLoaded` and `totalFrames` of the root timeline for level zero, and the `xscale` property of the bar graph) to make some pretty complex decisions on how to manage the loading of the site.

There are a number of things you can do to this preloader when your ActionScripting skills exceed the fairly simple methods we've used here to make it even more efficient. The two main options aren't preloading the entire main site before jumping to it and using the preloader as an advanced bandwidth manager.

Not preloading the entire main site before jumping to it means loading the first part of the main site, making sure that all essential components are in by then, and then jumping to the main site before it's 100% loaded. Obviously, this means that the user gets to see the site quicker. To force Flash to load up stuff before it's actually needed, you can stick it off stage somewhere, and possibly scale it down or set its `visible` property to `False`.

To turn your preloader into an advanced bandwidth manager means splitting the main site up into more than one SWF. The preloader will look at the current level's SWF, and if that has loaded, loads the next one. Each loaded level is 'parked' at a blank first frame so it's invisible, and the site only shows them (by running them with a `play();` action) when the user requests them. If the user requests a SWF that hasn't loaded, the manager discards the currently loading SWF, and starts loading the requested one, and restarts the loading of any missing SWFs later.

This advanced type of loader is very rarely seen on the Web. Obviously people still seem to think doing big intros and heavy Flash sites is more important than actually managing their efficient loading! To turn the preloader into this manager doesn't actually take much (hint – try a **do** loop that carries on running until all the levels are loaded fully. If the user forces the SWFs to be run out of sequence, re-run the loop from the start again, making sure that it skips any SWFs that are already loaded).

Now that we've used properties in a sort of housekeeping/site loading/check what's going on sort of way I think we can move on to show you some more fun things. At the end of this chapter I'll give you a hands on exercise that involves a scrollbar for navigation. For now sit back while I show you what lies behind a dynamic showreel on stun:design.

The stun:design Showreel

There are a lot of sites out there that use dynamic animation in a *functional* way. That's to say, the animation serves a purpose rather than just acting as eye candy. New navigation methods are perhaps one of the most useful ways to use ActionScript. This following example uses a sideways scrolling motion as part of a show-reel or portfolio. At the moment the show-reel contains pictures of myself and various friends in our younger years, but I guess you can use it for something more practical, like showing your current portfolio.

The showreel is in the zip download file for this chapter as **showreel.fla**. Load it up and test it to see what it does. Remember the ball scroll we did in Chapter 1, where the ball simply followed the x position of the cursor? Well, this is just a more polished version of the same thing. The ball scroll was done with two lines of ActionScript and this doesn't take that many more.

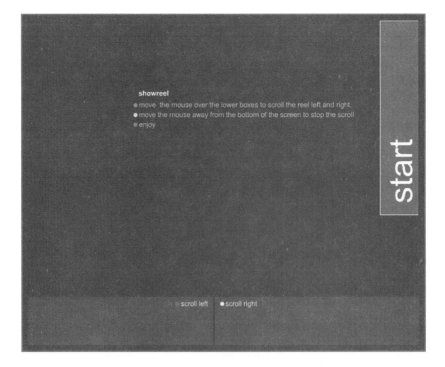

The site starts off with the screen pictured, with a set of instructions about how to use the showreel. Roll over the **scroll left** area and the reel will begin to show itself, as the gray block marked **start** glides from right to left, showing its pictures. The scrolling increases in speed as you move the cursor more to the left of the **scroll left** box, or more to the right of the **scroll right** box. If you move the cursor up towards any particular picture and out of the **scroll left** box, the scrolling will stop.

This is the type of site navigation that had long-time ActionScripters gazing in awe when it was first used with earlier versions of Flash. It's actually very easy to implement the basic scrolling action. If you open the library in **showreel.fla**, you'll see that there's very little in there. There's a single movieclip that contains the scrolling pictures and text, and the bitmaps for the pictures themselves:

If you do use bitmaps like this, be careful to individually optimize them. In case you need a quick reminder of how that's done, here's a brief step by step run through. In the library, double-click on the bitmap to bring up the bitmap properties window. Select **photo(jpeg)** from the **Compression:** drop-down and uncheck the **Use imported jpeg data** checkbox. You'll see a **Quality:** entry box. Try reducing the current value to various new values and click on the test button to see whether the picture quality is acceptable at each try. Sometimes selecting **lossless** from the **Compression:** drop-down menu can give you better compression:quality ratios, particularly for bitmaps with few color variations (that is solid colors). Test for this by selecting **lossless** for compression and then hitting the test button.

The ActionScript in **showreel.fla** is looking at where the mouse *x* position is in relation to a center line, and moving the **reel** movieclip based on that distance. The direction (left or right) takes care of itself as long as we also consider the *sign* of this distance – whether it's positive or negative.

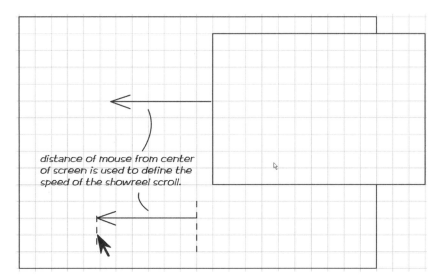

In terms of the ActionScript, we're only interested in the **actions** and **reel** layers, although the **diagnostics** layer was used in setting up some values for the ActionScript. (The arrow ⬆ on **Layer 3** shows that it's a mask layer and the 🕑 symbol on the **reel** layer shows that that's the layer being masked.)

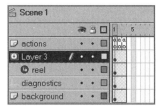

The layer **reel** contains the showreel movieclip, which I've given an instance name of **reel**.

Frame 1 of the **actions** layer contains the initialization of some variables we'll be using:

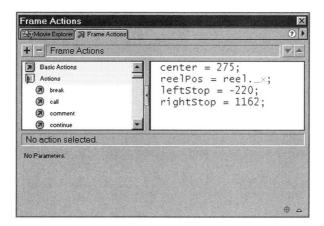

`center` is the position of the center line, which is exactly half way across the screen and so can be calculated from screen width/2. In the default screen width this is 550/2 = 275 so we have the line

```
center = 275;
```

`reelPos` is the postion of the **reel** movieclip. Rather than give it a number, I've just looked at the movieclip's *x* position property, `reel._x` and assigned this to `reelpos`, so we have:

```
reelPos = reel._x;
```

I'm not interested in the *y* position of **reel**, because we're only moving the movieclip from left to right. We're not moving it up and down at all, so it will always stay at the same y value.

We need to have the **reel** movieclip scrolling across the stage, but we need it to stop once it has scrolled entirely to the left or to the right. The user will have no interest in seeing a blank screen where the movieclip was for any length of time. We need to set the maximum leftmost and rightmost positions of the **reel** movieclip. That's where these lines come in:

```
leftStop = -220;
rightStop = 1162;
```

If you're wondering how I got these figures, I'll have to be honest and say that I came up with them only after I'd got the basic scroll to work. I'll explain things in that order too – I think things will make much more sense once you've seen how the thing works.

Before we start working on the code for the scroll, we need to make sure that we're very clear on what we need to do – remember, if it doesn't work on paper, it won't work when you code it. We need a diagram, so here's a cleaned up version of the sketch I drew to figure out how this scroll movement should work:

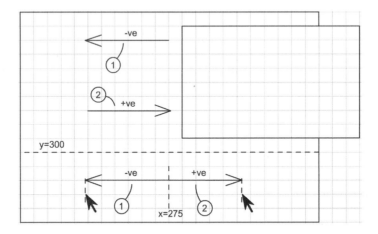

If we look at the actions attached to frame 2, we'll see the heart of the scrolling ActionScript. It may look a little daunting, but this is **all of it** - just 8 lines of ActionScript:

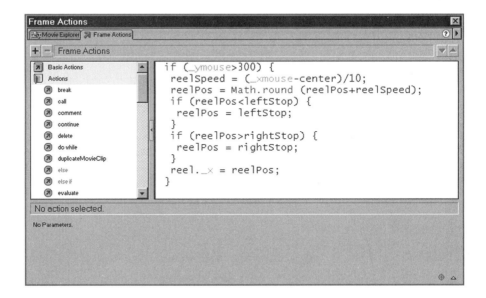

```
if (_ymouse>300) {
  reelSpeed = (_xmouse-center)/10;
  reelPos = Math.round (reelPos+reelSpeed);
  if (reelPos<leftStop) {
    reelPos = leftStop;
  }
  if (reelPos>rightStop) {
    reelPos = rightStop;
  }
  reel._x = reelPos;
}
```

We'll go through this line by line, which will show you that things aren't quite so scary once we break them down.

We need to tell Flash when to scroll and when we're not interested in moving **reel** from right to left or left to right. We can do this by checking to see whether the mouse is over or under the dotted line in our diagram, where the *y* value = 300.

If the mouse's *y* value is greater than 300 or under the line in the sketch, (remember that *y* values increase as we move down in Flash) then we want to scroll. If the mouse's *y* value is less than 300, then the mouse is over the line in the sketch and we don't want to scroll, we want to stay where we are thank you very much.

So we have the first line:

```
if (_ymouse>300) {
```

This `if` statement contains the rest of our code which will only run and let us scroll if that `_ymouse>300` condition is found to be true. If it isn't, the code won't run and nothing will happen.

According to our diagram, we now need to relate the distance between the mouse and the centre line to the speed at which the reel scrolls. In other words, we want the reel to scroll faster the further away from the center line the mouse gets. So we get this line:

```
reelSpeed = (_xmouse-center);
```

Except, in the finished FLA, it is:

```
reelSpeed = (_xmouse-center)/10;
```

The original line made it scroll too fast, so I just divided it by ten to make it scroll at a more sensible speed.

When we initialized some variables in the first frame of the **actions** layer earlier, we set the center as the middle line (275). So, if the mouse is to the left (shown by ① in the sketch) then the `_xmouse-center` will work out negative, and if our mouse is to the right of center (as in situation ②), we'll get a positive speed.

We need to tell the **reel** movieclip whether to move left or right by working out whether the `reelSpeed` that we got from the last line is negative or positive. If it's negative, we want **reel** to move left. If it's positive, we want it to move to the right. So we get this line, which sets the position of the **reel** movieclip to the previous position plus the value of `reelSpeed` from the last line:

```
reelPos = Math.round (reelPos+reelSpeed);
```

We now need to do something with the leftStop and rightStop variables that we set earlier. We need to know whether reelPos is going to go beyond their values. If it is, then we need to hold them at these values and let them go no further, so we have two if statements like this:

```
if (reelPos<leftStop) {
    reelPos = leftStop;
}
if (reelPos>rightStop) {
    reelPos = rightStop;
}
```

I got the values for these end-stops for the scroll action by scrolling **reel** around while looking at how reelPos changed. I did this with a test harness, which had some dynamic text set to show the changing value of reelPos. Temporarily return **diagnostics** to a normal layer by right-clicking on **diagnostics** and unchecking **Guide** by left-clicking it.

Now test the movie and you'll see a little window just above and a little to the left of **scroll left** which gives you the current *x* value of **reel** – it's 734 here:

I simply scrolled left until **reel** was about to disappear from the screen, read off the value and then scrolled right until **reel** was about to disappear from the screen, read off the value and assigned the two values to leftStop and rightStop in frame 1.

The last thing we need to do with our script is to actually make **reel** scroll – no, we haven't done that yet! We need to use the value of `reelPos` that we gained earlier to set the actual position of **reel**. Again, we're obviously only dealing with *x* values, because **reel** doesn't move up or down at all. This line is all we need:

```
reel._x = reelPos;
```

If you have a look at the actions in frame 3, you'll see the line

```
gotoAndPlay ("loop");
```

I've labeled frame 2 `loop` so this line simply creates a continuous loop that constantly checks for scrolling input and makes it all happen.

You now have the solid basis of a side-scroller – some professional sites use extras like acceleration and colored blocks moving about at different scroll speeds with the main bitmaps to create a parallax effect but that's just window dressing.

I'll round off this chapter with a look at how I've implemented and adapted all this scrolling business within stun:design. There are some pretty involved step-by-step instructions here, so get ready to practice what you've learned.

The stun:design Web Site

In these last three chapters I'll be showing you how all the ideas that we've been discussing came together to create the finished stun:design site. We'll be adding the final content in Chapters 10 and 11, but here I'll show you the process I went through to plan the site structure behind that. Up until now, the site has been ludicrously long and we've had to use the scrolling action of the browser to see all of it. You'll remember that at the initial planning stage I had the idea of using a 'side scroller' effect. As the finale to this chapter I'll show you how I created that, bringing in issues of linking movieclips that we've discussed in earlier chapters, as well as some of the interactivity that we've been looking at here.

You can see the finished product of what we're about to do here in the final FLA for this section **stunScroll1.fla** but if you want to follow what I do from the ground up use **stun_basic.fla** that we met in Chapter 5 as your starting point.

If you look at the library in **stun_basic.fla**, you'll see that I've used a naming strategy in the library. Most movieclip names are preceded with **mc**, symbols with **bu** and graphic symbols with **sy**, so you have **sy.lines** or **mc.thunder_spark** for example. It's well worth keeping to this (and changing any that don't to fit in with this strategy) so that you can find things more easily – buttons, movieclips and symbols will now be listed together because the library sorts alphabetically. You can also give closely related but different symbols the 'same name', such as **mc.apple**, **bu.apple** and **sy.apple**. We've not got there yet, but you'll see when we start to create specialized movieclip versions over the next two chapters how useful it is to create a meaningful subdivision. I've used **sp.** for sprite movieclips and **ma.** for movieclips that only contain ActionScripts such as the behavior movieclips we'll look at in the next chapter.

We'll add the scrolling finishing touches in a moment but the best place to start is with the structure of how things at stun:design fit together behind the scenes.

Creating Structure

As I prepared to build the side scroller, I realized that I had one main problem to deal with. I knew that I needed to fix the finished stun site so that the only parts of the site that move are those that need to move on screen or off screen. Any other content shouldn't have to move at all.

With the showreel example that included those cute photos we looked at earlier, the whole movieclip with all the photos in is loaded up at once. In other words, moving from left to right means moving content that couldn't be seen. The photos were relatively small, but you can see that if we start talking about moving an entire web site with animations that we can't see playing, then everything gets bandwidth inefficient to say the least.

I knew that I needed to start by dividing the site from one long strip into separate pages so that the user sees one page of content at a time. Those pages had to be separate to make it easy for me to effectively update parts of the site, modifying one part without having to change everything. That's the theory of modular design working in practice.

Open **stun_basic.fla** from Chapter 5 and I'll take you through what I did.

Creating Separate Pages

1. Before we start, select the 'this way' chevron on the far left and delete it, along with its associated library symbol. Delete the empty layers **starfield**, **vertline**, **hozline** as well.

2. Create three new movieclips called **mc.page01**, **mc.page02** and **mc.page03**.

   We're going to do some copying and pasting now. Don't worry too much about the size of the three pages you've just created at the moment because we're going to sort that out later by using **Modify > Movie**. This will change the size of everything in the entire FLA, so it's far easier to move everything first and then change the size.

   mc.page01 will be the initial Splash screen, designed to appear soon after the site starts loading. We'll create that now.

3. Select the big **stun:** text from the far left of the current main stage, and the **stun:** definition that appears above it and then copy the selection to the clipboard. Hit the ***Delete*** key to delete the selection from the screen after you've copied it.

4. Open **mc.page01**, paste in the selection and position it so that the left-hand side of the graphic starts at the registration point (the little + that denotes the origin of each movieclip), like this:

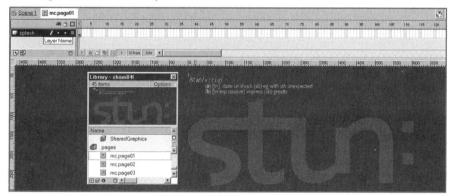

This makes sure that the _x property of each page is being counted from the left edge of each movieclip. You'll find that you have to do some scaling of the two items that you've cut and pasted (with the **Transform** panel) to make things fit.

mc.page02 is the intro, telling us about stun.

5. Create this in the same way that you created **mc.page01**. Cut the material from the middle of the main stage screen – principally the white stun logo and the **setyourbrowswertostun** text next to it – and paste it into **mc.page02**. Again, you need to line up the left-hand side of the graphic with the registration point like this:

As you'll see from the screenshot, I've included a new symbol in **mc.page02**, which is the left-hand side of the radar screen. The easiest way to do this is to duplicate the original radar symbol (**sy.lines**) and enter **edit in place** mode. Once you've done this, you can delete the right-hand half of the duplicate by zooming in and deleting the links between the left-hand and right-hand halves and then *Shift*-selecting and deleting. Then drag the new symbol out of the library into **mc.page02** and give it an Alpha value of around 40%.

mc.page03 is the show-page, with the stun portfolio and other goodies on it.

6. For this, copy across the entire original radar screen and all the buttons and associated graphics on the right-hand side. Don't forget to line the left-hand side of the radar graphic up with the registration point:

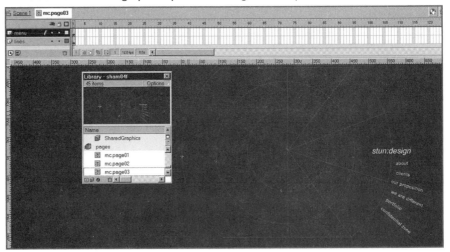

You should now have a completely blank main stage, with the exception of the lightning set of bitmaps across the top, which we'll come to in a bit (if the 'this way' chevron is still there remember that you should have deleted it in step 1.)

We've now created some sort of structure for the site, which relates back to what we talked of in Chapter 5 where we worked with **linking movieclips**. You may be used to seeing pages defined as separate scenes, but we've said that having them defined as separate movieclips is a definite advantage for ActionScript. Sure, with a scene-based site ActionScript can control which frame we're in, but it can do a whole lot more with pages that are movieclips because they have properties that we can change to alter their appearance or running order directly. We can make them appear or fade, change their size or color or orientation, make them act like turning pages, or even... make them scroll under the control of ActionScript.

Let's get back to work

7. Create a new layer called **pages** in the main timeline, select **View > Magnification > Show all** so that you can see it all and paste each of the three movieclips into it in roughly the same positions as they originally were on the main stage. You might need to do some more scaling to get them to fit, but don't fine tune their positions yet – that's the next step!

Our final movie will be an 800x600 size, the size of a browser set to 'fullscreen', so we want each of our pages to be no bigger than that. We'll create some guide lines to physically remind us how much of the web site can be seen within a single 800x600 screen, and will then scale each page to fit within an area of that size. Make sure that Show Guides is enabled before you start.

8. Still in the **pages** layer, with view set to **Show all**, make sure that rulers are turned on and snapping turned off. Then click and hold on the vertical ruler and with the mouse still down, drag away to the right. You'll see a solid green line appear. When you hit 800 on the horizontal ruler, release the mouse. Do this again to create a guide line at 1600 and 2400. The lines are there as helpers, and show a full 800x600 screen each, so you can now see how much room you have for each page. Scale each of the page movieclips so that they use the available screen real estate effectively, without going over the demarcation lines:

9. In the root timeline, layers **menu**, **lines** and **text** are now empty, so delete them. Your root timeline should look like this:

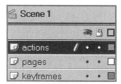

actions is currently empty but it won't be for long. **pages** contains your page movies, and **keyframes** contains the thunder bitmap strip.

If you test the movie now, you'll still be using the browser's scroll bars, but we now have the basic framework in place to carry on and do something *much* more interesting.

We've prepared the ground to do something with our site navigation by breaking it up into modular pieces, and now we've got to do some planning.

Navigation Overview

For a scroller we need *somewhere to scroll to*, and a *where we are now* for each page. As you can see in the diagram, we have our pages occupying one of three positions:

- The main browser window **front**

- The off-screen **left**

- The off-screen **right**

We'll always see **front** in our browser, but we can tell ActionScript to display our windows in **front** or **left** or **right**.

We have to set the co-ordinates of these three pages. Each page is 800 pixels across, but we also want to leave a gap between the pages to make absolutely sure that only one page is ever displayed in whatever browser the page is being displayed. A gap of 400 pixels is about right. So, 800+400gives us 1200, which is where we'll put the **left** screen. The **right** screen will be positioned at –1200. **front** is the viewable screen area, at x=0:

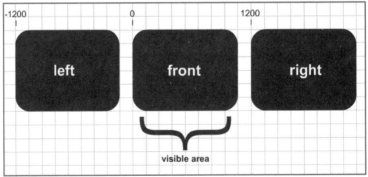

Why do it this way?

Well, imagine that our splash screen is in **left**, our intro is in **front**, and our main screen is in **right**. Intro is in front at the moment so that's what the user can see. The user then decides to move on from our intro to the main screen. To do this intro scrolls left into **left** and the main screen scrolls left into **front**, so that all the user can see is the main screen.

The splash screen which was in **left** isn't loaded any more because if the user really wants to go and see the splash screen, they'll have to scroll past the intro (now in **left**) first. So, you only have to move two pages which makes for a quicker site than moving three.

Now that we have the structure sorted, we need to design an interface to move around it. I rather liked the scrollbar interface that we came up with for the sound controllers so we're going to re-use the meter from the last chapter and modify it to produce our **navigator** bar.

The Menubar

1. Open **soundtrackcontrol.fla** from the last chapter's download file as a library, and drag the **soundcontrol** movieclip over onto the stage of your basic stun web site FLA, and then delete it. Although you've deleted it from the stage, the act of dragging it onto the stage forced Flash to put it in the library as well. You'll see **bargraph**, **soundcontrol** and **meter** appear in your library. For neatness, put all three movieclips into a new folder called **scroller stuff**.

> Notice how modularity has saved the day yet again, by saving me some time and allowing me to re-use previous work, which will save you time and money on every job when you're doing this for a living.

The sound controller consisted of a bar graph that could be dragged to any position 0 to 100, but for the navigation I don't want this. I want a scrollbar that 'snaps' to three positions corresponding to the three pages. I also want some indication of the page that we'll navigate to on the navigation scrollbar. Some more planning to do, I guess.

I'm willing to forgo my embarrassment for the sake of the education of others, so have a look at my planning sketch, followed by the final effect:

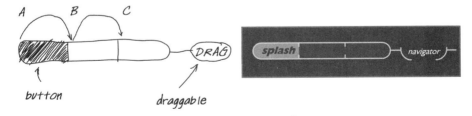

The sketch may be untidy, but it's a quick and precise description of the functionality I'm after, and when you're doing this for a living, what more do you need?

What I want to happen is that when the user drags and releases the bar/button, it will snap to the nearest position, A, B or C, corresponding to the three pages (as shown on my sketch above). The text **splash** should also change to reflect the current page location once the visitor has released the mouse button.

The sound control bargraph looks like the diagram shown. This isn't what we want because the bar is too long and can be dragged to a value of zero (just look at the FLA for Chapter 8 to see what I mean; you can drag the bar off the left hand screen area totally so that it disappears).

2. Go into your library and double-click on **soundcontrol** to enter **edit in place** mode, and make some changes. Delete the top half and replace the **pan control** text with **navigator**. I've given you some before and after pictures here:

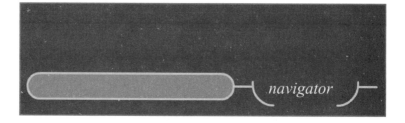

3. In **soundcontrol**, delete the **actions** and **buttons** layers and all of their contents. Re-name it as **menubar** in the library.

    Rather than have a bar graph, we'll use a 'sliding button' for our navigator (as I showed in my pencil sketch earlier). The slider will snap to one of the positions A, B or C when released, so we need to make it approximately a third of the length of the total meter.

4. Go into **bargraph** and make your bar – but not your button – 36 pixels long. You'll probably have to hide the **button** layer to get at the bar. Use the **Info** panel if you don't trust your ruler/eye combination, or use some more of those guides as we have in the screenshot to make things clearer for you:

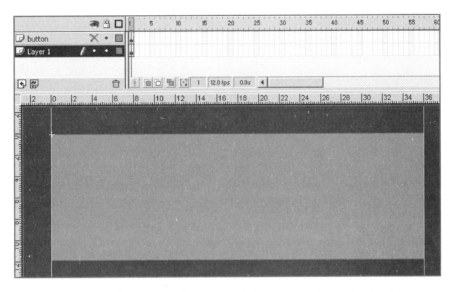

5. Make sure that the registration point of the new bar is on the far left edge so that we can constrain the lowest value that the dragbar can go to as 0 (the left-most of our three positions, or position A) and the highest as 72 (the right-most position, C).

6. Still in **bargraph**, add another layer. Call it **text** and bring that layer to the top. In layer **text** we need to add a dynamic text field covering the same area as our 36 pixel bar. Draw your box, bring up the **Text Options** window, set it to **Dynamic Text** and select **Single Line** from the drop-down menu, and enter menutitle into the **Variable** field, as pictured. Check the lower-case box as well. I used the humanist521XBdBT font and italicised it.

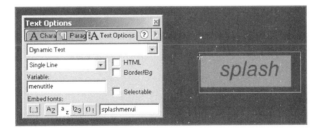

We want ActionScript to set the text to read **splash**, **intro**, or **main**, depending on whether it's forced to snap into position A, B or C. We'll create the 'snap' by looking at the button position pos, and using an if action to force it to go to the nearest position as soon as it's released.

Look at the diagram, then we can see these three possibilities illustrated by **i**, **ii**, and **iii**.

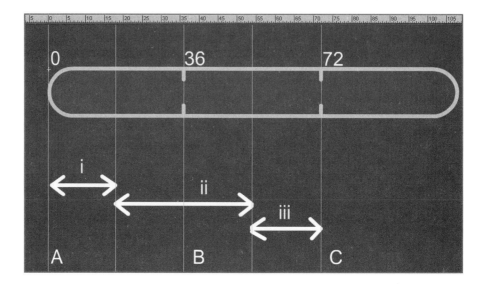

7. Unlock the **button** layer, select the invisible button and bring up the Actions window. There will still be some actions in there, from the button's previous incarnation in the last chapter. Delete them all and enter:

    ```
    on (press) {
        startDrag ("", false, 0, 0, 72, 0);
    }
    on (release, releaseOutside) {
        stopDrag ();
    ```

    This sets up the drag and constrains the limits of the drag to 0 and 72, as we talked about earlier.

8. On the next line, initialize our variable:

    ```
    pos = this._x;
    ```

9. If `pos` is less than 18 (and therefore the button's left edge is within area **i** in the diagram), `pos` needs to be forced back to position x = 0 or position A when the button is released:

    ```
    if (pos<18) {
        pos = 0;
        menutitle = "splash";
    ```

10. If pos is between 18 and 54 (via the else if, making the button within area **ii**), pos is forced to go to x = 36 or position B:

```
} else if (pos<54) {
    pos = 36;
    menutitle = "intro";
```

11. If pos is greater than 54 (which it must be by the time the if gets to the final else, because it's now 'not less than 54'), the button is within area **iii**, and is forced to go to x = 72, or Position C:

```
} else {
    pos = 72;
    menutitle = "main";
}
    this._x = pos;
}
```

12. Your **Object Actions** window should now look like this:

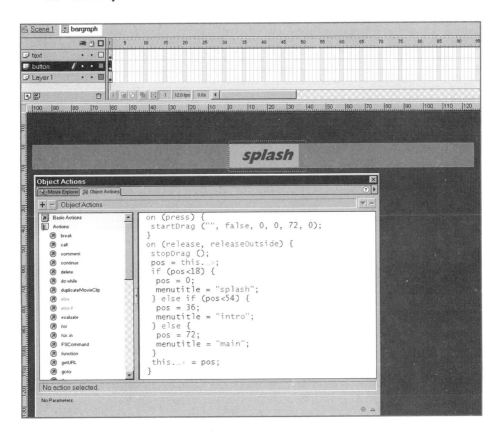

There is a further complication for us to address in the movieclip **meter**. The original soundcontrol passed back a value from 0 to 100, whereas we want a value corresponding to the number of pages to allow selection of pages 1, 2 or 3.

We need to extend the movieclip to include a simple loop that includes the following script action at frame 2, which divides the scale into 3 values only; 1-3 (I have to add 1 because as it stands, the division would give 0, 1 or 2). We also need to send the result stunpage to the _root timeline, making it a variable accessible to everything, because it's an important value for the site.

13. Go to frame 2 of the **actions** layer in **meter** and delete the value = graph._x; line and replace it with:

```
_root.stunPage = Math.round(graph._x/36)+1;
```

Your actions window should now look like this:

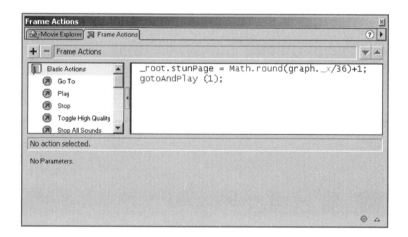

14. Select the **bezel** layer and add some little 'pips' to the scale on the meter to give an indication of the three places the scroll bar will snap back to when released. The little pips need to go at the 36 and 72 pixel mark:

15. Make the whole bar draggable in **menubar** by adding an invisible button from the library and scaling it to fit over the **navigator** text.

Give the button the standard dragbar actions:

```
on (press) {
    startDrag ("");
}
on (release, releaseOutside) {
    stopDrag ();
}
```

> *Visitors to the site may miss the fact that the menu bar is draggable. There are a lot of sites out there that have functions that are not really needed. Purists may argue that making the menu bar draggable is not necessary, because it is in the 'right place' to start off with. I would agree, but one of the cool features of the web is the need to explore. A site that throws up new avenues and interfaces is not necessarily bad when you remember that entertainment is important in keeping the user's attention.*

The Main Timeline

Back in the `_root` timeline, we want to convert our changes in the sliding button position into actual changes in the page positions. For now, we will make them move instantly to the next page but in the next chapter we will give them some movement.

1. Using the **Instance** panel, give the instances of **mc.page01**, **mc.page02** and **mc.page03** on the stage the instance names **page1**, **page2** and **page3**.

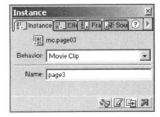

2. Extend the timeline to three frames on all three layers. In the first frame of the **actions** layer add this script to initialize our left, front and right positions and set the initial positions that the pages will take up. Go back and look at our initial diagrams if you're unsure about the positions.

```
// initialize page positions
left = -1200;
front = 0;
right = 1200;
// move pages to initial positions
page1._x = front;
page2._x = right;
page3._x = right;
```

3. Insert a new keyframe at frame 2 of the **actions** layer. We've set the page positions at the beginning, now we need to tell the pages to swap around depending on the variable stunPage, which we set when we use the navigator. Then:

```
if (stunPage == 1) {
    page1._x = front;
    page2._x = right;
    page3._x = right;
} else if (stunPage == 2) {
    page1._x = left;
    page2._x = front;
    page3._x = right;
} else {
    page1._x = left;
    page2._x = left;
    page3._x = front;
}
```

4. We'll want to be constantly checking this, so label this frame **mainloop** so that we can set up a loop between this frame and the next one easily.

5. Add another keyframe in frame 3 of **actions**, and enter a simple Goto action back to **mainloop**:

```
gotoAndPlay ("mainloop");
```

Note that I'm actually using the page movie _x property paths just like any other variable, and am writing to and reading to them at will, which is rather more efficient than using intermediate variables.

6. Now go into **Movie > Properties** and change the movie width to 800.

7. Create a new layer and call it **navigator**. Select the first frame and drag an instance of **menubar** out of the library and place it just above the thunder strip of bitmaps on the left-hand page.

8. Run the FLA. You'll see that you can drag the navigator about, and that if you drag its sliding button about, the pages will immediately appear as you move it. They don't scroll yet because I want a special kind of movement; **inertial** or accelerated movement, and we will look at that in the next chapter.

    You can see what is happening if you pull the bandwidth profiler right down so that the movie area is a squashed strip. The middle of the strip below is the middle area, and you can just see page 1 at the extreme left (at x = -1200), and page 3 at the right (x = 1200).

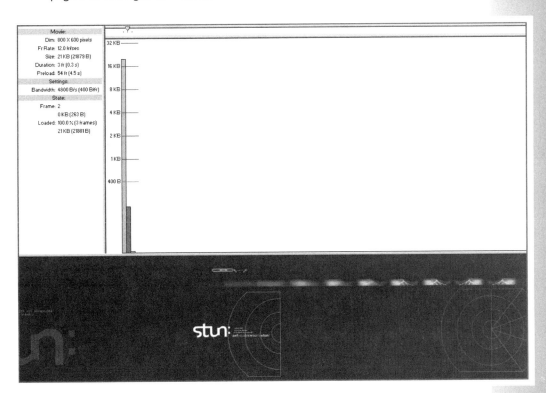

Summary

In this chapter we've looked at how Flash 5 ActionScript has been dvevloped into a powerful object-oriented language. We've covered:

- ActionScript methods, properties and behaviors

- Using object properties for advanced interactivity

- Building a preloader and cache detector

- Creating a showreel for stun:design

In the next chapter we will finish this effect by creating not only inertia, but a parallax effect in the scroll, as well as integrating a loading strategy. As I said at the beginning of the section, it's amazing how fast everything comes together when you've done the planning.

ぬふあうえおやゆよわ

10 Modular ActionScript

What we'll cover in this chapter:

- *Creating re-usable ActionScript*

- *Building a movieclip that can be used within any FLA*

- *Creating movieclips that will impart behaviors onto any timeline*

This chapter holds out the tantalizing prospect of being paid many times over for the same piece of code.

I've written this book to help you get down to doing stuff in the minimum amount of time, using the simplest and easiest methods available. I don't want you to get bogged down with irrelevant stuff that you'll never use in the real world. I've been assuming that if you're like me, you want to learn enough to make your Flash skills commercially valuable so that you can get something back for all the hard effort you've put in.

This is what **modular**, object-oriented ActionScript is all about. It's efficient and re-usable. Because it's efficient, you need less of it, and because it's re-usable, you have to write it less often. You can have a bag full of standard routines that just need tweaking to be usable on a new project. I like being paid twice for the same piece of coding. You can have lots of identical little movieclips following the same short simple bit of code, but when taken together, the overall behavior is *complex*. This is a good concept to explore because the code you actually need to write to create this apparent complexity is *short* and *simple*.

This chapter will introduce you to creating re-usable Actionscript to create graphic effects that you can use over and over again. We'll expand on that theme by creating behavior movieclips that you can use to apply particular movement behaviors anywhere you want to. As if that's not enough, we'll look at a new Flash 5 feature, the Smart Clip, that allows you to configure and modify your movieclips to suit every situation.

Once you have these techniques under your belt you'll be on your way to harnessing the power of Flash 5 dot notation and movieclip class structure, which puts you up there with the professionals, and no doubt about it.

First, let's look at modular good practice.

Modular Actionscript

There are some effects or functions that require Flash to be doing a lot of things at the same time. You need multiple timelines all handling a bit of the problem and working at the same time. You can't do that with what you've come across so far, because you're used to working with a single timeline (usually _root) to control everything.

This diagram shows the basic single timeline structure:

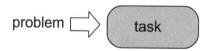

You have a big problem that you throw at the timeline, and have a big multi-part task that solves it, sprawling all over the place in the process. Your code will be difficult to structure or document because of its size. Writing it becomes a real hassle because it's difficult to add new functionality. You have to test the whole thing to see whether the addition works, and there's lots of documentation to wade through.

This diagram shows the modular approach:

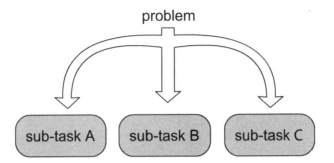

You have separate timelines in movieclips or loaded SWF levels that each look at a sub-task that solves a part of the problem. Each sub-task is now more compact, with a better defined problem to solve, which makes it easier to read and code. More subtly, because you've split the problem down into generic sub-tasks, if a similar problem arises somewhere else, you can now re-use the sub-tasks on their own in less time than it would take to re-write what's essentially the same overall problem structure.

So, modular programming involves building a particular function that can be re-used or easily re-engineered. We can pluck sub-task B out of that site very easily, but we can't really do the same with our tangled up timeline. We can uproot sub-task B fairly easily, but we still need to be careful that we can use it in its new location. We're going to have a look at an approach called the **black box approach** which makes sure that when we uproot sub-task B from its original home, it doesn't take a whole load of earth with it.

Black Box Programming

In programming, a black box is a piece of code that you can reuse without necessarily knowing all the details of how it works. You can't see inside the box because it's black, but you don't need to. The black box approach stipulates that all code must be **self contained** and distinct from any other code. You're only interested in two things – what it does to the outside world (its function, method or behavior) and what it needs from you and will give back to you (its interfaces). Browser plug-ins work like this. The organization that designed your browser isn't going to want to let their secrets become public knowledge so that their rivals can see exactly what they're doing. Your Internet browser has a well defined set of interfaces that third parties, such as Macromedia, can use to add plug-ins for Flash, or Director or whatever they want without having to know how all of the browser works.

How does this black box relate to what we're doing then?

The first rule for us is that to make code self-contained it really should be within a movieclip and not on the main timeline. The main timeline isn't portable in the same way that a movieclip is because it's not self contained and is consequently not a library item. To integrate the movieclip into our site, we simply have to add it to our library and make minor modifications to integrate it into its new environment. We've already seen examples of this, but we haven't really looked at how to create them for ourselves. That will change when we look at sound control sliders in a moment.

So, self-containment is an important feature of modularity, and the movieclip captures this requirement beautifully. But... there's always a *but* isn't there?

But... unless the movieclip controls itself (which we'll be seeing in the next chapter), the movieclip isn't totally self contained. It might come into contact with the world outside in two ways:

- By addressing other timelines in Flash

- By receiving or outputting data

The black box approach has ways of dealing with these areas of contact.

You might think that it's impossible for a movieclip to address other timelines while still being totally self contained and distinct from any other code. As soon as you address another timeline, you're setting up a relationship with something else in that particular FLA that won't be there in another FLA. Our black box movieclips must only access what we know will be there in any situation, so any actions we use in them should be independent of what the target is called and where the movieclip has been put.

We've already met the solution to this problem. That solution is that we need to use what we know will always be there in any situation. If you think about it, this includes properties of the parent timeline, and _parent paths like the ones we used in the last chapter for our button wrapped in a movielip. We'll see how to use these with the black box approach in a moment.

> *It goes without saying that black box code should be well documented so that we know what interactions to expect when we use it. This is important normally, but when we're writing code so that we can re-use it later it becomes absolutely **vital**. You'll never remember the intricacies of something you wrote when you come to re-use it while chasing a deadline six months later. Even if it seems like a waste of time now, document it!*

You don't learn these techniques by reading about them. You learn by doing them, which is exactly what we will do in the next section. As you look at the particular examples, see if you can spot how I'm adhering to the rules above.

We're going to have a look at an example of all the high level programming concepts that we've just talked about. To keep it simple, we will stick to control of movement, which opens up all kinds of possibilities for ActionScript animation and realistic motion.

There are a fair few cartoons and other full length features on the Web at the moment, and it would be a good idea to have the sort of control over some of them you get with a normal video. In this exercise we'll create a modular set of video controls that you can drop onto any timeline containing tween type animations.

As well as showing how to create a modular movieclip, this exercise will show you how to create **continuous feedback**. Continuous feedback involves not having to keep pressing a button to make something keep increasing or decreasing, but just having to press and hold for as long as you want the quantity to vary. This is a bit like pressing the volume button on a radio to increase the sound – you don't keep pressing again and again, you keep it pressed and take your finger off when the volume has increased to the level you wanted. If you get stuck at any point, you can get my version of this file from the download file for this chapter, **videocontrols.fla**..

Creating a Modular Movieclip

The first thing we'll need is the video control buttons. I got mine from **Window > Common Libraries > Buttons**, in the rectangle button set, where you'll find a set of buttons complete with all the play, rewind symbols.

1. Arrange your video control buttons into a strip, like this:

This strip consists of five buttons. The **Pause** button should freeze the target timeline at the current frame. Then, every time it's pressed, it should advance to the next frame. The **Play** button should undo any other button and start to play the movie from the current frame. The **Rewind** and **FastForward** buttons should work like standard video *fast-search* buttons: they will cause the movie to play at a faster rate (say x4) either backwards or forwards. The **Stop** button should stop the movie at its current frame.

2. Select all of your buttons using the *Shift* key to select multiple items and convert them to a movieclip symbol called **videocontrols**. Double-click the movieclip to enter **edit in place** mode and rename the layer with your buttons on in the movieclip **buttons** and create a new layer called **actions**:

OK, let's start adding the actions to the buttons. The Play and Stop buttons sound relatively painless, so we'll look at them first.

3. The Play button simply has to make the timeline that our video controls are on (which will be its _parent timeline) start to play. All we need to make this happen is an on (release) action, with the line _parent.play(); added afterwards:

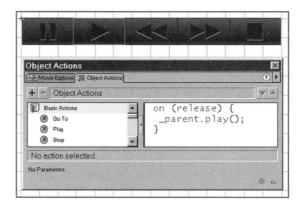

4. The Stop button needs to do exactly the same as Play, but this time we want a _parent.stop():

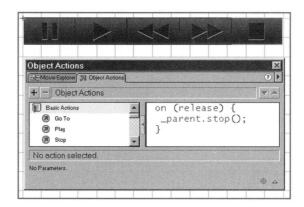

Now we come to the difficult ones.

The Pause button sounds like it needs to do two things. Obviously, it needs to freeze on the first press. If you click on it, release and press again, you'll expect the movie to act as if it's playing for a moment and then stop. In other words you want it to go to the next frame of the movie and freeze. If we're sneaky and just got to the next frame and pause for *all* Pause button presses, how many people will actually notice? How many people have ever noticed that's what real video recorders with this sort of pause function do? That's right. Nobody, because the frame rates are too fast for anyone to realize that's what's happening.

The `on (press)` action for this button is actually the same as the Stop button: a simple `_parent.stop()`. The `on (release)` action is a little harder. We want the `_parent` to `gotoAndStop` to its next frame. If you think back to Chapter 9 you may remember that there's a movieclip property to tell us which frame a movie is currently on: `_currentFrame`. To go forward one frame we just do a `gotoAndPlay` to the parent's `_currentFrame+1`. There are three possible ways to write this command, but two of them won't work. Here they are:

- `gotoAndStop(_parent._currentFrame+1);`
  This sends the timeline we are in, `videocontrols`, to whatever the `_parent` timeline is plus one. We don't want **our** timeline to go to `_parent + 1`, we want the `_parent` timeline to go to `_parent + 1`. If `_videocontrols` timeline pauses, the movie on the parent timeline is going to carry on playing and not a lot will happen!

- `_parent.gotoAndStop(_currentFrame+1);`
  This sends the `_parent` timeline to whatever is `videocontrol`'s current frame, plus one. This isn't a runner either - we still end up on the wrong timeline, and we've got nothing to play for the user on this one.

- `_parent.gotoAndStop(_parent._currentframe+1);`
  This sends the `_parent` timeline to whatever frame it's on, plus one, which is where we want it.

This one had me hot and bothered the first time I met it. You may be aiming an action like `gotoAndStop` at a different timeline through a pathname, but, unless you explicitly say otherwise, Flash assumes that any properties you describe, such as `_currentframe+1`, are based on the actual timeline that the action is attached to. This means that we have to put a path to `_parent` in for both the Goto command and the property.

5. Now that we've finally got that sorted, go and give your Pause button the `on (press)` and `on (release)` actions that we've just worked out:

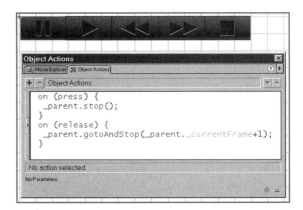

The FastForward and Rewind buttons are also a little tricky because we want to implement continuous movement. As I said earlier, we want them to keep increasing or decreasing the rate at which they rewind or fast forward our movieclip while they're selected. To do this, we need to set up some timeline actions in the **videocontrols** movieclip first. Rather than make the buttons themselves create the actions, we need something to start happening and keep on happening until the user stops it. How do we do this? Just as we have with other problems that have required something to happen until something else happens – with looping.

6. In frame 1 of **actions**, add a keyframe and assign a `stop();` action to it. Label this frame **stop**. Then extend both layers up to frame 11.

Don't worry that all the layers seem to contain the `stop();` action at the moment, we're going to insert some keyframes in a moment to fix that.

7. Now add two keyframes in the **actions** layer at frame 5 and 6. These two frames will handle the FastForward button's stuff. Give frame 5 the label **fastforward** and attach the action:

```
_parent.gotoAndPlay (_parent._currentFrame+3);
```

Notice that this states the _parent path for both method and property, just as we did for the Pause button. We decided earlier that x4 would be a good approximation of a faster rate for a fastforward or rewind function. When we're calculating this, we need to bear in mind that Flash advances at the rate of 1 anyway, so for a FastForward button, we want Flash to advance at this rate +3

8. To give us a continuous loop that runs on FastForward as long as we stay in frames 5 and 6, go to frame 6 and attach the action:

```
gotoAndPlay ("fastforward");
```

Note that this action is directed at the **videocontrols** timeline:

We need to do the same for the **Rewind** button.

9. Still on the **actions** layer, add two keyframes at 10 and 11. Label frame 10 **rewind** and add these actions:

```
_parent.gotoAndPlay(_parent._currentframe-5);
```

As with the FastForward button, the movie will be playing forward at the rate of 1 at the same time. To counter this, we need to add an extra number to our rewind value giving us –5 to rewind x4.

10. In frame 11, add this action:

```
gotoAndPlay ("rewind");
```

The label again sets up a simple looping structure that continues until the user stops it.

We've created our simple (stop); action in frame 1, our FastForward loop between frames 5 and 6 and our rewind loop between frames 10 and 11. We now need to move away from the timeline and add some actions to the buttons to tell them to go to our nicely choreographed timeline.

Bring up the **Rewind** button and add:

```
on (press) {
    gotoAndPlay ("rewind");
}
on (release) {
    gotoAndStop ("stop");
}
```

When you press the Rewind button, it will cause Flash to go into the rewind loop at frames 10 and 11 until you release the button, when it will go to frame 1 (which we labeled **stop**) and halt. This button shows how to *continuously* do something until the user releases it, a vital building block for all sorts of advanced interactive games and web site interfaces.

What if your user goes back until Flash is told to go to frame beyond the end of or before the beginning of a movie? The movie will just stop at the beginning or end. Macromedia haven't made any reference to this, so I'm a little uneasy about depending on it but it's been like this in previous versions of Flash, and seems to be a programmed function rather than a 'feature'.

11. The **FastForward** button is almost identical, except that it goes to the loop at frames 5 and 6.

```
on (press) {
    gotoAndPlay ("fastforward");
}
on (release) {
    gotoAndStop ("stop");
}
```

12. Save the FLA here before we move on.

You can now use this set of controls on any timeline that consists of tween animations anywhere in any FLA. All you have to do is drop it into the target timeline! How have we achieved this feat of coding?

The video controls don't refer to any specific timeline to control, but refer to it as _parent, which is the timeline that **videocontrols** finds itself on. This is a *general* interface and will work with anything because the controls need to know nothing about this timeline, not even how many frames it has.

The controls are modular because you can simply drag them onto any timeline, and they'll work. The fact that the whole thing is wrapped inside a movieclip means you just open this FLA as a library, drag the videocontrols movieclip onto the target timeline and, uh, that's it... it works! Let's test this out.

A year ago, when we were all still on Flash 4, people were beginning to use Flash for e-greeting cards. Most of them were pretty saccharine, so I came up with an altogether darker example which used some photography I came across on the Internet by a man called Martinus Versfeld. I asked him if I could use some of his pictures for one of my pieces, and like most people on the Web tend to (if you ask nicely), he said OK. You can find the results of this in the download file for this chapter as **dark.fla**. This exercise will show you how easy it is to drop those videcontrols onto another timeline.

Re-using a Modular Movieclip

1. Open **dark.fla** now and in the root timeline, create a new layer **controls**. Make sure that it's the topmost layer, otherwise our controls could be obscured by things on a higher layer moving in front of them:

2. Now using **File > Open as library**, open the **videocontrols** library window, switch to **dark.fla** and drag the movieclip **videocontrols** onto the stage. Place it in layer **control**:

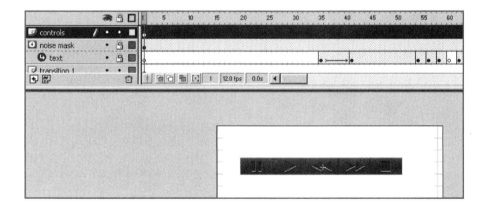

Close the library for **videocontrols** and open the library again. The library that comes up will be the one for **dark.fla**, and you will see **videocontrols** and all the associated buttons in it. You can tidy the library up by creating a new folder and putting all the video control bits and pieces in it, as I've done here:

Name	Kind	Use Count
anim frames	Folder	
bitmaps	Folder	
controls	Folder	
Grey button-ffwd	Button	1
Grey button-pause	Button	1
Grey button-play	Button	1
Grey button-rwd	Button	1
Grey button-stop	Button	1
videocontrols	Movie Clip	1
Futuremedia logo	Folder	
mask	Graphic	1
noise line	Graphic	33
text	Folder	

A tidy library is always a good idea in an FLA as complicated as this, and you don't need me to tell you why.

If you run the movie now, the video controls will operate as you would expect.

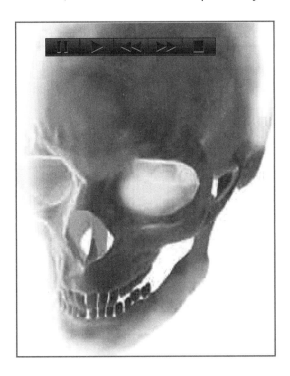

This set of controls will only act on a single timeline. If your animation consists of other movieclips as well as the timeline that holds **videocontrols**, it won't control them, just the timeline that it's placed on. You could modify the controls so that they can be hidden, perhaps in the same way that the stun:toys were. You could even add a dragbar or use the `_alpha` property to make them semi-transparent when they're not in use. You could build up a whole site navigation system using a little TV remote control unit for your navigation; press the channel buttons to move about, and the video controls to control the movies. Enough of my ideas – I'll leave you to experiment.

Thus far, we've looked at reusing a movieclip that contains pre built graphic effects that we can use in different situations. I'll move things on now to look at how we can reuse something a little more subtle: a **behavior movieclip**.

Behavior Movieclips

Sometimes you want a movieclip called, say, **blob**, to do lots of things at the same time. You might want it to move about the screen in a particular way based on one set of criteria, but you also want it to change its appearance based on a different set of criteria as it moves. These two things could be implemented in your movieclip's timeline in a long multi-frame script, but that may not be the ideal way to do it. The two things are *independent*, and are going on at the same time. They are essentially separate **behaviors** that the movieclip needs to follow. If a movieclip has no content but scripts in it which apply effects to their `_parent`, we call it a **behavior movieclip**.

To code this, you could have a separate movieclip for each behavior, each of which exists within **blob** and *imparts* a particular behavior on it. The other possibility is to have each movieclip imparting this behavior by controlling not **blob**, but `_parent`. This is the start of modular design, because our movieclip doesn't need to know anything about its parent other than the fact that it's a movieclip with the defined set of properties that a movieclip possesses. We can do anything to it because we know what general properties the parent will have. For example, we don't need to know how big it is because we know that there is a general property that contains this information and it's always in the same place – we can use `_xscale` and `_yscale`. We've already done something like this in earlier chapters, with simple commands where we used relative paths such as `_parent` and alluded to another useful path called `this`.

We'll look now at adding behaviors to a movieclip that we can use again and again to different effect. Now that we know all about properties and are well on the way to the top of the ActionScript mountain, we won't settle for just any behaviors here. We'll go for the big one: **real movement**. This is motion based on real physics, and takes into account the fact that objects in the real world have weight and move in an intelligent interactive way. There's very little math involved here, but there's a lot of common sense and some precise observations that you may need to think about carefully. If you find it hard going, take it slowly. It's not difficult, just different, and it's well worth knowing if you want to go on to building the kind of sites and effects that have everyone else gaping in awe.

Creating Real Movement

Real movement is different from anything else we have done in Flash because real things have *mass*. They can't stop immediately, and when they start to move they take time to build up speed. The way this all works out involves a lot of physics if we let it. I prefer a more fundamental science called Common Sense, which can be quite powerful in looking at real life situations.

Think about the equation below.

Where we want to go = where we are + the distance we have to travel

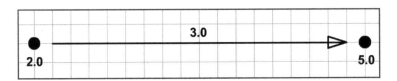

In this diagram, we're at a position 2 meters down from the start of a path, and we want to be 5 meters down the path. Where we want to be is 3 meters away, so from our equation we have:

5(where we want to go) = 2(where we are) + 3(the distance we have to travel)

We can simplify our initial equation by removing the vague term **the distance we have to travel**.

The distance we have to travel is:

where we want to go – where we are

This is 5 - 2 in our example. So, where we are at any given time is:

Where we want to go = where we are + (where we want to go – where we are)

This equation isn't good for animation in Flash because it describes our whole journey in one go. If taken literally, it implies that we reach our destination in zero time because there is no reference to time in the equation. It's simply saying **We're not where we want to be** and then **We are we want to be**. There are no intermediate steps between leaving **where we were** and arriving at **where we want to be**. As much as we would all like to be able to travel around like this in the real world, there's usually a tedious wait between leaving and arriving. To understand how we build this reality into Flash, we need to understand how computers model reality or **continuous existence**.

Real motion is a continuous process. When we walk from A to B we exist for an infinite number of instants between those two points. It's a common sense part of reality that we exist 'continuously' and don't disappear for even a fraction of a second on our journey.

Computers can't handle this type of reality because it would take more processing power than all of them put together to properly simulate a millionth of a second's worth of what really goes on in something as simple as a glass of water. Instead, we've taught computers to cheat. What they do is split time up into a series of instants or *snapshots* in time, called frames in Flash. We calculate what's happening for each frame and freeze that condition until the next frame. While we're waiting for the next frame, reality is skipped, and we cease to exist, or rather, we're frozen at our last known position. If the computer plays this fake reality back to us sufficiently quickly, we see **motion**. Film works on exactly the same principle, feeding our eyes with a sequence of static images that together present motion.

The computer moves everything along by a fraction of the distance it needs to move, and then looks at where we are now. This process of jumping forward a little, looking at what the conditions are now and plugging them into our equations of motion to get a new set of positions for the current frame is called **iteration**.

Our model of reality is called a **time-sliced** or **iterative process**. It's the basis of all computer simulation and real-time games that model true physical motion. What we essentially do is take the last set of results from our equations and reapply them to the current frame each time to get changing motion.

Let's consider real movement then, but in terms of iteration. What we need to do is split the motion into 'slices of motion'. We don't want to travel the whole distance in one go because that would give us too big a jump and would just be unrealistic. Neither do we simply want to split the journey into equal distances because that wouldn't properly model us slowing down or speeding up as we travel, a process caused by our having *mass*.

As we get closer to our destination we want to be traveling less and less every frame, or to put is simply, *we want to slow down*. What we're saying is that we want to travel a reducing proportion of the distance every frame. We could do that easily if we looked at the **distance remaining** rather than the **total distance**, because the distance remaining is always reducing.

Think about what would happen if we traveled only half the remaining distance every time:

Where we want to go = where we are + ((where we want to go – where we are)/2)

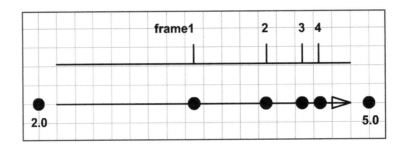

What actually happens is that in each frame we travel half the distance again. If we applied this equation every frame we would actually slow down the closer we got to our destination, as you can see in the diagram.

As we approach our destination, there are three possible outcomes:

- If we don't slow down fast enough, we go past where we want to stop.

- If we slow down just right, we stop right on the spot.

- If we slow down too quickly, we stop before our destination.

If you look at the next equation, the variable **n** is a measure of how quickly the equation reacts to change. It's essentially the *stiffness* (or for the technically minded, the *feedback*) of the system. In terms of motion, it can represent how fast we accelerate or decelerate on our journey, or the amount of force we are applying to continue us in our motion.

Where we want to go = where we are + ((where we want to go – where we are)/n)

If the value of **1/n** is much less than 1, we never reach our destination because the distance we travel on every iteration falls off too quickly. In plain language, we slow down too much. If the value of **1/n** is close to but less than one, we've hit the brake pedal at the right point and will reach our destination. If the value of **1/n** is exactly 1, we reach our destination immediately, on the first iteration.

If the value of **n** is less than one, the value of **1/n** is obviously greater than 1 and we'll go past our destination without stopping, but will have time to turn back and make another attempt. We've overshot, but it's OK, we can just reverse back up. If the value of **1/n** is greater than, say, 2, making **n** less than 0.5, we go too fast past our target, our distance increases too fast for us to slow down for another attempt and we shoot off towards an infinite speed. We tried to stop for that stop sign, but we were just going too fast and now we want to get out of there before anyone crashes into us.

How do I know all this? Well, it's down to a bit of math that's beyond the scope of this chapter. If you're interested, go and find out about **Control Theory**. The actual value of **1/n** for each type of movement can be calculated, but you can find it much easier by just playing with the numbers. To summarize:

- If **n** is less than 0.5, the motion accelerates past the target and never stops. This is an unstable motion and it's best to avoid it as it won't be realistic (and that's what we're trying to achieve here, right?).

- If **n** is equal to 0.5, we'll *oscillate* around our target; we'll reach our target, but overshoot and do the same coming back the other way... forever!

- If **n** is greater than 0.5 but less than 1, we'll slightly overshoot our target but will come back the other way, and will stop on the target after a few 'bounces'.

- If **n** is equal to 1, we'll immediately get to our target. This isn't a realistic movement and should also be avoided.

- If **n** is between 1 and 2, we'll slow down the closer we get to our target and stop without overshooting. n = 1.8 to 2 will usually give the most aesthetically pleasing motion; we'll slow down to just over half the speed each time we travel half the distance.

- If **n** is over 2, we'll never reach the target.

We've looked at slowing down – what about getting faster? How does our equation handle that? We need to look at the other part of the equation. Where do we want to go? So far, this has stayed static and we've been moving towards it. If where we want to go gets further away from us, the equation forces us to speed up because the distance left to travel goes up. Think of catching that bus – the further away the bus is, the faster you run.

Our equation doesn't have a speed limit, but, because the speed is specified by how far away we want to be, the speed is limited by how far away we can be (in other words, the size of the stage area in Flash). The equation we've ended up with is important, and we can re-write it as:

Where we want to go = where we are + ((where we want to go – where we are)/constant)

Where **constant** is a number above 0.5.

Why is this important? It's important because it is the simplest, most processor friendly equation we can use to get believable true to life movement. This is because it simulates **acceleration**. Acceleration is important because it implies a number of physical quantities, such as weight, viscosity, friction, inertia, and all sorts of other real world parameters. We're about to use this equation in three particular types of movement behavior, and you'll see how we can build on it to create some complex looking motion.

Although this equation is about how motion changes with time, it has no reference to time. That comes into it because of the nature of our simulation method: **time slicing**. Our iterative process is based on frames, and it's the frame interval that creates our time-based motion.

What has this all got to do with web design? Haven't we gone a little bit off the beaten track here? Well no, because interactivity is found mainly in two places: games and web sites. As web sites become more advanced, this relationship between games and web design has become more symbiotic, which is why this book has kept dipping into games as well as web design. I've recently noticed that real world kinematics – or, more simply, organic behavior – has made the crossover from games to web sites. Don't believe me? Take a look at any number of cutting-edge sites. Have a look at the little moving calendar that seems to accelerate and decelerate rather than just scroll at the bottom of praystation.com. Guess what that movement is – the one you've just learned about. It's a motion that looks realistic because it shows objects *accelerating* and *decelerating*. In short, the calendar is moving as if it has *weight*.

We've been looking at some serious concepts here. Let's lighten up a little – in fact let's lighten up a lot with a cute image to illustrate what we're doing next to practice what we've been talking about.

Jell-o wobbles. Prod it and it squishes and contorts for a bit but gets back to its original size. What if we applied the same sort of movement to something, say a button, in Flash?

Jell-o wobbles as a result of temporary changes to its shape and size. We'll start by looking at size. When a user rolls over a button we usually to make the button bigger to tell them that it's about to be activated. We'll make it do this by giving it a jell-o wobble. What is a jell-o wobble? It is when something undulates or vibrates slowly.

We've seen that to work out a real-life movement we always have to:

- Work out what your **where we want to go** and **where we are** values actually are.

- Apply these values to the equation with an iterative or looping process, inserting a value for **constant** of about 1.

- Taking into account my earlier summary, fine-tune **constant** until you get the movement or change you want.

So, in jell-o terms, what are our **where we want to go** and **where we are** values? They are *sizes*. The **where we want to go** is *the size I want to be* and the **where we are** is *the size I am now*. This occurs when **1/constant** is slightly greater than 1. We go past our target and the distance then becomes negative, forcing us to move back towards our destination, in wobble fashion. **1/constant** needs to be greater than 1, so **constant** needs to be less than 1 but greater than 0.5.

Our equation now looks like:

The size I want to be = the size I am now + ((the size I want to be – the size I am now)/a value between 0.5 and 1)

Let's transfer this jell-o wobble to something that we can use on a web site.

If you get stuck, the FLA file for this exercise is in the download file for this chapter as **jello.fla**.

Creating a Jell-o Button

1. Create a square invisible button called **invisible**, and then create a shape of your choice and make it a symbol. Mine is a circle called... um, **circle**.

2. Create a new movieclip **behaviorJello**, and inside it rename layer one **button** and add a new layer called **actions**.

If you remember, **where we want to go** is **the size I want to be**. So this will be a defined variable, buttontarget. 'Where we are' is 'the size we are now', so we'll define this as a variable, buttonscale.

Initially, we'll make the two variables the same size, 100%, which means that **where we are** and **where we want to be** are both the original size. If we rollover the button, we'll make buttontarget (where we want to go) bigger. When we press the button, we'll make buttontarget bigger still.

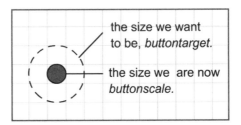

3. The button is the bit that makes our buttontarget bigger or smaller, as we shall see in a moment, but first let's go to frame 1 of our **actions** layer in the **behaviorjello** movieclip and add those variables:

```
// initialize wobble parameters
buttonscale = _parent._xscale;
buttontarget = buttonscale;
```

These two lines initialize our two variables, which are both set to the current _parent movieclip's size in percent, which will be 100%. Our behavior hasn't got a parent yet, but because it's modular, _parent will be any other movieclip you put it into, just as it was with our **videocontrols** earlier. We're only looking at the x scale, because we'll be using that to scale in the y direction as well.

4. Drag an instance of the invisible button we prepared earlier onto the stage on frame 1 of the **button** layer. We need the button to change depending on what the user is doing. If we rollover the button, we want the parent to inflate to 200% of its size. If the user presses the button, we want it to inflate by a massive 400%.

Add these actions to the button to give us want we want:

```
on (rollOver) {
    buttonTarget = 200;
}
on (releaseOutside, rollOut) {
    buttonTarget = 100;
}
on (press) {
    buttonTarget = 400;
}
on (release) {
    buttonTarget = 200;
}
```

Go back to the **actions** layer.

5. Insert two new frames and select frame 2. Give it the label wobbleloop. In this frame we need to add an if action to check whether we've reached where we want to be (buttontarget). If we haven't reached where we want to be, we apply our equation:

```
// Apply wobble equation
if (buttonScale<>buttonTarget) {
buttonScale = Math.round (buttonScale+(buttonTarget-
buttonScale)/0.6);
// perform animation
_parent._xscale = buttonScale;
_parent._yscale = buttonScale;
}
```

I've set constant to 0.6. This means that, although we'll go past our target size, we'll have time to slow down and come back the other way and try again. We'll do this a number of times, slowing down our change in size as we do so, until we reach our target size.The resulting changes in size will look like a 'wobble'.

The math.round(); is there to make sure we get a whole number value.

The if action that we've just inserted into frame 2 needs to be constantly repeated – we need to constantly check on whether we've reached where we want to be. To do this, we need to set up a loop.

6. Put a gotoAndPlay("wobbleloop"); action into frame 3. Although this is the simplest part of the code, it's the bit that is producing our *iteration*. It's causing us to constantly re-apply the *previous* frame's results to define a motion for *this* frame.

7. Now create a new movieclip **myshape**. Rename layer 1 **shape** and create a new layer called **behavior**. Drop a copy of **circle**, or whatever you called your shape in step 1, into layer **shape**. Then drop the **behaviorJello** movieclip into **behavior** and scale it so that it fits over the circle.

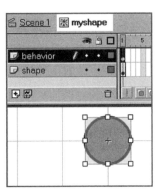

What have we done? We've made **behaviorJello**'s `_parent` the new movieclip **myshape**. This means that if you roll over or prod **myshape** it should act like jell-o.

8. Drag **myshape** onto the main stage and test the movie. See that? It wobbles, and that's just the start of what we're going to do.

You can drop **behaviorJello** into any movieclip, and it will force that movieclip to wobble. A bit of text, even an animation - *anything* can be made to take on this behavior. You can also play about with the constant value. At just above 0.5 it becomes something called an **oscillator**. The math makes it into a wobbler that can never stop wobbling once you start it off! If you make the value less than 0.5 what happens? It iterates right out of the frame because we've gone past 0.5 and into unstable motion.

At a value of 1, the wobble effect disappears. This is because the wobble starts to slow down as you approach the target size value so that it never goes past where it needs to get. It just expands and deflates like a balloon. Make the constant something really big, say 20, to see this at an extreme.

The jell-o wobble applies our equation to *size*, but we are not limited to that. We have all those properties we looked at in Chapter 9 to play with. We looked at size last time, so this time we will look at *position*.

Inertia Behavior

We are going to create a movieclip that tries to catch up to the mouse cursor. Remember our equation:

Where we want to go = where we are + ((where we want to go − where we are)/constant)

Here, **where we want to go** will be the mouse position, as denoted by the mouse object's properties _xmouse and _ymouse. The shape that attempts to follow the mouse will have position shapeX and shapeY. What we want to go into the equation is the distance between the shape's position and the mouse's which is distX, distY, as shown in the diagram:

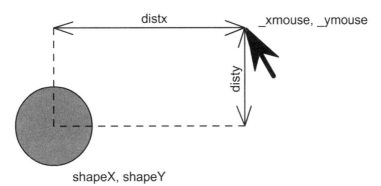

Apart from the fact that we have no button this time, **behaviorInertia** is pretty much the same as **behaviorJello**. It has an initialization frame, a main script frame, and a final frame that creates a loop between itself and frame 2 (in fact, this FLA started off as **behaviorJello.fla**, and I just changed the lines around a bit).

This exercise is contained in **inertia.fla** in the download file for this chapter if you get stuck at any point.

Creating Intertia

1. Create a new Flash movie. Like last time, make a circle and convert it to a graphic symbol called **circle**. Delete the original instance of it on the main stage. Now create a new movieclip called **behaviorInertia**. In this movieclip, rename layer 1 **actions**, and insert three keyframes into the first three frames.

2. In frame 1 initialize these variables:

   ```
   // initialize inertia parameters
   shapeX = _parent._x;
   shapeY = _parent._y;
   targetX = 0;
   targetY = 0;
   ```

   The shape variables are set to whatever the _parent movieclip's position is. targetX and targetY will soon become the mouse position. I've called them this to suggest that anything can be the **where we want to go** position whether that be the position of a scrolling calendar menu, or the target of a diving alien. Remember that behind all this we have the theme of creating reusable code.

3. In frame 2, we're going to enter some pretty complex ActionScript, but don't worry, what we're actually doing is pretty simple. First of all, we need to get the mouse position and work out how far away we are from it:

```
// Capture mouse positions
targetX = _root._xmouse;
targetY = _root._ymouse;
distX = targetX-shapeX;
distY = targetY-shapeY;
```

4. We now need to use the **how far away** term and add it to where we are through the equation. We're using _root to capture the mouse positions because that is where the mouse really lives, on the main timeline. We would get the same motion if we used _parent in any case, because our equations are not really concerned with absolute positions, but where we are *relative* to where we want to be:

```
// Apply inertia equation
shapeX = Math.round(shapeX+(distX/5));
shapeY = Math.round(shapeY+(distY/5));
```

5. Finally, we need to actually perform the animation:

```
// perform animation
_parent._x = shapeX;
_parent._y = shapeY;
```

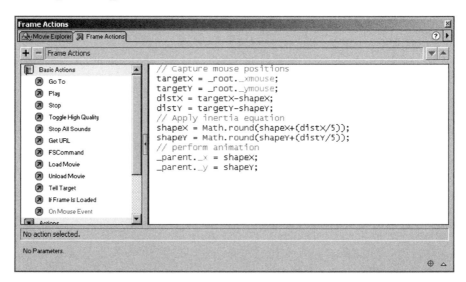

6. To set up our loop, label frame 2 **inertialoop** and in frame 3 add a `gotoAndPlay();` to **inertialoop**.

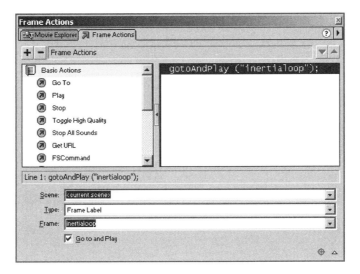

If you place the **behaviorInertia** into *any* movieclip it will follow your mouse. Let's test this with a new movieclip.

7. Return to the main timeline, create another movieclip (I've called mine **myshape**), and drag your **circle** graphic onto the stage. Create another layer, name it **behavior**, and drag your **behaviorInertia** movieclip out of the library and scale it over the circle.

8. Return to your main stage and drag **myshape** out of your library onto it. Test your movie.

If it looks similar to the jell-o behavior then that's because it is *exactly* the same; motion with acceleration, or rather changes in properties that vary in a smooth lifelike transition.

What if you had a few of the **behaviorInertia** balls on the screen at the same time? You can try it by putting a few **myshape** balls onto the screen. The problem is that they follow the same path after a while, so they all overlap one another and you only see one ball. I looked at this motion and thought about it, and how swarms of flies or shoals of fish move.

Let's develop what we've done in the last exercise to create a swarm.

Swarm Behavior

behaviorSwarm looks daunting from a distance, but it's based on **behaviorInertia**, and took me half an hour develop. I've had a bit of practice with Flash of course, but I guarantee that you'll be doing the same within six months if you stick with it. All I've done with **behaviorSwarm** is start off with a simple set of premises, and slowly built it up. The story doesn't end here either – there is much more I could do with swarm and we'll talk about that in a moment.

> *If you go away with one thing from this section, remember that Flash allows you to quickly visualize behavior-based changes under the control of ActionScript. Once you have the basic ingredients, it's easy to build up to a stunning, dynamic and re-usable effect.*

The swarm as a whole may travel to a single destination, but individual swarm members have slightly different destinations. Why? Because in real life it's difficult to occupy the same place as something else! So a swarming fly will land slightly to one side of its neighbor. That is the nature of **swarming**. The individual members of a swarm are actually trying to all go to the same place, but they can't, and are always trying to maintain a position in an area with limited space.

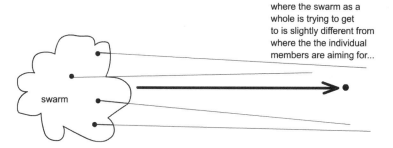

where the swarm as a whole is trying to get to is slightly different from where the the individual members are aiming for...

There is also the *type* of motion. A swarm in motion will tend to be more spread out when it's traveling because each member needs space to fly. When it's at rest, the swarm can become more tightly packed, because speeds are now much lower, and some of the members may be just stationary and hovering rather than actually moving. There is a something here about the *density* of a swarm.

Where did I get all that information from? Nowhere. No books on flies or queuing theory, chaotic motion or fluid dynamics. I just used my observations of two **Inertia** balls moving around following my cursor, and combined that with the memory of walking down a canal path with my partner last summer, having to dodge past the odd congregation of flying insects.

behaviorSwarm is exactly the same as **behaviorInertia** except for a few things. I've added two new terms: flockX, flockY. This is a random position around the target destination (which is again the cursor), where the _parent heads for. Because it's random, it's different for all individual members of the swarm. flock changes depending on whether the cursor is stationary. If it's moving, the swarm gets bigger. If the cursor is stationary, the swarm will become smaller and more dense. I used the variable oldTargetX to tell whether the cursor is moving. If the current TargetX is the same as oldTargetX, the cursor is stationary.

Every now and again, there's a chance that each swarm member changes where it wants to get to, due to its neighbors getting in the way. We can simulate this and apply it to multiple instances. Although the code looks bigger, those are the only changes. You can see the final FLA as **swarm.fla**.

Creating a Swarm

1. **behaviorSwarm** is just another three frame script movieclip. In frame 1 we need to set the initialization for the variables:

```
// initialize parameters
shapeX = _parent._x;
shapeY = _parent._y;
targetX = 0;
targetY = 0;
oldTargetX = 0;
FlockX = (Math.random()*200)-100;
FlockY = (Math.random()*200)-100;
```

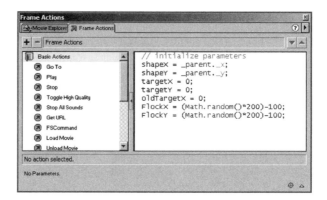

Notice the addition of the `flock` variables I mentioned just now and the `oldTargetX` variable. We're setting the `flock` variables to a random number between -100 and 100.

2. The first part of our code sets our target position (where we want to get to) as the current mouse position. We don't want to know the current mouse position so much as *how far we are* from it, which is what the *dist* variables are. This is equated to the difference between our current position (*shape*) and where we want to be (*target*). To make sure all of the swarm doesn't head for the same exact position, we have also added the `Flock` offsets, which we have already defined above to be random. This offset is not only random, but a *different* random number for each member of our swarm, so they will all head for the mouse position plus or minus a bit. This will mean that we will see our swarm not actually head for the mouse itself, but *swarm around it*. The only difference from **behaviorswarm** so far is the addition of the `FlockX` and `FlockY` variables to `distX`, `distY` in lines 4 and 5.

```
// Capture mouse positions and distance from mouse
targetX = _root._xmouse;
targetY = _root._ymouse;
distX = targetX-shapeX+FlockX;
distY = targetY-shapeY+FlockY;
//
```

3. The next bit is new – we need to allow the values of the `Flock` variables to change depending on whether the cursor is still or moving. There are two motions the swarm will take up, based on this code. If the current mouse position is the same as it was last time (if `targetX ==oldTargetX`), the mouse hasn't moved, so the flock variables have a chance (1 in 10, via `Math.random();`) of becoming a random number that is closer to the mouse (between –50 and 50). So if the mouse stays still, the swarm gets closer, as if it is about to settle. If the mouse has moved (`targetX<>oldTargetX`), then we make the swarm bigger by increasing flock:

```
if ((targetX==oldTargetX)&&Math.random()>0.9) {
// add small scale random darting if mouse is still
FlockX = (Math.random()*100)-50;
FlockY = (Math.random()*100)-50;
} else if ((targetX<>oldTargetX)&&Math.random()>0.8) {
// add large scale random darting if mouse is moving
FlockX = (Math.random()*400)-200;
FlockY = (Math.random()*400)-200;
}
```

4. Finally, we apply our motion equation. We're currently at shape and need to travel a distance Dist. I've set n = 20, so we'll travel 1/20 of the remaining distance every iteration, which is quite slow, in keeping with the speed of a swarm of bees or similar small creatures. The new bit here is keeping a record of of the previous targetX mouse position to help us decide whether the mouse is moving or stationary.

```
// Apply inertia equation
shapeX = Math.round(shapeX+(DistX)/20);
shapeY = Math.round(shapeY+(DistY)/20);
// perform animation
_parent._x = shapeX;
_parent._y = shapeY;
// remember the current mouse pos so we can tell if
// it has moved next time around
oldTargetX = targetX;
```

5. Again, you need to add a label ("swarmloop") to frame 2 and send frame 3 to gotoAndPlay it.

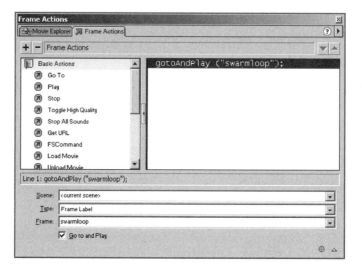

6. You now need to create a graphic symbol that will swarm around your mouse. In my FLA, I've set my background to black, and created a graphic symbol called **bug** which is just a small white cross:

7. As you did with **behaviorInertia**, you need to create a new movieclip (as you can see, I called mine **bug movie**) and drag your graphic symbol into layer 1. Then create a new layer called **behavior** and drag the **behaviorSwarm** movieclip onto that layer, over your graphic symbol.

8. Return to your main stage and drag several instances of the **bug** movie (or whatever you called the movieclip that you made in the last step) out onto the stage. How many you drag out will depend on the size of your original 'bug' graphic symbol – you can see that I made my symbol quite small and used quite a few instances:

9. Test the movie. If you leave the mouse still, you'll see the swarm bunch up and flit around it as a dense swarm. If you move the mouse, the swarm gets less dense as its members move apart to enable them to move for the journey. Here's a happy bonus - leave the cursor still for a bit and then move it slightly. It's almost as if the swarm has been disturbed and is getting angry! Funny how when you model simplicity, complex behaviors seem to just emerge...

Sometime, I want to develop this further. Instead of swarms chasing the cursor, I want them chasing *food*. The food would be a plant called *spore* growing on a distant planet. The user could cause *spore* to grow or die out by changing the climate. The behaviors of the swarm aren't fixed but can mutate in response to the changing conditions. The members can be grazers that eat *spore* or evolve to be stronger and eat other grazers, or become scavengers, eating *spore* but keeping an eye on the weaker grazers. I've had ideas for all sorts of other possible behaviors, like *pollution*, *growth* and *aggression*.

I would call this game *Ecology*, and I've managed to get as far as modeling the spore growth at the moment. Maybe you'll see all of this game in another book, but for now you can see that each iteration in this exercise is just another step to something more complex. Where will *you* end up with this?

The last stage in our tour of reusing ActionScript for maximum output from minimum input takes us to Smart Clips.

Smart Clips

Smart Clips are new to Flash 5, and they streamline the process of making movieclips modular. They're designed to allow you to make individual movieclips **configurable**, which means that, as well as being able to drag and drop your modular movieclips into new applications, you can also tailor them to make them more versatile within your creations.

To build a Smart Clip, you first need to build your movieclip, then decide which part of it needs to be configurable – which aspect will need changing when you use it again. This could be a variable that's used to decide the strength of a behavior, the color or any other property, or the text that appears on a button. The difference here is that you don't define this variable in your movieclip's initialization phase. The next stage is to make the variable that you want to be configurable one of the Smart Clip's parameters. When you drag each instance of the Smart Clip onto the stage, you can change this variable value for each separate instance, allowing each one to behave differently.

So much for the theory, let's see what happens when we actually do this. When we built the jell-o button, you may have been asking "Well, that's all very well, but how do get button to take you somewhere else?". To show you, I've built an FLA that makes the jell-o button into a Smart Clip. It's in the download file for this chapter as **jelloSmart.fla** if you want, but we're going to start from the beginning anyway.

To run through things quickly, we're about to change the button associated with the jell-o behavior in **behaviorJello** so that it's capable of causing the timeline to jump to a label. The label will be the configurable aspect of this Smart Clip. The movieclip we want to make into a Smart clip is **myshape**. We'll add a property to this Smart Clip called dest, which defines the label we want to jump to when a viewer presses the button.

Making a Smart Clip

1. From the library select **myshape** and then with the window's **Options** menu select **Define Clip Paramenters**. A new window will appear, called **Define Clip Parameters**. Click on the top left **+** button to add a new property. A new field with **Name varname**, **Value defaultValue** and **Type Default** will appear. Click on **Name** and change it to **dest**:

2. In the **Description** field add a description of how to use the Smart Clip. This allows other people to use your Smart Clips but what's more important is that is helps me remember what it was all about in six month's time!

3. The **Lock in instance** checkbox defines whether the user is allowed to change what you've just defined. You should tick it without hesitation to make sure they can't. Once you close the window, you'll notice that the icon for **myshape** has changed. It's now a Smart Clip, so its icon now shows a list on the right side, to signify that it has additional Smart properties:

So far, we have a variable `dest` that is passed to **myshape**. Our button is actually embedded in **myshape**, so to retrieve this value, we have to look at `_parent.dest`. Also, we actually want the jump to occur on the timeline that **myshape** is sitting on, which to the button is the `_parent`.

4. So we need to add a line like this to the `on (release)` event of the button inside **behaviorJello**:

```
on (release) {
    buttonTarget = 200;
    _parent._parent.gotoAndPlay(_parent.dest);
}
```

5. Your button is now ready for use. To test it, I've set up a couple of layers. **actions** has a `stop();` at frame 1 and 10, and a frame label **gohere** at frame 10. This will cause the timeline to stop at frame 1 until the button forces it to jump to frame 10. **Smart Button** is the layer with our Smart Clip in it:

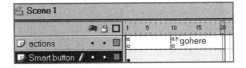

Now that we've made our Smart Clip configurable, we have to *configure* our button.

6. Select the **myshape** instance and bring up the **Clip Parameters** panel (listed in **Window > Panels**) You'll see **dest** listed. In the **Value** column, add the value you want this button to have, which is **gohere**:

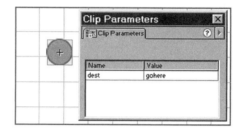

If you test the movie, you'll see that when you click the button, it goes where you wanted it to.

This is a really simple example, but you can see already how we can define other, more basic properties that affect the behavior or appearance of each particular instance of a Smart Clip. It would also be useful where you were, say, producing a Flash site that had to interface to a database or other server-side stuff. If you weren't sure of the exact protocols, you could just define all the interfaces as documented Smart Clips, and let the server-side programmer select all the required protocol values from the Smart Clip list. Something to remember when you're a Flash web design star and landing that sort of assignment on a regular basis. Send me a postcard when you do!

We'll carry on the theme of movement by taking a look at how I used the movement equation as the basis for some scrolling effects at stun:design and how they're combined with the sound controls we saw in Chapter 8.

The stun:design Web Site

My first step was to define how I wanted the scroll to work. Rather than have a single scroll movement, I've used three separate scrolling movements on the site - a background, middle ground and foreground motion. This will create a parallax scrolling effect, where different elements scroll in at different acceleration rates. I'll show you how I achieved this by defining a different motion equation for each of the three depths, or rather, the same equation with different values.

I also had to find a way of 'switching off' pages that aren't currently in view, so that Flash doesn't concern itself with animations that the viewer can't see. It's particularly important to do this because scrolling can be a bit processor intensive and animations make further demands on processor power. The situation is aggravated by the fact that the Flash plug-in tends not to grab its fair share of the available processor time and lets everything else have first pick. This factor has improved a little in the Flash 5 plug-in, but it's still too polite for its own good when we designers are trying to produce advanced interfaces and games.

You can see my version of the web site with the final scrolling added as **stun_scroll2.fla**. I'll start off taking you through how I created three movements by simply defining three different values of 1/n from our **where we want to go** equation and applying them to the relevant movieclips.

Creating the Scroll Movement

1. Open up **stun_scroll1.fla** from the last chapter. Go to the main timeline and select the first frame's ActionScript, which should read like this:

    ```
    // initialize page positions
    left = -1200;
    front = 0;
    right = 1200;
    // move pages to initial positions
    page1._x = front;
    page2._x = right;
    page3._x = right;
    ```

    In our equation, the lower the value of **n**, the quicker the movement accelerates to its final destination. So we need some values for our three scrolling movements. The objects in the foreground need to be the fastest, and those in the background the slowest. How did I arrive at values for the three?

    As we discussed earlier, **n = 1** gives a motion where the pages will go straight to their destination in one go, which is the fastest possible movement, and also the least realistic. I wanted something for the foreground that was fast but not quite that fast, and so I started at **n=1.0** and worked up in units of 0.1. Two attempts and I was there, with **n=1.2**. The middle level is the classic 'move half the remaining distance every time' motion. I find **n=2** to be the most aesthetically pleasing for this, so there wasn't really much thinking in that one. The background will contain the far off stuff, so it should move pretty sluggishly. I started this off at 50 and moved it down to 30 because at 50 it was taking too long to stop and was becoming too much of a distraction when it was the only thing still moving.

2. Add these lines to the end of the script in frame 1 to initialize the movements:

```
// initialize movements
nFore = 1.2;
nMiddle = 2;
nBack = 30;
```

3. The last version of the FLA had this script in frame 2:

```
if (stunPage == 1) {
    page1._x = front;
    page2._x = right;
    page3._x = right;
} else if (stunPage == 2) {
    page1._x = left;
    page2._x = front;
    page3._x = right;
} else {
    page1._x = left;
    page2._x = left;
    page3._x = front;
}
```

As you can tell from lines 2 to 4, the starting positions are page 1 in **front**, and pages 2 and 3 are in **right**.

Instead of jumping straight away to our destination, we need to create motion to the destination with our equation. page1X through to page3X are the **where we want to be** term, and the _x property of each page is **where it is now**, so alter the code to read like this:

```
if (stunPage == 1) {
    page1X = front;
    page2X = right;
    page3X = right;
} else if (stunPage == 2) {
    page1X = left;
    page2X = front;
    page3X = right;
} else {
    page1X = left;
    page2X = left;
    page3X = front;
}
```

4. Add these three lines to the end of this code in frame 2 to define the motion:

```
page1._x = Math.round(page1._x+(page1X-page1._x)/nMiddle);
page2._x = Math.round(page2._x+(page2X-page2._x)/nMiddle);
page3._x = Math.round(page3._x+(page3X-page3._x)/nMiddle);
```

The pages are been treated as if they were in the middle ground (hence the 1/n*Middle* 1/n term).

5. Run the FLA with these code changes and you'll see that the movement from **behaviorInertia** is being applied to our pages, which are effectively mini web pages within our FLA. This shows how simple it can be to make a mountain out of a molehill - the idea itself hasn't got bigger or better, it's just that we have *applied* it to something bigger and better to get the biggest reward from the minimum effort.

We still have one big stationary element in our site: the strip that contains the thunder animation frames. I'll show you how I added movement to that.

6. Zoom out and select the two strips of the version onscreen with *Shift*-select and convert them into a movieclip called **mc.thunderstrip**.

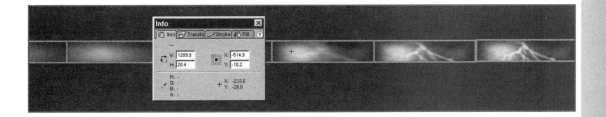

Once I'd placed the bitmap strip onscreen, it felt right to move it as a background object because it's small and has a very subdued color, just like a far off object.

7. Select the movieclip on stage (if you want to edit it in great deal, you'll need to enter edit in place, because it's much bigger than the stage) and scale it down in size, before giving it the instance name, **back**.

I now needed some sort of foreground object to whizz around in front. I initially considered a star field, but I decided that wouldn't feel quite right as stars are millions of miles away. I felt that the style and movements were creating quite a techno feel, but the soundtrack sounded more restrained than the usual techno bass thumper.

This made me think oriental, and after a quick search on the Web, I came up with some suitably heavy Katakana and Hiragana fonts:

ぬふあうえおやゆよカ

The particular typeface I used is called cozmism, and I found it at Digital Dream Design (http://member.nifty.ne.jp/digitaldreamdesign/). Take a look at the download files on friendsofed.com too.

Creating Scrolling Textfields

1. Create text in a graphic symbol and call it **gr.stunCool Katakana**. Create some text using the font - I used *su'tan cho sugoi* (one for you to ponder on...):

2. Now create a new movieclip and call it **mc.katakana**. Add a couple of instances of **gr.stunCool Katakana** and position them about four hundred pixels left and right of the center of the movieclip (if you don't get the position right, just drop back in and edit the movieclip after the next few steps):

3. Add a little gray background and a dark gray outline to the two sides and bottom of your graphic symbol for extra style points:

4. Add a new layer on the main stage and call it **Katakana**. Select the first keyframe and drag an instance of **mc.katakana** into it. Don't worry that both instances of your graphic symbol don't fit into the front 800x600 window for the moment.

Position it so that one of the text 'tabs' is above the **stun** defintion text and below the thunderstrip bitmaps, like this:

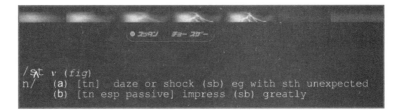

Give it an instance name of **kata**.

5. Create another new layer and call it **backstrip**. Select the first keyframe and create a long rectangle with a black fill and dark gray outlines that starts just above the **mc.thunderstrip** instance and comes down so that the bottom outline ties up with the side outline of your katanka text tab.

You'll need to make sure that this layer is behind (lower than) both the **Katakana** layer with your text tab and the **keyframes** layer with **mc.thunderstrip** on it. Check your layer order against the screenshot if it doesn't work for you:

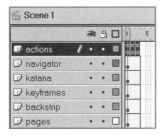

6. To get this all moving with a funky parallax scroll, we need to alter the ActionScript on frame 2 of the **actions** layer. We need to add movements for the katakana text and the strip, through their instance names **kata** and **back** so that they scroll as well. We also need to reduce the left and right positions for the text and strip so that they don't go off the front viewable screen area.

This means adding two lines to the end of each statement like this:

```
if (stunPage == 1) {
    page1X = front;
    page2X = right;
    page3X = right;
    backX = right/4;
    kataX = right/2;
} else if (stunPage == 2) {
    page1X = left;
    page2X = front;
    page3X = right;
    backX = front;
    kataX = front;
} else {
    page1X = left;
    page2X = left;
    page3X = front;
    backX = left/4;
    kataX = left/2;
}
page1._x = Math.round(page1._x+(page1X-page1._x)/nMiddle);
page2._x = Math.round(page2._x+(page2X-page2._x)/nMiddle);
page3._x = Math.round(page3._x+(page3X-page3._x)/nMiddle);
kata._x = Math.round(kata._x+(kataX-kata._x)/nFore);
back._x = Math.round(back._x+(backX-back._x)/nBack);
```

Run the movie now and you'll see the parallax effect. Notice that the katatana text is been treated as if it's in the foreground (it's using nFore) and the backstrip is in the background (it's using nBack).

You may be wondering why we're not using loops and arrays for this repetitive code. Well, I tried that at this point, but once I'd initialized all the extra variables and added all the looping structures I ended up with a piece of code about a third longer than this. That goes against my best practice of only using loops if they're going to give me fewer lines of ActionScript, not more. So without using loops and arrays I have this code that's faster and clearer.

If the user re-sizes their browser so that it's long and thin, there's a risk that they'll see the off-screen pages, so we need to add a mask over the visible screen.

7. Create a new layer and call it **mask**. With the first frame selected, create a borderless rectangle with its top left corner at 0,0 and a size that matches our stage size (800, 600). Drag so that it fits our stage area exactly.

8. Make layer **mask** into a mask and drag all layers except **actions** and **navigator** beneath it. If you're unsure about the correct order, have a look at the screenshot:

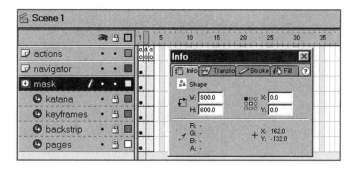

Run your movie now, or look at my version (**stun_scroll02.fla**). I've broken apart the katakana font in case you don't have it on your system.

You may want to alter the pages of this web site to add your own content. There's a potential problem here in that you may add lots of animations and effects, and as it stands, Flash would keep playing them even when the pages are off screen and the user can't see them. This would result in loss of performance in the page that the user *can* see, and they won't know why. I'll show you how I put this right.

Hiding Pages

I found that this was quite easy. Within each page I introduced a movieclip to keep a watch out for when the page is off the viewable screen area. When it is, the movieclip makes the page go to a blank frame. As soon as the page is back onscreen, the movieclip reverses this behavior and makes the page show itself again. You may have expected me to use the _visible property. That really wasn't an option because it wouldn't have stopped the animations but merely made them invisible. In any case, the movieclip is already invisible as it's off the screen. What we're really trying to do here is not to make it disappear, but to stop all processor intensive animations and calculations happening when the page isn't being viewed.

Our new movieclip is another **behavior movieclip** because it makes its _parent take on a simple behavior: to make the _parent appear and disappear. I've called the behavior movieclip **ma.detectOffScreen**, using the **ma** prefix to remind me that it's a movieclip containing only ActionScript. You can see this part of the exercise in **stun_scroll03.fla**.

Follow me through as I explain what I did.

Hiding Pages

1. Create a new movieclip and call it **ma.detectOffScreen**.

   If the page's left-hand side is greater than x = 1100 or less than −1100, we know it must be off screen, because the pages are only 800 pixels wide. The Math.abs(); object allows us to check for both the positive and negative outcome because it strips the number of its sign to give an abs(*olute*) value.

   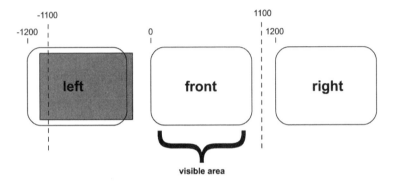

   When the movieclip is off the screen area I made the behavior go to a label **hide** in the page movieclip's timeline. If the page isn't past 1100 on either side, it must be either in the visible area **front** or in transit between our three positions, which will take it past the visible area. In these cases, I needed to force the page to be shown by making it jump to a label **show**, where all the content exists.

2. To make this happen, select frame 1 of the new movieclip and enter these actions:

   ```
   if (Math.abs(_parent._x)>1100) {
       _parent.gotoAndStop("hide");
   } else {
       _parent.gotoAndStop("show");
   }
   ```

3. Add a keyframe and then a gotoAndPlay (1); to frame 2 to make the behavior constantly apply its actions onto the parent page. Your timeline should now look like this:

   We now have to modify the three page movieclips to take account of these changes.

4. For each of the three **mc.page** movieclips add two new layers: **actions** and **behavior**. Add a second keyframe at frame 2 in the **actions** layer and extend layer **behavior** by one frame. In frame 1 of **actions** add the label **show**, and in frame 2 add the label **hide**. Drag a copy of **ma.detectOffScreen** into frame 1 of **behavior**. Here you can see how I've consistently dragged them all to just above the registration cross of each page so that I know where they are:

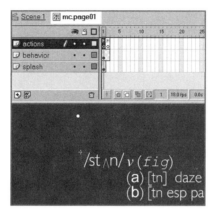

The actual content is only ever in frame 1, so as soon as our **ma.detectOffScreen** behavior kicks in and causes a jump to label **hide** in frame 2, the whole page will disappear and won't cause undue processor overhead when it shouldn't.

You can check this by testing the movie. Make sure that you've saved your file, then make the **mask** layer into a guide layer. Test the movie and make the viewable screen long by dragging down the bandwidth profiler, like this:

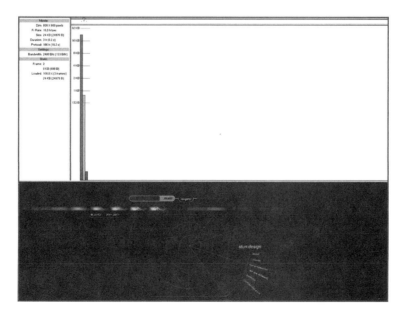

You won't be able to see anything except the front page. You might think that this doesn't show anything, but you've turned the mask off so we've successfully made the pages go to their **hide** labels and stop. If you still don't believe me, try the same trick with **stun_scroll2.fla** and you'll see the extra pages appear.

The file **stun_03.fla** is the bare stun web site with no added content. You can use this file to build up your own site by changing my graphics for some of your own designs. Use what's there as inspiration for trying out what you've learned in this book. It's given me some ideas myself. For example, I've built up a soft spot for the little tabbed katakana text, because the tabs could easily become a drop-down menus for each page, which would produce a really cool clutter free interface to add to a side scrolling site. I haven't seen this done before as most side scrollers tend to use floating windows.

I made an effort to make the file size of the bare site as small as possible. The site comes in at 21K (I was aiming at 20K) which will load up within five seconds on a 56K modem. Because our actual content will load up as separate movies, the user won't have to wait any longer than that to enter our site. Expecting the user to wait for anything much more than ten seconds for a Flash site to come is hoping for the impossibe. There are many designers out there who would argue otherwise, but remember that their sites are usually designed for a particular crowd (other Flash designers and clients with fast connections) and not the general public.

We all talk about cable and optical communications that will transform the Internet, but they aren't here yet in enough numbers to make a difference. They probably won't be for some time to come and until that day arrives, think 56K modem.

OK, let's round things up with a little stun sound.

Adding the Sound Control

You can see the finished version of what we're about to do in **stun_scroll4.fla**. You'll have to run it from a location that contains **soundtrack.swf** from Chapter 8 in the same folder, otherwise Flash won't be able to locate the soundtrack file.

Because we've made our sound controller modular, we can just drag it onto the stage as we did for our navigator menu slider.

1. Open **soundTrackControl.fla** as a library in **stun_scroll3.fla**. Drag the **soundControl** movieclip onto the stage and then delete it, because that puts it into our library.

   You always need to make sure that you keep your library tidy, so I've moved all three files that have now appeared in my library into the interfaces directory. The files are **invisible**, **soundcontrol**, and **meter**. I've also renamed these to fit in with my two-letter prefix (remember that **mc**). Be very careful though; you need to make sure that you don't end up duplicating library names as a result. We now have two invisible buttons, so if you rename invisible as **bu.invisible**, you'll have two **bu.invisibles** in the library, which isn't a good idea. Call it **bu.invSound** instead. There are now two identical invisible buttons (**bu.invisible** and **bu.invSound**) when I can actually do with one, but swapping buttons will only save a few bytes so it's not really worth the trouble to get rid of one.

You'll meet the same problem with **meter**, as there's already a **mc.meter** in the library, so call it **mc.meterBig** instead. I've renamed **soundcontrol** as **mc.controllerSound**, in keeping with **mc.controllerNavigator**.

The soundtrack comes in at about 150K, making it pretty hefty. Even though this streams in, I've noticed that sound-streaming is quite processor intensive for Flash, and it makes our side scrolling slow down noticeably on some machines. The number of times I've been looking at Flash sites in a quiet, busy office and had the Mac suddenly start thumping out a drum'n'bass number is 'more than once'. These two factors make me believe that a soundtrack should be off and unloaded by default, so that the user has to click on something to hear it.

To do this, I decided that the sound controller should be minimized somehow, and the user will only see it if they press a 'I want a soundtrack' button. Bring up **mc.controllerSound** in **edit in place** mode and I'll show you how.

2. Safe in the assumption that the user doesn't want to hear the soundtrack again if they stop it change the **stop** button text to **kill** or something similar. You may need to hide the button layer temporarily to do this. This button will make our sound controls disappear and unload the soundtrack SWF file. The soundtrack will stop after around four minutes anyway, because it's a composition rather than a looping rhythm, which I wouldn't want to impose on anyone irrespective of bandwidth limitations.

We need to change the level that the soundtrack is loaded at to `_level99` so that it's out of the way of all the other SWFs that we'll be loading later.

3. Do this by bringing up the actions for frame 1 of **mc.controllerSound** and changing both references to level `1` to level `99`. Your script should now look like this:

```
// start streaming in the soundtrack
loadMovieNum ("soundtrack.swf", 99);
// initialize sound object
soundtrack = new Sound();
soundtrack.attachSound(_level99);
// initialize meter positions
soundpan.graph._x = 50;
soundvol.graph._x = 75;
```

Change the action attached to **kill**'s invisible button pad from:

```
on (release) {
    soundtrack.stop();
}
```

to:

```
on (release) {
    soundtrack.stop();
    unloadMovieNum (99);
    gotoAndStop ("blank");
}
```

The last action will make the soundcontroller disappear by making it go to a keyframe with nothing showing. This is a frame we'll add in a moment.

4. Staying with the buttons, change the ActionScript attached to the **restart** button so that it now references _level99, not _level1;

```
on (release) {
    soundtrack.stop();
    _level99.gotoAndPlay(1);
}
```

Frame 3 of the **actions** layer currently has a gotoAndPlay(2); action. Because we'll be moving frames around in a moment, we'll make this into a gotoAndStop("label") first.

5. Give frame 2 a label **soundLoop** and change the Goto action in frame 3 to:

```
gotoAndPlay ("soundLoop");
```

We need to modify the timeline by adding a new frame 1, which will shift the existing frames 1-3 along so that they're now frames 2-4. The new frame 1 will be the minimized soundcontrols, and in this state they'll consist simply of the **stun:soundtrack** text and associated invisible button pad.

6. Add new keyframes at frame 2 for all layers except the **actions** layer. With frame 1 of the **actions** layer selected, delete everything on the movieclip's stage (drawing a big box around everything with the Arrow tool and then pressing **Delete** is the fastest way of doing this). This will give you blank keyframes appearing in frame 1 of all four layers.

7. Go to frame 1 of **actions** and create a new blank frame, which will appear at frame 2. Copy frame 1 and paste it into frame 2 (copy and paste frames by selecting the frame and right-clicking to bring up a menu).

8. In the new frame 1 of the **actions** layer, delete the script, (which is now in frame 2) and add a `stop()`; command. This will cause the sound control to stay minimized until the user says otherwise, and the soundtrack won't be loaded. Extend layers **buttons**, **text** and **sliders** to frame 4, so that your timeline now looks like this:

9. In frame I of layer **text** add the **stun:soundtrack** text that you see. I used Humanst521LtBT bold italic in 11 and 10pt. In layer **buttons** add an invisible button that covers it. Attach an `on (Release)`; `play()`; ActionScript to the button. As soon as the user presses this button, the **mc.controllerSound** movieclip will now go to frame 2, thus showing the sound control sliders and loading the soundtrack in.

10. Create a new keyframe in frame 5 of the **actions** layer and add the **blank** label. When the timeline goes to this frame (via the **kill** button's ActionScript), the controls will disappear and the soundtrack will be unloaded.

   In frame 2 of the **buttons** layer, drag an invisible button over the **vol control** and **pan control** text so that the sound controls are draggable in the same way as the navigator.

11. Give both buttons the usual actions:

```
on (press) {
    startDrag ("");
}
on (release, releaseOutside) {
    stopDrag ();
}
```

12. Create a new layer called **back** and make sure that it's at the bottom of the list of layers. Add a new keyframe at frame 2 and with this selected add some backgrounds to the controls in the same color as the web site background. See what I've done here:

Doing this is a lot easier if you change the movie background color while you make the change. This should mean that if the controls overlap a white background (such as the **stun** text), you can still make out the text. As a final step, turn the backgrounds into graphic symbols and give them 60% Alpha. Make sure that the **back** layer has four frames, like all the others.

13. Open up your **mc.page02**, and add a new layer called **soundcontrol**. Drag it down so that it's under **behavior** and **actions** in the layer order. If it doesn't already have two frames, add another frame so that it does:

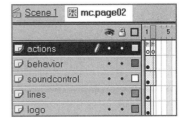

14. Drag our finished **mc.controller.sound** onto the stage with frame 1 selected. I've put mine just to the left of the bottom of the radar graphic and scaled it up to about 220%, as you can see:

Test your movie. If it doesn't work, compare it with **stun_scroll4.fla**.

> *You might remember, long, long ago, in the introduction, that we introduced you to the **Movie Explorer**. We said that it was the only place where you could print out an entire listing of your ActionScript from any part of your site. You probably thought "Uh, yeah, good idea" at the time. Now that your scripts are getting complex, you might start to see why this is such a great idea. Printing your code, sitting down with a mug of coffee and a red pen to see where things went wrong is often a very useful exercise. Here, you've the added luxury of being able to print my code as well and make a comparison.*

You might've noticed that the sound control also exists on frame 2 of **mc.page02**, which is where the page goes to when it's off screen so that it doesn't take up unnecessary processor power. We don't want the sound controls to disappear when the user changes pages and reset the sound every time the page re-appears, so we'll leave the controller in frames 1 and 2. The user always has the opportunity to kill the sound, after all.

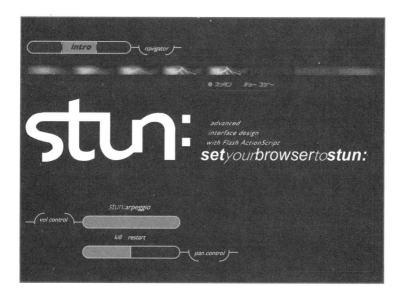

You *could* design the controls so they don't reset the sound object or reload the soundtrack every time the sound controls reappear instead. This would mean checking whether the soundtrack is already running with property `_level99._framesloaded`. The result of this would be 0 if the soundtrack hasn't started yet, so you know when not to re-define the sound object. You'd also have to make the `volume` and `pan` values global, because if they live on `_root` they won't reset every time that **mc.controllerSound** disappears from its timeline. This option is quite elegant, but I don't like it because I would prefer the sound controls to stay maximized until the user decides otherwise, rather than disappearing and leaving the sound playing.

Summary

In this chapter we've taken a look at seriously professional ActionScript techniques. We've covered:

- Best practice for modular, black box programming

- Creating modular movieclips

- Building ActionScript to create real movement

- Creating behavior movieclips

- Adding scrolling effects to stun:design

We're about to launch into the all important final chapter where you'll add the finishing touches to both the stun:design web site and the bottom line to the Extra Skills section on your resume: acommplished ActionScript programmer. Face it, that's what you are now.

11 Sprites

What we'll cover in this chapter:

- Creating sprites and assigning movement and collision behaviors

- Creating the stun:zapper game

- Adding a splash page and loading message to stun:design

- Creating a ticker tape message display for stun:design

In this chapter we'll go over what we mean by *sprites* and tie them into the related building blocks that you have already learned about in the last two chapters. Then we'll look at basic sprite functionality and how to create it, before deconstructing an entire game so that you will know enough about sprites to go away and start making your own games.

In reading this chapter, you are entering a new level of advanced ActionScript programming. This isn't the steep cliff-face at the top of the mountain it may seem at first, but is rather the integration of the concepts you have been looking at in isolation in earlier chapters. We're going to take the separate areas of ActionScripting and put them together to create something that is much bigger than the sum of the parts. The glue that holds advanced ActionScripting together is your ability to see through the problem with forward planning and be totally familiar with the separate building blocks.

What is a Sprite?

A sprite is a screen-based object whose behavior and actions are controlled by dedicated code that is integral to itself. This means that our main code can let the sprite get on with whatever it's doing in terms of movement, collision, appearance and so on, safe in the knowledge that it can look after itself.

It can be a space invader, or a happy little spider that follows you around the web site helping you when you get into difficulty. The sprite should be able to do three things without you having to keep an eye on it, none of which should be new to you. It needs to:

- Move

- Detect collision

- Act independently

The first point is that a sprite should be able to move around the screen in an intelligent way, and know if it's moving into areas where it shouldn't be (such as off the visible screen area), and take its own remedial action. This is really just an *advanced behavior*, which we looked at in the last chapter.

To create movement and other changes in the sprite, we have to alter *movieclip* properties, which you looked at in Chapter 9. The behavior ActionScript that we use will be slightly more advanced in its structure in that it doesn't control its parent but *itself*, with a new pathname called `this`. You already know about paths, so this should be just a variation on a theme.

The second point involves collision detection. A sprite should be able to detect when it's hit another sprite, and take the appropriate action – move away, explode, or cause what it's hit to explode. This is a new way of using old techniques – collision detection is just a new **method** that's applied to the movieclip object with (you guessed it) dot notation.

The last point involves the programming techniques we learned in the last chapter. Our sprite should keep the main program informed of what it's doing and what its status is. This strongly implies that our sprite routines should be designed using a **black box** or **modular** approach. The main program shouldn't have to bother with taking care of the sprite's movement or collision detection, and only needs to know what is necessary. The sprite is really just an advanced object that has methods that it applies to itself to control its own behavior.

In the last chapter, we covered the principles of something that went beyond animation, and moved into the realm of **simulation**. Simulation is a cornerstone for all that's related to advanced behaviors and specifically the behaviors' interaction with each other. To create a believable game world, we define rules for it, and everything in the world has to conform to them. The inter-interaction of the game sprites with each other is the difference between creating real time games and creating separate advanced animated effects for web sites.

We've already covered the principles that underpin the basic elements of sprite construction – it's just that you never knew you were a games programmer. There are three basic factors we need to consider for sprite construction:

- Control

- Movement

- Collisions

Let's take them one at a time.

Control

Control is all about simulating intelligence and giving the impression that the sprite is aware of what's going on around it.

Control is just a *behavior*. For our game, we'll steal the behavior for the aliens from the **behaviorSwarm** in the last chapter. We have to modify it to control itself so that it doesn't talk to Flash unless it has to. This is quite easy. At the start of all the paths, we remove _parent and replace it with _this.

For example, the **behaviorSwarm** movieclip (in **swarm.fla** from the last chapter) uses the following lines to move its parent:

```
_parent._x = shapeX;
_parent._y = shapeY;
```

To make them apply to the current movieclip itself, we change the lines to:

```
this._x = shapeX;
this._y = shapeY;
```

Rather than controlling another movieclip with _parent, we're controlling our own movieclip with this. Although that looks like a small change, it's a big change in scope. The behavior is now controlling its own actions rather than those of a separate movieclip.

Now that we're giving the sprite some independence, we need to remember that it has to be aware of its own surroundings and their rules. It's not talking to the main program any more, so it needs to know this itself. It's a big boy now, it's moved out into the real world and it has to do its own washing. As well as knowing about what is going on around it, our sprite also needs to be aware of its own internal status. These are two separate *levels* of influence: local and global.

Global and Localized Data

Think of sprites as people. As people, we have internal influences, such as our own thoughts and emotions. We also have information coming to us, say what's going on in the immediate environment, or television news about what's going on in another country. Our internal influences are the most important, but we need to be aware that we may have to adapt them in reaction to what's going on around us.

Sprites are the same. Their internally generated behavior controls them in the same way that our emotions control us. At the same time, though, the sprite must also look to see whether its actions are beginning to break the external rules by looking at the immediate environment. The sprite doesn't have the same level of complexity that we do. Its repertoire of interaction is:

- Step 1: Set my next movement as per my behavior.

- Step 2: Check whether I'm breaking any rules.

- Step 3: If I'm breaking no rules, modify my behavior as per the rules of my environment, otherwise move me as per my behavior (and keep repeating the three steps).

The simplest way to illustrate these steps is to look at **boundary violation**.

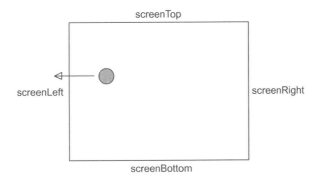

The sprite in the diagram has a behavior that causes it to move off the visible screen boundary. How do we tell it not to do that? One option would be to put something about the size of the screen into the sprite behavior itself, but that's not true to life. In real life, how far we travel depends on the circumstances surrounding us. If it's raining, we won't walk so far. Putting the size of the screen in the behavior also makes the behavior less adaptable. In future, we might want the behavior to change depending on a different external factor, something else that's happening. Having to build everything again doesn't really fit in with the modular lessons that we've been learning.

In real life we don't carry around with us information about our immediate, we perceive the *environment itself*. An easier and more consistent way to tell our sprite not to move off the visible screen is to realize that the screen boundary positions are a *worldwide* set of attributes, or something that everything in our world should know about. In other words it's a **global** piece of information that every sprite needs.

The contrast to this is **local** information that's contained within the sprite's immediate environment and not in the wider world. As an example, once the sprite moves, it would look at where its environment ends by looking outside of itself and onto the global (or _root) timeline. It would check global variables on the external timeline that tell it that it's violating a global rule and modify its behavior. In the same way, the internal thoughts of the sprite (I'm getting rather close to this other sprite) are only required by the sprite itself, and if anything else wants to know this information, it should have to ask the sprite.

We can see that information in our game world is also in two **levels**. The global information about the world is the lowest highest level, and as we get more and more specific, it gets less centralized and more concerned with individuals within the world. One sprite on one side of the screen doesn't really need to know that two sprites on the other side of the screen have just collided, it might put him off trying to kill the evil human at the bottom of the screen!

The key word here is **levels**, because it's something that Flash has already and something that we've been talking about in this book. We've seen that _root is the lowest level, and that the individual movieclips or embedded behaviors (if any) have their own level, which is their own timeline. So, to know global information about the world, any movie needs to look at the lowest or shared timeline, _root. If it needs to talk to or know anything from an inhabitant within the world, it looks at the movieclip timeline owned by that inhabitant's movieclip. Our world data is therefore structured around levels, and these levels are based on timelines.

We'll see how to apply this in the next section when we'll have a game world that consists of a section of deep space. Its inhabitants will be SwarmAliens and our courageous Lone Crusader© in his Starfleet SpaceCruiser™ that we met way back at the end of Chapter 1.

Our next issue surrounding sprite construction was quite a vital one: movement.

Movement

Movement is the most important attribute to the gamer, but to the programmer it's merely a consequence of control. We've already seen this in things such as the *swarm* behavior, which wasn't a movement so much as a section of code that controlled properties of a number of movieclips. The fact that these properties were actually associated with position is how the movement occurred, but we could just as easily have applied it to size (which we did with the Jell-o behavior), or color, and so on.

We don't need to say much more about movement. Movement is a visual property that we think is important in real-time applications, but to us as programmers, it's really just a consequence of all the control and relationships that we've set up in our game world. Talking about movement in isolation isn't meaningful. Instead, we'll be concentrating on the control we define that creates this movement in the first place.

If we want to create movement, we have to say "What's the behavior that is causing that movement, and what are the important features that I have to simulate to reproduce it?" We did exactly this with our *swarm* movement, by breaking down the swarming behavior, deconstructing its movement back to a set of rules that are followed to create the movement in the first place.

Now to our last point: collision.

Collision

Collision is a vital ingredient in a believable game world because most sprites have to know something is near them before they can interact, or change their behavior in some way. In the game we'll be looking at, collision means just that. In other, more sedate games it may mean something more fundamental: the initiation of complex interaction between the two sprites. In other words, sprites don't necessarily have to try to blow each other up!

In the *Ecology* game I mentioned in the last chapter, collision would mean that two creatures that are in significant proximity start interacting. The two sprites would have to be able to signal each other and retrieve information about exactly what type of creature the other one was. This information would allow the sprite to decide whether the other sprite was a potential mate, or food, a predator, or just another like-minded creature with which to swarm with for safety.

Collision is something new, so we'll show you in practical terms how it works in Flash. The file for this FLA is in the download file for this chapter as **collision.fla**.

What is collision? Two things are in collision if their boundaries intersect. This is almost the same as real life collisions. In real life, the boundary is the shape's outline but in the virtual world, this boundary can be bigger or smaller than the sprite outline, so two circles can 'collide' without ever touching each other.

In this exercise we'll create some basic collision detection. We'll create two circles and set up some dynamic text to tell us whether or not Flash sees a collision between them. We need to move the 'hitter' circle towards the 'target' circle somehow, and the easiest way to do this is by making it draggable.

Detecting a Collision

1. The first thing we'll need is our ubiquitous invisible button. Create a square one as usual, called **invisible**.

   Next, we want to create our two movieclips.

2. Create the first movieclip, which will be our target and call it **hitarea**. It has to be a single frame movieclip that has a definite shape, so make a circle and convert it into a graphic symbol called **circle**. Drag an instance of **circle** onto the stage of the movieclip.

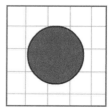

   Next, we want to create the 'hitter'.

3. Create a new movieclip called **hitter**. Name layer 1 **circle** and drag an instance of **circle** from the library into it.

4. Create a layer called **button** and drag an instance of **invisible** out of the library into it. Scale the invisible button to fit around the circle:

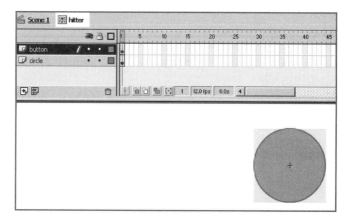

5. The button needs the to be draggable, so attach these actions to it:

```
on (press) {
    startDrag ("");
}
on (release, releaseOutside) {
    stopDrag ();
}
```

6. Still in **hitter**, create a layer and call it **text**. Put a dynamic text box just underneath the circle. This will contain a bit of dynamic text set up to display a variable coll (as in collision) so enter coll into the **Variable** box in the **Text Options** menu. Check the **Border/Bg** checkbox so that the text has a border we can see. Uncheck the **Selectable** checkbox:

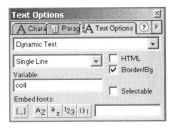
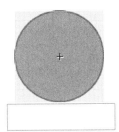

7. Create another new layer in **hitter**, and call it **actions**. Give it two frames and extend the other three layers to two frames as well. In the first frame, we need to add these actions:

```
coll = "";
```

The variable coll is the one we're displaying in the text. Here we set it to nothing by simply putting nothing in the **Value:** field of the setVariable action, and leaving the **Expression:** field unchecked. This is because we want it to show 'nothing' as opposed to 'Undefined'.

```
if (this.hitTest("_root.hitarea")) {
    coll = "hit";
}
```

You need to type in the expression in the if(); statement by hand. (I guess you're adept at typing rather than using drag-and-drop by now, so I won't say you can also find hitTest() in the toolbox panel in **Objects > MovieClip**). Make sure that the this.hitTest part of it comes up blue when you've finished entering everything.

This script checks whether *this* movieclip (the one that contains our ActionScript) is touching our **hitarea** instance (which is the 'target' of our 'hitter'). The expression is **true** if an overlapping is seen, and **false** if it isn't. If it's true, our `if` will set `coll` to "`hit`", and we'll see this in the dynamic text field.

8. In frame 2 of the **actions** layer, add a keyframe and add a `gotoAndPlay(1)` action so that we'll be continuously repeating our hit test.

9. Drag two **hitters** and one **hitarea** onto the stage. Give the circle an instance name **hitarea** with the **Instance** panel. Test the movie.

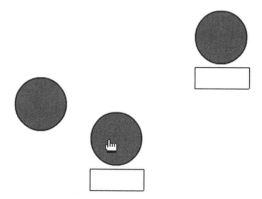

You can drag either of the two **hitters** around. If you drag either one over the **hitarea** instance, you'll see the dynamic text change to tell us a that a collision has taken place between the two.

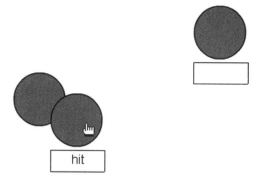

This would make a nice drag-and-drop interface. You could have the user physically drag and drop products (which would be the equivalent of our circles) into a shopping basket for example, or have a MP3 downloads page where the user chooses the music they want through record icons dropped into a DJ's record bag.

Before we continue I should draw your attention to a couple of things. You have to name the item you want to detect the collision with, so you must know its instance name. This means that you can't just detect a collision with anything. To do this would require a loop that looked at all available instances, which would mean that you have to know the names of all available instances at any time. We've got out of having to know what the instance name of the **hitter** is by simply calling it this.

Why did we drag two instances of **hitter** onto the stage instead of just one? We did it so that we could see that coll could be true for one **hitter** and not necessarily true for the other. The two variables have the same name but a different path, which makes them unique. Each instance's local variables are *unique* even though they share the same names because they are in different movieclips.

The hit detection sometimes gives a **true** when the circles are close but not touching. This is because we're checking whether the *boundary boxes*, which are the little outlines that appear when you select a movieclip on the stage of the movieclips, are touching:

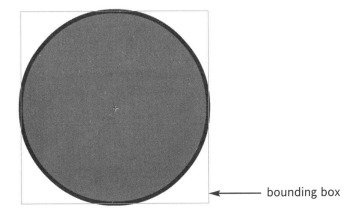

bounding box

You can modify the command to check for outlines rather than the bounding box, but this is a bigger job, and might slow Flash down in a video game. Talking of games, it's time to get on to the main project of this chapter – creating stun:zapper.

Planning stun:zapper

We'll create a space invaders type game, with swarming aliens at the top and the player's ship at the bottom. This is a pretty well known setup, so I won't waste your time by showing you a design breakdown of a game that's been in the public domain since the late seventies.

But this doesn't mean I haven't thought it through! To shape my initial concept and develop an idea of what will happen I thought of all the arena games I've played and broke down all the functions. I will live and die by my statement that introduced this book "If it doesn't work in paper, it won't work when you code it."

For simplicity's sake I've decided that the player will only be allowed one life and one bullet (so that there's only ever one bullet onscreen). Also, we won't have the invaders attacking by firing on the player. This is entirely possible, but I feel a little uneasy about defining a game with too many sprites on the screen at the same time. Instead, the aliens will perform some form of swooping or diving attack, which calls for fewer sprites and therefore a faster game.

One of the major reasons that Flash is disadvantaged is that it's forced to play its game inside a browser window and can't control the screen attributes, such as what size the full screen will be. Unlike dedicated consoles which actually play games on fairly small screens, usually no bigger than about 600x400 pixels, Flash has to play on a screen of unknown bit depth. This could be a screen size of 1280x1024, on which currently only the highest specified desktop computers can render acceptably fast games, and then only with some form of graphic hardware support. Flash has to do this on a platform that wasn't built for speed - the browser. The Flash player itself doesn't do us any favors either, as it doesn't grab all the available processor time for itself as most video games do. So, we'll keep things simple for the moment.

In the early arcade machines, they always made the games last a calculated amount of time for the average player. The difficulty level was graded so that the player would think they had got their money's worth. An important consideration at the planning stage, and one often overlooked by Flash games is how long do we want an average game to last? This affects all sorts of usability issues like 'is it too challenging?', 'does the game last long enough?', and 'does the player see enough of the game on the first turn to want to have another go?'. I generally assume that a good web game should last no more than one minute for the first go, have immediately obvious controls, and have no long preloads that break up the game. The player should also be able to get better from this abysmal start by practicing.

The next step is to plan how the game will work from a programming perspective. The block diagrams that you see here all relate to different aspects of the game and are taken directly from the three pages of handwritten notes and sketches that I scribbled down before I wrote the game.

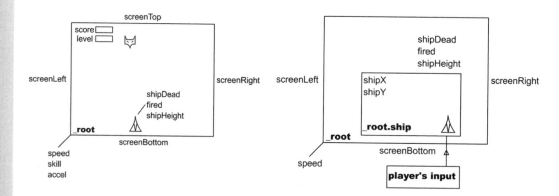

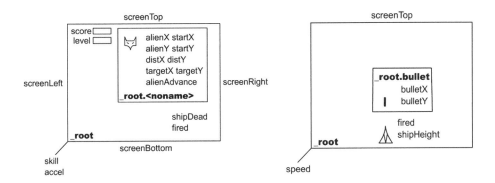

We'll come back to look at each of these in more detail as we look at the ActionScript behind each section. I wanted to show them to you here so that you could see how they're as useful as the flowcharts that we looked at in Chapter 2, but on a slightly higher level. Flowcharts would be more concerned with the detailed logic while these block diagrams are high level overviews that helped me to mesh together a game world with no logical flaws. Once I had these, I dropped down a level and began flowcharting the smaller ActionScript cogs of that world.

I found that these were a lot more useful than flowcharts because they imply *relationships* rather than logic and are easier to formulate. They really show objects and their interfaces, which is useful for getting an overview of what each game piece can see and interact with in the game world, and what in the game world will influence its behavior.

It took me half an hour to create these, and by the time I had finished I knew I could complete this game, because all the information was in front of me. This is the way you must work if you want to reach this level of ActionScripting, and it's more or less mandatory if you expect to do it commercially. I wrote this game in around eight hours, including planning, which isn't far from the timescale that you'll be used to in the real world. To turn ideas around that quickly you must plan everything out first in the same way that I've done. At first it may seem like something that is slowing you down, but with time you'll be able to quickly home in to the important bits very quickly, and you'll find that the time spent reaps massive savings when you come to code it all up.

I don't propose to go through the whole program as a tutorial in this section, because you should have developed far enough in ActionScript at this stage to be able to see what's happening. I'm guessing that you're probably more interested in seeing how our plans are converted to ActionScript so you can go away and do the same thing with *Missile Command* or *Defender*. I'll do a breakdown of the code and tell you what each bit does and my reasoning at every stage.

As I've said, you need to plan all aspects of a game before coding it. What I'm going to do here is show you the plans and the code separately for each section so that you get a clear view of what the ActionScripting is doing in each section. Don't think for a moment that I only planned one section at a time!

The Game World (the global level)

One of the important issues in designing your game world is *approximation*. You want to concentrate only on those things that are important in your game. Deep Space has all sorts of things that we are not interested in, such as temperature, radiation intensity, even gravity (which we are simulating indirectly). They won't affect anything in our game world, so we don't need them. This is an important thing to have a feel for, and it is one of the defining features of good simulation; knowing what to leave out and what to leave in...

The things I think we need to look at, the things that define the world in which our sprites will live and play are shown here in the finished game, followed by the first block diagram that I showed you:

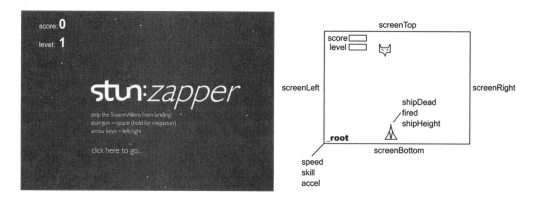

All of these properties are defined within the root timeline and are all **global parameters**, that represent something about the environment of the game world that affects every instance in it. I'll define each one in turn and in a little more detail

screenTop, Bottom, Right, Left

These are the game world limits and represent the visible screen area. We'll see later that the game actually allows some sprites to start off outside the game world, but their behaviors will force them to move back into the game world.

score

score is really there for the player and represents the carrot that keeps the player wanting to have another go. In the final game, I've never got more than 600 points. So now you have an incentive. As we'll see, score also feeds into the level parameter.

level, skill, accel

level is an important world parameter, because it controls how well the *SwarmAliens* will play. It's derived from the score, and the higher the score, the higher the level gets. The longer the player survives, the harder the game gets. level works by feeding into several other parameters that control the alien behavior; skill and accel(eration). As the aliens get more skillful, they will attack more, and as the accel parameter changes, they will get to their top speed faster, and therefore get from A to B quicker.

speed

speed is how fast things move in pixels per frame. The aliens will have a slightly different movement strategy, based on the equation in the last chapter, but the stars and player's ship will have movement based on this parameter.

shipDead, fired, shipHeight

These are some parameters about the player's ship that will be needed by the other sprites, so I decided it would be more convenient to make them global. ShipDead represents whether the player has died or is still fighting the good fight. Fired tells us whether a bullet is in the process of being fired. ShipHeight is an odd one. I put it in because I could see it being important for at least some other sprites. One of these would be the bullet, which needs to start off at the top of the ship because that's where it's fired from. I thought it might also come in useful if the game ran too slowly. The aliens can't hit the ship until they are ShipHeight above ScreenBottom. We don't really need to test for collisions between the aliens and the ship until then. As it happens, the game ran fast enough and I didn't need to do this, but if you decide to develop the game further – and I hope you do – then you have this option to consider.

Let's go and have a look at how I have coded this. Dealing with global issues involves the main timeline, so open **stunzapper.fla** from the download file for this chapter and have a look at the main timeline:

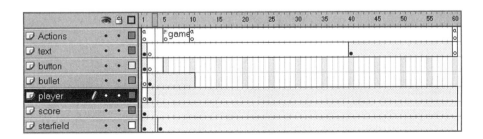

Frame 1 of the **Actions** layer shows the start screen:

Frame 1 of layer **Actions** also initializes all the global parameters that we've just discussed:

```
// set up screen
screen_left = 20;
screen_right = 530;
screen_top = 20;
screen_bottom = 380;
// general game constants
speed = 10;
skill = 0.04;
accel = 20;
score = 0;
level = 1;
fired = false;
shipDead = false;
shipHeight = 40;
stop ();
```

The script then stops and waits for you to click on a button to start the game.

This is required because there is a bug in Flash 5 (at the time of writing) that prevents keyboard presses being detected until at least one mouse-click has been seen. The Flash movie can be one of several things in a browser window, so when you press anything on the keyboard, the browser doesn't know which plug-in or textbox or whatever the key press is supposed to communicate with unless you give the browser a hint by selecting the target by clicking on it. Waiting for the user to click to start a game tells the SWF that we want to select it as well as starting our game.

Once the player has clicked the invisible button behind the **click here to go...** text, the game proceeds to the loop in frames 5 to 10.

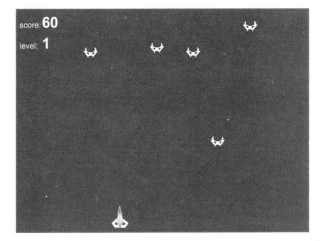

The game loop continues until the player has died, signified by `shipDead` being true. A check is also constantly being made during this loop to see whether the score is above `score x level`. If so, then the skill level of the aliens is doubled and the level increased by one. The first time this will happen is at `score=200`, and it will then occur every 200 points thereafter. The script that does this is attached to frame 10 of layer **Actions**, and it looks like this:

```
if (score>(level*200)) {
   skill = skill*2;
   accel = accel/1.5;
   level = ++level;
}
if (shipDead==false) {
   gotoAndPlay ("gameLoop");
}
```

This will continue to loop back to frame 5 (`gameloop`) if the player is still alive.

The other important feature of the main timeline is the starting positions of the aliens:

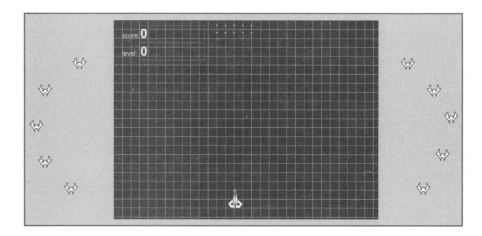

There are 10 aliens, arranged in two semi-circles just off the screen area. This is to make sure that they don't just 'appear' when they re-spawn, but rather scream in from the sides.

Frame 40 is the *GameOver* screen and, in true video game tradition, there's a short pause between frames 10 and 40 before it appears. Frame 60 simply sends the game back to the start so the player can try again.

The Player (the ship object and its interfaces)

The player's sprite has no intelligence or behavior of its own, but rather takes its movements from the player's keypresses. All it really has to do is move left and right, and fire on demand from the player. It also has to check that it's always within the game world.

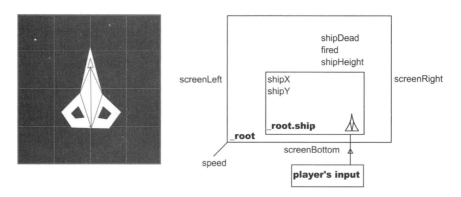

I've defined two **local variables**, ShipX and ShipY, that tell me the current position of the ship. By looking at the players inputs, I'll know whether the player is asking for the ship to move left (shipX = ShipX-Speed) or right (ShipX = ShipX+Speed). I also want to check that I'm not going too far to the left (ShipX<screenLeft) or to the right (ShipX>screenRight).

The ship movieclip needs to control the firing of the bullet. If the user hasn't already fired so that there is already a bullet on the screen, and fired==true, we want to allow the bullet to be fired. We then need to make fired==false so that the player isn't allowed to fire again until this shot has completed.

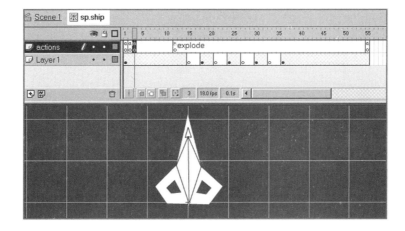

If you look in the ship's timeline, you'll see that it contains three action frames. The timeline will jump to that label **explode** to make the ship blink and explode if it's hit (which means that shipdead==true). The three action frames are really where it all happens, so we'll look at those in detail.

The key codes are the values used by the **key** object, which you haven't met yet. The key object is very simple to use, and to detect a particular keypress all you have to do is find the key code for the key you want to detect. Use the action Key.isDown(key code) to detect whether the key is currently down. Placing it in an if statement's argument is usually the best way of handling the detection.

> *The codes for each key are listed in the Macromedia documentation for each particular key, which you can access via* **Help > ActionScript Reference**, *and look under the* **Keyboard Keys** *and* **Key Code Values** *section. It's also in Appendix B of the* ActionScript Reference Guide *if you have the printed material.*

I've defined the codes for the keys we use in the game – the left arrow, the right arrow and the spacebar:

```
// define key codes
left_arrow = 37;
right_arrow = 39;
space = 32;
```

Frame 1 initializes the sprite: the initial position of the sprite is to be the middle bottom of the screen, which equates to half way between screenRight and screenLeft, and at screenBottom:

```
// set up ship variables
shipx = (_parent.screen_right-_parent.screen_left)/2;
shipy = _parent.screen_bottom;
// move ship to initial positions
this._x = shipx;
this._y = shipy;
```

Frame 2 is the main controlling code and I've done this for the three keys:

For the left arrow, we want to reduce the ship's x co-ordinate by speed as long as it won't take us past screenLeft.

```
// user inputs
if (Key.isDown(left_arrow) && (shipx>_parent.screen_left)) {
    shipx = shipx-_parent.speed;
}
```

For the right arrow key, we want to increase the ship's x position by speed as long as it doesn't take us past screenRight.

```
if (Key.isDown(right_arrow) && (shipx<_parent.screen_right)) {
    shipx = shipx+_parent.speed;
}
```

The spacebar allows us to fire the bullet but only if there is no bullet currently in the process of being fired. If we're OK to fire, we need to make the bullet's x position the same as our ship's x position so that it fires from the same position that the ship is at.

```
if (Key.isDown(space)&&(_parent.fired==false)) {
    _parent.fired = true;
    _parent.bullet.bulletX = shipX;
}
```

Finally, we need to move the ship. Notice that I'm only changing the ship's *x* position. I don't need to change the *y* position because the ship doesn't move up or down, just sideways.

```
// ship movement
this._x = shipx;
```

All this script above is useful as a template for anything that's required to move or happen as a result of keyboard inputs, so we have re-usable code again. Remember that the key object is a bit buggy, and will only work if at least one mouseclick has occurred since the browser window was opened (it seems to work OK in test mode within Flash though!).

Frame 3 is a looping action that looks to see whether the ship has died (through shipdead) and either causes the ship to carry on moving or explode, depending on the outcome:

```
if (_parent.shipdead) {
  gotoAndPlay ("explode");
} else {
  gotoAndPlay ("shipLoop");
}
```

The SwarmAlien (the alien1 object and its interfaces)

In many ways, the *SwarmAlien* is the only thing in the game with intelligence. Its movements are based around a real motion that uses acceleration, and it defines its own behavior, attacking or swarming based on a fairly advanced script. It also advances down the game world as time goes on, getting closer and closer to the hapless player. It is only a matter of time... The *SwarmAlien* makes all the collision detections in the game, which is fairly impressive considering it's the main target. Altogether quite an intelligent lifeform!

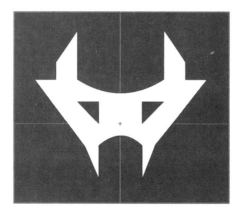

In logical terms, in our game the aliens are hitting the bullets rather than the other way around. It's actually easier to do it this way because each alien has to make one check for a bullet, rather than the single bullet having to check for all aliens. This seems a bizarre way to model our 'bullet hitting' detection, but it actually results in less code.

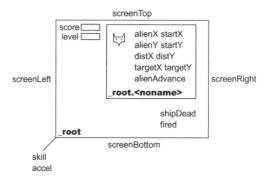

The first surprising thing to notice about the alien is that it has no instance name. This is because it doesn't need one; it doesn't divulge any information to the other sprites so there's no need to reference it.

The alien has a scary number of local variables. AlienX and AlienY are its position on the screen, and StartX and StartY are its starting positions. The starting positions are used because the alien never actually really dies. Once it's been hit it waits a short time and re-spawns at the original start position, which is just off screen. There are, actually, *always* the same number of aliens about at any one time.

distX, distY are variables that we've met before; they are the **where we are – where we want to go** terms in our real motion equation from the last chapter. targetX, targetY is our *where we want to go*. The alienAdvance variable is a modification to the *swarm* behavior we saw in the last chapter which the aliens will be using. It represents the distance from the top of the screen that the alien is allowed to swarm in. As the game progresses, this variable gets higher and the alien swarms lower down the screen, making it closer to its target theat ship. As soon as the alien has been shot, the respawned alien has to start again from the top, and alienAdvance is reset to its start value to make this happen. The secret of the game is to shoot at the lowest aliens, because they will, on average, have the highest alienAdvance, and therefore give you the biggest headache.

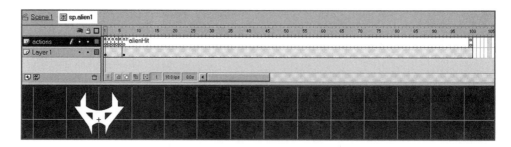

The alien timeline consists of seven action frames. We'll look at them in order.

The first frame initializes the alien. I've looked at its `_x`, `_y` properties and equated `alienX`, `alienY` and `startX`, `startY` to them. The alien acts rather like a salmon in that when it dies, it's re-spawned at its original birthplace, the positions off-screen you saw earlier. It's important to keep a record of the start position, because it's different for each instance.

The last line sets `alienAdvance`, which is a measure of how low the alien is allowed to swarm.

```
alienX = this._x;
alienY = this._y;
startX = alienX;
startY = alienY;
alienAdvance = 4;
```

Frame 2 is one of two large scripts (don't worry, there's only one more). The first `if` looks at `skill` and compares it with a random decimal number between 0 and 1, as supplied by the Math object's `random()` method. If `skill` is higher than the random number, the alien will perform a diving attack motion, and if it's lower, the alien will simply swarm. As `skill` gets larger, there's an increasing chance that the alien will attack rather than swarm aimlessly. In other words, it will become more *skillful*.

So how does it attack? Well, we'll be using the **behaviorSwarm** behavior that we defined in the last chapter. That had a target set of variables which was our **where we want to go** term.

If the alien decides to swarm, our `target` is a random position somewhere in the top `1/alienAdvance` of the screen. `alienadvance` is 4 to start off with, so we're initially looking at the alien swarming somewhere in the top quarter of the screen, well away from the ship and posing no real threat (the words 'sitting' and 'duck' come to mind).

```
if (_parent.skill<Math.random()) {
   targetX = Math.random()*(_parent.screen_right-
_parent.screen_left);
   targetY =
_parent.screen.top+Math.random()*(_parent.screen_bottom/alien
Advance);
```

If the alien decides to attack, we set the `target` to be the ship's position, plus or minus a small random value. This means that the alien will now attempt to swarm to a position that's very close to the ship, it not directly *at* it! These lines will cause the alien to switch from the benign swarming motion into a kamikaze dive bomb...

```
} else {
   targetX = _parent.ship._x+((Math.random()*100)-50);
   targetY = _parent.ship._y-5;
```

The second `if` caters for the fact that there's no bottom limit to how far down the aliens can advance. If the alien intended to go lower than the bottom of the screen, it's constrained to just above the bottom of the screen. In this way, if the alien actually intended to move across and behind the ship, it will actually now sweep towards the ship on a collision course:

```
}
if (targetY>_parent.screen_bottom) {
   targetY = _parent.screen_bottom+10;
}
```

Frame 3 is the big one. Here's where our modified **behaviorSwarm** comes in. Here's where you see code re-use at work, because it's essentially the same idea with a few tweaks. The first five lines are almost the same as the ones you saw for **behaviorSwarm** except we have added a '1/constant' term that is now `1/accel`. As `accel` gets smaller, the aliens will get quicker and more efficient.

The first block of code works out how far the alien is away from where it wants to be and stores this distance as the `dist` variables. This is then used in the movement equations to create a new position part-way towards our target, `alien`.

```
distX = targetX-alienX;
distY = targetY-alienY;
// Apply inertia equation
alienX = Math.round(alienX+(distX/_parent.accel));
alienY = Math.round(alienY+(distY/_parent.accel));
```

The first `if` checks whether our alien has reached the bottom of the screen, or 'landed'. If it has, the code jumps to label `alienLanded` in frame 5.

```
if (alienY> _parent.screen_bottom) {
   gotoAndStop ("alienLanded");
}
```

The second `if` looks at whether we are close to our `target`. If we've reached our destination (or rather, are within 10 pixels of it), we allow the alien to swarm a bit further down the screen in recognition of its bravery in getting so far. We then jump to `alienInitialize`, which will set a new target for the alien to move to. This will, on average, be slightly lower down the screen and closer to the ship. In this way, the alien will slowly advance down the screen towards the hapless ship. Notice that I've reduced `alienAdvance`. This variable decides which fraction of the screen the alien can swarm in, and reducing its value will increase that fraction (sanity check: a third is less than a half; as the bottom number decreases, the fraction goes up in value).

```
if ((distX<10)&&(distY<10)) {
    alienAdvance = alienAdvance-0.05;
    gotoAndPlay ("alienInitialize");
}
```

The final part of this block of code performs the sprite movement and checks to see whether our alien has hit either the bullet or ship. If the bullet has hit our alien, we jump to frame 6 (alienHit) and set fired to false (which allows the user to fire again). If we've hit the ship, we want the ship to die (and we communicate this by setting shipdead). For added realism, you could also make the alien explode as well by going to alienHit as before, but I kinda think the alien deserves a break for its bravery.

```
// perform animation
this._x = alienX;
this._y = alienY;
// check for collisions
if (this.hitTest(_parent.bullet)) {
    _parent.fired = false;
    gotoAndPlay ("alienHit");
}
if (this.hitTest(_parent.ship)) {
    _parent.shipdead = true;
}
```

Frame 4 simply sets up a loop so that the previous frame is constantly re-run with a gotoAndPlay.

Frame 5 is the frame we jump to if the alien lands. In this case, the alien just freezes where it is. This means it's now level with the ship, the ship has less room to maneuver, so it's not something you want to happen to often. The initial version of the game ended the game when this happened, but this felt a bit unfair, so the final version of the game lets the player soldier on.

```
this._y = _parent.screen_bottom;
stop ();
```

Frame 6 is what happens when the alien is hit. This is a simple script that adds the points for this kill to the score (10 for each alien, multiplied by the current level, so you get more points the longer you last), and sets alienAdvance back to its initial value. Although it's not obvious by looking at the timeline picture, the alien graphic is replaced by an explosion at this point, and disappears after the explosion has faded.

```
_parent.score = _parent.score + (_parent.level*10);
alienAdvance = 4;
```

The alien sprite stays at the position it died for approximately another 95 frames, and the final frame in the timeline sets the alien up for another attack, re-spawning it off screen at its original birth place.

So the aliens never really die, but wait a while and are re-spawned behind the scenes! Killing them is really a bad policy, because they just come back stronger (but it's fun trying).

The Bullet (the bullet object and its interfaces)

The bullet is the thing that comes out of the player's gun. There is actually only one bullet in the game – you are actually always firing the same one, although it's no less potent with each use. I hope for humanity's sake that your aim is better than the joker in the picture... miles away from the target! (well, OK, it was me).

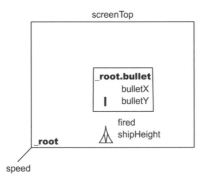

You can tell that the bullet is a simple object just by looking at its object diagram. At the instant it's fired, it takes on the *y* co-ordinate of the ship (bulletX=_root.ship.shipX). It continues up the screen until either it hits an alien on the way up, or it reaches the top of the screen (bulletY==screenTop). While it's traveling up the screen, it moves at 2*speed. Obviously, our bullet has to travel faster than the other elements in the game to be believable, and making it travel at twice the game speed is how we're achieving this bit of reality.

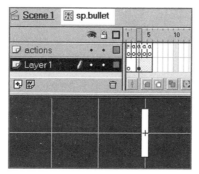

The bullet has two states. It can either be 'not being fired', or 'being fired'. If it's not being fired, we want it to be invisible. If it *is* being fired, we want it to be visible and move up the screen until it either reaches the top of the screen, or it has hit an alien.

Frames 1 and 2 are the bullet being invisible. **Layer 1** is empty, so the bullet movieclip is empty. The corresponding ActionScript for these two frames keeps looking for the bullet is 'being fired' condition.

Frame 1 is a blank keyframe labeled blank. Frame 2 created a loop that goes back to frame 1 (thus keeping the bullet stationary and invisible) as long as fired==false, signifying the bullet hasn't been fired. As soon as this condition is true, the bullet timeline will go to frame 3, and the gun has been fired.

```
if (_parent.fired==false) {
   gotoAndPlay ("blank");
}
```

Frame 3 initializes the bullet for its journey towards the aliens. The ship object has already initialized the bullet's *x* position, and the bullet now does the same for its own *y* position. It needs to fire from a height equal to the top of the ship, a distance given by screenBottom - shipHeight. The bullet is now made visible via Layer 1. The fuses have been lit...

```
bulletY = _parent.screen_bottom-_parent.shipHeight;
this._y = bulletY;
this._x = bulletX;
```

Frame 4 simply decreases the y co-ordinate of the bullet, bulletY, causing it to move upwards in a straight path:

```
bulletY = bulletY-_parent.speed*2;
this._y = bulletY;
```

Frame 5 checks the bullet's condition. If it goes beyond the top of the screen or fired becomes false for any reason, the bullet is no longer being fired, and it goes back to its invisible state by jumping back to frame 1 (blank). Notice that I set fired to false before this jump. This is because if the bullet has gone above the screenTop, we need to set fired to false, because nothing else in the game will.

The OR logic in Flash looks like this: ||. It's called a **pipe symbol**. On the rare occasion that you use it you may find it difficult to reproduce manually. So I guess it's lucky then that Flash gives it to you ready made - it's the last in the list in the **Operators** set.

If the bullet hasn't reached the top nor hit anything, we want it to continue on its journey by looping back to frame 4 ('bulletloop'). This also sets the bullet back to its 'ready to be fired again' condition if it goes outside the top of the screen:

```
if ((bulletY<_parent.screen_top)||(_parent.fired==false)) {
  _parent.fired = false;
  gotoAndPlay ("blank");
} else {
  gotoAndPlay ("bulletLoop");
}
```

There are a couple more things in the game, such as the explosions, but they are just a modified version of the stun web site star fields, which we'll be going through in the end of chapter exercise in a minute.

The Debris of War

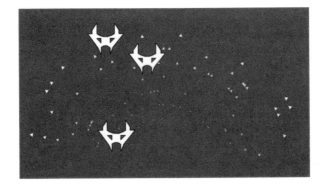

As well as the combatants, no laser battle in space is complete without some level of pyrotechnics. This game includes separate explosions for the aliens and the ship. The previous picture shows the *SwarmAliens* victoriously moving through the expanding plasma cloud that was once my spacecraft.

This is all about the scrolling starfield that is the backdrop to the battle. No space game is complete without one. You might also want to look at an additional file, **stunZappersound.fla**, which shows the game, plus the sound that goes with it.

Now for our final look at the stun:design in its finished state.

The stun:design Web Site

Before I started on the final push, I decided to step back and look at the site so far, and scribbled a few ideas.

Looking at the main site options (under stun:design on the **main** page), I figured that the **about** content could safely go to page 2 (which would otherwise be looking a bit redundant), the **we are different** button was looking too much like **our proposition** so I would substitute it for **stun:toys** (sounds like more fun as well; we're different because we like to play, and more to the point, are capable of coding some cool games and Flash applications).

Confidential zone is something that tends to appear on corporate design sites (it's usually a gateway to work in progress for those clients who haven't discovered the knack of jumping straight to the 'work in progress' URL for their commissioned site). I've never used a system like this so I decided to kill it.

Jake Smith of Subnet (a design house in England) provided me with three FLAs for our content, consisting of three FLAs for the menu options, so we're ready to start integrating them.

I'll take you through the three sections of the site:

- Splash page with its loading message

- Intro page with a ticker tape message

- Contents pages

I'll give you some background explanation and step by step instructions on doing something similar.

Page One: Splash

Page one of the site is the first thing that will appear. I've designed it to be static so that it doesn't look odd during the initial download, and I don't propose to add any content to it. It's a 'splash', or introductory, screen to set the style and I don't want it to be heavy on the eye. In particular, I need the user to quickly see that the navigator bar is the means of site navigation. Because it's slightly non-standard in its appearance, I don't want other controls, buttons and animations going off to confuse them.

The actions layer will be the last thing to load up (Flash will load the first frame of your movie bottom up in layer order unless you set **File >Publish Settings > Flash > load order** differently to this default). The navigation won't work until the code to drive it is in the cache. Because our FLA has the full basic site on all frames (although some movie clips will be hidden off screen, the whole site is actually there on the stage from frame 1), the site is ready to work as soon as frame 1 is loaded, and won't start working until then.

You can see this on the bandwidth profiler when you test the movie:

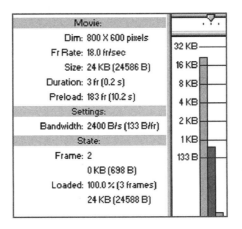

Frame 1 loads in 100% of the movie.

We'll add a loading screen because, although the main site is a mere 20 – 30K and the site has been designed to do without a preloader, there's something fundamentally different about Flash ActionScript sites over their tween-based cousins that makes it difficult to give the user feedback of the sites loading status. So, although it breaks my heart to add a loader screen to my compact little main site, I must remember that the site is there for your education... This loader is actually a much simpler version of the loader we saw earlier in the book, but don't worry, we'll be extending that particular system later to the heady status of streaming manager. Because we've already seen something very similar to this preloader before, I'll skip quickly through it. You can see the finished effect in **stun_scroll05.fla**. Don't forget to test the movie with **Show Streaming** enabled.

Creating the stun:design Loader

1. Create a new scene using the **Window > Panels > Scene** panel and call it **loader**. Make it the first scene by dragging it to the top of the list. Flash will load the scenes in the order shown by this panel, top to bottom:

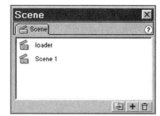

We'll create a percent loaded indicator in the **loader** scene, so the user is kept aware of the site's loading status.

2. If you're not already in **loader**, double-click on it to jump to it. You'll now have an empty scene to play in. Create three layers, **actions**, **percent** and **logo**.

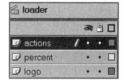

3. Add two keyframes in the **actions** layer and in frame 1 add the action:

```
siteLoaded = Math.round((_framesloaded/_totalframes)*100);
```

siteLoaded has been assigned the percentage of the site loaded in so far. We're using the properties _framesloaded and _totalframes to create a fraction of the total frames loaded over the total frames, and turning it into an integer percentage value. For example, if our site has 30 frames, and 11 of them have loaded:

11 / 30 = 0.3666 recurring
0.3666 * 100 = 36.66
Math.round (36.66) = 37

Therefore Flash will display that 37% of the site has already loaded.

Incidentally, notice that because there's no path Flash 5 knows I'm talking about the main timeline (you might even see the invisible this. path at work here). Although it's common knowledge amongst many professional Flash designers that this is the case, it amazes me that more people don't use the more visually arresting properties in the same way to affect the whole site. For example, if you use _alpha, in this way you could actually fade in/out the whole site. Why not try it on your next project!

Instead of showing a percent loaded value on a boring bar graph or numeric, get it to fade in by setting...

```
_alpha = Math.round((_framesloaded/_totalframes)*100);
```

...from the main timeline. Alternatively, you could zoom into the whole site as it slowly appeared with the _xscale, _yscale properties... or... need I go on?

4. OK, now that I've diverted you with yet more Flash food for thought, let's get back on track. On frame 2 add the action:

```
if (siteloaded<98) {
    gotoAndPlay (1);
}
```

We've set up a loop between the two frames that is constantly calculating the percent loaded for the site. I've set the siteloaded value to be 98 instead of 100 or 99 on the off chance that the rounding function rounds down and we never reach 100.

All we need to do now is display this percent value:

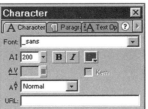

5. In layer **percent**, add a dynamic text field and assign it to our siteloaded variable. Choose the **_sans** font, so that Flash isn't weighed down by having to stream in the fonts.

The three fonts that start with an underscore are system fonts and Flash will get them locally from your computer, so there's no additional download time. Notice that I've made the font relatively huge (200 points). There are lots of preloaders out there that are tiny, but of course because we are using vectors, this is a false economy, so to be different I've gone for the opposite extreme.

6. Finally in layer **logo**, pull a copy of **sy.stun text** out of the library, and scale it to fit with the numbers. Put another, smaller, text box containing a % sign, after the number. The whole preloader comes in at a touch over 400 bytes, so we won't need a preloader to load up our preloader (not a joke, I've seen it been done).

So when we test the site now, with **View > Show streaming** enabled, we should see the percent loaded value go up smoothly to the high nineties, whereupon the preloader will get past our `if` action on frame 2 and go into our main site. Is that what happens with you? No? I'll explain why...

We're not measuring the percent of the SWF that has streamed in, we're measuring frames and turning that into a percentage value. Because ActionScript sites tend to have very few frames, a percent loader is next to useless, more so on our site because nearly all the site loads on one particular frame, causing unhealthy looking jumps and stops in the percent value. Not very visually appealing, and gives no information to the user. However, there is one way out – cheat.

Here's what we're going to do:

- We increment the percent loaded value by one every loop if it's less than the actual percent loaded value.

- If our fake percent loaded value is equal to the real percent loaded value, we stop cheating and wait at this real value.

- Once we've reached 98% loaded in real money, we immediately set our fake value to 99%.

The thing to remember is that the user isn't really worried about real values, but rather wants to see things happening to tell them that we're reaching some sort of conclusion.

Here's the timeline showing you that we have actions in four frames. I'll take you through frame by frame.

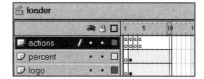

7. In frame 1, put the actions:

```
if (_totalframes == _framesloaded) {
    gotoAndPlay ("Scene 1", 1);
}
loaded = 0;
```

This is our skip frame. If we don't need a preloader (the site is already loaded, and the user has used the back button), we want to go straight to the main site.

8. We now have a fake counter called `loaded`, so change the dynamic text field to show this variable instead of `siteLoaded`, which is our real percent loaded value. The screen is blank on this frame because we want to skip seamlessly into the main site if there's nothing to load.

Frame 2 looks at the true `_framesloaded` value, and if it's higher than our fake value `loaded`, then we increment `loaded`. In this way, we'll see every percent value from 0 to 98%:

```
siteLoaded = Math.round((_framesloaded/_totalframes)*100);
if (loaded < siteLoaded) {
    loaded = ++loaded;
}
```

Frame 3 is simply our looping command. If we're not up to 99 percent, we'll go back to the last frame:

```
if (siteloaded<98) {
    gotoAndPlay (2);
}
```

Frame 4 sets the final value of loaded to 99 via the command:

```
loaded = 99;
```

You can see that I've then added six more frames, taking us up to frame 10 in all three layers. This will leave the preloader up at 99 percent long enough to show the user we've finished. If we go straight across to the next scene it looks a little rushed. Try it and see what you think. When you've spent some time taking a look, move on to page two.

Page 2: Intro

For page two, I wanted some sort of visual text for the **about stun:design** message. I didn't want any faddy swirling text effects as they are becoming a bit cheap and cheerless these days. Instead, I went for ticker tape or typewriter type messages, where text appears in a narrow window, sometimes scrolling in left-right (ticker tape) or one letter at a time (typewriter style). This gives a nice solid text effect, but with just enough movement to keep the message visual.

You can see the effect in **stun_scroll05.fla**. Go to page two of the site and wait a moment. You should see the text appear below the main strap-line (it's the line that currently reads **jake smith: webdesigner@subnet**.)

The way that the text message is printed is in a typewriter style, so it looks a little like this:

j
ja
jak
jake
jake
jake s
jake sm

And so on a letter at a time. When the line is finished, the typewriter text clears and starts on the next line.

So how do we print out a paragraph of text, a letter at a time? Well, we print a sentence at a time, and within each sentence, we print it a character at a time. To do this, we have two loops, one inside the other.

For each line in this paragraph {
**   clear the display**
**   For each character in this line {**
**   display what is already on display plus this character**
**   }**
**   }**

I expanded on this using a flowchart, which did a particularly good job of showing the workings of these nested loops. The text on the right-hand side is a dry run to show what is happening for the first line of a paragraph consisting of the two lines **hi there**! and, **how are you!**

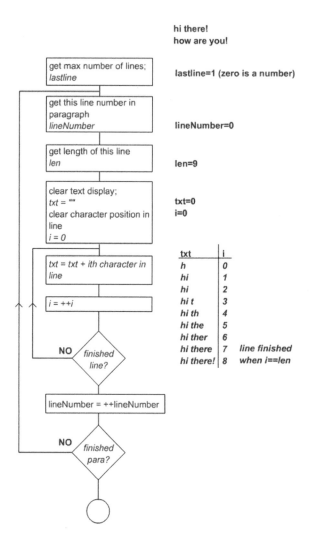

We'll be using arrays to solve this flowchart. Something that always trips people up with arrays is that zero is counted as a number, so that the second element in an array is myArray[1] not myArray[2], something to bear in mind as you read on...

So, running down our flowchart, from Block 1 at the top:

- **Block 1** – The maximum number of lines for our paragraph is 1, because we have two lines numbered 0 and 1.

- **Block 2 and 3** – The first line is line 0 and this includes 9 characters (including spaces), which is characters 0 to 8. (Yes I know, this zero business can get very fiddly. My advice is to always write it all down on a scrap of paper to keep some sense of sanity.)

- **Block 4** – My text to display is **txt** and I am using a loop counter **i** (the letter **i** is a traditionally used convention in coding to represent a loop counter). I clear both of these, noting that **txt** is a string variable and **i** is a numerical variable.

- **Block 5, 6, and decision** – This is a loop that runs through the sentence, adding the next character to **txt** in turn. The loop ends when we have done all of the characters. Notice that the check on **i** is done at the end of the loop so we are looking for **i==9** not **i==8** to finish the loop.

- **Block 7 and 8** – Set up a second loop around almost the whole flowchart to look at the next line.

So, the flowchart shows up our two loops, one on the outside to handle each line, and an inner one that looks at the characters in the line itself. You may have thought our earlier hangman game was a bit redundant for web design, but you can see here that we're using something very similar (and simpler). That's the magic of being able to code games - they give you an advanced understanding of ActionScripting techniques. If you can write Flash games, you'll walk over the simpler scripting needed for web sites.

We can code this now, but remember that we won't be using looping actions. This is because we don't want to loop within a frame, but between frames so that we can actually see the effect work over a number of frames, rather than being completed in a single frame so that we don't see anything.

The final text effect is in **mc.titles** (which you will find in the library folder **pages > page02**). Here's what its finished timeline will look like:

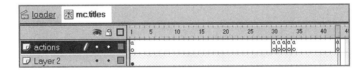

The next exercise will show you how I got there.

Creating the stun:design Ticker Tape Message

1. Create a new movie clip symbol named **mc.titles**. Add another layer and call the first layer **actions**. Make both of the layers 43 frames long.

2. On **Layer 2** add a dynamic text box to show our string variable **txt**:

*Be sure not to use the _sans, _serif or _typewriter fonts. These are system fonts and Flash doesn't treat them in the same way as the others. In particular, if you try to put them inside a movie clip such as mc.page02, they won't move about with the rest of the movie clip on the stage. They probably won't show up at all because they've been left behind outside the visible screen area when the page scrolls in via ActionScript control. I've chosen to use the Arial font. To save time and space, because Flash will have to download this font, I have told it to use the letters a-z only, plus the additional characters . : ' * @ , .*

Frame 1 of **actions** will contain the initialization code. This creates an array `line` and fills it with all the sentences to be printed typewriter style. Notice that some sentences have trailing spaces at the end. These are used to add pauses, Flash will be printing the spaces, but you won't see them so it looks like a pause. The last action gets the `length` of the array, which in this case is 15 (0 to 14, that pesky zero element again!).

3. Type the following code into frame 1:

```
// initialize titles.
line = new Array();
line[0] = "we are stun:design.";
line[1] = "specialists in advanced website design.";
line[2] = "*web multimedia.......";
line[3] = "*advanced user interfaces.......";
line[4] = "*web based applications......";
line[5] = "we have the weapons you need.";
line[6] = "don't forget to set them to stun:";
line[7] = "our work can be lethal.          ";
line[8] = "stun:design by:";
line[9] = "jake smith: webdesigner @subnet.     ";
line[10] = "anders dhyr: webdesigner @kpms.      ";
line[11] = "melanie o: content architect @friends of ed.  ";
line[12] = "sham b: webdesigner, freelance.          ";
line[13] = "to learn how to create your stun:designs";
line[14] = "get *foundation flash actionscript*.        ";
lastLine = line.length;
```

Frames 2 to 29 are blank, because I wanted to delay the start of the effect for a few seconds, to allow the page to settle and for the user to read the other text before they are compelled to read the animated text.

4. Insert a keyframe at frame 30. This is the initialization needed to start printing our text. It isn't in frame 1, because, unlike in the flowchart, I want my text to repeat over once all the lines have run through. To do this I only have to point Flash back to the first line via frame 30. Label this frame **lineStart**, so that you can easily set up a loop back to it later on. Finally, attach the following code to the frame:

```
lineNumber = 0;
```

Block 2 of the flowchart is something we've got by implication. The current line we want to look at is `line[lineNumber]`.

5. Insert a keyframe into Frame 31, and add the code:

```
len = line[lineNumber].length;
```

This represents **Block 3**. Notice that the `length` method has been used twice on a string object in two different ways so far, and given two different results. For example, if we apply it to the string object `line.length` Flash knows that we want to know the number of separate items in the array, but if we ask for the length of a particular array element in the object, it gives us the number of characters. This is consistent, because the method always gives us the length in terms of the number of elements at the object level we're looking at.

> *Implied here is the power of methods over simple actions. Methods are intelligent in that they know about object hierarchies and levels within an object, which is why you should use them over non-method based implementations (the power of dot notation yet again).*

Because the flowchart jumps to this block, I know I will be looping to here, so I've given it the label **lineLoop**.

6. Put another keyframe in frame 32. This is our **Block 4**, and has the following code:

```
i = 0;
txt = "";
```

7. Frame 33 is going to be **Block 5**, the first block in our inner loop. I therefore need to give it a keyframe and a label called **wordLoop**. Type this code into the frame:

```
txt = txt+line[lineNumber].charAt(i);
```

8. The keyframe in frame 34 is our **Block 6** and the first **decision** combined. If we haven't printed all the characters in this line, we want to print the next character via our inner loop with this code:

```
i = ++i;
if (i<len) {
    gotoAndPlay ("wordLoop");
}
```

After Frame 34, I've added another short pause, because the period in a line always signifies a pause. The final frame goes back either to our outer loop, having first incremented lineNumber, so next time around we'll be looking at the next line in the array line. If we've actually finished, we jump all the way to the beginning, starting with line 0 again.

9. To do this, put a keyframe into frame 43 with the following code:

```
lineNumber = ++lineNumber;
if (lineNumber==lastLine) {
    gotoAndPlay ("lineStart");
} else {
    gotoAndPlay ("lineLoop");
}
```

10. Now, go into your **mc.page02** clip and create a new layer called **ticker**. We only want this layer to be 1 frame long, so if 2 frames are automatically created, delete the second. Pull a copy of your **mc.titles** movie clip out of the library into this new layer underneath the logo, and finally, test the movie.

If you want to, you can easily alter the 'typewriter' effect to give a 'tickertape' effect by changing the code in frame 33. I'll leave this as a little project for you, but here are a couple of hints to start you off:

■ The new code needs to be something that, as well as adding char(i) to the right end of the string, also takes the leftmost letter away to create scrolling.

■ You will also need to initialize it so that:

txt = "<spaces equal to the number of characters in string>";

Rather than:

txt = "";

...as we have done for our typewriter effect.

Now for the main course.

Page 3: The Main Content

Almost all of our content is found in page three. We have to be careful though, because we don't want it to make our current slim file size shoot up dramatically. To address this, we'll load up the content separately. As well as freeing us from a bigger download as we add more and more content, this has the added advantage that our site consists of separate (and dare I say, *modular*) FLAs, and we can update the content of each separately.

Way back in Chapter 5 we briefly looked at adding windows to the site. We did this via loaded levels, which was an introduction to how we're actually going to do it here. Within stun:design we're going to load our content not external to level0 as additional levels (as we did then) but rather inside existing movie clips. Don't worry, this is the same principle, just a little more advanced. Now that you're comfortable with levels after what we did in we did in Chapter 5 I think it's time for you to try something that will be more useful to you in the long run.

OK, theory first.

Because levels are essentially 'new stages' in front of the main one at level0, when we use them to load content, we're limited somewhat by the size and shape of the levels. This makes them rather cumbersome to use because:

- You're limited to *absolute paths* (ones that start with *_leveln*). This kills all the structured modular movie clip design that we've talked about so far, because you have a great big dirty absolute path with which to talk to the new content.

- Rather than bringing content into your SWF, what you're actually doing is to layer it on top of your existing content, meaning that these layers have to be referenced individually.

- Levels come in only one size (the stage size) and their registration point is in the most annoying place possible – no, not their center, but their top left corner. You can't change it easily, which is an almighty pain. If you want to ever do some interesting ActionScript-based transformations on a whole level, it takes so much planning you'd be better off not bothering. Believe me, I've tried

- You can't refer to a level until it's been loaded, so any external ActionScript that does anything to it (for example, ActionScript in level0), can't communicate with a level until it knows that it's started streaming

We can gather from all of this that levels are good for overlaying simple animation content, or for segmenting largely unrelated content, but when you want ActionScript to talk across levels, the complexity really does go up exponentially.

Now, consider what I'm about to say.

A level is basically a timeline. OK, it's split into scenes, but that's just for ease of use. When the final SWF is created, the scenes are merged so that you end up with a single timeline.

A movie clip contains the same thing, a single timeline. So what if you could scoop out the timeline in an existing movie clip and replace it with something else and all during runtime over the Internet. What would that give us?

The most important point is that the movie clip would always be there, even if the content hadn't arrived yet. The movie clip still has the most important thing as far as ActionScript is concerned - an instance name with which to refer and control it. So, if we wanted to, we could be rotating the movie clip at the same time as content was streaming into it and our ActionScript wouldn't care. More importantly, our ActionScript could merrily do the same thing before the content had even started to load. You can use relative paths to refer to your loaded content. This means that your structure stays modular, so that your interface would always remain loaded, but the content could easily be changed. In essence, the loaded content that's in the target movie clip will look like it has always been there once it has loaded. Before the content is loaded up, you can have something else there as a placeholder, and this placeholder is what's in the movie clip when the main site comes up. If you want to lose your content, just jump to a place on the timeline where your movie clip doesn't exist. This is easier than using levels where you have to worry about unloading them.

Sounds incredible... How does it work in practice?

Consider the following. You have a site with lots of bitmaps in it, so you place a low-resolution bitmap in each of many movie clips. As soon as the user tells Flash that they want a closer look at any bitmap, you just load a higher-resolution (and probably bigger) bitmap into the movie clip. The part of the picture viewer that lets the user zoom and pan around the bitmap won't actually care whether there's a low-resolution or high-resolution picture there, or even if it's already in the process of loading.

The capability to replace the timeline of any movie clip during runtime actually exists in Flash. It's called a **load target** as opposed to a **load level**. For an ActionScript guru, the load target has to be the one to choose, but the best bit is that they use the same command: `loadMovie`.

The only difference is that instead of selecting a **Location:** of **Level**, you use the drop-down menu to select **Target**:

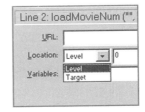

Then in the entry box to the immediate right of the **Location:** drop-down menu, you add the instance name, including any path from the timeline that your load movie command is attached to. This will cause Flash to replace the contents of the specified movie clip instance with the content of the SWF.

But that's not all.

When you created the SWF, you could have built it as a level0 timeline with scenes but you can still put it into a movie clip once it's been converted to a SWF. You've effectively built a movie clip that can have scenes! I can't emphasize how much this is the way to go if you want to build really big ActionScript/data-based sites. The ability to control such a monster has only really appeared in Flash 5, so most current Flash web sites are really just simple sites based around a single complex visual effect, or multiple loaded levels.

Now, how to use this practically...

We'll create a general window that has an embedded empty movie clip called **content**. Whenever we want to add content into the window, we just load a timeline into **content**, and it will show up in the window. The window will be a modular object that can load in any of our content. It will take care of things like loading content, maximizing and minimizing, dragging, etc, so that all our main timeline has to say is 'show this content'. The window will find it, load it, and allow us to do most things that you can do with a window.

Our window will have three states:

- blank (i.e. 'invisible')

- minimized

- maximized

There's a slight problem here because we can also have the content 'not loaded' or 'loaded'. Although we could just show a maximized window with blank content while loading takes place, this isn't really a good thing to do because it gives no indication of what's happening. For this reason, we'll have a fourth window state, called **loading**.

Our window will initially be in its **blank** state. Once the user requests that the window opens, there are two possible situations: either the content has loaded, or it hasn't. If the content *has* loaded, then fine - we just maximize the window. If it *hasn't* loaded, we have to go to the *loading* state.

> *The window object is actually a simple case of a rather fundamental programming structure called a* **state machine***. This is something that's used in high level programming in real rocket science, like industrial process control or computer systems that control missiles in air combat. It's a modal system, which means that the software can find itself in one of a number of different modes such as, 'unarmed', 'armed', 'locked on target', 'launching', etc, and does different things according to the state (or mode) it is in. I have never seen this discussed with reference to ActionScript, but then ActionScript was never up to the job of representing such software until Flash 5.*

We can use a state diagram to represent our window:

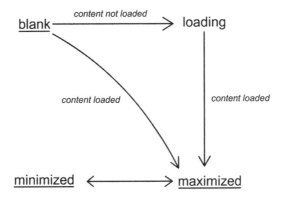

- The direction of the arrows connecting the window states is important because you can only go between states in the given directions.

- The **content loaded**, **content not loaded** conditions that are set have to be true before we can go along any particular path.

- The **maximized**, **minimized** and **blank** states are ones that we want to get to.

- The **loading** state is one that the user won't actually request to go to, but we have to take it into account because of the nature of the problem.

Looking at things in this way helps us out because we can look at each state in turn and say "Where can I go to, given I am at *this* state, and I want to go to *that* state, what has to be in place before I can?" You can then use a set of if... else structures to see where you are on the state diagram and what you can do next. It's also quicker to create than a flow chart for modal structures and easier to convert into basic code.

I'll break the problem down into its two main areas: the windows themselves and the content to go in them. Taking each in turn I'll show you what I did.

First, the window. It consists of four components:

- The window graphics and buttons

- The empty *content* movie clip

- Some simple ActionScript to interface the window with the content movie clip

- The controlling window behavior, which contains the code to drive our window as per the state diagram

The Window Graphics and Buttons

Here's a run through of my thought process for the windows and how I want them to look. I've based the design on the navigator and sound controllers to try and keep an integrated feel. The first thing I did was to design the window button icons as separate graphic symbols. These are the maximize, and minimize buttons:

They are 30 pixel circles with the appropriate square or rectangle drawn inside them. There was originally a close button as well, but it didn't last long. We'll see why in a moment.

Next, I had to design a window. I liked the rounded shapes of the navigator and sound controls and thought about using them as a theme. The window ended up as a rather simple affair, as you can see in the shot below. It's just a simple rounded square of fixed size. The content goes in the area currently occupied by my test animation (the film-reel countdown, currently at '3').

When the user clicks the minimize icon ⊖ at the top left of the **portfolio** window, it will become like the **clients** and **proposition** windows; just a title bar and a maximize icon. The viewer can use the icon to toggle between a maximized and minimized window. I decided not to have a close icon because the minimized windows just looked so cute. Yes, I know... Sometimes the most compelling reasons are also the least technical.

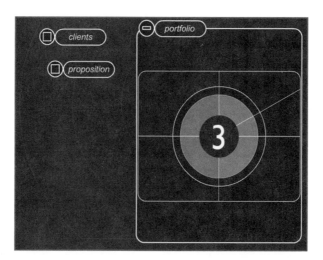

Now I'll take you through the details of how I created these, but rather than step through all of the instructions for drawing squares, I'll just give you a list of what's on each layer, and how it all fits together. Don't worry, I'll go back into more detail when things get difficult again.

The finished FLA for this section of the exercise is **stun_scroll06.fla**.

Creating the stun:design Windows

1. Create a new movie clip called **mc.clientWindow**, and fill it with the following:

Layer Name	Contents
Win Border	A 300 x 400 rectangle, with 20 pt rounded corners. Starts in frame 20, ends in 30.
background	To make this layer, cut the fill out of the **Win Border** layer and paste it in place here – I'll explain why in a minute.
WinBar	A similar rectangle 100 x 30, with 20 pt rounded corners Starts in frame 20, ends in 40.
WinIcons	Contains the minimise symbol from frames 30-39, then the maximise symbol in frame 40.
button	This layer contains 3 instances of our old friend, the invisible button. 1 over the **WinBar** icon running from frames 20-40. 1 over the minimise icon in frames 30-39, and finally, 1 over the maximise icon in frame 40.
title	This is just the name of our window – in this case **clients** – over the **WinBar** icon in frames 20-40.
loading	The text **loading...** which goes underneath the **WinBar** icon, and appears in frames 20-23.

The final window should look like this:

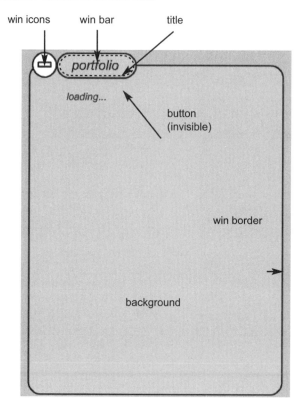

2. You need to add three more layers: **actions**, **WinBehavior** and **content**. When you've created all of your layers, rearrange them into this order:

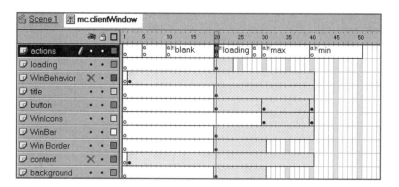

You can now see why I split the **Win Border** layer into two, so the content can go between them. This means that if our content is bigger than the window, it will show over the background, but under the border where we can easily clip it. You can also see a whole host of actions and labels in the **actions** layer. Don't worry, it looks more complicated than it really is.

> As an aside before we carry on, the reason that there's nothing on frame 1 of this movie is because from time to time there are problems with ActionScript in the first frame of movie clips being skipped. The way to get around this is just to move all of your layers forward one frame, it's as simple as that.

We'll cover the **content** and **WinBehavior** layers in a minute, but first let's turn our minds to that jam-packed **actions** layer. You may need to refer to our earlier state diagram here to recap on what we need each of our windows to be doing.

The whole window state machine revolves around a single variable win. This can be equal to the string values blank, loading, max and min, denoting the four window states. The only thing that can actually *change* the window state is the controlling behavior **ma.winBehavior**, which we'll be looking at last of all. The ActionScript on the timeline is really only designed to control the value of win, plus setting up a couple of other variables to enable content loading.

3. Frame 5 contains my initialization script:

```
// initialize
win = "blank";
oldWin = "blank";
startLoad = false;
movie = "WinClients.swf";
stop ();
```

We set win to blank to tell the window to start off in the *blank* state, which means that when the site starts, the window is still there, but it's currently sitting at a blank frame, and so not visible. I've also set a variable oldWin. This is set to be the same as win, but you won't see why it's so useful until we look at the behavior later on. We also have a couple of other variables to define: startLoad tells us whether the window has started loading its content yet, and movie is the location of the content.

4. At frame 10 is the label **blank**. At this keyframe the window graphics aren't yet on the timeline, so, although the window is actually there (in fact it's always there in the final web site) the user can't see it. This corresponds to my *blank*

state in the state diagram, and it just has a stop(); action attached to halt the timeline at this frame:

```
// Blank window
stop ();
```

5. Insert a keyframe into frame 20, and label it **loading**. This frame is the beginning of our loading loop that will run until frame 28. This loop will keep the window in the loading state until the content has completely loaded. All of the code for our loop goes in frame 28. The actions below check to see whether our content has loaded in. We know that it's finished when totoalframes = framesloaded. If this hasn't happened yet, we loop back to frame 20. Otherwise, we set oldWin and win up to force the behavior (which we'll look at in a moment) to send us to the *maximized* window state:

```
if (content._framesloaded <> content._totalframes) {
    gotoAndPlay ("loading");
} else {
    oldWin = "min";
    win = "max";
}
```

6. Frame 30 is labelled **max**, and contains the script for our *maximized* window state. Basically, this code just starts the content playing and stops the timeline from running on until we want it to:

```
// Maximized window
content.gotoAndPlay("show");
stop ();
```

7. The opposite case is true for the minimized state, which hides the content. At frame 40, insert the following code, and the label **min**:

```
// Minimized window
content.gotoAndStop("hide");
stop ();
```

8. The invisible button over the windows text is simply a button with the startDrag – stopDrag actions we are all familiar with by now, the code is as follows:

```
on (press) {
startDrag ("");
}
on (release, releaseOutside) {
stopDrag();
}
```

And that's the code done.

So to recap:

- Frame 20 is the first time that the window shows itself. This is the *loading* state.

- During this time the window shows up maximized (and cannot be minimized – as in the state diagram).

- The timeline loops between frames 20 and 28 (frame 28 has `gotoAndPlay("loading");`) on it, which causes the **loading...** text to flash during the load (it's the only thing on layer **loading**).

- Frame 30 is the *maximize* state. This is just like the *loading* state, except that there is now also a minimize icon:

- Finally, frame 40 is the *minimize* state. This state has just the title bar and an icon to get back to the *maximize* state.

The invisible buttons over the max and min icons simply request that the window is put in its maximized or minimized state as follows:

```
on (release) {
   win = "min";
}
```

or

```
on (release) {
   win = "max";
}
```

We'll see how the behavior that controls the window state handles this in a moment.

> *You may have realized that the only thing that will change between windows is the movie variable in frame 5 (and possibly also the position of the content within the window). That means that there's very little stopping you from turning the basic window design into a Smart Clip for use in your own sites. Simply use the movie variable to define the new content SWF per window. This will give you a Graphic User Interface (GUI) extension for Flash; the ability to display loaded content in a draggable window within the Flash player!*

We'll move on now to the empty content movieclip and the simple ActionScript that interfaces it with the window.

The Content Movie Clip

This is just an empty movie clip. It has nothing inside it except a blank frame 1. I've called this movie **mc.content** and placed it on the window movie clip's timeline. Our content will be loaded in this empty shell, so although it seems to do nothing, it is pretty crucial. So that the ActionScript can reference it, you *must* give it an instance name. I've called mine **content**.

You can see the **content** movie clip as the little filled dot in the top left of this picture:

The content can be anything, but it must have two frame labels on its timeline: **hide** and **show**.

hide is a frame that has no content. We can jump to this frame with a `content.gotoAndPlay("hide");` action. In the picture below it's on frame 2. It has a `stop();` action attached to it so that when the content first comes up, it's blank.

show is a frame that contains the main content, in our case a series of movie clips. To get to the content we have to do a `content.gotoAndPlay("show");` command. All the content SWFs are built around this scheme (you can find them as **winPortfolio.fla**, **winClients.fla** and **winProposition.fla**).

Now it's on to the behavior.

The Window Behavior

The **ma.winBehavior** movieclip converts our state diagram into code.

> You'll notice that the code in the final FLA **stun_scroll06.fla** *is commented. I've taken some of it out for the book because I am explaining the code as I go along.*

The behavior timeline is just a simple two-frame loop. Frame 1 is the code that implements our state machine, and frame 2 is a simple `gotoAndPlay` that takes us back to frame 1.

The crux of the state machine that you must understand before you can go off and design your own is this: although the user might want the window to go to a particular new state, the state machine may not be allowed to do so. Instead it has to go to another, intermediate state first (which I introduced briefly when I discussed why we needed a loading state).

So, we really need two variables to control our window state:

- The state we're at

- The state we would *like* to go

Our state machine looks at where we *are*, and how we can get to where we would like to go. If we can't get there, it will try to get us *closer* to it by jumping to another state.

> *This is a basic software concept, and an expanded version of this simplified description is used in such complex environments as microprocessor design (the microprocessor inside your computer is a prime example of a state machine, because almost everything in it is such a device).*

Back on planet earth, our two variables are win and oldWin. OldWin is our last good state (where we are) and win is our latest user request to change the window state.

The state machine knows that there's a change of state required if win and oldWin are *different*. For example, if we were at the maximized state and wanted to change the window to minimized, win would become "min", whereas oldWin would still be our current state "max".

So, the first line of the behavior looks to see whether the two controlling variables are unequal, to judge whether a change in state is needed:

```
if (_parent.oldWin<>_parent.win) {
```

Once we've decided that a state change is required, we need to work out which state we're currently *at* and which one the user is looking to go to.

The first if looks at 'I am at blank and want to go to maximized' (which is the only thing the user can request from the *blank* state):

```
// 1. User attempt to open window from blank...
if ((_parent.oldWin == "blank") && (_parent.win == "max")) {
```

The nested if statements run through all the possible situations that could be present when we try to go from blank to max;

No content downloaded yet. Our state machine looks at whether we can go to a maximized window or whether we have to go to the loading mode first. startLoad tells us if the content has started loading in yet, and if it's **false** we have no content. In this case we need to start loading off.

```
if (_parent.startLoad == false) {
loadMovie (_parent.movie, "_parent.content");
_parent.startLoad = true;
```

Of special note here is our loadMovie command. We're loading into the **content** movieclip in our _parent. The SWF name we're loading is held by variable _parent.movie (which we defined in the initialization frame, frame 5).

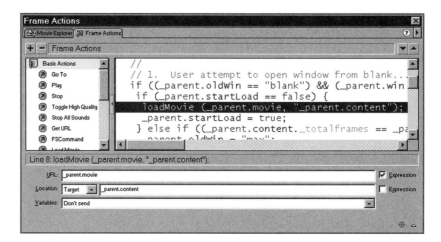

The **URL:** field is an expression (because it's held within a variable), and the target's **Location:** is *not* an expression (because it's a string literal specifying a path).

Otherwise, if loading has actually completed (which we'll know by looking at our content movieclips _totalframes and _framesloaded properties), we can make the window movie (our parent) go to its **max** state. Whenever we complete a state change, we flag up the fact that we have reached a new and 'stable' state (that is, one that we can stay at) by making *both* win and oldWin equal to the new state ("max" in this case).

```
} else if ((_parent.content._totalframes ==
_parent.content._framesloaded) && _parent.framesloaded <> 0)
{
  _parent.oldWin = "max";
  _parent.gotoAndPlay("max");
```

If we haven't started loading and we haven't gone to the *maximize* state, then we must be in the process of loading content, so we make the window go to the *loading* state.

```
} else {
  _parent.oldwin = "loading";
  _parent.win = "loading";
  _parent.gotoAndPlay("loading");
  }
}
```

The second big if looks at the state changes available from the maximized state. We can go to only one other state from here: minimized. To get to here, the content for this window must have already loaded in, so we have no checks to make (this is shown on the state diagram by the fact that there is no text on the connecting arrow).

```
  // 2. User Attempt to go from max window to min...
  if ((_parent.oldwin == "max") && (_parent.win == "min")) {
     _parent.oldWin = "min";
     _parent.gotoAndPlay("min");
  }
```

Finally, we can go back from the minimized state to the maximized state (and nowhere else).

```
  // 3. User attempt to go from min window to max...
  if ((_parent.oldWin == "min") && (_parent.win == "max")) {
     _parent.oldWin = "max";
     _parent.gotoAndPlay("max");
     }
  }
```

And that's it.

This state machine may look a bit complex, but state machines *always* look like this, and *always* use the same single action; `if` and `if... else`.

Think what you'll be doing in Flash with it in six months time once you've embraced and understood all of this.

Integration

To get our windows working, all we have to do is place them inside our third page movieclip **mc.page03**, and cause the existing menu buttons to bring up the windows by doing a `win = max;` request to the window.

After my little re-organization at the beginning of this exercise, the buttons I now have are as follows:

I created a new layer **windows** to put the window movieclips in. In all, we will have three windows: one for **portfolio**, one for **clients** and one for our **proposition**.

Because these movieclips will be invisible, and show up as little filled circles, it's a good idea to label them with a guide layer, as I've done here. The guide layer won't show up during actual runtime, so it's there as a reminder to us about what invisible movieclip is where:

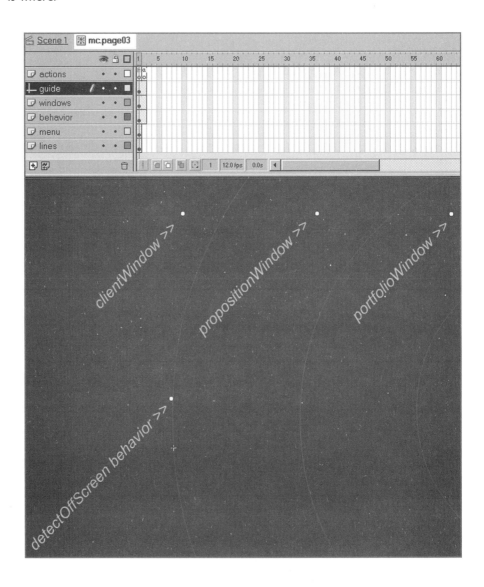

The window movieclips (which are called **mc.portfolioWindow**, **mc.clientWindow** and **mc.propositionWindow**) need to have instance names so I've called them **portfolioWindow**, **clientWindow** and **propositionWindow** respectively.

To call up any of the windows you simply place this request to open the window and the content within it:

```
windowInstancename.win = "max";
```

The state machine will go away and handle all the streaming, and so on, to get to a full open window with associated content. Cool.

I've made the button actions slightly more complex, because I decided that there wasn't enough room for all the windows to be open at the same time. The final script minimizes any other windows that are open as well as maximizing the requested window. Here's the script for the first window (**clients** and **proposition** are almost identical):

```
on (release) {
    portfolioWindow.win = "max";
    if (clientWindow.win == "max") {
        clientWindow.win = "min";
    }
    if (propositionWindow.win == "max") {
        propositionWindow.win = "min";
    }
}
```

The first action requests the **portfolio** window to be opened, and the next two if statements request the **client** and **proposition** windows to be minimized if they're currently maximized.

The final thing is to minimize all the windows if they're ever off screen (that is, page 3 isn't in the *front* position). Easy! Just add the following script to the **hide** label of **mc.page03**:

```
clientWindow.win = "min";
propositionWindow.win = "min";
portfolioWindow.win = "min";
```

You'll see that, although getting to here was hard, once we *are* here, and have our generic window created, controlling it is easy. We just tell it to maximize or minimize, and all the other stuff is handled by the window itself. Of course, since I created the movieclips, it goes without saying that the required movieclips are modular, so if you want to use the same system... you know what to do - just drag-and-drop, plug and play!

This basic window system is just itching to be added to though. You could:

- Make the window a Smart Clip. This is so easy I will leave it to you to figure out (there's a big hint in the text on how to do it anyway).

- Start the window content loading in without the user requesting it, making a sort of 'background load'. You would have all the windows looking for a global variable, _root.nothingIsLoading (a Boolean) to be `false`. The first window to see it could take it (by setting it to `true`) and use the spare bandwidth time. When you load anything in, you would make sure Flash took control of this Boolean, and if any window had taken control of it outside a user request, it would have to give it back and stop loading, discarding the content so far. This is actually using something called a **semaphore**. The nothingIsLoading Boolean is a semaphore variable that denotes ownership of a resource (the available bandwidth) that only one movieclip can use.

Let's finish off with a look at the last two buttons: **stun:toys** and **contact**.

The Last Two Buttons

I have made the stun:toys open in a new browser window rather than in their own Flash windows because of two reasons:

- The Flash player doesn't like taking too much by way of processor overheads. If instead you cause another browser to open another Flash SWF, they seem to take more of the processor time together (a useful thing to remember if you want to create more Flash videogames!).

- There isn't that much space left after the first three windows have been opened!

The action to open the stun toys is:

```
on (release) {
    getURL ("stun_toys02.html", "_blank");
}
```

If you look at this FLA you'll see that the stun:invaders have been re-packaged in the same way as the calculator and wire game... a welcome addition!

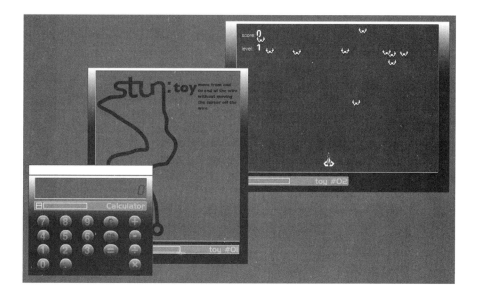

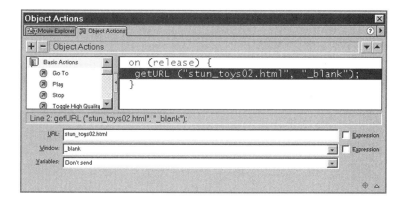

The **contact** button will be used to open a blank e-mail message that the user can send to the stun team. The action to do this is:

```
on (release) {
   getURL
("mailto:f_actionscript@friendsofed.com?subject=stun
website");
}
```

This is the same sort of thing as the last getURL except that we're not specifying a web address this time, but an e-mail address and a title for the e-mail

mailto: tells the browser this is a e-mail address, and if there's a default e-mail program set up, to open it with the e-mail address as f_actionscript@friendsofed.com with the subject as stun website:

Finally, because we'll be finally putting the main SWF into a properly sized browser, we no longer need to mask **layer** in the root timeline (it slows up the site in any case), so you can get rid of it.

All done!

The list of files you need to run the stun site is;

stun_scroll06.swf (and associated HTML, which you should rename **index.html** when you upload it to the internet).

The site content;
winPortfolio.swf
winClients.swf
winProposition.swf

The stun toys;
stun_toys02.swf (and associated HTML file)

The soundtrack
sountrack.swf

You need to run **stun_scroll.swf** from a location that contains all these files to see the full site with all the options.

The Last Farewell

This last chapter has been the hardest. I've included so much detail here that you may need to read it once, then come back to it after a while. The best way to learn this is to go away and try to build your own game, and come back and look at how I did it when you get stuck.

In this chapter, just as in the rest of this book, my reasoning has been to give you plenty to think about. I've wanted to make this book useful to you not just for a couple of weeks while you're learning the ActionScript ropes, but for a for a few months to come as you take on board everything that we've covered here in the context of what you do every day. We've looked at the fundamentals of what advanced ActionScript programming should look like, with multiple timelines, levels of variables, and a graphical method to plan it all out in the design stage.

There are particular additions to Flash 5 that make the creation of video games and advanced interactive presentations in general much easier, and this book has followed a path that covers all of them in detail. We've concentrated on Flash 5's use of dot notation. We have had more time to concentrate on varied *techniques* rather than having to look at every command and way of using them.

Knowing commands such as `setProperty` or the original way of doing `tellTargets` isn't as important as knowing really cool stuff like the principles of computer simulation, how to integrate soundtracks, explanation of the different available web site topologies, and sprite emulation. You haven't missed out, you have just been taught much more efficient ways of implementing these commands.

We've created an ActionScript-based site from the ground up, right from the planning stages, through setting up the navigation, adding interactivity, integrating sound capabilities seamlessly into the interface, making the site modular and ready to accept content.

This may be a book on ActionScript, but always remember that you're a designer first, and a programmer second. ActionScript has become a new and important design tool that you can use just as well as all the others.

Welcome to the peak of the mountain, and award yourself a chocolate biscuit and a cup of tea from that battered thermos. Take a look around – you can stay here, but there is a particularly enticing range just to the North with fewer tourists and better views, just waiting to be climbed. Hopefully, one victory has left you thirsty for more. Happy traveling!

stun

/stʌn/ *(-nn-)*

(a) [tn] daze or shock (sb) eg with sth unexpected

(b) [tn esp passive] impress (sb) greatly

*set*your*browsertostun:*

A Glossary

FLA

The editable Flash authoring file. This is the editable file that is created by the user during development.

SWF

The **S**hock**W**ave for **F**lash file is the final Flash output file, suitable for running by the Flash player or browser plugin. This file will be considerably smaller than the FLA and is no longer in an editable form. It is the file that must be uploaded to your server (along with the HTML file) when you come to publish your Flash site on the web.

Absolute (number)

A number stripped of its sign. Both +3 and −3 are 3 as an absolute number.

Absolute (path)

A 'route map' to get to a destination starting from the lowest level, which is always _root.

Action

A single ActionScript instruction. This term is identical to *command* as used in some other languages.

ActionScript

The programming language used in Flash 5. This language is a subset of the existing *JavaScript* language. It conforms to the ECMA-262 implementation of the language, but does not support some browser specific and other specialized commands within this standard. ActionScript includes some additional commands to this standard for compatibility with Flash 4.

Alpha

This percentage value refers to the transparency of an object. An Alpha of 0 is fully transparent, 100 is opaque.

Argument

Information given as part of an *action* that is required by the action to complete its task. It may include data to be manipulated or may be the name of the object that is the target of the action.

Bandwidth Profiler

The tool used to fine tune a Flash project before final publication. The bandwidth profiler will indicate how much bandwidth or download time a file is using.

Behavior

A term used in this book to describe a movieclip containing ActionScript only, whose function is to make its _parent behave in a certain way. The behavior can do this by controlling the _parent playhead (via gotoAndPlay actions for example) or by varying the _parent properties, which can alter position or appearance. Behaviors are a fundamental building block for advanced ActionScript-based animation.

Browser cache

An area of memory used by the browser to store downloaded content. A SWF file that has been loaded once before and is still in the browser cache does not need to be downloaded from the internet again.

Dynamic text

Text that changes as the variable assigned to the particular field changes during the movie.

ECMA

European Computers Manufacturers Association. A group concerned with setting standards for computer languages (amongst other things), and it does this on a copyright/royalty free basis. In particular, the ECMA-262 standard is the variant of JavaScript upon which *ActionScript* is based.

Event

A named occurrence, such as a mouse press, that can be used to start off the running of an associated set of actions called the *event handler*.

Flowchart

A graphic method of representing the flow of logic in a piece of code. Useful for representing branching or looping logic.

Instance Layer

A system used to place items on the screen into a number of imaginary 'depths' so that the items can seem to move in front and behind each other, and also so that the current tool can be made to affect only one (or a group of) depths.

Integer

The whole part of a number, minus any fractional or decimal part. The integer part of 3.14 is 3.

JavaScript

A scripting language launched jointly by Netscape Communications and Sun MicroSystems to create online applications. Most common browsers can run JavaScript, and it used to be the main way of adding interactivity into traditional HTML before the advent of Flash. The similarity between 'JavaScript' and 'Java' is a marketing ploy only; Java is in a totally different league and is much more powerful.

Literal

A symbol within an *action* representing a fixed value, such as 3 or "dog".

Modular

A design or portion of a design that has been written with re-use and extensibility in mind. This is achieved in software by using a number of features such as well-defined interfaces, self contained code and well documented code.

Movie Explorer

New to Flash 5, the Movie Explorer is a tool used to view all the components of your Flash movie and their positions within it.

Panel

A tabbed window used by Flash 5 to show information about the selected tool or the currently selected screen element. Panels replace what were previously called Inspectors in Flash 4.

Panning

The method of varying the sound volume in a stereo signal to give the impression of sound coming from an area rather than from the two point sources that are the two speakers emitting the sound.

Playhead

A marker that signifies the current frame of a timeline.

Relative (path)

A 'route map' to get to a destination which starts from where you currently are. An action that issues a relative command is said to be relative if the path is taken to be from the timeline the action is attached to. Code that uses relative paths is not modular.

State diagram

A graphical method for representing the individual positions, modes or levels of activity that a real or software object can put itself into, showing how these modes interlink. The state diagram is used often in top level software design, where the software *functionality* is represented as a *state machine* or a 'machine with a number of definite states'.

Sprite

A term used in this book to describe a movieclip that controls its own properties and local variables so that it alters its own movements and appearance independently from any other code. A sprite can be released onto a stage and will require little or no external guidance in making its own decisions, moving about or interacting with other sprites. The difference between a sprite and a behavior is that the sprite is designed to look at all its inputs (and responses to them) via a single centralized body of code, whereas a behavior is only concerned with one relatively simple set of actions, and complex movement usually requires many separate behavior movieclips.

Note this terminology is specific to this book only and does not refer to Macromedia's term *sprite* as used in Director.

Streaming

A Flash file that begins to play before it has totally loaded in at the user's *browser cache*. The use of streaming can give the illusion that content is loading in quicker, because the content plays while it is still loading in.

Syntax

The structure of a language. Applies equally to human and computer languages.

stun

/stʌn/ vt [Tn]
    (a) [Tn] daze or shock (sb) eg with sth unexpected
    (b) [Tn esp passive] impress (sb) greatly

set*your****browser****to****stun:***

B. Events

Button Events

Interactivity in Flash is largely created by detecting button events. All the basic events you need to be familiar with are listed below. The examples assume that you've created the button and timeline set up to show the text **event detected** as per the buttons section of Chapter 4.

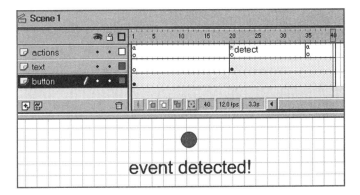

What we will do is set up the button to detect all the various available button events, and get the button to jump to label **detect** and start playing as soon as it does, which will bring up the **event detected** text. At frame 35, the timeline is told to go back to the start and stop, ready for you to press the button again.

Select the button and bring up the **Actions window** using either the little arrow icon in the bottom right of the screen, or via **Window > Actions**. Notice that the window is now called **Object Actions**, instead of the **Frame Actions** window you have used before.

Press

This option detects a mouse press. It doesn't wait for you to release the mouse button before executing the Go To. It may surprise some beginners to realize that this option is not actually used that often. It doesn't wait around, so in most situations you don't see the Down state of the button, which can look bad. If you uncheck **Release** and check **Press** in our button example, you'll notice that the **event detected** text disappears rather faster because it appears as soon as you click the mouse, giving you less time to read it.

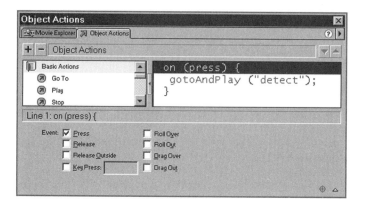

Release

This is the default option because most buttons use it. It's used in preference to **Press** because it waits for a mouse **<press><release>** action, allowing all three button states (Up, Over, Down) to be seen.

Release Outside

This option detects a **<press><move outside the hit area><release>** sequence. It doesn't really sound useful until you realize that you can check more than one on mouse event to detect. For small buttons, you can detect the **Release** and **Release Outside** events by checking both. Then, if a user inadvertently moves outside the Hit area before releasing their mouse button, the click is still detected.

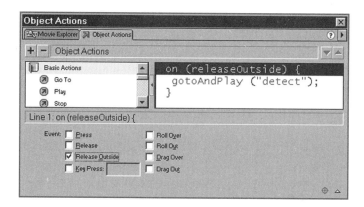

Key Press

This looks for the user to hit a key – they don't actually need to be able to see the button to do this so it's sometimes a good idea to use an invisible or off-screen button when you're detecting just keypresses.

Be aware that when you publish your movie, keypresses are sometimes not detected until at least one mouse-click has occurred because this is required to give the embedded SWF focus within the browser. Keypress buttons are a good way of taking inputs from the user for Flash games. To select the key to detect, simply enter it in the text entry area to the left of the **Key Press:** checkbox. This function is case sensitive, so be careful with those Shift keys. You could use this event to have a 'press spacebar to continue' type function instead of the more usual mouse-click, or allow the user to select an option from a numbered list by pressing a numbered key rather than having to point and click. The more considerate web designers would of course allow both mouse-clicks *and* keyboard entry by having *both* events checked...

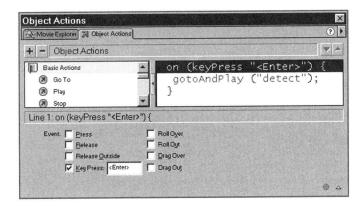

Roll Over

This event executes the `gotoAndPlay()` command as soon as you are in the button's Hit area. The event takes place without the user pressing anything. It's useful for detecting whether the mouse is within a particular area. If you had, say, a picture of a farmyard, you could use rollover events to make the sound of each animal as the mouse went over them.

Roll Out

This event executes the `gotoAndPlay()` as soon as the mouse rolls back out of the Hit area, having previously been inside it. It's something you would normally use in conjunction with **Roll Over**. The sound or movieclip that was started with the **Roll Over** would be stopped by the **Roll Out**.

Drag Over

This event detects a mouse that is pressed over the button and rolled out of the Hit area and then dragged back into the Hit area, whilst kept pressed all the time. It's not used that often, except for some rather specialized buttons used in draggable interfaces and games. When you're using this event remember that the Hit area *doesn't* have to be solid. (See the figure below for a hint... the left circle would be an *Up* button state, and the second circle on the right with the outer donut would be the *Hit* area.) Now that you've seen the wire game, stun:toy, created out of simple buttons, you may already have some cool ideas for another game. The possibility for designing a game where you have to drag a puck out of some kind of maze without touching the sides of the maze springs to mind (chased perhaps by an angry sprite that wants it back?!). A whole game based on a single button action. Whatever next!

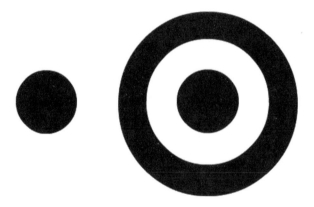

Drag Out

This detects a mouse that is pressed over the button and then moves out of the button while it is still pressed. You would use this event if you were allowing the user to drag something within a constrained area, and you wanted the dragging to stop if the user went outside the area (thus leaving the draggable button behind).

Movie Events

Load

The first frame that the movieclip appears on the parent timeline **loads** the movieclip. This event happens on the first frame that a movieclip appears on a timeline. You could use this event to play a sound on the first occurrence of a particular clip, or more usefully, you could use it to initialize related variables on the timeline in readiness to dynamically control the movieclip in some way.

Unload

This event occurs as soon as the movie disappears from the parent timeline it is sitting on. This event could be used to reset the variables in the *load* example.

Mouse up/down/move

These events check the mouse button or for mouse movement. Notice that this event doesn't care where the mouse is when the button is pressed or the mouse moved. You might use this to attach sounds to the two mouse buttons, irrespective of whether the click and releases occur over a button or not. It can also be used to set animations or other interactivity off on a mouse movement. I would avoid these events because they sound too much like precursors to eye candy! These events could, however, be used to detect a long term *lack* of interactivity from the user, and you could set in motion a number of increasingly humorous and/or aurally loud movies to bring the errant user back in line...

Key down/up

These events check for a key press and release. Note that you can't specify *which* key. This would be an advantage if you wanted to add a 'press any key to continue' type function, and is better than using a button's **on keypress** event (as described in the button section above). This is because you wouldn't really be bothered which key was pressed for the continue to occur.

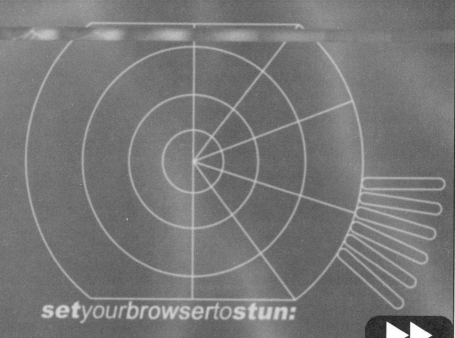

stun

/st n/ *vt[t:v]*
    (a) [tn] daze or shock (sb) eg with sth unexpected
    (b) [tn esp passive] impress (sb) greatly

set**yourbrowserto**stun:

This appendix lists selected properties of the movieclip object that will be useful to the Flash programmer. Examples of use are included for each property to get you started in ActionScript based animations. The examples all assume that you have a movieclip with instance name *shape* on the stage. You can quickly create this symbol by:

1. Draw a filled square on the stage. (NB - make sure the square is selected in all the following steps.)

2. Make it 50 pixels in width and height using the **Info** panel's **H:** and **W:** boxes.

3. Press *F8* to create a new movieclip symbol. Call the new symbol **myshape** and make it a movieclip.

4. Bring up the **Instance** panel and enter **shape** in the **Name:** field.

5. Call the layer that the square is in **symbol**.

6. Add a new layer above this called **actions**. Attach the actions stated below to frame 1 of this layer (unless directed otherwise).

You might want to save this FLA at this point to use as the starting point for all the examples below, by the end of which you will be a master of properties!

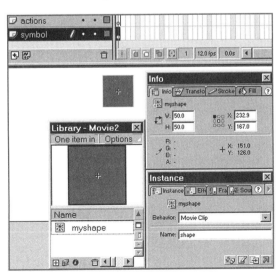

Alpha

Affects the transparency of the movieclip and gives the same transparency variation as the Alpha effect in the **Effects** panel.

Example of use:

```
shape._alpha = 50;
```

This gives the symbol an Alpha of 50%.

Height

Affects the height of the movieclip bounding box in pixels. You can see the starting height of the movie via the **Info** panel's **H:** field, or by reading the _height property itself (via ActionScript) before you start writing to it. You should not set this to a negative value.

Varying this property will also affect _yscale (the percent height property) listed below. If your movieclip changes its size over time (like the circle below, which gets bigger due to a tween animation within the movieclip itself), you should realize that the _height and _width properties will change as well from one movieclip frame to another, making the _height and _width properties pretty meaningless. Unless you want to scale your instance to a definite pixel value, you should use the _yscale property instead.

Example of use:

```
shape._height = 200;
```

This gives our symbol a height of 200 pixels. Note that this won't scale the shape by a proportional distance in width at the same time, resulting in an elongated rectangle. To scale the circle proportionately, you'll need to add the line below to the end:

```
shape._width = 200;
```

Rotation

Controls the angle of rotation of the movieclip. You can see the starting angle by looking at the angle field in the **Transform** panel, or by reading the _rotation property itself before writing to it. Entering a positive angle will result in a clockwise rotation, and negative will give you counter-clockwise. An angle of 90 will cause quarter clockwise rotation, and an angle of 180 will cause a half clockwise rotation.

This is how to rotate our **square** instance smoothly by a quarter turn:

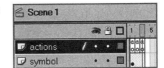

Extend both layers to three frames via the f5 key. Add keyframes to the **actions** layer at frames 2 and 3:

In frame 1 of **actions** add the action:

```
rotationAngle = 0;
```

In frame 2 of **actions** add the action:

```
shape._rotation = rotationAngle
```

In frame 3 of **actions** add:

```
rotationAngle = ++rotationAngle;
if (rotationAngle<=90) {
  gotoAndPlay (2);
} else {
  stop ();
}
```

This code sets up a loop between frames 2 and 3 that increases the _rotation property from 0 to 90 in steps of 1 degree, resulting in a smooth animated rotation. The if statement at frame 3 stops the looping when our angle rotationAngle is greater than 90.

Visible

This is a Boolean value that can be set to true (visible) or false (invisible). The invisible state is more like a 'disable' state, because buttons that are in an invisible state can't be clicked (which makes it a good shortcut way of doing pop-up menus and the like). You don't want the buttons active when the menu is invisible and 'un-popped'.

The following code will toggle the `_visible` property to make our symbol flash:

Extend both layers to frame 10 with **F5**.

Add a keyframe at frames 5 and 10 of layer **actions** with **F6**.
In frame 1 of **actions** add:

```
shape._visible = false;
```

In frame 5 add:

```
shape._visible = true;
```

In frame 10 add:

```
gotoAndPlay (1);
```

This code sets up a loop between frames 1 and 10. The symbol isn't visible between frames 1 to 4, and visible between frames 5 and 10 of the loop, resulting in a flashing effect.

Width

This is the same as `_height` above, but concerned with a movieclip's width.

X and Y

These two properties are the *x* and *y* positions of the centre point of the movieclip (denoted by the little cross when you edit any movieclip). This is a very important pair of properties because changing them will let you *move* your movieclip, so they're the two properties you're most likely to use in ActionScript-based animation. The rulers can be used (via **View > Rulers**) to show the *x* and *y* values and how they vary across the stage. Also, be aware that each movieclip has its own set of internal *x,y* co-ordinates, with 0.0, 0.0 at the center point of the movieclip. So, ActionScript on the timeline of a movie and ActionScript on the root timeline that both move something to 20.0, 20.0 *will move their respective objects to different positions on the stage.* You can see this by selecting **View > Rulers** and looking at what the rulers show as 0.0, 0.0 for the stage and the movieclip when you edit it. The figure below shows what you'll see when you edit a movieclip. 0.0, 0.0 is at the center-point of the movieclip, and not at the top left-hand corner, as it is for the stage:

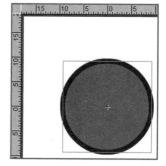

The following code will move our symbol horizontally across the screen from left to right until it reaches the far right end, and will then repeat the action.

Extend both layers to frame 3. In layer **actions**, add keyframes at frames 2 and 3.

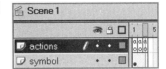

In frame 1 of layer **actions** add:

```
xPos = 0;
```

In frame 2 of **actions** add:

```
xPos = xPos + 5;
shape._x = xPos;
```

In frame 3 of **actions** add:

```
if (xPos>=500) {
   gotoAndPlay (1);
} else {
   gotoAndPlay (2);
}
```

This code varies the _x property between 0 and 500 in increments of 5 pixels. If we've moved the symbol all the way to the right-hand side of the screen, the if on frame 3 takes us to frame 1, where we reset our position xPos to zero, taking us back to the left-hand side. If we haven't got to the far right, the if goes back to frame 2 and continues to be moved 5 pixels to the right.

xscale and yscale

These are the same as _height and _width above, but they're measured in *relative* percent values. *100%* is the value of the movieclip before you do anything to it. This means that if a movieclip increases its own size due to tween animations (as described for the _height property above), then although the pixel size values will change, the % value will stay at 100%. Because of all this, _xscale and _yscale are usually more meaningful than _height or _width when you're using ActionScript to perform size transformations. Varying the _xscale and _yscale properties will obviously also affect _height and _width pixel values.

The following code will reduce the size of our symbol by 50%:

```
shape._xscale = 50;
shape._yscale = 50;
```

This sets both the _xscale and _yscale property to 50%.

xmouse and ymouse

These tell you the current position of the mouse cursor. These are read only values. Asking for the mouse position from the root timeline and asking for the same thing from a movieclip's timeline will give you different results.

Movieclip Properties

Currentframe

Returns the number of the frame where the playhead is currently located in the timeline. See examples of how to use this property in the video controls in the Chapter 10.

Droptarget

Specifies the name of the movie that the movieclip was dropped on to. for more information see Chapter 9.

Framesloaded

Shows the number of frames that have been loaded from a streaming movie. For more information see Chapter 9.

Name

Allows you to change the instance name of a movieclip. For more information see Chapter 9.

Quality

Refers to how the Flash player renders each frame. For more information see Chapter 9.

Target

Finds the path of a specified named movieclip, so you don't even have to bother with knowing the path of a movie to be able to control it. For more information see Chapter 9.

Url

Tells you the URL that the movieclip was loaded from. For more information see Chapter 9.

Totalframes

Shows the number of frames in a movieclip. For more information see Chapter 9.

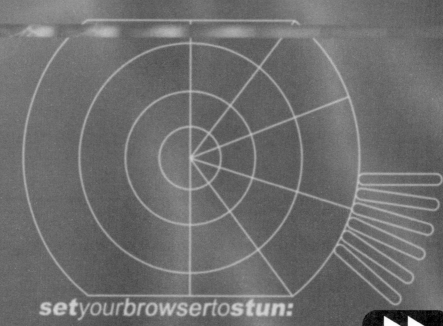

stun

/st n/ x r g

(a) [tn] daze or shock (sb) eg with sth unexpected
(b) [tn esp passive] impress (sb) greatly

set_yourbrowserto_**stun:**

D Operator Precedence

When you use variables and literals to create expressions there are a number of rules you need to follow to ensure that Flash works out the expression the way you intend. The following sections give rules to ensure that you and Flash know what to expect of each other when you start writing ActionScripts with complex expressions within them.

Variables

If you enter an action

   $a = b + c;$

it's normally obvious what type *a* will end up as if you keep *a*, *b* and *c* the same type. For example, if *b* and *c* are the numerics 3 and 2, *a* will be the numeric 5. However, it isn't always obvious what the result will be if you mix types:

1. If *b* or *c* are both string variables, *a* will be a string. If *b* was the string literal *"calling car number"* and *c* was the number 3452, *a* would be the string literal *"calling car number 3452"*.

2. If *b* is a string and c is a Boolean *a* will be a string. If *b* was the string literal *"please be"* and *c* was the Boolean *true*, *a* would be the string *"please be true"*. Some users might have expected this to work out as *please be 1*, because *true = 1* and *false = 0*.

3. If both *b* and c are Boolean variables and c is also a Boolean. This is actually a useful feature if you want to do something only if two out of the three Boolean conditions *x*, *y* and *z* are *true*. If you add them, the majority is true if the answer is 2 (because *true = 1, false = 0, and* 0+1+1=2). This can be very useful when you want to simulate a *majority* gate, which is true when *most* of the inputs are true (useful in creating expert systems and games).

▶

So the rules of combining variables are:

string + string = string
string + numeric = string
string + Boolean = string

numeric + numeric = numeric
numeric + Boolean = numeric

Boolean + Boolean = numeric

The best way to learn this is to build a single frame movie with the script:

a = "hello ";
b = true;
c = 5;
d = a + b;

and output *d* as dynamic text. Try setting *d* to all the combinations of *a*, *b* and *c*, and use the minus operator as well.

Operators

This book hasn't exhaustively covered every operator because it's not designed to be a reference manual. The Macromedia reference material doesn't provide a complete reference on how to use operators that would be useful to the beginner either, so we've included examples of the use of each of the main operators below. You can find the full list of operators under **Operators** in the **Actions** panel:

Logical NOT (!)

This will give the *inverse* value for a Boolean. If the bracket would have worked out as true, putting a ! in front will make it false:

```
b= 1;
a = !(b==2);
```

The script above will give **a = true** if **b** isn't equal to 2. Putting a ! in front of this condition in an `if` statement is like saying **if this is not true**:

```
if !(myBoolean) {
    //these actions will only be reached
    //when myBoolean is false
}
```

Logical AND (&&)

This gives the Boolean **AND** result. You would use it in an `if` statement if you wanted to say:

if this and that is true, do these actions:

```
if (this) && (that) {
    //do these actions
}
```

this and **that** are expressions that must work out to true or false, such as (x ==5) or (myBoolean).

Logical OR (||)

This gives the Boolean OR result. You would use it if you wanted to say **if this is true or that is true, do these actions:**

```
if (this) || (that) {
    //do these actions
}
```

this and **that** are expressions that must work out to true or false, such as (x ==5) or (myBoolean).

Test inequality (!=)

This will give **c** true if **a** doesn't equal **b** in:

c = (a != b);

You would typically use this in the condition of an `if` action:

if (a != b) {
// do these actions
}

It replaces the old Flash 4 way of writing it (<>), which has been used in the main text in some places of this book. It's noted that you would see the same result to the above if you used:

c= !(a == b);

Modulo (%)

This gives the remainder of a division. 11 divided by 4 is 2 remainder 3. If we wanted to know the remainder of this calculation and place it in variable c we could write:

a = 11;
b = 4;
c = a % b;

Increment and Decrement variable (++ and --)

These operators either add or subtract 1 from a variable. There are two ways of writing either:

y = 5;
y = ++y;

will perform a +1 first to give y as 6.

y = 5;
z = y++

will do the equal first (to make **z** equal to 5) and then add 1 to **y** to make **y** equal to 6. A similar case exists for the decrement version of this operator.

Less than, less than or equal, greater than, greater than or equal (<, <=, > , >=)

These operators can be used to test the whether the left side of the expression is 'less than', 'less than or equal', 'greater than' or 'greater than or equal' to the right side. The result is a Boolean.

```
a = 3;
b = 4;
c =  a < b;
```

Would give **c** = **true** because 3 is less than 4.

```
a = 4;
b = 4;
c =  a < b;
```

Would give **c** = **false** because 4 is equal to 4 and not less than it.

```
a = 4
b = 4
c = a <= b;
```

Would give **c** = **true** because 4 is less than or equal to 4.

```
a = "a";
b = "b";
c = a < b;
```

Would give **c** = **true** because the string 'a' is alphabetically before 'b' (as would a = "A")

```
a = "d";
b = "b";
c = a < b;
```

Would give **c** = **false** because the string 'd' is alphabetically after 'b'.

A similar case exists for the 'greater than' and 'greater than or equal' tests. These operators are usually used in if statements to see if one variable is greater than another variable or numeric:

```
if (a > 10) {
// these actions will be run only if
// a is greater than 10
}

if (b <= c) {
// these actions will only be run if
// a is less than or equal to c
}
```

Operator Precedence

The order that Flash performs an expression can have an impact on the final result. Consider the expression below:

```
b = 2;
c = 3;
d = 4;
a = b * c + d;
```

a will work out as either 10 (if **b*c** is evaluated first) or 14 (if **c+d** is evaluated first).

When you learned elementary math, you may have been taught to remember the word BODMAS. This is short for Brackets Open, Divide, Multiply, Add, Subtract, and is the standard order that expressions should be evaluated in math. First, evaluate everything in the brackets, then do all divisions, then multiplication, then additions, and finally subtraction. So, applying BODMAS to our equation, **b*c** will be evaluated first, and the answer will be 14. If you wanted Flash to calculate the **c+d** term first, you would have to force Flash to do so by adding brackets:

```
a = b * (c + d);
```

Using BODMAS, you can see that the following expression would give you 2.6667:

```
b = 2;
c = 3;
d = 4;
a = b / c *d;
```

The divide is evaluated before the multiplication (D comes before M in BODMAS) to give (2/3)*4.

As a general rule, if you're not sure about operator precedence, use brackets. This practice will make for more readable code for non rocket-science mathematicians, and is unlikely to result in noticeably slower code (animations and the physical drawing of vectors takes up the lion's share of processing time).

The order of operator precedence can be confusing because you have so many operators other than +, -, * and /. You also have logical operators and string and Boolean variables to consider. Rather than try to remember any BODMAS type acronym for the total number of operators (a failed attempt before you start; there are aproximately 50 different operators you can have!) you're much safer if you use brackets or split long expressions up into manageable chunks.

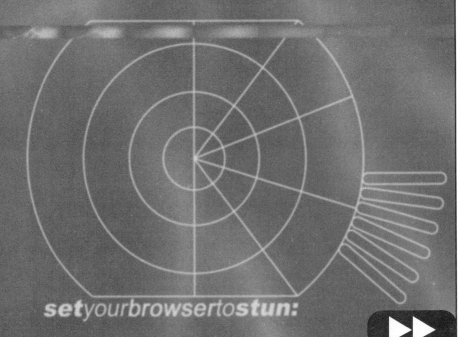

stun

/stʌn/ v(-nn-)
    (a) [tn] daze or shock (sb) eg with sth unexpected
    (b) [tn esp passive] impress (sb) greatly

set *your* ***browser*** *to* ***stun:***

E Flash 5 Compatibility

In this appendix, we'll see how to convert FLAs created in older versions of Flash and how to prepare Flash 5 FLAs to run on the widest possible number of machines.

The Flash 4 plug-in is installed as part of the standard 5.x browser. That initial coverage, plus those users who have downloaded it directly from Macromedia makes it one of the most commonly installed plug-ins for web browsers. You can expect around 90% of all potential visitors to your site to have it already installed.

The Flash 5 plug-in isn't expected to have the same sort of coverage until it's been out there for a while, as part of the install for the latest browser version. This makes compatibility a big issue as you're creating your content in Flash 5.

On the positive side, Flash 5:

- Allows you to produce SWF content for Flash 1, 2, 3 and 4 from the Flash 5 environment.

- Opens FLAs created in previous versions of Flash and lets you edit them with full Flash 5 functionality.

- Makes a fair job of converting Flash 4 ActionScript to Flash 5 (although it doesn't convert certain deprecated Flash 4 commands into the more efficient Flash 5 forms, and neither does it convert Flash 4 code to use the more efficient Flash 5 dot notation).

- Is a very good environment for writing content for Flash 1, 2 or 3, and because of the better interface, is usually a better choice in terms of workflow than the original versions of Flash themselves.

On the negative side, Flash 5:

- Doesn't let you save your source FLA files as Flash 4 compatible formats. It allows you to open Flash 4 files, but once you save them, they will be saved only in Flash 5 format

- Saves all FLA files in a Flash 5 readable format whatever version it was loaded up as. When it saves, Flash 5 overwrites the original,

▶

and gives you no warning of what it has just done. You will only become aware of the problem when you later come to try to open the same FLA in Flash 4 and find you no longer can. This has caused outrage in some quarters, particularly by people who opened some of their previous web sites in the Flash 5 trial, poked around the interface, and then saved the work, assuming that they could load the same file in Flash 4, but they couldn't...

There is no way of telling which Flash version a FLA is until you try to open it, they all come up as a 'Flash movie' if you try to look at the file properties.

- Flash 5 specific SWFs not being compatible with the latest version of Macromedia Director. You just wouldn't want to work on the Macromedia support line when a few of the people who make CD-Rom presentations for point of sale kiosks and the like found out about that particular undocumented feature!

My two overriding pieces of advice are:

- Keep legacy Flash and Flash 5 FLA files in separate places.

- As soon as you open a Flash 4 or previous version FLA, get into the habit of using **File > Save** as to save it elsewhere as a Flash 5 FLA, thus avoiding losing the legacy readable version.

We'll take a look at compatibility issues in more detail, and from both angles:

- Converting your old Flash 4 files up to Flash 5

- Exporting Flash 5 content into Flash 3 or 4

Converting Legacy Flash FLAs into Flash 5

It's very easy to convert FLA files created in previous versions of Flash up to Flash 5: simply open them in Flash 5. When Flash loads up the file, it will create all conversions necessary to make the FLA work with Flash 5.

The thing that will be impacted the most in this process is Flash 4 ActionScript. The problem is that although the FLA will now work with Flash 5, the conversion creates some pretty inefficient code and makes no use of much of Flash 5's superior functionality.

Be aware that some of the changes listed below may prevent you creating Flash 4 compatible SWFs though, which we will look at in the next section.

Here's an old Flash 4 version of a site:

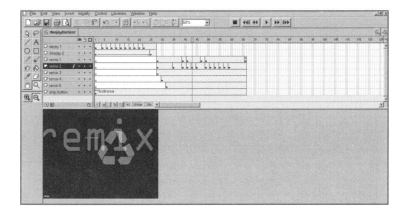

If you load the same site in Flash 5, you'll get an output window informing you of all the changes that Flash has made in the current scene:

Flash doesn't tell of you the changes that will be made in subsequent scenes unless you open them. So, once you've loaded your legacy Flash FLA into Flash 5, select each scene via **Window >Panels >Scene** and select each scene in turn, watching what appears in the Output window. You can save the contents of the Output window to a file via its Options drop-down menu for later reference:

As soon as you've done this to all the scenes, save the converted Flash 5 file with **File >Save As** before you do a bit of work and forget, thus overwriting and losing forever the legacy FLA!

This is probably all you need to do to convert FLAs from Flash 1 to 3. Flash 4 was the first ActionScript-heavy version of Flash, so it's the one where you'll need to make some more detailed changes. Although the conversion will most likely work first time, there are a number of things you might want to do to tidy up the code ready for future enhancements:

Remove all the unnecessary and annoying Number(); commands

Flash 4 allowed you to use only numeric variables with all operators (such as +, <, >), but Flash 5 now allows you to use string variables too. Because of this, Flash 5 ActionScript may now produce a string result where previously it was a numeric, thus totally screwing up any calculations involving the affected variables further down the line (which will now produce a string or NaN (Not a Number) result). To protect your ActionScript against this, Flash 5 will force all variables that are potentially affected to be numbers by enclosing them with `Number()`;. Although this is a sure-fire way of maintaining compatibility, it creates some really ugly code!

For example:

The Flash 4 code below....

```
Set Variable: "diff" = pl-y+Random(2)
Set Variable: "y" = y+INT((diff*1.72)+oy)
If (y<-40)
        Set Variable: "y" = -40
Else If (y> 140)
        Set Variable: "y" = 140
End If
```

becomes this monster:

```
diff = Number(pl-y)+Number(random(2));
y = Number(y)+Number(int(Number((diff*1.72))+Number(oy)));
if (Number(y)<Number(-40)) {
    y = -40;
} else if (Number(y)>140) {
    y = 140;
}
```

when it would work just as well as this:

```
diff = pl-y+random(2);
y = y+int((diff*1.72)+oy);
if (y<-40) {
    y = -40;
} else if (y>140) {
    y = 140;
}
```

...which is more understandable than either of the two versions of the same code above it, making it easier to modify.

The only times you'll actually need the Number(); command to be there are:

- **For the Flash 4 GetProperty action**. Leave the Number() actions for this command, because there are differences between how this command works in Flash 4 and 5, which the Number() action is crucial in fixing.

- **When you're first assigning a user inputted variable to something else**. Suppose you had an input text field with associated variable in1. If you transfer this variable to another one with userInput = in1, you should instead use userInput = Number(In1);. Flash 5 has a fairly unpredictable habit of assuming that most inputs are string values, whereas Flash 4 was more comfortable with most variables being numerics.

Convert Flash 4 Paths to Flash 5 Dot Notation

Flash 5 retains the old Flash 4 slash path notation, which is, well, 'not very good' to put it mildly. If you don't convert the old Flash 4 slash notation to Flash 5 dot notation now, be aware you're your web site probably won't work at all when Flash 6 comes out.

I've listed the Flash 4 and Flash 5 path identifiers here to help you make the necessary conversions from Flash 4 to Flash 5:

Flash 4 Slash Notation	Flash 5 Dot Notation	Comments
/	root	root timeline.
/apple	root.apple	A movieclip with instance name apple that sits on the main timeline.
/apple:myVariable	root.apple.myVariable	A variable within *apple* called *myVariable*.
..	parent	The parent timeline.
..:myVariable	parent.myVariable	Accessing a variable *myVariable* in the parent timeline.
../apple:myVariable	parent.apple.myVariable	Accessing a variable in movieclip apple from another movieclip that is on the same timeline as apple.
level5/:myVariable	level5.myVariable	Accessing a variable called *myVariable* on the level 5 SWF.
Not implemented	this	New to Flash 5.

Be aware of these points:

- Any Flash 4 paths that begin with a forward slash / are absolute

- Any Flash 4 paths that begin with two dots .. are relative.

- Flash 4 had a colon : before a variable name, so it was quite possible to have a movieclip and a variable of the same name because the pathnames made a differentiation. Flash 5 dot notation does not, and the Flash 4 to Flash 5 conversion will give very unexpected results because of it, unless you make the names of all variables and instances unique from each other.

- The **this** pathname is new to Flash 5. Any Flash 5 FLA that contains it cannot be exported back as a Flash 4 compatible SWF. More on this later.

Assuming that you have access to Flash 4, by far the best way of converting Flash 4 paths to Flash 5 is:

- Set the frame rate to 1 – 5 fps and test the FLA in Flash 4. Bring up the Output window and save the resulting output to a file from the windows **Options** pop-up window for every point where you know new variables have been defined, or movieclips appear for the first time.

- Do the same for Flash 5.

- Compare the two outputs. Flash 4 will show all variables in slash notation and Flash 5 will show them as dot notation (even though the actual ActionScripting may still use slash notation throughout). A veritable Rosetta stone to allow you to convert any path between the two notations has now been produced...

Convert Deprecated Commands to the Equivalent Dot Notation.

Perhaps the most used Flash 4 'advanced' action (I put *advanced* in quotes because Flash 5 makes the same functionality easy), was the Flash 4 **TellTarget** action. TellTarget was required in Flash 4 because it did not have a system like dot notation.

This Flash 4 TellTarget command

```
tellTarget ("/title") {
    gotoAndStop ("unnofficial");
}
tellTarget ("/downloadTitle") {
    gotoAndStop ("unnofficial");
}
```

Becomes much clearer with Flash 5 dot notation:

```
title.gotoAndStop("unofficial");
downloadTitle.gotoAndStop("unofficial");
```

You'll see the *TellTarget* command crop up a lot if you download tutorials and sample files from the Internet, many of which are Flash 4 or Flash 4 conversions.

Convert non-deprecated commands to the equivalent dot notation.

Setproperty is another command that is much better as dot notation. It was a command used in Flash 4 to set properties of movieclip objects. You're much better off doing the same thing in Flash 5 as dot notation;

```
setProperty ("buttonMe", _alpha, 50);
```

becomes

```
buttonMe._alpha = 50
```

Although this command and the related **GetProperty** are not yet deprecated in Flash 5, I can see little reason for them surviving much past Flash 6, given that there's a shorter and easier way of writing the same thing via dot notation. Don't wait for this to happen, change it now, and make your skills focus on the structures likely to be more prevalent in later versions of Flash.

Exporting Flash 5 Content for Compatibility with Legacy Versions

You'll need to tackle this when you want to:

- Export as a Flash 4 compatible format for the maximum audience, or if your FLA did not make use of the Flash 5 specific functionality.

- Convert to Flash 3 for compatibility with some Web TV or Videogame consoles with integral surfing capability that do not (and in some cases, will never) support Flash 4 or 5.

- Convert to Flash 3 when you're designing simple animated Flash banners for advertising, where the use of ActionScripting will be minimal and you want the maximum possible compatibility. (Experience has shown that although minority users are few in number, on the Web they have a habit of being the most vocal, something that would not look good to the client, so take no chances!)

Telling Flash 5 to produce content as SWFs compatible with previous versions of the plug-in is easy. Simply go to **File > Publish** Settings, select the **Flash** tab, and pick the version you require from the **Version:** drop-down menu:

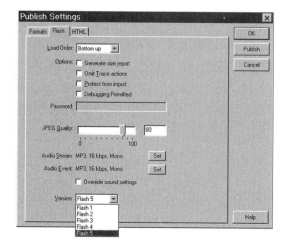

When you've done this, Flash will highlight in the Actions window all ActionScript that's not compatible with the target version of Flash you've selected. In the toolbox panel, it will also highlight all commands that aren't compatible with the current version:

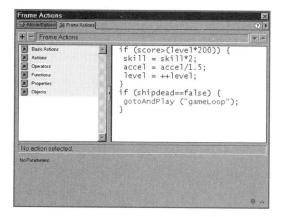

To get it working for the target version, you have to get rid of all the yellow highlighting in the code by re-coding it, or by reducing functionality.

I think it would be unusual for you to want to export anything to Flash 1 and 2 because support for Flash 3 is almost total (whether by the Flash 3 plug-in, of by the Flash 4/5 plug-ins).

Flash 3 supports all Basic Actions, and a few commands in the Actions set. You can view them by setting the **Version:** drop-down menu to Flash 3 and taking a look at the Actions window. Yes, I know. Amazing isn't it? We old timers had to get by without variables in Flash 3...

Flash 4 support is actually pretty good for general ActionScript commands, so you should find that you can convert most of your Flash 5 commands into something that will work. You can use full dot notation (except the `this` path, which means that you would have to convert all the sprites in the stun:zapper game to be behaviors that controlled a `_parent`).

You can use almost all properties. The only real notable exceptions are `_xmouse` and `_ymouse`, so you can't find out the position of the mouse directly. You can work around this by creating an empty movieclip that's constantly being dragged with a `startDrag`, and use the x, y co-ordinates of that instead.

The major omissions for Flash 4 are the new Flash 5 **objects**. The only new Flash 5 object that you can use in Flash 4 is the **Math** object. This is converted to Flash 4 compatible code via added ActionScript code that produces approximate values. This will make your Flash 4 SWF bigger than the same SWF in Flash 5 because the Flash 5 SWF will use code that's in the plug-in itself.

The **for** loop isn't supported either, but because you can't use the **Array** object that accompanies it, it's really no loss.

Flash 5 is eminently suitable for writing content destined for a particular target version from scratch. You have a better authoring environment than any of the previous versions, and have a good indication of the actions that won't work via the yellow highlighting. The use of Flash 5 to create Flash 4 content is particularly useful, because you can use dot notation and have the better scripting environment.

This was probably Macromedia's reason for assuming that nobody would want to keep previous legacy versions of the FLA if they had Flash 5 on their hard-drive, which happily, is largely true.

stun

/stʌn/ v(-nn-)

(a) [tn] daze or shock (sb) eg with sth unexpected
(b) [tn esp passive] impress (sb) greatly

*set*yourbrowserto*stun:*

F Debugging

Avoiding Errors in the First Place

- Know what you want to do in plain English first, or if you're just playing about looking for effects, keep each little trial separately in its own test program, and only try to build them into your final site when you have got them working.

- Where possible, keep your code well commented. If not in the code itself, keep a notebook describing the code.

- Keep your code modular where possible, so that each frame does a very specific task, or where this isn't possible, keep bits of code that do the same thing together. If you were writing some code that moved something about, keep all the code that calculates the variables together, separately from the code that does the final moving.

- Use sensible variable names and comments that tell you what they're doing.

- If you use test harnesses (such as the dynamic text fields that I introduced in Chapter 9), keep them in the code for as long as possible, because code doesn't work more often than it does during development, and you never know when you will need them again.

- When you're working on large sites, keep a revision list. This enables you to record any changes and identify when errors are introduced. Whenever a change is implemented, save the FLA as a new version with a revised name (**filename>revision+1>.fla**).

- Keep all your cool effects modular. This means that you can add all the elements into the finished site already tested, making for a less error-prone process.

- Build your site using separate scenes to handle particular areas. This way you can constrain errors to a single scene, and are therefore looking at smaller bits of code when you come to debug. The ability to test one scene at a time using **Control > Test Scene** makes this method extremely workable in practice.

- Know your commands before you try to use them in existing code. Learn coding techniques and commands that are new to you away from 'live' code, and only apply them when you're confident in how to use them.

- Write your code so that it becomes testable at the earliest opportunity. This means that you'll get early reassurance that the method you're developing is correct and robust.

- Make sure your code checks that everything is in range and sensible. Try all the non-sensible button combinations as well as the sensible ones

Common Mistakes

- **Trying to refer to non-existent instance names.** A movieclip instance can only be referred to if it is on a timeline. As soon as it no longer exists on a timeline, ActionScript can no longer reference it or any variables it had on its timeline. If you have the same instance across scenes, make sure you have named it the same in both places, because spelling mistakes can always make fools of us all!

- **Assigning actions to things on the stage, not in the library.** This also applies to Smart Clips.

- **Forgetting to check an Expression box.** This makes Flash assume that arguments are strings. It will therefore evaluate expressions as NaN (Not a Number).

- **Forgetting to add input = Number(input); before you start using your variable input as a number.** Flash will usually assign any input from the user via a text field as a string, even if you enter numerals only. If you want to take in a numeric not a string, always make sure that it's converted to a numeric first, with input=Number(input) with before you start using your variable input as a number.

- **Forgetting to stop the timeline from continuing straight onto the next scene.** If you have a timeline split into several scenes, remember that the timeline will continue straight onto the next scene unless you stop it from doing so.

- **Calling an instance and a variable by the same name.** In general, try to make all Instance names and variable names unique, unless you are using local variables.

- **Inserting a label in a gotoAndPlay(); command that is wrong or has been deleted.** Flash won't tell you that you've done this, and will just carry on, potentially ploughing into ActionScript further down the timeline that isn't expecting it. If the bandwidth profiler shows the playhead carrying on when you would've expected an unconditional jump, before you panic, look at the label and make sure that where you're asking Flash to jump actually exists.

- **Entering an incorrect path**. Flash won't warn you and will get lost during run-time.

- **Trying to make your site go to a frame that hasn't yet loaded when it is streaming into a target browser.** Flash goes to the most recent frame loaded, which might be the right decision for a basic animation, but is completely the wrong thing to do in an ActionScript site because you may jump into the middle of ActionScript that isn't expecting you.

Debugging Tools

There are a number of debugging facilities open to you as an ActionScript programmer. I strongly advise you to use them to **confirm that things will behave as you expect them to**, as well as for debugging when you know there's a mistake. Prevention is always the best long-term strategy. Note that when Flash isn't working properly, some of the real time diagnostics available are just too fast to make out what's happening. In these cases, it's sometimes sensible to make the site run much slower than it will in the final finished site by setting the frame rate down.

The Output Window

The **Output** window appears whenever Flash wants to communicate that it has detected errors. Most usually, you'll see this window if you try to test Flash 4 FLAs. It will open to tell you that Flash has made changes to your code to update it to Flash 5 syntax. You can also use it at any time during the running of a SWF file (i.e. when you're using **Control > Test movie, Debug Scene**, or **Test Scene**). You can use it to display either all the objects or variables in the current frame using either **Debug > List Objects** or **Debug > List Variables** respectively. The window shows a snapshot every time you use it, but this doesn't update.

List Variables

This option lists all variables with full paths. It allows you to:

- See the full paths, using _level0 instead of _root as the lowest level. (The advantage of this is that if you're using loaded levels, you can see what's happening in each level of your movie.) This is useful if you don't know the path for a particular variable.

- See variable value snapshots immediately before and after the error. This means that you can go away and have a think about what's happening. The window also allows you to print the output via its **Options** drop-down menu.

List Objects

The **List Objects** window shows you which symbols are on the timeline at any particular frame. Although not as useful as the last window, you could use it to get a listing of exactly what's on stage at any particular frame.

The ActionScript *Trace* Command

The **Output** window described above can also be used with a rather useful action called `trace();`. You can use this to send a number of useful information items to the **Output** window.

Variable Values

The **Output** window can be used to send the current value of any variable.

Remember to check the **Expression** tick box when you want to use variables. If you want to show more than one variable, you have to use one `trace();` command per variable because you can only enter one thing in the brackets.

Branching and Program Flow

You can also use the `trace();` command to see which blocks of commands within your ActionScript are being run and when. It's particularly useful for finding out things about conditional statements and loops such as:

- Which part of an `if` statement was run.

- How many times a loop actually ran.

- What you have to do to get a particular bit of code to run, and if program execution *ever* gets to a particular block of code.

- If you ever get to the unfortunate situation where your ActionScript crashes, you can see how far it actually gets within the offending script before it dies.

The Debugger

The **Debugger** is new for Flash 5 and in many ways looks like a real-time version of the Output window. This is a real-time tool, so as I've said, consider dropping the frame rate when you use it, otherwise it may move a little too quickly.

The **Debugger** window becomes active if you select the **Control > Debug Movie** option. The **Debugger** is a particularly useful tool, because not only does it present all the information you can derive from the other methods that we've seen so far, it also lets you *change* variable values and properties in real-time. I'll give you more explanation on all of the tabs here.

Properties Tab

The **Properties** tab allows you to see all the properties of the selected movieclip. Select the movieclip you want to watch in the top panel and you'll see all its property attributes fill with actual values.

Notice that these are changing in real-time. You can see this directly if you move your mouse about. You'll see the _xmouse and _ymouse properties vary to signify where the mouse is in terms of the movieclip's origin.

Some of the properties are grayed out and others are displayed in black. The ones in black are those properties that the **Debugger** window will let you change in real-time. Simply select the current value in the right-hand column and put in a new value. This is really useful for testing out property-based animations. You can easily recreate particular situations to see what the code will do, such as 'What happens if my space-invader goes off the screen?'.

You can also use it to manually change properties before you start coding to see what the effects of changing each property will be in visual terms.

Unfortunately, you can't assign variables or expressions to the right-hand side of the **Debugger**, only numbers or literals such as *2* or *cake*.

Variable Tab

This tab works in much the same way as the **Properties** tab, except that it displays all the variables on the currently selected timeline. The first variable, **$version** is a system variable. It gives the revision number of the Flash player. After this variable, all the other ones listed will be those you've defined.

As with the **Properties** tab though, you can throw a few spanners in the works by changing a few variables to see how the code would react to extreme situations.

Watch Tab

The **Watch** tab allows you to build up a list of variables you want to look at together. There are two ways to do this:

- Right-click or *Ctrl*-click on a variable name in the **Variable** tab. Click on the **Watch** option that comes up. The variable will now have a blue circle next to it, and if you look in the **Watch** tab, you'll now see the variable listed.

- With the **Watch** tab selected, Right-click or *Ctrl*-click to bring up and select **Add** or **Remove** from the menu to either add or remove variables from your list. If you add a variable, a new blank field will be listed. Click anywhere in the **Name** column of the new field to enter your variable name, noting that you'll need to add the full path.

You can choose to make the Debug window available for the final exported SWF via the **File > Publish settings > Flash** tab, by selecting **Debugging Permitted**. You can also enter a password to prevent anyone else having access to debugging via the field next to this option.

You can then access the **Debugger** by right-clicking or *Ctrl*-clicking on the SWF and selecting **Debugger** from the pop-up menu.

stun

/stʌn/ *v*(*-nn-*)
- **(a)** [tn] daze or shock (sb) eg with sth unexpected
- **(b)** [tn esp passive] impress (sb) greatly

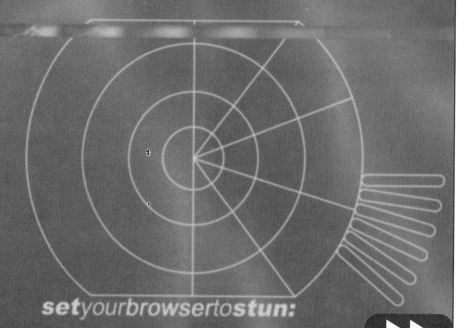

*set**your**browser**to**stun:*

Index

W